Whigs and Cities

WHIGS AND CITIES

POPULAR POLITICS
IN THE AGE OF
WALPOLE AND PITT

Nicholas Rogers

CLARENDON PRESS · OXFORD
1989

Oxford University Press, Walton Street, Oxford OX2 6DP

Oxford New York Toronto
Delhi Bombay Calcutta Madras Karachi
Petaling Jaya Singapore Hong Kong Tokyo
Nairobi Dar es Salaam Cape Town
Melbourne Auckland

and associated companies in
Berlin Ibadan

Oxford is a trade mark of Oxford University Press

Published in the United States
by Oxford University Press, New York

British Library Cataloguing in Publication Data
Rogers, Nicholas
Whigs and cities: popular politics in the age of
Walpole and Pitt.
1. England. Urban regions. Politics, history
I. Title 320.9'42
ISBN 0–19–821785–4

Library of Congress Cataloging in Publication Data
(data available)

Typeset by Pentacor Ltd, High Wycombe, Bucks
Printed and bound in
Great Britain by Biddles Ltd,
Guildford and King's Lynn

To
My Mother
And In Memory of Alan

Preface

THIS book began many years ago as a Ph.D. dissertation on London politics in the age of Walpole and Pitt. It has been substantially revised and expanded to include a section on provincial politics so that firmer generalizations could be advanced about the nature and scope of urban politics. Parts of Chapter 1 and much of Chapter 5 have already appeared in print, and I wish to thank the editors of the *English Historical Review* and *Past and Present* for permission to reproduce work which originally appeared in their journals.

In writing this book I have incurred many lasting obligations. I am particularly indebted to the staffs of the Avon Central Library, the Bristol Record Office, the British Library, the Corporation of London Record Office, the Greater London Record Office, the Guildhall Library, the Norwich City Library, the Norwich and Norfolk Record Office, the Public Record Office (both at Chancery Lane and Kew), and to the Westminster Public Library for their help and assistance. I also wish to acknowledge the financial assistance of the Social Science and Humanities Research Council of Canada, which enabled me to spend long periods of time in British archives.

My intellectual debts are many. George Rudé and Edward Thompson gave me much encouragement and advice at the beginning of this project and have always been a source of inspiration. John Brewer shared his enthusiasm and knowledge of popular politics with me on many occasions. In Toronto I have benefitted from the advice and criticism of a number of colleagues in my own department, especially Joe Ernst and Douglas Hay, and from a rich cluster of seventeenth- and eighteenth-century historians in the Toronto area, who for several years now have held regular seminars on subjects of common interest and have commented on my own work. Other academics in the field have been kind enough to share their ideas with me and to engage my own, notably Jonathan Barry, Henry Horwitz, and Kathleen Wilson. In particular I should like to thank Joanna Innes for her rigorous and thorough reading of the final sections of this book. I should also like to thank my former supervisor and friend, John Beattie, for his encouragement, support, and constructive criticism over the years. It is a pleasure to have worked with him.

Finally, I am grateful to my siblings and my own family for all their support. This book is dedicated to my parents. I am only sorry that my stepfather, Alan Powell, did not live long enough to see this project in print.

Contents

List of Tables

1
Introduction

Come listen ye Gulls whom Bribery coaxes
For Lucre to mortgage your votes to C—t Foxes
With Feasting and Boozing, tho' now they may treat
Ere a year's at an end they will prove sour Meat.

> [Mark Freeman], *The Downfall of Bribery*
> (London, 1733), p. 20.

All degrees of people, who have leisure and abilities, . . .
acquire rational ideas of liberty and submission, of the
Rights of the Church, and of the Power of the State, of
their duties as Subjects, and of what they may justly claim
as Freemen.

> Anon., *The Liveryman, or Plain Thoughts on Publick
> Affairs* (London, 1740), p. 9.

THE urban politics of the early Hanoverian era have not
been the subject of sustained historical inquiry. It might
be tempting to ascribe this to a Namierite legacy, to the
continued fascination with high political life and with those
structures of power that allowed a relatively small group of
landed gentlemen, lawyers, and merchant princes to preside
over Britain's destiny. Whatever the truth in this answer, it
would be incomplete. The last two decades have seen a
substantial reaction to Namierism, a renewed concern with
political argument and ideology and a new sensitivity to the
diverse modes of communication and redress which signalled
the presence of a lively extra-parliamentary public. Yet our
knowledge of urban politics, in particular, remains curiously
uneven and impressionistic. Beyond London we know little of
how townsmen acted or felt, or indeed how we might gauge
their collective presence.

Part of the reason for this lacuna lies in the particular way in
which historians reacted to Namier. The reception of Namier's

work, initially at least, followed the well-beaten tracks of Whig historiography.[1] It protested against his categorical dismissal of party, his strictly legal definition of royal privileges and responsibilities, his scepticism of political idealism, and his cynical assessment of political argument. It did not challenge centrally his subjectivist notion of power; that is, it did not question the assumption that power resided exclusively in those leading families and decision-makers who exercised formal political authority and in the various lines of dependency which secured their right to rule. To be sure, the next generation of historians substantially qualified this perspective. The re-emphasis upon party and ideological strife in the Augustan age raised serious objections to a widespread application of Namierism, but it did not dispute its appositeness for the middle decades of the century. Rather, it generated a new interpretation of English political development which highlighted the swift transition from the politically volatile and divisive society of Queen Anne to the high summer of Hanoverian oligarchy.[2]

According to this view, the constitutional issues which so animated the politicians and the electorate during the reigns of William and Anne reached a climacteric with the Hanoverian succession and ebbed perceptibly with the consolidation of the Whig supremacy. After the proscription of the Tory party and the subordination of the Church to the State, politics became increasingly a matter of preferment and patronage, directed by Walpole and the great Whig grandees. What dissonant voices remained were swiftly neutralized or pushed to the margins. Although the smaller gentry periodically objected to Walpole's political priorities and resented the alliance of aristocratic and moneyed power at the apex of Hanoverian society, they proved too fragile and fragmented a base for a concerted challenge to

[1] See e.g. Richard Pares, *George III and the Politicians* (Oxford, 1953); Herbert Butterfield, 'George III and the Constitution', *History*, 43 (1958) 14–33; and W. R. Fryer, 'King George III: His Political Character and Conduct 1760–84: A New Whig Interpretation', *Renaissance and Modern Studies*, 6 (1962), 68–101.
[2] Geoffrey Holmes, *British Politics in the Age of Anne* (London, 1967); J. H. Plumb, *The Growth of Political Stability in England 1675–1725* (London, 1967). For their reflections on the electorate, see J. H. Plumb, 'The Growth of the Electorate in England from 1600 to 1715', *Past and Present*, 45 (Nov. 1969), 90–116; and Geoffrey Holmes, *The Electorate and the National Will in the First Age of Party* (Lancaster, 1976).

the Whig regime. Bolingbroke's efforts to rally the gentry and merchants against Walpolean corruption consequently proved a failure. They simply added to the vocal but ineffectual voices which deplored the growth of oligarchy or envied its benefici- aries. 'The greatest threats' to Walpole's position, claimed W. A. Speck, came 'not from the besieging opposition, but from mutinies within the guarrison'.[3] Amid the Whig triumph, political conflict became largely a matter of ins versus outs, immobilizing the momentum for reform and narrowing its constituency, to a point that one historian has argued that 'the case for reform was deployed mainly by bookish radicals with antiquarian tastes'.[4] It was not until the reign of George III that a genuinely popular movement for political reform would gather momentum.

Within the last decade or so, this view of British political development has not gone unchallenged. Edward Thompson has called for a re-examination of the popular, informal resistance to Whig rule and has highlighted both the self- consciously heretical Jacobitism of the crowd and the militant protests of the forest yeomen and cottagers in defence of their customary rights.[5] But by and large historians have preferred the more traditional byways of high politics, in order to question the foundations of political stability which Plumb predicated upon élite integration and one-party Whig govern- ment. Several insisted that the Tory party was a far more resilient and organized force than the orthodoxy of the 1960s presumed, and questioned the cohesion of high society. Eveline Cruickshanks and J. C. D. Clark both made a case for the persistence and intensity of dynastic conflict until 1750.[6] Linda Colley, on the other hand, portrayed the Tories as a pre- eminently Hanoverian party, broadening its base and consoli- dating its position in the larger constituencies by some

---

[3] W. A. Speck, *Stability and Strife: England 1714–1760* (Cambridge, Mass., 1977), p. 229.

[4] John Cannon, *Parliamentary Reform 1640–1832* (Cambridge, 1973), p. 45.

[5] Edward Thompson, 'Patrician Society, Plebeian Culture', *Journal of Social History*, 7 (summer, 1974), 382–405; id., 'Eighteenth-Century English Society: Class Struggle without Class?', *Social History*, 3/2 (May 1978), 152–64; id., *Whigs and Hunters: The Origin of the Black Act* (London, 1975).

[6] Eveline Cruickshanks, *Political Untouchables: The Tories and the '45* (London, 1979); J. C. D. Clark, *English Society 1688–1832* (Cambridge, 1985), chs. 1, 3.

'opportunistic sorties' into reform politics.[7] This re-emphasis upon party polarities has tended to underscore the subordination of the extra-parliamentary public to high political manœuvre, to insist upon its intrinsic conservatism, sectarianism, and role as gentlemanly surrogate. Even the new experiments in extra-parliamentary association have been attributed to the political acumen of the great rather than to the complexities of urban political culture. Voters were generally too ductile, deferential, and dependent upon upper-class clientage to constitute an independent voice; their world was too local to have much impact. Electoral participation was so spasmodic, Clark assured us, that political élites virtually created their own constituencies. In any case, 'the daily business of government was conducted at St. James's and Westminster in terms which usually owed relatively little to a sense of popular pressure or wide accountability.'[8] On this last matter, at least, Colley largely concurred. 'Of course the plebian readers of Swift and Defoe in the 1710s, of Bolingbroke in the 1730s, and of Wilkes in the 1760s could evolve political opinions of their own', she declared. 'But the public opinion which impinged on the political centre, the public opinion with which politicians *in office* were normally concerned, was the opinion of the educated, the prosperous, and most especially, the landed.'[9]

The new 'party' interpretations of the Hanoverian era, then, have largely subsumed popular politics under the banner of high political manœuvre. Indeed, in some respects they have gone further. For while the Namierite revisionists were sometimes prepared to acknowledge the uneasy relationship between the political élite and the informal political nation and attributed the growth of political stability to the consolidation of new money and land and the consequent *impotence* of the less powerful,[10] the new historians of party have laid greater stress upon the ideological and material *subordination* of the populace at large. Both assessments of popular politics, I

[7] Linda Colley, *In Defiance of Oligarchy: the Tory Party 1714–1760* (Cambridge, 1982).

[8] Clark, *English Society 1688–1832*, pp. 19–20.

[9] Linda Colley, *In Defiance of Oligarchy*, p. 19.

[10] See J. H. Plumb, 'Political Man', in James L. Clifford (ed.), *Man versus Society in Eighteenth-Century Britain* (Cambridge, 1968), pp. 1–21.

shall argue, are in many respects misleading. Most crucially, they minimize the presence of the cities and great towns.

It is the thesis of this book that the cities and large towns were more intractable sources of political support than is conventionally assumed. At important junctures in Hanoverian politics they constituted critical sites for a popular challenge to the Whig regime and an important source of support for William Pitt during the Seven Years War. I shall endeavour to show that while a handful of towns were dominated by landed grandees, the great majority were open, independent boroughs, with active electorates whose political horizons were both local and national. Although many of the large urban boroughs were prepared to support the Whig defence of the Protestant succession during the early decades of the Hanoverian accession, by the 1730s they had been progressively alienated from the Whig regime. The sources of this discontent, I shall argue, originated in part from the government's attempt to contain electoral participation and popular assembly and from the series of financial scandals which tarnished its public integrity. But it was also boosted by Walpole's fiscal policy, which threatened to undermine business credit and inflate the government's sources of patronage and powers of surveillance over exciseable commodities. In addition, important sectors of mercantile opinion became increasingly disenchanted with the government's Eurocentric policy and its lack of commitment to transatlantic trade. The result was a dramatic campaign to purify Parliament of executive influence and render it more accountable to the electorate. It was a debate, I shall suggest, that was neither visionary nor archaic but did address the representation of non-landed interests in Hanoverian society. Even after its failure, the demand for a more venturesome foreign policy attuned to commercial and industrial expansion continued to resonate from the middling ranks of the large cities and to reach those in power.

In advancing this argument I shall begin, predictably, with the City of London. As the principal open constituency and port, whose activities were closely scrutinized in the provinces, the City was the centre of extra-parliamentary opinion, the critical source and springboard for nation-wide campaigns.

Within a decade of the Hanoverian accession, the City's role as a watchdog of liberty was threatened by legislative attempts to circumscribe its democratic processes and to consolidate the civic presence of the powerful moneyed interest, that relatively exclusive body of big financiers and fundholders whose affiliation with the Whig party dated from the mid-1690s. By the late 1730s this policy of containment had failed. Led by the middling merchants and tradesmen of the Common Council, the City moved on to the offensive, facilitating a national campaign for Walpole's dismissal and parliamentary reform, and popularizing Country coalitions against the Court. Although this alliance of opposition Whigs and Tories, first founded in the 1720s, collapsed in the wake of an upsurge of loyalism during the Forty-Five, the City continued to advocate the cause of representative government and to inhibit the diversion of British resources to Hanoverian priorities. During the 1750s it proved a crucial, although not uncritical, base of support for Pitt, whose rise to prominence owed much to his professed patriotism and charismatic war-leadership.

However, charting the tortuous route of City politics is not my sole concern. I am particularly interested in determining the social configurations of the City opposition and the social penetration of Country ideas in the metropolis as a whole. Following George Rudé's pioneering social analysis of the Wilkite movement,[11] I examine the electoral sociology of four London constituencies at critical points in the campaign against Walpole and his successors. In the City, I hope to show the extent to which the financial revolution was a crucial determinant of political allegiance, polarizing the moneyed companies and the chartered companies against a diverse group of civic populists, whose main strength rested with the domestic trades. In Westminster, I chart the ways in which the luxury economy served to buttress the significant presence of Court and aristocratic power and how this was temporarily challenged by a group of dissident lawyers, tradesmen, and gentlemen with the help of the parliamentary opposition and an artisanal rank and file. Outside these two cities, however,

---

[11] George Rudé, *Wilkes and Liberty* (Oxford, 1962), esp. ch. V and apps. V–X.

the metropolitan appeal of the anti-ministerialists was more limited. In Surrey and Middlesex, the support given to Country candidates was rural as much as urban, with local reputations and power structures playing as significant a role in determining voting patterns. Unlike Wilkes, the Country candidates of the mid-century failed to win over the lesser freeholders of the urban suburbs. The political independence of the urban freeholder remained fragile, suggesting that the mid-century battles in the metropolis represented a transitional stage in the development of a middling political consciousness. Outside the City, where there was a strong tradition of civic service and participation, electoral politics were still mediated by clientage, connection, and localism.

If the metropolis none the less witnessed some significant challenges to Court power in the halcyon days of the Whig supremacy, what was the provincial experience? To date we know remarkably little about the provincial towns,[12] yet no satisfactory discussion of popular politics can exclude them. Generally speaking, historians have presumed that provincial politics were localist, pragmatic, and gentry-dominated, isolated from the mainstream of national politics prior to industrialization; or, alternatively, brought within its orbit through the factional in-fighting of its élites. Yet gentry domination of provincial town politics arguably declined in the eighteenth century. It only persisted in towns with declining economies. With renewed urban growth and the expansion of the press, the interaction between the provinces and the capital became more complex and intense, the mediation of the gentry less necessary. In electoral terms, as I shall show in Chapter 7, the experience of the large towns ran counter to the national trend, to a point that more contests were recorded in the Hanoverian era than in the Augustan. Equally significant, the pattern of provincial politics followed the London trend. It registered the deepening unpopularity of Walpole during the 1730s and the call for parliamentary reform. It also witnessed the emergence of Country coalitions

---

[12] The notable exception is Kathleen Wilson, 'The Rejection of Deference: Urban Political Culture in England 1715–1785', Ph.D. thesis (Yale, 1985), to be published in a revised form as *'The Sense of the People': Urban Political Culture in England 1715–1785* (New York, forthcoming).

against government candidates, despite the continued resilience of party affiliations in many towns. Indeed, it is possible to talk of a Country 'moment' in urban politics, national in scope and radical in character. Such a phenomenon questions the current interpretations of the Walpolean opposition as a crypto-Jacobite or backwoodsman movement, and calls for a reappraisal of the linkages between incipient imperialism, trade, and parliamentary reform. By extension it queries the conventional chronology of the reform movement and the neatness of the distinction which John Brewer has made between the custodial, Country politics of the 1730s, and the open, participatory politics of the Wilkites.[13]

If Chapter 7 attempts to redraw the psephological and ideological map of Georgian England, the subsequent Chapters offer two contrasting case studies in provincial politics. For while there was a convergence between the metropolitan and provincial politics at crucial junctures, there were noteworthy differences in their rhythms, traditions, and outlook, differences that can only be explored at the local level. Bristol was chosen because it was a party-riven town which contributed to the Country 'moment', yet relapsed into oligarchy. Norwich was chosen because it was a quintessentially open constituency whose political record ran counter to the urban trend. How can we explain these different trajectories and seeming paradoxes? What does their experience add to our understanding of party affiliations and local power structures, and of the ways in which economic interest and ideology might intersect? The answers to these questions are not straightforward, but they will, I hope, serve to deepen our understanding of popular politics, both within the provinces and between the provinces and the metropolitan area.

As a final foray into urban politics, I propose to examine the role of the crowd. Since George Rudé's pioneering studies in the late fifties, studies of popular disturbance have become one of the staples of eighteenth-century social history. Yet our understanding of the crowd in politics remains largely metropolitan and fragmentary, centred almost exclusively upon the major political crises of the eighteenth century. This has not

[13] John Brewer, *Party Ideology and Popular Politics at the Accession of George III* (Cambridge, 1976), pp. 253–7.

only given crowd studies an episodic quality; it has both reified the crowd and imbued it with a radical teleology. In Chapter 10 I challenge the assumption that crowds were necessarily radical, or even devoted to opposition, pin-pointing those occasions when they were mobilized on behalf of government or local patrons. I also argue that crowds must be situated within a context of popular festival and political ceremonial in which all sectors of society were accorded a role, whether as benefactors, participants, or spectators. In this way it becomes possible to see street politics as a contested terrain between groups and parties competing for popular allegiance, as well as a struggle between the labouring poor and the propertied over customary festive privileges and the boundaries of the political. This dual articulation gave political festivals an unpredictable quality and frustrated the establishment of a stable ceremonial order. As a result, it imbued street politics with an energy that periodically unsettled, without fundamentally challenging, magnate rule. Crowds were traditional, not reformist, but their actions continually tested the boundaries of authority and preserved, at least until 1780, a critical space for libertarian politics. It was a space that the middling citizens of the large towns were often able to exploit to advantage.

PART I

The City of London in National Politics

1

City Politics and the Rise of Whig Oligarchy

The Country very justly looks upon the Londoners to have the greatest interest with publick Safety, to know best wherein it consists, and to have the fairest Opportunities of discovering what Attacks are made against it. When any Invasion upon the Publick is attempted, the first Beacon is lighted up here, to give Warning to all Parts of the Land of the approaching Danger.

Freeholder's Journal, 28 Feb. 1722

THE City of London was the premier constituency in eighteenth-century Britain and enjoyed a quite unique status within the political realm. It was among the first political communities to wrestle Corporate privileges from the Crown and to enjoy a semi-autonomous existence within the state. This was a recognition of its economic importance as much as its close association with government. The city's geographical proximity to the continent and its natural facilities for overseas traffic quickly enhanced its economic standing, and by the early fourteenth century it had grown into a self-confident port, dominating the wool, cloth, and wine trades as well as the profitable field of war purveyance, becoming in turn a crucial nucleus of inland commerce. By 1700 London was responsible for roughly 60 per cent of all foreign exports and, together with its immediate environs, for the manufacture of all manner of articles for foreign and domestic consumption. The principal source of government credit, London was also a vital tax-base. Nearly 20 per cent of the English and Welsh land tax was raised in the greater London area and over a third of the 1697 subsidy.[1] The City, with its

[1] *A Scheme of the Proportions Several Counties in England Paid to the Land Tax in 1693 and to the Subsidies in 1697, Compared with the Number of Members then Sent to Parliament* (London, 1698), p. 1.

deep strata of wealthy and middling citizens, was too important to be ignored.

The City of London's prestige was further advanced by its
dramatic interventions in national politics. Eighteenth-century
contemporaries were acutely aware of London's contribution
to the civil war, both in its moderate and radical phases; and
the role it played in the final defeat of Stuart absolutism and
the framing of the 1688/9 settlement was within living
memory.[2] To be sure, London's military importance declined
with the advent of a permanent standing army. Its trained
bands no longer occupied the strategic place they did in 1642.
But there remained a keen appreciation of the City's ability to
mobilize popular support for and against national governments
and to set agendas for discussion and debate. London's civic
and parliamentary elections frequently involved national as
opposed to local issues. The deliberations of Common Hall,
whose 8,000 liverymen prided themselves on their discernment
and freedom from electoral interference, were anxiously
watched in Whitehall and elsewhere.[3] Traditionally independent
of the Court and aristocracy, London came to be regarded as a
barometer of public opinion, its Addresses, Instructions, and
elections tokens of the popular tide. Writing to the duchess of
Marlborough in 1705, the duke of Halifax commented that 'the
country always take the rule from hence, and the true pulse of
the nation is always felt at the heart'.[4] In this respect London
politics had a genuinely national dimension, attracting a
broader audience within the political nation as a whole. This
explains why London elections and Addresses to the Crown
were regularly featured in provincial newspapers and by the
mid-century even found their way into colonial journals.

[2] For London's contribution, see Valerie Pearl, *London and the Outbreak of
the Puritan Revolution* (Oxford, 1961); Brian Manning, *The English People and
the English Revolution* (London, 1976); David Underdown, *Pride's Purge:
Politics in the Puritan Revolution* (Oxford, 1970); John Miller, 'The Militia and
the Army in the Reign of James II', *Historical Journal*, 16/4 (1973), 659–79; J. R.
Jones, *The Revolution of 1688 in England* (London, 1972).

[3] Membership of Common Hall doubled in the second half of the
seventeenth century, reaching 8,200 by 1710, rising to around 8,500 in the
1720s, and after the 1725 act falling to approximately 8,100 by 1734. The
participation rate at parliamentary, shrieval, and other civic elections (such as
that of Chamberlain in 1734) was in the region of 80%. These calculations are
based on the extant voting-lists and poll-books.

[4] W. A. Speck, *Tory and Whig: the Struggle in The Constituencies 1701–
1715* (London, 1970), p. 95.

As the classic independent constituency and premier port, close to the hub of national politics, the City of London inevitably became embroiled in the struggle for power between Whig and Tory during the last decades of Stuart rule. In fact, it became the crucial extra-parliamentary site for the party battles which reached their climacteric with the Hanoverian accession and the subsequent triumph of Whig government. It is the purpose of this Chapter to highlight the central configurations of this struggle, focusing especially upon its local roots and ramifications. Much of this story has already been chronicled by Gary De Krey, and I have no wish to duplicate this fine work.[5] What I wish to explore more fully is the particular alienation of many Londoners from Whiggery by 1720 and the ways in which the Whig party under Walpole sought to contain City disaffection and to undermine its democratic processes. For it was these developments which largely defined London's stance in national politics before 1750 and influenced its capacity to act as a watch-dog to government. Or, to echo the words of the *Freeholder's Journal*, as a beacon to liberty.

One distinguishing feature of London politics in the first half of the eighteenth century was the continuing tension between the City and the moneyed interest, the specialized creditor class which rose to prominence with the establishment of the funded debt and the expansion of the money-market. This conflict was noted some thirty years ago by the late Lucy Sutherland in a pioneering essay;[6] but this insight has not been developed. By and large historians have approached the political debate over the financial revolution in terms of the frictions between land and credit.[7] Echoing Swift and Bolingbroke they have tended to see the emergence of the great financial syndicates as a challenge to the traditional authority of the landed gentry, disrupting the conventional parameters of

---

[5] Gary S. De Krey, *A Fractured Society: The Politics of London in the First Age of Party 1688–1715* (Oxford, 1985). See also Henry Horwitz's useful synopsis, 'Party in a Civic Context: London from the Exclusion Crisis to the Fall of Walpole', in Clyve Jones (ed.), *Britain in the First Age of Party 1680–1750: Essays Presented to Geoffrey Holmes* (London, 1987), pp. 173–94.

[6] Lucy Sutherland, 'The City of London in Eighteenth-Century Politics', in A. J. P. Taylor and Richard Pares (eds.), *Essays Presented to Sir Lewis Namier* (London, 1956), pp. 49–74; see also her *City of London and the Opposition to Government 1768–74* (1958 Creighton Lecture in History; London, 1959).

[7] Isaac Kramnick, *Bolingbroke and his Circle: The Politics of Nostalgia in the Age of Walpole* (Cambridge, Mass., 1968), esp. chs. 2, 3.

political power and responsibility, and enhancing the power of the executive over a gentry-dominated legislature. This, of course, was a crucial theme of eighteenth-century political discourse which enlivened the party strife of the Augustan era in particular. But it is also true that the social tensions between high finance and trade were far from inconsequential, especially in the nation's principal commercial constituency, the City of London.

Let us begin with the question of civic participation, a theme at the heart of Country notions of public responsibility. During the late seventeenth and early eighteenth centuries, the purely economic advantages to big business of joining the civic community declined. The regulations governing the trading activities of 'unfree' merchants had become largely inoperative. The security of the Orphans' bequests had been disastrously shaken by the scandals of the 1690s. And—what was of paramount importance—the key to spectacular wealth lay with the joint-stock companies and the interlocking business syndicates which controlled important sectors of overseas enterprise and quickly superseded the City itself as the major source of government credit. Although livery membership might widen the range of business contacts for the ambitious parvenu and provide him with incidental benefits, social prestige, perhaps, or the right to charitable assistance in old age and bankruptcy, the rise of the financial companies associated with the London money-market made membership less imperative, if not largely irrelevant. The trend in recruitment is unmistakable. Among the directors of the Bank of England, for example, livery membership declined from 50 per cent in the period 1694–1714 to 26 per cent in 1739–63. Within the East India directorate, livery affiliations fell from 50 per cent in 1710 to 35 per cent in 1739, to 22 per cent in 1763. Among the more important insurance companies too, where Dutch and Huguenot affiliations were particularly important, the same conditions prevailed. An analysis of 375 individuals who formed the directorship of the six major moneyed companies of the capital in the mid-decades of the century reveals that only 22 per cent were liverymen.[8] Even within the creditor élite as a

---

[8] The six are the Bank of England, the East India Company, the South Sea

whole, the proportion who joined Common Hall was a third. To the mid-eighteenth century London plutocrat, City membership was clearly a less attractive proposition than it had been fifty years earlier.

The reluctance of the financial plutocracy to join the London Corporation and to contribute substantially to its welfare at a time when the City strove, with comparatively inelastic financial resources, to meet mounting administrative expenses, was bitterly resented. The argument voiced in the post-Restoration era that those who had 'acquired Great Estate' in the City should owe some obligation to it, was re-echoed by the smaller retailers, who were compelled to bear the burden of increased taxation at a time when their privileged position in the metropolitan market was seriously undermined by the demographic expansion of the metropolis beyond the City limits and the changing structure of merchant capitalism. Among the Common Councilmen, too, who were broadly representative of the middling trades and professions, the aversion of the moneyed men to civic life was a vexatious issue. In 1702, the Common Council had tried to force the members of the United East India Company to take up the City freedom. Eleven years later, the Court petitioned Parliament to enforce the discriminatory legislation against 'unfree' merchants, many of whom combined overseas commerce with public investment, on their own account or as attorneys for international finance.[9] Both these efforts proved unsuccessful. The City failed to attract the new creditor class, quite apart from those who, on account of their ethnic origins, were barred from civic life. Outside the Levant Company, the few merchant-capitalists who did take out the freedom and perhaps the cloth of one of the livery companies did so for honorific or

Company, and the three major insurance companies in London: London Assurance, Royal Exchange Assurance, and the Sub Fire. The period examined was 1739–63.

[9] J. R. Kellett, 'The Causes and Progress of the Financial Decline of the Corporation of London 1660–1694', Ph.D. thesis (London, 1952), pp. 381–94; for the 1702 petition see Corporation of London Record Office (hereafter CLRO) Small MS, box 23, no. 31. See also Henry Horwitz, 'Testamentary Practice, Family Strategies and the Last Phases of the Custom of London 1660–1725', *Law and History Review*, 2/2 (autumn, 1984), 224–5.

cogently political reasons. For the well-connected plutocrat, particularly the more cosmopolitan, the burdens of civic responsibility outweighed the advantages.

The aversion of the financiers and large creditors to civic life might have been little more than a rankling grievance had it remained divorced from politics. But the political role of the plutocracy was far from unobtrusive and was hardly commensurate with its increasing isolation from formal civic life. The quest for the lucrative windfalls of government contracts and loans disposed financiers to increase their political visibility, and the turn of the century saw the greater financiers scrambling for seats in the House of Commons. This upsurge in 'Parliament-jobbing' was viewed with alarm by the independent-minded freemen and freeholders of the larger constituencies, for it magnified the trade in rotten boroughs and accentuated the drift of British politics towards oligarchy. Not surprisingly, the carpet-bagging financiers sparked a new debate about the under-representation of the counties and larger towns. 'It seems not equal that all the Freeholders of a County should be represented by only two men, and the Towns in the same County be represented by above Forty, as it is in Cornwall', claimed one pamphleteer, who went on to note that 'the City of London itself, though some say it bears a proportion to six parts of the Kingdom, sends but four members of itself and but eight in the whole Circumference.'[10] Consequently he demanded the disfranchisement of the depopulated, desolate boroughs and a redistribution of seats to the more populous and commercially vibrant centres.

In the mind of the independent voter, the political implications of the new financial age did not end there. It was also feared that the influx of plutocrats into Parliament would broaden the powers of the executive and adversely alter the equilibrium of interests represented in the Commons. There was a special concern that the priorities of the larger commercial constituencies would be undermined by high finance, particularly those of a City as complex as London. This message was brought home in a concrete way during the general election of 1701, when the broader preoccupations of

---

[10] Anon., *The Freeholder's Plea against Stock-Jobbing Elections of Parliamentary Men* (London, 1701), pp. 16–18.

the London citizenry were subordinated to the bitter rivalry between the two East India companies. 'We are plagued with the Impertinence of the two East India Companies', quipped one commentator, 'as if the Interest of either Company were to be named in the Day with the Protestant Religion and the public Peace.'[11] It was not that merchant-financiers were necessarily insensitive to the needs of their constituents in places like London, but, travelling the fast lanes of parliamentary politics and relatively indifferent to civic service, they were less likely to be model representatives.

The rise of high finance, then, was seen as essentially antagonistic to the development of a more open structure of politics which many hoped would accompany the 1694 Triennial Act. The role of the new fundholders within City politics itself only confirmed this view. The plutocracy's basic commitment to Whiggery was apparent from the foundation of the Bank of England, notwithstanding the few financiers, often goldsmith bankers, who were Tory in sympathy. Robert Harley's difficulties in 1711, when he attempted to find financial backing for the new Tory ministry, clearly illustrates this fact.[12] After 1714, moreover, when the Tories were proscribed from office, the Whig allegiances of the cosmopolitan plutocracy were unquestionable. Indeed, the financial community as a whole proved to be ministerial devotees in City politics, ready to lend their weight to curb dissonant voices which might unsettle the new economic order.

Even before the Hanoverian accession the close association of Whiggery with big business had resulted in some remarkable political reversals. The Whig merchants of the 1680s, active in the long-distance trades and opposed to the traditional monopolies, courted freeman opinion during the Exclusion era and came out firmly against the confiscation of the City's Charter. As late as 1690, they proposed radical changes in the City's constitution, demanding direct ward elections of the City's Mayor, Sheriffs, and Aldermen, as well as the legislative supremacy of Common Council.[13] In this way they hoped to

[11] *The Freeholder's Plea*, p. 7.
[12] B. W. Hill, 'The Change of Government and the "Loss of the City" 1710–1711', *Economic History Review*[2], 24 (Aug. 1971), 395–413.
[13] Gary S. De Krey, 'Political Radicalism in London after the Glorious

prevent the City magistracy from frustrating the popular will. Yet within five years this policy had been abandoned. Entrenched in power within the Corporation and availing themselves of the new opportunities in war-finance, the Whig mercantile élite quickly exchanged its radical coat for a more establishment cut. In 1692 Whig leaders pared down the ward franchise to freeman householders paying scot and bearing lot, eliminating many inhabitants who had customarily voted in Common Council and aldermanic elections. Three years later, in an effort to improve the City's finances, the Whigs permitted the Court of Aldermen to accept fines from sheriffs-elect unwilling to take office. In so doing they compromised the right of Common Hall to choose the sheriffs, a right they had defended in 1682 and again in 1690.

The new, oligarchic stance of the post-Revolution Whig leaders was reaffirmed by the next generation. Merchant-financiers like Sir Gilbert Heathcote, one of the rising stars of Revolution finance, who became Alderman of Walbrook in 1702, had little sympathy with the small-to-middling tradesmen who demanded a greater stake in City politics. Along with his Whig colleagues on the aldermanic bench he resisted the move to open aldermanic elections to direct representation by the wards and strenuously fought the claims of Common Council to adjudicate contested elections. He also abused his authority as returning officer in order to frustrate open scrutinies, peremptorily refusing in the Broad Street aldermanic contest of 1711 to declare which voters he had accepted or disqualified. In this respect he was scarcely less brazen than some of his fellow merchants such as Sir Robert Beachcroft, lord mayor of London in 1712. In the Langbourn aldermanic contest of that year Beachcroft had the audacity to preside over his own candidature along with Peter Delmé, a Bank Director, against the Tories Sir William Withers and Sir Samuel Clarke. In the election the Tory candidates appeared to have the majority of votes, but in the face of the evidence Beachcroft

Revolution', *Journal of Modern History*, 4/4 (Dec. 1985), 591–7; and *A Fractured Society*, ch. 2. See also Margaret Priestley, 'London Merchants and Opposition Politics in Charles II's reign', *Bulletin of the Institute of Historical Research*, 29 (1956), 205–19.

declared for the Whigs: and when forty-two petitioners raised the issue in Common Council, 'It pleased God that the Right Honorable the Lord Mayor was suddenly taken ill, so that the Court rose without coming to any resolution.'[14]

Such high-handed tactics only served to intensify the struggle over city governance, both in Common Council and the courts. In 1712 the Tory majority on Common Council passed a by-law to regularize ward elections and to limit the powers of the presiding officer, insisting that he publicly declare which voters he had disqualified. Two years later it overturned the old system of electing aldermen by nomination and co-option, in favour of direct ward representation, striking a blow for freemen democracy. These victories brought only modest gains. Although the Whig aldermen did not openly challenge the 1712 and 1714 by-laws, they continued to deny the right of Common Council to judge the legality of ward elections, especially those pertaining to aldermen, and persistently flouted legally constituted procedures. When the Tory-dominated Common Council sought redress in the courts it was regularly obstructed. In April 1714 Lord Mayor Samuel Stanier, at the prompting of Bank director Sir William Ashurst, left the chamber rather than admit two Tory councillors for Cheap ward on a writ of mandamus from Queen's Bench, 'the members crying out justice, liberty, English privileges and the like, but all to no purpose'. On other occasions writs of mandamus were countered by writs of prohibition. When the Whigs blocked a petition on a disputed return for Bread Street ward in 1720 with yet another writ of prohibition, the Tory printer John Barber was heard to remark 'a good night to our liberties and privileges . . . instead of a Court of Common Council we shall sit here as a Court of Clots'.[15] For this indiscretion he was hauled before King's Bench for contempt of court, and although ultimately pardoned, ordered to pay costs.

This obstructive policy of the aldermanic bench, masterminded by some of the best-known exponents of Revolution finance, sharpened the suspicion of the moneyed interest as well as blazoning the conservatism of the Whigs. Indeed, as the Whig party became increasingly identified with high finance

[14] CLRO Misc. MS 241.1; British Library, Hargrave MS, 139, fos. 222–6.
[15] *HMC Portland* MS, v. 411–12; BL, Hargrave MS, 139, fo. 235.

and correspondingly oligarchic in its politics, so dissidents of the lower ranks of the electorate began to gravitate to their opponents. Admittedly, there were impediments to the Tories' popular appeal. Their support of a more open structure of politics fell short of radical expectations, for despite their opposition to the 1692 Act and their endorsement of direct ward elections, they never campaigned for an unqualified freeman franchise. Nor did they share the radicals' perception of Common Hall as the central forum of London opinion. What is more, the royalist, High Anglican heritage of the Tories cannot have sat well with the libertarian inclinations of many freemen. Fulminations from the pulpit against the Good Old Cause and the persistent eulogies of the royal 'martyr', Charles I, hardly cut ice with radicals who cherished London's democratic interlude, nor did it entirely square with the demands for a more representative and independent Common Council whose historical genealogy reached back to the Interregnum. Not surprisingly, some crypto-republicans remained riveted to the Whig party despite the oligarchic stance of its leaders, as did the Dissenting interest *tout court*, recognizing that Tory religious policy would cut a swathe through its ranks and deny its members even minimal civic rights. At the same time, the Tory party had not been greatly compromised by Charles II's reassertion of his prerogative powers in 1683. A substantial number of its leaders had disavowed his adventurist policies and those of his brother, and had defended the City's autonomy from royal intervention. Such men entered the post-Revolution era with their reputations intact and lent substance to the argument that London Tories were not unconditional supporters of monarchy nor ideologically hostile to civic independence. To vote Tory after 1688 was not necessarily to vote for a reactionary past.

Moreover, the appeal of London Toryism was never narrowly political. It drew its strength from important social and economic developments which compounded the Whigs' renunciation of radicalism. The Tory critique of occasional conformity as a self-serving, untrustworthy, and intrinsically immoral practice played upon the anxieties of civically minded Londoners who looked askance at the new constellation of moneyed power and its dissenting affiliations. As some 50 of the first 120 Bank directors were Dissenters or their close allies, religious and economic opportunism seemed intertwined. Many citizens resented the fact that the new barons of Revolution finance had displaced the City as a major source of government credit and baulked at the wealth of the central nonconformist congregations. The strains of war fuelled these animosities, for they accentuated the divergent interests of the fundholders from the trading rank and file. Like many landed gentlemen, London traders and manufacturers were piqued by the huge fortunes made from war, and the influence that such money could bring to bear upon government policy. No doubt they also chafed at the way in which wartime speculations cramped their supplies of credit, a crucial issue for men of middling means.

The emergence of new sources of power and credit in London society after 1688 thus gave rise to a Tory populism, rooted essentially in the manufacturing trades and middling crafts but reaching a much wider constituency. Within the Livery the Tories drew increasing support from the lesser companies in contrast to their opponents who had begun to consolidate their support among the Great Twelve.[16] To be sure, the social polarities between Whig and Tory were not as striking during the heyday of Sacheverell as they were to be under Walpole, for the battle between High Churchmen and Dissenters remained an important determinant of political choice. But a comparison between the 1682 and 1710 poll-books reveals a clear shift in the proclivities of those livery companies which genuinely represented their crafts. Marginally Tory in 1682, they were solidly so by 1710.

If social contrast between the parties was fairly evident in Common Hall by 1710, it was emphatically apparent among the freemen of the wards. At the time of the Exclusion crisis the Whigs commanded clear majorities in the populous outer wards of the City whereas their opponents dominated the

---

[16] Gary S. De Krey, 'Political Radicalism', *Journal of Modern History* (1985) 611–13; and *A Fractured Society*, pp. 165–70. In my view De Krey exaggerates the polarization of Whig and Tory liverymen on social lines before 1720. Taking the 20 companies with the lowest livery fines and/or no residential halls in the period 1682–1722, the pattern of allegiance was as follows: in 1682, 6 voted Tory, 4 Whig, 5 were divided, and 5 are unknown; in 1710 and 1722 the corresponding figures are 9, 5, 4, 2 and 9, 4, 7, 0.

inner mercantile quarters. By the turn of the century the Tories
were beginning to make gains in the wards bordering the city
walls, especially Castle Baynard and Farringdon Within, but at
the expense of their support in the predominantly mercantile
neighbourhoods which were becoming increasingly Whiggish
in inclination. By 1710, and certainly by the Hanoverian
accession, the political geography of the Exclusionist era had
been more or less reversed, with the Whigs well-entrenched in
the wards around the Exchange and the Tories making further
headway in the larger, more populous and industrial wards. As
a result the Tories firmly dominated the Common Council,
returning members who were drawn primarily from the
manufacturing, industrial, and retail trades. Led by merchant
aldermen who had themselves served as Common Councilmen,[17] the Tory party was strongly anchored in the domestic
economy of London and drew proportionately more of its
support from the poorer freemen. This impression is confirmed
from the few scrutiny-books that have survived. In the inner-
city ward of Walbrook, for example, the Tories drew the vast
bulk of their support from skilled craftsmen, domestic suppliers, and retailers in the food trades, in contrast to the Whigs,
who received the support and patronage of the overseas
merchants, factors, and packers. In the more populous but
merchant-dominated ward by the Tower of London,[18] the
Tories were better represented among the small-to-middling
trades. Some 68 per cent of their voters in 1717 occupied
dwellings rated between £10 and £39 per annum, compared to
42 per cent among their opponents.

At the end of Queen Anne's reign the Tories were poised to
win over some of the Common Council seats in the mercantile
quarter of the city and to renew their challenge to the Whig-
dominated Upper Court. The Hanoverian accession frustrated
this advance. Capitalizing upon the deep dissensions within
the Tory party and the highly ambiguous loyalties of some of
its leaders, the Whigs swept to power in the general election of

[17] De Krey, *A Fractured Society*, pp. 171–6; Alfred B. Beaven, *The Aldermen
of the City of London* (2 vols.; London, 1908, 1913), ii. 119–25. My calculations
reveal that, of the aldermen elected between 1694 and 1725, 65% of the Tories
had been Common Councilmen compared to 53% of the Whigs.

[18] CLRO MS, 83.3 (Walbrook ward); MS 77.3 (Tower ward). The rate-books
for Tower ward are located in Guildhall MS 11. 316/56, Land tax, Mar. 1717.

January 1715. In the City the Whigs won by a margin of over 500 votes and promptly pushed through a series of Instructions demanding a full-scale inquiry into the foreign and commercial policies of the Tory ex-ministry. The Treaty of Utrecht and the uncertainties of the succession had ultimately redounded to Whig advantage. But this dramatic reversal of party fortunes also intensified political rivalries at the grass roots and unleashed the forces of disaffection which had scarcely been contained since the final years of the war. While the proclamation of the new reign and George I's coronation passed without major protest in London, there had been clear signs that the popular acceptance of the Hanoverian regime would be contingent upon the political complexion of the government. A correspondent of Robert Harley noted that some London parishes had been extremely reluctant to ring in the new reign and that many Tories had stood with their hats on while the sheriffs read the proclamation.[19] Such displays of Tory dissonance were also evident at Marlborough's entry to London and at the Lord Mayor's Banquet in October, when the king was personally greeted with shouts of 'Ormonde, no Marlborough.'[20] They were quickly followed by a minor riot at Whitechapel where Dr Welton's High Church supporters attacked a visiting preacher from Berkshire who had gloried in the nation's 'deliverance' from Tory-Jacobitism.

By the spring of 1715 this disaffection had spread to the streets of the metropolis. On the anniversary of the late queen's accession, bells were rung, flags displayed, and a man pilloried at the Royal Exchange for speaking treasonable words against George I was released to cries of 'High Church and Sacheverell for ever' and 'Down with the Whigs.'[21] These outbursts escalated once Parliament had met and the full implications of the Whig revenge against the Tory ex-ministry became clear. In mid-April a Brentford wool-comber was indicted for condemning the king's speech and several other men were charged with drinking the Pretender's health, including one who laid fifty guineas against the king reigning

[19] BL, Loan 29/204, f. 400.
[20] BL, Add. MS 22,202, fos. 200–1, 212; Abel Boyer, *Political State of Great Britain* (60 vols.; London, 1711–40), viii. 439.
[21] *Post Boy*, 8–10 Mar. 1715; *St James's Post*, 11 Mar. 1715.

twelve months. Predictably, the next sequence of anniversaries brought a new flush of demonstrations. Queen Anne's coronation day was riotously celebrated in the western parishes of the city and an effigy of King William was burnt on the bonfire at Snow Hill.[22] The king's birthday on 28 May brought a riotous crowd to the Royal Exchange, 'armed with great Clubbs and crying out High Church and Ormonde'. At Cheapside they paraded effigies of Cromwell, William III, and Marlborough, shouting 'Down with the Rump' and 'No Hanoverian, No Presbyterian Government.'[23] Several arrests were made on this occasion and the London militia was called out, but this did not deter Tory crowds from celebrating Restoration day. On this occasion they smashed the windows that were not illuminated, including those of the Whig lord mayor, Sir Charles Peers, and burnt another effigy of Cromwell before Smithfield. More ominously still, the Pretender's birthday saw a flurry of white roses and cockades in Clerkenwell, Holborn, and Whitechapel and intimations of a second Sacheverell fever.[24] On the celebrated 10 June, 400 rioters, many of them 'masked or in women's apparel', sacked Wright's Presbyterian meeting-house in Blackfriars and the Pretender's declaration was tacked to the door of Burgess's chapel in Lincoln's Inn Fields.

The Tories hoped that the mounting discontent against the new regime would deter the Whigs from pursuing retributive action against their leaders. Before the coronation Swift predicted that 'If anything withholds the Whigs from the utmost violence, it will be only fear of provoking the Rabble, by remembering what past in the Business of Sacheverell.'[25] The same point was echoed by Bishop Atterbury. In an anonymous electoral pamphlet he had warned that a high-handed Whig policy would simply inflame popular prejudice against the new king and fan the fires of discontent. But in fact

[22] *Flying Post*, 23–6 Apr., 5–7 May 1715; Greater London Record Office (GLRO), MJ/SR indt. 75, recs. 56, 61, 212, 241, 270.

[23] Public Record Office (henceforth PRO), SP 35/74/33–4; Boyer, *Political State*, ix. 335, 444–5; CLRO, Lieutenant Minutes (1714–44), fo. 27.

[24] *Flying Post*, 11–14, 21 June 1715; *Dublin Post Man*, 4 July 1715; PRO, WO 4/17/144.

[25] Jonathan Swift, *The Correspondence of Jonathan Swift 1714–23*, ed. Harold Williams (5 vols.; Oxford, 1963), iii. 131.

the demonstrations simply stiffened the resolve of the Whigs to try the architects of the Treaty of Utrecht as quickly as possible. In Parliament, Lord Coningsby cited the provocative symbolism of 10 June as a reason for speeding up the trials, while from the pulpit, Thomas Bradbury asserted that 'nothing but an impeachment could destroy the Interest these men have with the Mob who then may be brought to consider what Devils they had worshipped'.[26] This determination brought substantial political dividends, for the defection of Ormonde and Bolingbroke appeared to confirm Tory complicity in the riots and strengthened the government's powers of repression. By the outbreak of the rebellion in the north the government had co-ordinated the local committees to administer the oaths of allegiance and supremacy and had begun to ferret out the printers, publishers, and preachers who had stiffened resistance to the ministry. In the next few months, several hawkers were taken up in St Giles-in-the-Fields, including Frances Chichester for dispersing 'divers scandalous and seditious papers against the government'; and Elizabeth Humphries of Long Acre, who was arrested for 'crying about the Street a scandalous paper called England or Great Britain's Run Mad, a Dialogue between George and James'.[27]

The outbreak of the rebellion and the evident disunity of the Tory party, gravely embarrassed by the flight of Ormonde and Bolingbroke to St Germain and the seditious militancy of its rank and file, provided the Whigs with a golden opportunity to consolidate their position in City politics. The Whigs were well prepared for this eventuality. Since the summer of 1714 the Whigs had begun to mobilize their resources for the Hanoverian accession. In May 1714 they had created a club to co-ordinate their electoral support in the City wards, and following the general election had established links with James Craggs, the postmaster-general, and by extension with the leading lights of the government.[28] By the summer of 1715 the Whig party was well placed to take control of the Common

---

[26] PRO, SP 35/3/167–8; Thomas Bradbury, *The Necessity of Impeaching the late Ministry* (London, 1715), pp. 28–9.

[27] GLRO, MJ/SR 2258 rec. 188; WJ/SR 2260 rec. 151.

[28] Henry Horwitz (ed.), *London Politics 1713–1717: Minutes of a Whig Club 1714–1717* (London Record Society, 17; London, 1981), *passim.*

Council from its opponents. Factious Tory councillors were under close surveillance; Tory control of the City lieutenancy had been broken and its officers removed from the militia; and the Whig party was able to mobilize the extensive government patronage of the Excise, Stamp, Leather, and Ordnance departments as well as its own clientage among the nonconformist community and the mercantile bourgeoisie. The Whigs had also calculated where they could gain extra votes from the nonfreemen and which common councillors they could detach from their opponents. Yet despite this battery of electoral support and the political advantage that they reaped from the Accession crisis, the Whigs failed to breach the last bastion of Tory power. While the Whigs narrowed the Tory majorities on Common Council in 1714 and 1715, they lost ground in the following year, securing 79 seats to their opponents' 115. By the time of the next general election in 1722 Whig fortunes had slumped even further, for they held only 50 seats to the Tories' 126 and secured outright majorities in only six wards.[29] Dominant in Parliament and in the circles of big business, the Whigs failed to win over the freemen of the wards.

Part of the reason for the Whigs' poor showing in ward politics stemmed from the manipulative policies of the aldermanic court, which persistently denied freemen their electoral choice and thwarted the efforts of Common Council to adjudicate contested elections. As we had seen, this was a major issue in City politics and one that was aggravated by the Lords' judgment of 1719 which excoriated Common Council for using public funds to finance its legal suits against the Court of Aldermen.[30] But there was also considerable opposition to the illiberal manner in which the Whigs had consolidated their power since the accession. Many Londoners resented the way in which the military had been used to disperse the frolicsome, irreverent demonstrations against the Whig ministry in 1716, especially on the Pretender's birthday, when six hundred guards entered the City to arrest all those wearing white cockades and shot down one freeman who

---

[29] Horwitz, *London Politics*, pp. 16–17; my figures are calculated from Christopher Layer's annotated list of the 1722 Common Council, located in PRO, SP 35/39/298.

[30] *Journals of the House of Lords*, 21 (1718–21), 145–9.

called them 'His Majesty's bulldogs'.[31] This intervention flouted the City's deep-rooted tradition of independence from government and standing army. It was especially galling because the government's proscription of street demonstrations during the Accession crisis was not extended to the equally provocative counter-demonstrations of the Whig mughouses. These clubs, financed by Whig grandees such as the Duke of Newcastle and linked to both military and paramilitary organizations such as the Artillery Company, were ostensibly created to boost loyalism in London and to stem the tide of disaffection. But their anti-Catholic, anti-Jacobite festivals were often highly inflammatory, replete with the symbols of Tory perfidy and disunity; and they generated a series of street battles between Tory and Whig demonstrators that kept Accession politics at fever pitch and arguably strengthened the government's militaristic tendencies.

Closely allied to these developments was a series of parliamentary acts which, in the eyes of many, confirmed the Whig's anti-libertarian proclivities. Early in the reign the open tolerance of popular disturbance in many provincial towns and the extreme difficulty in bringing the ringleaders to justice had convinced the Whigs that new anti-riot measures were necessary. Accordingly, the spring of 1715 saw the introduction of a new Riot Act which substantially modified the legal definition of popular disorder. Before the Act common and statute law had distinguished riots against the state (treason) from riots of a private nature (misdemeanour). The distinction gave a grand jury some leeway in the interpretation of popular grievances and, where it was compassionate or in sympathy with the rioters, effectively prohibited exemplary executions. It also mitigated the use of violence in suppressing riots, for civil and military authorities could be charged with using excessive force if the riot was regarded as a private matter. The new Act overrode such distinctions. Under its terms, rioters numbering twelve or more were guilty of a capital felony if they failed to disperse within an hour of the proclamation ordering them to

---

[31] *Weekly Journal*, 16 June 1716; James L. Fitts, 'Newcastle's Mob', *Albion*, 5/1 (spring, 1973), 41–9; Nicholas Rogers, 'Popular Protest in Early Hanoverian London', *Past and Present*, 79 (May, 1978), 78–83.

do so. Furthermore, magistrates and their agents were indemnified if, in the course of dispersing rioters, they happened to kill or injure them. In other words, the doctrine of constructive treason was supplemented by a behaviourist definition of riot, which ignored popular grievances and protected the forces of law and order from legal recrimination.[32] The intention of the Act was clear: to circumscribe the powers of juries; to enhance those of the bench; and to widen the opportunities for judicial terror and the swift suppression of public disorder.

In the Midlands the Riot Act was invoked to suppress the rash of meeting-house riots that had reached alarming proportions in the summer of 1715. In London it was used for more openly partisan purposes, to curb the attacks upon Whig mug-houses that had gathered momentum following the northern insurrection and the trials of the Preston rebels.[33] The most formidable of these attacks occurred at Robert Read's mug-house in Salisbury Court, deep in the Tory quarter of Farringdon Without. Here Tories and muggites traded insults and blows in a series of street scuffles until the landlord, allegedly provoked beyond endurance, fired on the crowd killing one of its ringleaders, Daniel Vaughan, a small-coals-man and former Bridewell apprentice. The guards from Whitehall were immediately called in to disperse the rioters, the new Riot Act was read, and about thirty were arrested. Most of the assailants were released, presumably through lack of evidence, but six were indicted and found guilty of capital felony under the terms of the Act. Five were hanged at the end of the street. Robert Read, by contrast, was acquitted of murder after a three-hour trial, despite a contrary verdict from the coroner's jury.

The Salisbury Court executions added a partisan flavour to the 'Bill of Riots', as one Tory satirist dubbed the Riot Act,[34] and only deepened its unpopularity. Together with 1 George I, st. 2 c. 30, which allowed the government to transfer all treason trials to suitably loyalist counties, the Riot Act signified the increasingly authoritarian drift of Whig policy and

---

[32] N. Rogers, 'Popular Protest', *Past and Present* (1978), 73–5.
[33] Ibid. 81–3.
[34] Charles Hornby, *The Second and Last English Advice to the Freeholders of England* (London, 1723), p. 25.

the party's deep suspicion of popular rights and privileges. The Septennial Act did nothing to detract from this image, for it was rightly perceived as a statute which would reduce the power of the electorate over its representatives and insulate the Commons from popular pressures. Indeed, Whig spokesmen admitted as much, defending the Act as a critical safeguard against popular anarchy and sedition and as a necessary fillip to magisterial authority, hitherto at the mercy of wayward shifts in political power. As Defoe opined, the continuation of triennial parliaments would likely produce 'a Triennial King, Triennial Alliances and a Triennial Constitution'.[35] This alarmist strain of thinking may have touched those troubled by the tumults of 1715 and 1716 and transfixed by the persistent rumours of Jacobite plots which fuelled the Whig politics of fear. But it ran very much against the grain of independent opinion in London and the custom of its citizens, who were habituated to annual Common Council elections and had recently pressed for an increasing voice in the election of aldermen. Predictably, the Septennial Act won little respect from those who cherished London's role as the pulse of the Augustan electorate, nor from those who remembered earlier transgressions of parliamentary power, justified, as in 1716, as a necessary counterpoise to electoral venality and political malevolence. Well might the Whigs smart at the bonfires which greeted the dissolution of 1722, 'imitating the Rejoicings which were made at the Dissolution of Oliver's Rump Parliament', and the 'cries of the hawkers who were dispersing *the last Will and Testament of the old deceased Parliament, the Character of the Rump Parliament* etc.'.[36] The London streets rang with seditious laughter.

The tough measures adopted by the Whigs during the Accession crisis underscored the illiberal, oligarchic tenor of their policies, a phenomenon which in London, at least, had become increasingly evident since the turn of the century. Together with the financial scandals of the era they formed the staple of a new Tory critique of Hanoverian England which

[35] Daniel Defoe, *The Alteration in the Triennial Act Considered* (London, 1716), p. 21.
[36] 'Cato' [Thomas Gordon], *A Short View of the Conspiracy with Some Reflections on the Present State of Affairs* (London, 1723), p. 24.

proved very popular in London circles. Weeklies like the
Freeholder's Journal brought a sharper perspective to
eighteenth-century politics in the light of post-1714 developments, casting the Whig party as the promoter of a new state
complex which profoundly altered the balance of forces in
British politics and degraded its standards of public service. In
this 'Age of Engraftments', with its 'Engraftments of Stocks'
and 'Engrafting one Parliament upon another', financial speculation and political opportunism were conjoined, and a 'Sett of
upstarts' were seen riding high upon public gullibility and
misfortune.[37] Among them were to be found some of the
foremost leaders of London Whiggery. They included Sir
Gilbert Heathcote, Spanish wine merchant, government contractor, Bank and East India director, a wheeler-dealer of
Revolution finance who believed it was 'more a man's business
to look forward and retrieve than to look backward and repine'
and whose hard-nosed attitude towards the poor was immor-
talized by Pope; and Sir John Eyles, the son of a Baptist mercer
from Wiltshire who made his fortune as a London merchant,
helped Walpole salvage the South Sea company after the
Bubble, and was deeply involved in the fraudulent sale of the
forfeited estates of the English Jacobites.[38] They also featured
new aldermen like Sir Harcourt Master, a money-lender and
South Sea director whose loyalist activities in 1715 and 1716
landed him several plum government jobs, including the
lucrative post of Receiver-General of the Land Tax for London
and Middlesex.[39] This windfall clearly went to his head, for by
1720 Master found himself in financial difficulties, having

---

[37] *Freeholder's Journal*, 23 Mar. 1722; see also 4 Apr. 1722. According to
Edmund Curll, the circulation of the *Freeholder's Journal* reached 8,000: see
Laurence Hanson, *Government and the Press 1695–1763* (Oxford, 1936), p. 65.

[38] Romney Sedgwick (ed.), *The History of Parliament: The House of
Commons 1715–54* (2 vols.; London, 1970), ii. 21, 123; Alexander Pope, *Epistle
III*, ll. 101–2. In Charles Hornby, *The Second and Last English Advice*, p. 50,
Eyles is referred to as one of 'Walpole's Pack-horses . . . void of all Honour and
Compassion'. Eyles was also attacked by Hutcheson in the *Freeholder's
Journal*, 16 June 1722.

[39] On Master see PRO SP 44/176/241; *Flying Post*, 8–10 Nov. 1715; *Weekly
Journal*, 4 Aug. 1716, 26 Nov. 1716, 21 June 1718. See also John Carswell, *The
South Sea Bubble* (London, 1960), pp. 74, 215, 277; P. G. M. Dickson, *The
Financial Revolution in England* (London, 1967), pp. 118–19, 126; Virginia
Cowles, *The Great Swindle* (London, 1960), p. 172; William Cobbett, *Parlia-
mentary History of England* (41 vols.; London, 1804–20), vii. 782, 835.

speculated unsuccessfully with government money. As a result he indulged in some sharp dealing in South Sea stock during the 1720 scandal, bringing in a list of £110,000 on the third subscription. Never one of the inner circle of directors who master-minded the plan, he none the less received the full wrath of the Commons for his unscrupulous dealings. Like 'Aminadah Cheat-all' in the anonymous *Essay in praise of Knavery*, he was 'a true Son of Exchange Alley' who epitomized the new moneyed order.[40]

The early years of the Whig supremacy thus threw up a series of issues and personalities around which the London Tories could reorganize. In the run-up to the 1722 election the accumulated grievances of the past seven years were put squarely before the London electorate. Archibald Hutcheson, a Whig lawyer who had managed the affairs of the exiled but popular duke of Ormonde, set the pace, centring his attack upon the government's anti-libertarian legislation as well as its complicity with the South Sea affair. 'You call yourselves Whigs', he thundered in an open letter to the government, 'but you have acted according to the Principles of the vilest Tories. Has there ever been a Bill for Public Liberty proposed, since the Revolution, which you and your predecessors, Pensionary Court Whigs, have not strenuously opposed?'[41] And he went on to mock the ministry's inquiry into the South Sea scheme: 'those that rattled the false dice were carried to the Horse Pond, while the confederate Sharpers, Setters and Officers of the Gaming-Table sat undisturbed, demure and innocent as Lambs, quite amazed at the Impudence of the Cheat.'

These words were heeded by the London Whig party, for it quite consciously adopted a circumspect electoral strategy, abandoning all candidates clearly identified with ministerial policy and the inner circles of Whig high finance. Neither of the incumbents closely associated with the Bank of England, Sir John Ward and Sir Thomas Scawen, both of whom had supported the Septennial Act, were put up for nomination. Rather the Whig leaders delayed advertising a slate until the disposition of the Livery at the initial nomination at Skinner's Hall was known, ultimately selecting only three candidates

[40] Anon., *An Essay in Praise of Knavery* (London, 1723), p. 30.
[41] *Freeholder's Journal*, 23 Mar. 1721.

rather than the customary four. These included the two Whig incumbents who since 1715 had consistently voted with the opposition; and Sir John Barnard, an independent Whig who openly disavowed any connection with the Bubble companies, professing his 'utter abhorence of all such vile methods of becoming rich'.[42]

This was more of a face-saving list than a conventional one. It indicates the despondency that riddled Whig circles when they faced an electorate smarting from the financial scandals of 1720 and the four-year postponement of voting rights.[43] In the event the Whigs were able to avoid an electoral humiliation by sailing close to the popular wind and profiting from the factionalism of their opponents, who could not agree whether to promote an impeccably Tory list or one more attractive to voters beyond the Blue constituency. Even so, the election of two nominal Whigs out of sympathy with ministerial policy was hardly an endorsement of the party. That was made clearer by the instructions issued to the new representatives demanding, *inter alia*, the repeal of the Riot and Septennial Acts and a further parliamentary inquiry into the South Sea scandal.[44] This strident anti-ministerialism admittedly evaporated somewhat in the wake of the Layer plot, which raised once more the spectre of Tory-Jacobitism. Yet the boost which these revelations should have given to Whig fortunes did not re-establish the party's former standing, and for the next two years the parties remained deadlocked. An analysis of the polling-lists of the 1722 general election, the shrieval election of March 1724, and the parliamentary by-election later that year suggests that roughly two-thirds of the regular voters voted consistently along party lines.[45] While the Whigs enticed

---

[42] *Daily Post*, 21 May 1722.

[43] In the shrieval election of June 1721, the Whig candidates were confronted by voters shouting 'No Courtiers! No South Sea!' Protests against the South Sea Scandal and against the Septennial Act were also heard in the Westminster election of 1722, three weeks before the election in the City of London: *Norwich Gazette*, 24 June–1 July 1721, 17–24 Mar. 1722.

[44] *Freeholder's Journal*, 30 May 1722.

[45] This statement is based on a 10% sample of the 1722 poll. The voting behaviour of the liverymen in the sample was then followed up in the two 1724 elections for which polling-lists have survived. The 1722 poll-book was printed separately. The lists for the 1724 elections can be found in *Daily Post*, 16 Mar. 1724; *Daily Journal*, 20 Mar. 1724 (shrieval); and *Daily Post*, 7 Dec. 1724 (parliamentary by-election).

slightly more votes from the Tories than vice versa, the liverymen who split their vote in 1722 tended to vote Tory rather than Whig thereafter. Since the regular voters were more or less evenly balanced between the two parties, electoral victories were to a great extent determined by the ability of either party to mobilize the casual and new voters, a factor which explains the heated controversies over voter-eligibility and the escalation of violence at the hustings.

This was the context in which the City Elections Bill was introduced in the Commons. Recourse to Parliament to resolve the bitter disputes over ward elections had been contemplated by the leaders of the Whig party since the early years of the Hanoverian accession. The issue was revived in 1723 when the Tory Common Council endorsed a liberal definition of the rate-paying qualifications for freeman voters and recommended stricter controls upon aldermen in their capacity as returning officers.[46] Neither of these propositions was acceptable to the Whig-dominated Upper Court, which in March 1724 invoked its veto to prevent the new electoral bill passing into law. This action made parliamentary intervention more or less inevitable, but what gave it a sense of urgency was the precarious state of Whig support in the City's other electorate, the eight thousand liverymen who chose the sheriffs, mayors, and representatives to Parliament. As we have seen, successive Jacobite plots had failed to consolidate the Whigs' impressive 1715 victory. Their appeal as the party of the Protestant succession, protecting liberty from a Catholic repossession of Britain, had become problematic.

In taking the question of electoral reform to Parliament, the Whigs posed as the party of electoral probity, anxious to restore some order and regularity to City contests and to avoid needless, expensive litigation.[47] The argument was not without some substance, for the Tories had overreached themselves in the shrieval elections of 1723 and 1724, flooding the polls with irregular voters and inhibiting orderly scrutinies. On the other hand, the Whig arguments about electoral chicanery and violence were hypocritical, ignoring years of Whig obstructionism in ward elections and the persistent efforts by Tory

---

[46] I. G. Doolittle, 'Walpole's City Elections Act (1725)', *English Historical Review*, 97 (July 1982), 508–10.
[47] *London Journal*, 8 May 1725.

councillors to bind Whig aldermen to open electoral procedures. They were also exaggerated, for apart from the
infractions of the mid-1720s and the adverse publicity thrown
upon Humphrey Parsons, the returning officer in 1723, livery
elections were relatively orderly affairs. Rarely did City
elections degenerate into violence so evident as that at
Westminster, where voters were ridden down and cudgelled in
Tothill Fields. To be sure, with some 6,000–7,000 liverymen,
roughly a third of whom lived outside the City, regularly
casting their votes, impersonations were not uncommon.
Humphrey Parsons allegedly allowed journeymen Joyners to
poll for the Tory Sir John Williams in 1723 as well as
Patternmakers and Coachmakers of dubious authenticity.[48]
Yet bad voters typically amounted to 3–5 per cent of all
participants—not a high percentage by eighteenth-century
standards. Only in March 1724 did the number of objections
approach 15 per cent of the total poll, and on that occasion the
Tories complained that their opponents swamped the scrutiny
with many 'hear-say Affidavits' on the last day, making it
impossible for them to muster counter-evidences.[49] For all the
publicity about electoral malpractice, then, Common Hall
elections were comparatively orderly, albeit litigious events.
Londoners were extremely touchy about their political independence and deplored both the bruising and the eat-and-swill
conventions of other constituencies.

The same was true of ward elections. Rarely were they
carried with violence and bribery, although they were certainly
litigious, more litigious in fact than those of Common Hall. It
was not uncommon for 20–30 per cent of the votes to be
contested, and in some cases the proportion of objections was
even higher. This was because the basic structure of ward
politics encouraged a wide range of inhabitants to vote,
especially those who had been active in their local vestries,
precincts, or ward inquests. The result was that considerable
numbers of 'unfreemen' and lodgers voted in ward elections,
despite the fact that both parties officially recognized that the
franchise fell upon ratepaying freemen householders. These
votes were regularly challenged, too, for local managers had a

---

[48] BL, Hargrave MS 139, fos. 285–8, 304.
[49] *Daily Post*, 25, 27 Mar. 1724.

keen knowledge of the prevailing affiliations and credentials of many of their citizens. A surviving voting-list for Walbrook ward in 1714 shows that the Whigs knew who were nonjurors, who had not paid the rates, who were politically passive, and who could be induced to vote with a little prodding.[50] Such information was readily available for scrutinies. In the Langbourn aldermanic election of 1712, for instance, objections were raised against the vote of Jeremiah Bold because he was a shopkeeper rather than a householder and had 'paid no Rent nor Parish duties from midsummer'. Complaints were also levelled against Joseph Watson, a haberdasher of Exchange Alley, who had paid scot to the neighbouring ward of Cornhill, and against William Potter, whose rents were paid by Hudson's Bay.[51] On the other hand, the scrutineer was prepared to defend the vote of Joseph Mott, a Vintner, whose eligibility had been challenged by the opposing party. Mott paid £60 per annum for his house, the scrutineer claimed, which is 'part in Cornhill ward, & part in Langbourn. He eats, drinks & lyes in that part of the house which is in Langbourn ward' and had paid scot and lot at the time of the poll.

Such intimate information suggests that local managers had both the sophistication and knowledge to arbitrate at electoral disputes, and that however contentious ward elections may have been, they were not teetering upon electoral anarchy. It also suggests that many of the arguments for parliamentary intervention in 1724 were superficial, exaggerating electoral excess and corruption. Indeed, far from being a disinterested measure designed to restore a modicum of civic harmony to London's troubled government, the City Elections Act of 1725 had partisan objectives, as an analysis of its clauses and amendments reveals.

In the original draft of the Bill it was proposed to restrict the growth of the lesser livery companies, none of whom were allowed to exceed their present membership without permission of the Court of Aldermen. This would have benefited the Whigs, who by 1722 had won over most of the Great Twelve Companies, while losing ground among some of the smaller. But it was not a crucial issue for the Whig party, who

---

[50] CLRO, MS 83.3.
[51] CLRO, Misc MS 248.1.

could depend upon the patronage of the government departments and the moneyed companies for a substantial phalanx of supporters, and who could confidently expect that the stricter regulation of the Livery by means of voter-registration would benefit their candidates. Consequently, after this clause had drawn a storm of protest, it was judiciously abandoned, thereby enhancing the conciliatory image of the ministerial party.

By contrast, the ward franchise was a more serious matter, for it was in the wards rather than in the Livery that Whig support was weakest. It was also a more difficult issue to resolve, for although the Tories were conventionally classified as the popular party, the Whig had benefited from the votes of the 'unfreemen' in the wealthier wards. In the closely contested Broad Street aldermanic election of 1711, for instance, the Whigs calculated that they would benefit from the 'unfree' vote in virtually all the inner wards of the City, as well as in Aldersgate and Bishopsgate where several Dissenting chapels were located.[52] Clearly a strict enforcement of the freeman franchise was of dubious advantage to the Whigs. They stood to lose a great deal of unofficial support in the wealthier wards, in return for some gains in the more populous Tory wards of the west.

The Whig solution to this dilemma was to reaffirm the freeman franchise but to offer some encouragement to the wealthier non-freemen to take up the freedom of the city. This *douceur* was the abolition of the customary regulations governing freemen's bequests, which were generally regarded as a major disincentive to civic membership among the rich, although in fact there were various legal stratagems for avoiding the custom.[53] To be sure, this proposal was welcomed on other grounds. It was hoped that it would improve the city's finances and it offered a plausible solution to the complaint that too many businessmen had reaped the advantages of trading in the city without assuming any of the responsibilities. But once the political complexities of the ward

[52] For the Broad Street election of 1711, see *Post Boy*, 27–9 Sept. 1722; Horwitz, *London Politics*, pp. 16–17.
[53] Horwitz, 'Testamentary Practice', *Law and History Review* (1984), 223–39.

franchise are unravelled—once it is recognized that the Whigs had a stake in the non-freeman vote, especially in the wealthier areas of the city—the party dimensions of the proposal seem clear.

The other qualifications surrounding the ward franchise were more directly aimed at the Tories. The disfranchisement of the freeman householders whose premises were rated at under £10 per annum, though less significant than historians have assumed, certainly hurt the Tories in the western wards of the city. By contrast, the allocation of votes to business partners whose yearly rent exceeded £10 per capita helped the Whigs. Similarly, the redefinition of scot to include a broader range of public taxes, or a total contribution of 30 shillings per annum, benefited the wealthier Whig voters, as the Whig aldermen themselves recognized in 1723. What is more, the expansion of scot to include the scavenger, orphans, and watch and ward contributions exposed voters to a wider and more complex qualifying process and strengthened the power of the Whig-dominated Court of Aldermen over its adjudication. Finally, and most significantly in view of the Common Council's continual campaign for an open review of electoral disputes, the regulations governing the supervision of polls and scrutinies were less rigorous than those currently in force under the 1712 by-law. In the initial draft of the Bill the presiding officer, whether Mayor or Alderman, was no longer obliged to specify which contested votes he had allowed or disallowed, only the number of true votes.[54] In view of the aldermanic record since 1709, strong protests were raised against this clause, and the Lords subsequently passed an amendment which made such votes public. Such a list, however, could not be used in evidence before any court of law, and the only deterrent to a partial returning officer, apart from adverse publicity, was a modest fine of £200. As the dissentients in the Lords declared, this was an insufficient guarantee of electoral impartiality.

The cumulative impact of the clauses was therefore weighted towards the Whigs, notwithstanding the amendments made to the Bill and the superficially impartial manner

[54] Doolittle, 'City Elections Act', *English Historical Review* (1982), 513.

in which the measure was promoted. Clearly, the political advantages of these electoral reforms remained somewhat in doubt, for they were ultimately dependent upon the superior organization of the Whig party and its ability to attract new votes from the ranks of the 'unfreemen'. Even so, the risks involved were minimized by strengthening the appellate powers of the Court of Aldermen and confirming its powers of veto over the acts and ordinances of the Common Council. This last proposal was crucial, despite recent claims to the contrary,[55] for it prevented the Common Council from presenting Addresses and petitions that did not square with the prevailing Whig sentiment of the Upper Court, the twenty-five aldermen elected for life. Of course, the Whig monopoly of the Upper Court could be broken; but in 1725 it was reasonably assumed that the tremendous influence which the ministry could bring to bear upon the aldermen of London, many of whom were closely associated with the moneyed companies, would prevent such an eventuality. As one of Walpole's friends wrote to the British envoy at Turin, the aim of the 1725 Act was 'to strengthen the Court party, for if they reduce the government of the City to only the Lord Mayor and the aldermen's power, the Court can at any time gain their worships'. Two months later he confided, 'it was a great shame that the cits should oppose the designs of the government at all elections with so much mutiny'.[56] The 1725 Act would 'bring them to reason'.

Whig 'reason' meant a further retreat from the Whiggery of old and a conception of City governance that constrained popular representation with a reassertion of patrician authority. In this respect the City Elections Act was consistent with the drift of Whig policy since the 1690s and the oligarchic disposition of the Hanoverian regime. Like the Riot and Septennial Acts, the 1725 statute expressed a fear of open politics untempered by the sinews of patronage and magnate power. It also confirmed, beyond question, the alliance of Whiggery and big business, nullifying the efforts of the smaller merchants and traders formally to question the economic

[55] Doolittle, 'City Elections Act', *English Historical Review* (1982), 523–8.
[56] *HMC Clements* MS 384, 391; cited by Alfred J. Henderson, *London and the National Government 1721–42* (Durham, NC, 1945), p. 110.

ramifications of high finance. This became clear in 1727 when the Whig-dominated Court of Aldermen vetoed a Common Council Address to the new monarch lamenting the decline of 'real Credit' and highlighting the current hazards of trade caused by the activities of the South Sea Company, whose exploitation of the Assiento beyond the terms laid down in the Treaty of Utrecht soured Anglo-Spanish relations and disrupted transatlantic commerce.[57] This last issue was to be an important factor in the final mobilization of support against Walpole.

While the City Elections Act clarified the relationship between the Court and high finance so central to Whig support in London, it also facilitated an alliance between the Tories and opposition Whig opinion. Such a combination had been in the offing since the early 1720s, for the journalists who had taken the lead in developing a more secular critique of Whig government were by and large of Whig pedigree, men like Hutcheson and the wayward, mercurial duke of Wharton. In fact, Hutcheson denounced party labels in the first edition of the *Freeholder's Journal* and the following month urged liverymen to make an exemplary rejection of corrupt government for 'the Country very justly looks upon the Londoners to have the greatest Interest in the publick Safety'.[58] But such words went unheeded. Although there was some talk of putting Robert Heysham and Sir John Barnard on an antiministerial list, the habit of party proved too strong.[59] While Barnard himself picked up a good many stray votes, two-thirds of the electors opted for the party slates, forfeiting one vote in the process.

The aftermath of the City Elections Act, however, provided another opportunity for developing a Country opposition. Independent-minded Whigs might have reluctantly accepted the tough measures taken by the government to curb the popular unrest of the accession years, especially if they were convinced that the Tory party was riddled with Jacobitism and still bent upon pursuing a draconian religious policy. Certainly, successive Jacobite plots did little to allay their

---

[57] Henderson, *London and the National Government*, pp. 117–20.
[58] *Freeholder's Journal*, 31 Jan., 28 Feb. 1722.
[59] Henderson, *London and the National Government*, pp. 63–4.

anxieties. But the City Elections Act could not be defended upon grounds of national emergency; it was a frontal attack upon London's political autonomy, constraining its democratic processes in the interests of Whig oligarchy. Never as radical a measure as the forfeiture of the charter, to which it was sometimes compared, it cannily exploited the government's resources of patronage and made it more difficult for London to act as the pulse of the political nation outside Parliament. These considerations weighed heavily upon citizens proud of London's political inheritance.

Changes within the Tory constituency itself also eased the promotion of a broader-based opposition. Before the 1720s the principal guardians of orthodox Toryism were the High Church clergy, ever ready to rally Anglicans against the Dissenters, whose numbers and visibility increased markedly in the two decades after 1688. Indeed, it was the 'Gown Incendiaries', as Defoe called them,[60] who were the most outspoken critics of the Hanoverian regime during the Accession years, even to the point of inciting popular disorder. After 1720, however, the High Church divines were no longer the conscience of the party in quite the same way as they had been earlier. Denied a voice in convocation, they also lost some of their more formidable leaders in London. By 1724 two of their foremost demagogues, Luke Milbourne, rector of St Ethelburga, and Henry Sacheverell, rector of St Andrew Holborn, were dead; and Bishop Atterbury, the former lecturer of St Brides and Bridewell, acknowledged chieftain of Westminster, had been harried into exile. Bereft of such charismatic leadership, the High Church divines found it difficult to adjust to the changing religious context, for the Whigs did not pursue a policy of unqualified religious toleration as was predicted. While the Occasional Conformity and Schism Acts were repealed in 1719 and the Corporation Act was modified to preclude a vigorous persecution of nonconformists, Dissenters were not admitted to full citizenship. They failed to secure the

[60] Daniel Defoe, *The Pernicious Consequences of the Clergy's Intermeddling with Affairs of State* (London, 1715), pp. 38–9. See also my 'Riot and, Popular Jacobitism in Early Hanoverian England', in Eveline Cruickshanks (ed.), *Ideology and Conspiracy: Aspects of Jacobitism 1689–1759* (Edinburgh, 1982), p. 73 and p. 85 n. 11.

repeal of the Test and Corporation Acts and their acceptance of royal or civic office remained conditional upon local discretion or intermittent Acts of Indemnity. The Anglican fear of a Church overrun by 'schismatics' did not materialize.

This did not mean that sectarian strife was altogether absent from London politics or that High Churchmen were totally denied the opportunity to pour forth on the iniquities of Dissent, which remained riveted to the Whig party despite the modest concessions it received from the government. Notwithstanding the national decline of nonconformity after 1715, the City of London continued to attract spirited preachers to its more prestigious meetings, and funds for new buildings were forthcoming. Edmund Calamy had a new meeting-house built for him at Long Ditch, Westminster, in 1721; Samuel Wright's congregation was housed in a new building in Carter Lane, Doctors Commons, in 1734; and Isaac Watts's chapel outgrew its Mark Lane premises, moving first to Pinners' Hall and later to Bury Street.[61] In fact, the total number of meetings of the three Dissenting denominations and the Quakers continued to grow. Whereas eighty congregations existed at the turn of the century within the wider metropolis, some ninety-nine were to be found in 1740.[62] Certainly, this growth was largely to be found in the metropolitan suburbs and populous parishes outside the City walls and probably concealed a levelling-off, if not decline, in active membership. But the wealthier congregations within the City still held their own, both in terms of numbers and meeting-houses, and continued to provide the social and political leadership of the nonconformist interest in London.

Even so, the religious passions which animated Augustan politics lost much of their vibrancy. With the eclipse of High Church clerical leadership and the lower profile of Dissent, which sought to elicit further concessions from the Whig ministry through discreet lobbying rather than through the electoral process, religion ceased to be such an important

[61] Michael Watts, *The Dissenters* (Oxford, 1978), p. 311; Edmund Calamy, *An Historical Account of My Own Life* (2 vols.; London, 1829), ii. 441. For Calamy and Wright, see also DNB.

[62] For an important commentary on the strength of the Dissenting interest in London in 1731 see Dr Williams Library, MS 38.18. See also ch. 4.

touchstone of London politics. This is evident in the 1727 general election, for despite the open opposition of the Dissenters to Sir John Barnard, who was accused of being a former Sacheverell supporter,[63] the major issues of the campaign were the aldermanic veto, electoral bribery and corruption, and the South Sea Assiento. Indeed, the *Craftsman*, echoing the Common Council's condemnation of South Sea Company policy, urged liverymen to differentiate between 'fair merchants and notorious Stock Jobbers, between the true promoters of our Manufacturers and most Beneficial Commerce, and the overgrown Monopolies which are destructive of both'. It also questioned 'whether all overgrown Companies are not prejudicial to, and in some Measure, inconsistent with the Liberties of a free People, as well as the true Interest of a Trading Nation, with regard to the Influence which they have in the Elections of Members of Parliament, particularly for this great and honourable City'.[64]

The 1727 election was notable in one other respect. It saw the first real break with Augustan party politics. After some initial campaigning on party lines the London opposition eventually agreed to set up an anti-ministerial list consisting of three Tory candidates and the popular Sir John Barnard, who had come out strongly against the City Elections Act and had collaborated with the Tories several months earlier to return Sir Thomas Lombe for Bassishaw ward.[65] This strategy proved successful, for singularly few opposition liverymen voted for the Tory candidates alone; most supported the entire opposition slate. In a hard-fought contest the opposition ultimately picked up two seats; one going to Sir John Barnard, whose reputation at Common Hall transcended partisanship, the other to Humphrey Parsons, an extreme Tory who had replaced Sir Francis Child on the opposition list when the latter agreed to stand for Middlesex. Although this election was technically a draw between ministry and opposition, anti-ministerial spokesmen regarded it as a victory, for the Court Whigs had gone out of their way to mobilize the support of

---

[63] *Daily Journal*, 11, 16 Aug. 1727. The fear that Tories would persecute Dissenters is mentioned by 'Philo-Londoniensis' in the *Daily Journal*, 7 Oct. 1727.

[64] *Craftsman*, 7–9 Oct. 1727.

[65] Henderson, *London and the National Government*, pp. 135–6.

government placemen. Writing to Harley, Dr Stratford commented that

The carrying of two in the City, under the present circumstances, is a great victory. Had all that were influenced by Bank, South Sea and East India, by custom house, excise, post office & c, and all that did not vote at all, been left to themselves, it must have been carried by at least 4 to 1.[66]

This was certainly an exaggeration, but the result did suggest that a ministerial victory at Common Hall would henceforth be dependent upon superior electoral organization, if not the intimidation of subaltern voters.

This became clear as early as 1728, when the Court Whigs failed to coordinate their campaign for a new chamberlain and consequently put up a poor showing against Colonel Samuel Robinson, a former ally of the duke of Wharton and one of the principal Tory opponents of the City Elections Act. Coming in the wake of the 1727 election, in which accusations of electoral bribery and influence showered the hustings, Robinson deliberately appealed to the independent spirit of the Livery, declaring his 'only Dependence' to be upon the 'Free and Voluntary votes of my Fellow-Citizens'.[67] This stance was contrasted, predictably, with the influence which his opponent could muster among the great moneyed companies and government departments. 'Do you think, sir,' wrote one 'liveryman' to a fictional ward manager on the eve of Robinson's contest, 'I am to be bought and sold, transferred from one another, or chopped and changed like old Frippery? . . . I scorn both Buyer and Seller; and every honest Citizens detests such practices. Nor am I to be Jockeyed out of my Reason by any set of Tricksters, or Influenced by Courtiers, Companies and their Creatures.'[68] Robinson's victory was a sign that the City's tradition of independent politics could not be legislated into docility. It remained to be seen whether the Tory opposition, now leavened by independent Whig opinion, could nullify the 1725 Act and wrest control of the Court of Aldermen from the financial barons of the new Whig order.

[66] *HMC Portland* MS vii. 453.
[67] For accusations of electoral bribery see *Daily Journal*, 27 Oct. 1727, and *Daily Post*, 5 Feb. 1728 (Robinson's declaration).
[68] *Mist's Weekly Journal*, 10 Feb. 1728.

2

The Struggle for Control of the City
1728–1747

THE opposition victories of 1727 and 1728 revealed that the struggle for control of the City of London would probably be a hard and protracted one. But they by no means represented a clear-cut defeat of Walpole's policies. The opposition alliance of Tories and independent Whigs was still confronted with the problem of undermining Walpole's majority on the critically important Court of Aldermen and of eroding the solid support that the Whigs enjoyed at Common Hall and within the inner-city wards. This was a formidable task. Quite apart from the financial barons, the government had attracted the votes of those who identified the Hanoverian regime with commercial stability and social order. These included the Dissenters, who never forgot the High Church assault upon their civic rights and educational institutions. It also included the bulk of the wealthier merchants and tradesmen. Despite the efforts of the opposition press to differentiate the financiers from the merchants, most big businessmen continued to opt for a Whig government which promised peace and prosperity after decades of war. In the shrieval election of 1724, for example, prominent merchants and tradesmen voted Whig rather than Tory by a ratio of 2 : 1.[1]

Developments in the 1730s went some way towards unsettling this electoral base. While the Dissenters continued to vote for Whig candidates in City elections, they did not always play the active role that was expected of them. In some critical contests, in fact, some of their leaders abstained from voting.[2] This absenteeism probably stemmed from the refusal of the

---

[1] I used *Kent's Directory* of 1734 and *An Alphabetical List of the Livery 1733* (BL, 1303 d.12) to locate 100 merchants and leading tradesmen who voted in the March 1724 shrieval election. The polls are to be found in the *Daily Post*, 16 Mar. 1724 and the *Daily Journal*, 20 Mar. 1724.

[2] Of the 25 leaders of the Protestant Dissenting Deputies who were entitled

government to grant them full citizenship, a concession which the Dissenters fully expected after 1714.[3] Even a preacher like Samuel Wright, whose meeting-house had been ransacked by Tory mobs on two occasions in the period 1710–15, felt compelled to sound a note of discord. In a 1733 pamphlet which explicitly recalled the Sacheverell fury, he asked why the Dissenters had not been rewarded for their loyalism to Hanover and their contribution to the state: 'The Glorious Revolution, by which we were delivered from Wooden Shoes and Wooden Gods, was not brought about by the Power nor the Principles of the Church whose Maxims were non-Resistance and Passive Obedience, but by a set of Principles borrow'd from Protestant Dissenters.'[4] In 1719 Wright had declared there was 'nothing too great or generous to expect from the present administration'. Now he thought it time that his brethren demanded the right to full citizenship as 'natives and freeborn Englishmen'.

The smouldering resentment of the Dissenters thus tempered their contribution to City politics and weakened what had hitherto been a reliable and energetic source of Whig support. The situation of the merchants was somewhat different. On the whole the mercantile community had benefited from Walpole's early fiscal reforms, specifically the removal of export duties upon manufacturing goods and the import duties on raw materials. It had also witnessed the slow but steady growth of the economy since 1715. But growth itself, especially in the rapidly expanding sectors of the transatlantic economy, brought a fresh set of problems in its train. The overproduction of sugar in the Caribbean saw a fall in prices after 1728 and demands by planters for privileged

---

to vote in city elections, 19 voted for the government candidate in the 1734 Chamberlain's election and 6 abstained. For the Deputies see Guildhall MS 3083/1.

[3] For the repeal agitation see N. C. Hunt, *Two Early Political Associations: The Quakers and the Dissenting Deputies in the Age of Sir Robert Walpole* (Oxford, 1961), pp. 134–5, 146–53.

[4] Samuel Wright, *The Church in Perils among False Brethren* (London, 1733), pp. 29; cf. 38–9. For the earlier eulogy to Hanover and the Whig government see his *Sermon Breach'd on the Fifth of November in the year 1719* (London, 1719), p. 36.

access to New England and European markets. The commercial penetration of the Caribbean led to renewed tension
between British merchants and the Spanish authorities and
appeals for greater naval protection and diplomatic representation. And the expansion of the tobacco industry led Virginia
planters to demand better terms from London and provincial
consignment merchants and a revision of the regulations
governing the import and re-export of this enumerated
product.[5]

Walpole was not insensitive to these demands for a freer
trade in the transatlantic economy. He raised the duty on
foreign sugar and molasses to boost the English Caribbean
sugar and rum trade and in 1739 allowed the West Indian
planters direct access to European ports. But he miscalculated
the mood of the London merchants when he proposed to
replace the customs duties on tobacco and wines with a new
excise tax. In this instance the demands of the Virginia
planters coincided nicely with his own fiscal priorities: a
reduction of the Land Tax; a renewed emphasis upon indirect
as opposed to direct taxation; and a campaign against smuggling and customs fraud that was costing the Treasury thousands
of pounds each year.[6] Sir Robert hoped that the London
tobacco merchants would accede to his proposal because it
would hit their Glaswegian competitors harder. It was in
Scotland that the evasion of tobacco duties was most marked.[7]
But the Londoners were more concerned with the general
repercussions of the tax, which would not only subject them to
stricter governmental supervision, but would weaken the
credit facilities they enjoyed in a major re-exporting industry.[8]

---

[5] R. B. Sheridan, 'The Molasses Act and the Market Strategy of British Sugar
Planters', *Journal of Economic History*, 17 (1957), 62–83; Jean O. McLachlan,
Trade and Peace with Old Spain 1667–1750 (Cambridge, 1940), pp. 60, 96;
Jacob M. Price, 'The Excise Crisis Revisited: The Administrative and Colonial
Dimensions of a Parliamentary Crisis', in Stephen Baxter (ed.), *England's Rise
to Greatness 1660–1763* (Berkeley and Los Angeles, 1983), pp. 270–7.

[6] For a concise discussion of Walpole's economic policy see Michael Jubb,
'Economic Policy and Economic Development', in Jeremy Black (ed.), *Britain
in the Age of Walpole* (London, 1984), pp. 121–44.

[7] Robert Nash, 'The English and Scottish Tobacco Trades in the Seventeenth and Eighteenth Centuries: Legal and Illegal trade', *Economic History
Review*, 35/2 (May 1982), 354–72.

[8] Price, 'The Excise Crisis Revisited', pp. 287, 305–6.

In fact, as soon as the government hinted at an excise, opposition was organized against it. In December 1732, London merchants met at the Swan tavern, Cornhill, to appoint a watch-dog committee, and to advise the four City members to oppose any extension of the excise.[9] Within weeks other groups in the City had followed suit and communications with provincial towns were opened in earnest. 'The affair of the Excise makes a great noise,' Lady Irwin informed Lord Carlisle in early January, 'Bristol and Leicester have already sent instructions to their Members to oppose it, and 'tis said all the great towns in England will do the same. The merchants of London having informed their correspondents in the country, the apprehension is become general especially amongst the traders in wine and tobacco, those being the first branches that will be attempted.'[10]

As Lady Irwin's letter suggests, the opposition to the tax was well advanced before the government had tabled any specific motion in the Commons. This enabled Walpole's enemies to press their case in the widest possible terms. Accordingly, the excise laws were depicted as prejudicing 'that great and useful body of Man, the Trading People of England ... those who neither seek nor expect Post or Preferments, and who have nothing in view but quietly to reap the Fruits of their honest Industry'.[11] They also bore harshly on the poor, who already shouldered the burden of excise taxes upon basic commodities such as candles, coals, soap, and leather; not to mention the restoration of the tax upon salt, which was seen as part of the same fiscal strategy. As Mist emphasized, excise taxes 'increase the Expense of the labouring and manufacturing people more, in proportion, than that of others in a higher Rank'.[12] Walpole himself made no bones about the socially discriminatory nature of his tax policy. Both the salt duty and the excise were intended to relieve the landed interest and place the tax burden more squarely (in his view, more equitably) upon the consumer. What he would have objected to was the

---

[9] Henderson, *London and the National Government*, p. 141.

[10] *HMC Carlisle*, p. 95, cited by Henderson, *London and the National Government*, p. 140.

[11] *Fog's Weekly Journal*, 13 Jan. 1733.

[12] Ibid., 20 Jan. 1733.

opposition's assertion that such policies harmed production and failed to alleviate the agricultural depression that had hit the country.[13]

Economic considerations were only one source of contention over the new tax proposals; indeed, the historical consensus is that they were less important than the libertarian.[14] It was emphasized that the excise laws denied trial by jury and forced traders into expensive and time-consuming litigation. They placed traders at the mercy of intrusive officers who might exact 'unjust perquisites' and tyrannize wives and daughters.[15] What is more, further excise laws would probably extend government patronage to unparalleled depths, and sap the last rivulets of English liberty. Such arguments were without doubt hyperbolic: the opposition had correctly sensed the political importance of the salt tax as a source of patronage, but its speculations that the country would be overrun by excise officers were wide of the mark. Sir Philip Yorke protested that the government's proposals envisaged an increase of 150 at most; and he went on to emphasize that the ministry had made the appeal procedures more public and less subject to Court interference by vesting the former powers of the Commissioners of Appeal in three judges at Westminster Hall.[16]

Certainly, the opposition exaggerated the anti-libertarian incursions of the excise proposals and cleverly projected the Monster Excise devouring the people. But we should not infer from this that the campaign was simply a question of what J. M. Robertson once described as 'panic-mongering that beggared burlesque'.[17] The suspicion of Walpole's intentions ran

---

[13] Chandler, *The History and Proceedings of the House of Commons*, vii. 160–2, 169, 318–24. On the select nature of this depression see J. V. Beckett, 'Regional Variation and the Agricultural Depression 1730–1750', *Economic History Review*, 35/1 (Feb. 1982) 35–52. On the way in which grain prices were buoyed up by a dramatic increase in exports in 1733–5 see Jeremy Black, 'Grain Exports and Neutrality: A Speculative Note on British Neutrality in the War of Polish Succession', *Journal of European Economic History*, 12/3 (winter, 1983), 593–600.

[14] Raymond Turner, 'The Excise Scheme of 1733', *English Historical Review*, 42 (Jan. 1927), 34–57; Paul Langford, *The Excise Crisis: Society and Politics in the Age of Walpole* (Oxford, 1975).

[15] [W. Pulteney], *The Late Excise Scheme Dissected* (London, 1734), p. 35. See also the *Craftsman*, 4, 11 Nov. 1732.

[16] Chandler, *The History and Proceedings of the House of Commons*, vii. 193, 333.

[17] J. M. Robertson, *Bolingbroke and Walpole* (London, 1919), pp. 143–4.

deep because the Excise crisis broke at a time when the Whig party was riven with scandal. At the time of the revival of the Salt Tax in 1732, the leading City Whig, Sir John Eyles, was publicly reprimanded by the speaker of the Commons for a breach of trust in the fraudulent sale of Lord Derwentwater's estates. Had he been actively involved in the deal he would have been expelled from the House, as was Sir Thomas Hales, described by Egmont as 'a constant friend of the Revolution and the present Government'.[18] A month later another prominent Whig, Sir Robert Sutton, was under attack for pumping the stock of the Charitable Corporation and defrauding the creditors. Within a few weeks Eyles had to weather another storm; this time over the proposal of the South Sea Company to convert 75 per cent of its capital into annuities. This project raised fears of another speculative ramp by unscrupulous directors, and prompted some forthright accusations from Edward Vernon about Eyles's own boardroom dealings.[19] It led the *Craftsman* to reflect that 'monopolies' were not only 'destructive to all free commerce' but were 'wealthy Combinations which might prove fatal to Liberty'.[20] This aura of sharp practice and scandal continued right up to the Excise crisis, for in February 1733 the Commons ordered the seizure of the records of the York Building Company. The directors of this project had been party to some speculative dealings by their fellow-travellers in the Charitable Corporation surrounding the purchase of some Scottish lead mines. When these deals fell through and the company became insolvent, with net liabilities of over £450,000, the treasurer, George Robinson, absconded to France with the books. The stockholders demanded an inquiry, only to be blocked by the governor, Solomon Ashley, a London merchant and MP for Bridport, who packed the meeting with his own cronies.[21]

Scandals involving Whigs with contacts in the highest

---

[18] *HMC Egmont diary*, i. 247.

[19] Sedgwick (ed.), *The House of Commons 1715–54*, ii. 456–8; *HMC Egmont diary*, i. 263; J. M. Bullock, 'The Charitable Corporation', *Notes and Queries* 160 (Apr. 1931), pp. 237–41.

[20] *Craftsman*, 13 Jan. 1733. For other comments about the scandals see *Fog's Weekly Journal*, 24 June, 12 Aug. 1732.

[21] Sedgwick (ed.), *The House of Commons 1715–54*, i. 423, ii. 77; *Brit. Parl. Papers*, i. 661–2; David Murray, *The York Buildings Company* (Glasgow, 1883), pp. 71–3.

quarters hardly improved the government's credibility and deepened the scepticism of the public over the excise. To *Fog's Weekly Journal* 'Cheating according to Law' had 'become a Proverb'.[22] It was in this climate that the City of London formally entered the lists against Walpole. At a special meeting convened by Lord Mayor John Barber, in February 1733, the Court of Common Council voted to instruct London's MPs to oppose any extension of the excise. According to Nathaniel Mist, Barber surprised the government by this move, although it cannot have been altogether unexpected because the merchants had canvassed the aldermen and common councilmen at least a month earlier.[23] Barber's initiative none the less boosted the campaign against the excise and prompted a closer collaboration between the City and the parliamentary opposition. Sir William Wyndham and William Shippen, the leading Tories in the Commons, paid their compliments to Barber soon after the Council meeting and the upshot was a political dinner held at Guildhall. The company included opposition Whigs such as William Pulteney and Samuel Sandys as well as Tories. It also featured Sir John Barnard, Humphrey Parsons, and Sir John Williams, all members of the 1727 opposition slate; Sir Francis Child, the moderate Tory banker and MP for Middlesex; and Alderman Micajah Perry, the leading tobacco importer in the metropolis, elected as a ministerialist in 1727 but now predictably in the opposition camp.[24]

By the time Walpole formally announced his intention to investigate the frauds in the tobacco trade, the London opposition was well organized. In the week before his motion anti-ministerial deputies conducted an extensive canvass of the wards, and a large number of citizens joined the merchants in lobbying Parliament. Walpole was not impressed by this solid array of strength. 'I hope it will not be said', he declared, 'that all those People came there of themselves naturally and without any instigation of others.' Most, he opined, 'did not speak their own Sentiments; they were played by others like so

[22] *Fog's Weekly Journal*, 12 Aug. 1732.
[23] RA, Stuart MS 160/21; *Northampton Mercury*, 8 Jan. 1733.
[24] RA, Stuart MS 160/21, 31.

many puppets'.[25] This line of argument was echoed in the government press, which depicted the campaign as superficially popular, serving narrow mercantile interests and a frustrated political opposition. While tobacco factors looked to their pockets, anti-ministerial hacks had 'Ballad-sung the Mob out of their senses' with the spectre of a general excise and had courted the citizen's fear of further taxation. 'Gain is certainly the Citizen's blind side,' noted one writer, 'nothing is more easy than to alarm them when the Craft is in danger.'[26]

These accusations were not without substance, for the threat of further taxation upon trade proved more potent than the reality. Even so, Walpole's dismissal of the merchant-led protests, his contemptuous reference to 'sturdy beggars', drew Barnard's ire. 'He look'd upon it', Mist reported, 'as the most glorious Day of his Life that Day he was chosen as one of the Representatives of the City of London, and therefore he could not sit still and hear the whole Body of the Merchants of that great City represented by that hon. gentleman as a parcel of Rogues, Smugglers and unfair traders.'[27] Certainly Sir Robert's disparaging remarks only stiffened the City's opposition to the Excise scheme. Toasts were drank to the 'Glorious Two Hundred and Four' who voted against Walpole's proposal; the hostile references to merchants in the *Daily Courant* were burnt by the common hangman;[28] and further deputations were planned against the Bill, including a petition from the Common Council. By the second reading the momentum of protest was such that Walpole abandoned the whole enterprise. Outside the House Sir Robert was jostled and several of his coterie were physically assaulted. When local JPs attempted to read the Riot Act, they were met with 'Damn your laws and proclamations'. In the ensuing celebrations, Lord Egmont recalled, the mob 'broke the windows of the Post office and of all other houses not illuminated, and would have done it of the Parliament House while we were sitting if they could have

---

[25] Quote from Boyer, *Political State*, xlvi. 409; see also Cobbett, *The Parliamentary History of England*, viii. 1305–6.

[26] Quotes from *Daily Courant*, 12 Mar. 1733; *London Journal*, 17 Feb. 1733; see also quotes from *The Citizen's Procession* (London, 1733).

[27] RA, Stuart MS 161/16A.

[28] *London Evening Post*, 27 Mar. 1733.

come within reach of them'.[29] Predictably, Sir Robert was burnt in effigy, in some instances alongside Sarah Malcolm, a murderess recently hanged before the Inner Temple gate in Mitre Court. In Fleet Street, *Fog's Weekly Journal* reported, 'a clumsy figure of a Man made of Straw, dress'd up with Ribbons, a Pipe in his Mouth and a Bottle in his Hand, was burnt with great triumph.'[30] Here, as elsewhere, crowds stopped carriages to demand money for their anti-Walpolean festival and insulted those 'who refused to join in their tumultuous proceedings'. According to Sir Thomas Robinson, the celebrations continued on into the following day with bell-ringing, public rejoicings, and 'bonfires in every street'.[31]

The withdrawal of the Excise Bill was a personal humiliation for Walpole who clearly miscalculated the ability of the merchant community to muster such support against the government. Part of this success, I have suggested, lay with the opposition's ability to generalize the conflict, to cast the Excise proposal as but one symptom of a broader theme, one of overbearing and irresponsible government. Walpolean Whiggery was increasingly identified with the cultivation of private interests, sycophancy, jobbery, the exploitation of public office, and overweening, opportunistic politics. The critique was not new: it had been voiced quite vigorously during the South Sea scandal and its aftermath. But in 1733 the ministry found itself on the defensive. It was the opposition that was winning the battle of words, juxtaposing 'the prudent vigour of the mercantile Part of the Nation' and the 'public spirit of the landed gentlemen' against Whig parasitism and its incursions upon liberty.[32] 'As it always was,' remarked the *Craftsman*, 'so it ever will be the chief Business of a Court Minion or Prime Minister to enrich himself with the Spoils of the Public.' And it went on to portray Britannia being dragged by bum-bailiffs to the bar of a disreputable House of Justice, through a gate whose inscription read 'No Juries, No Magna Carta.' In this analogy to the Excise crisis, Britannia was rescued by men 'dressed in plain habits, with the figures of

---

[29] *HMC Egmont diary*, i. 361–2.
[30] *Fog's Weekly Journal*, 14 Apr. 1733.
[31] *Northampton Mercury*, 16 Apr. 1733; *HMC Carlisle*, p. 110.
[32] See the *Craftsman*, 21, 28 Apr. 1733.

Looms, Ploughshares and Anchors emboss'd on their breasts', and taken to the Temple of Liberty. Britannia had been nobly defended by the 'people' against power-hungry politicians and their mercenary crew. As the opposition began to dictate the terms of political discourse, liberty was increasingly identified with the productive classes and the public-spirited, whether landed or mercantile, and increasingly juxtaposed to the Court, the big monopolies, and the servants of the state. The older association of liberty with the Protestant Succession, an important signifier in the 1720s, had been displaced.

The new-won confidence of the opposition was not temporary. It was important to the run-up of the general election of 1734. Just prior to the anniversary of the Excise, which was joyously celebrated in London as it was in other parts of the country, the City opposition won a narrow victory in the Chamberlain's election. In a hard-fought contest, the leader of the tobacco merchants, John Bosworth, defeated the ministerial candidate, William Selwin, by a mere four votes. The result enraged Walpole, who refused to give Bosworth the traditional accompaniment to the post, the receiver-generalship of the Land Tax.[33] As a further endorsement of Walpole's unpopularity, the contest was a bad omen for the Court party, who had canvassed hard for Selwin and mobilized many retainers. Two months later they declined to field any ministerial candidates in the general election, but concentrated their energies upon attacking John Barber, whose flamboyant Toryism and outspoken endorsement of the Excise riots, while Mayor, had alarmed conservative elements in the City.[34] The Court faction rallied the Dissenters against Barber and ran a smear campaign in the *London Journal*, which described him as 'a thorough, hardened, compleat Jacobite, in Practice and Principle'. In this they proved successful, for despite Barber's enormous popularity with the London crowd, he failed by almost 600 votes to win a seat.[35]

[33] W. R. Ward, *The English Land Tax in the Eighteenth Century* (Oxford, 1935), pp. 111–12.

[34] Henderson, *London and the National Government*, p. 156; the government appears to have investigated Barber's culpability in the riots, perhaps with a view to prosecution: see Cambridge Univ. Lib., Cholmondley (Houghton) 65/91/2.

[35] *London Journal*, 20 Apr. 1734; see also the *Free Briton*, 16 May 1734;

1734 nevertheless saw the resurgence of the opposition in the City. First there was Bosworth's triumph; then four parliamentary seats. In the Common Council elections later that year the Tory-Patriots failed to oust ministerial candidates from the inner-city wards; but within two years they had made some headway in at least four—Tower, Cheap, Coleman Street, and Aldgate. In the aldermanic elections, too, the opposition wrested seats from ministerial control. Deputy John Lesquesne held Broad Street for the Court in 1735, but in Walbrook, the West India merchant and critic of Walpole, George Heathcote, replaced the Whig merchant, Sir John Tash. The next two years brought further changes in the political disposition of the Upper Court. Robert Willimot, a merchant-insurer who played a prominent role in the Excise crisis, defeated the pro-Walpole deputy in Lime Street. Daniel Lambert, a wine merchant, defeated the sub-governor of the South Sea Company, Peter Burrell, in the port-side ward of Tower. And in the staunchly Tory ward of Farringdon Within, the MP for Amersham, Henry Marshall, defeated William Selwin, the Receiver-General of the Land Tax and Walpole's candidate for the Chamberlain's office in 1734.[36] The political tide was turning in favour of the City opposition.

Against this background the question of British commercial rights in the Caribbean re-emerged as an important political issue. Since the mid-seventeenth century Britain and her colonies had engaged in a lucrative contraband trade with the Spanish empire. Efforts had been made to regulate this illicit commerce in 1667 and subsequently by the Treaty of Utrecht, but neither settlement had proved satisfactory, and to a large extent good relations between Britain and Spain depended upon the latter's tolerance of smuggling.[37] From the late 1720s, however, Spain adopted a tougher policy. Local shipowners were sworn in as *guardacostas* and in partnership with local governors raided British shipping. Redress for the British

---

London Evening Post, 7–9, 9–11 May 1734; *Newcastle Courant*, 11, 18 May 1734. The Newcastle paper reported that Barber ended up with 577 single votes (24% of his total).

[36] Henderson, *London and the National Government*, pp. 168–9.
[37] Richard Pares, *War and Trade in the West Indies 1739–63* (London, 1936).

merchant proved virtually impossible. Litigation was endless; captured goods were quickly distributed in local markets; ships were confiscated to reappear under different names. The commissaries established by the Treaty of Seville in 1729 to deal with illegal seizures had produced few significant decisions by 1737.[38]

American and Caribbean traders grew increasingly alarmed by the scale of confiscations and in October 1737, 153 merchants signed a petition drawn up by the colonial agent for Jamaica complaining of Spanish privateering on the open seas. The following year a merchant lobby was organized from the Ship Tavern, behind the Royal Exchange, to press the government to take firmer action.[39] On 3 March, Micajah Perry, the London alderman and consignment merchant who played a conspicuous role in the anti-Excise campaign, presented a petition to the Commons from the London American and West India merchants. Within a few weeks it was joined by others from the out-ports, from Bristol, Glasgow, and Liverpool, confronting the ministry with a formidable array of mercantile grievances.[40]

The merchants' complaints were essentially threefold. First, they demanded adequate and swift compensation for illegal seizures. Second, they wanted an unambiguous affirmation of rights recognized by the 1670 treaty, such as the right to cut logwood in the Bay of Campeche. Third, and most important, they contested the legality of Spanish *guardacostas* inspecting British ships on the high seas, demanding free navigation from one British dominion to another. Closely linked to this issue was the argument that the articles of illicit merchandize enumerated under the 1667 treaty (for example, pieces of eight) were so common in the Caribbean that they were no longer evidence of smuggling.[41] Government sources privately admitted that this was true, but in Parliament their spokesmen prevaricated and insisted that it was better to settle these issues through the existing machinery of redress. War, they

---

[38] McLachlan, *Trade and Peace with Old Spain*, pp. 60, 96.
[39] *Gentleman's Magazine*, 8 (Mar. 1738), 163; BL, Add. ms 35, 909, fos. 82–3; *London Evening Post*, 4–6, 23–8 Feb. 1738.
[40] *Commons Journals*, 23, pp. 54–5, 63–5, 94–6.
[41] Pares, *War and Trade*, pp. 29–43; Cobbett, *The Parliamentary History of England*, x. 648.

argued, would only disrupt other sectors of British commerce, particularly trade in Mediterranean waters. To drive this point home the government even attempted to promote a counter-petition from the Spanish merchants supporting diplomatic negotiations in the interests of the whole mercantile community.[42]

In the early debates on Spanish depredations, the government successfully fought off the demand for an immediate recognition of the British right of navigation. But the clamour for tougher measures had a more conspicuously patriotic appeal. In the press much was made of the Spanish ill-treatment of British sailors, idealized in Richard Glover's poem *London* as the 'chosen train of Liberty and Commerce'.[43] The disclosures of Richard Copithorne, for example, a captain whose vessel had been captured by Spanish pirates in 1727 and whose petition for redress was presented to the Commons in February 1739, were amplified in pamphlet and journal. He told of Britons enduring torture, butchery on the island of Tortuga, and 'free-born English subjects' dwindling to 'Spanish Galley Slaves'.[44] A good deal of political capital was made of such incidents, and the traditions of popular Protestantism and libertarianism merged into a blistering indictment of Spanish barbarism, best-illustrated by the story of Captain Jenkins, whose loss of an ear was duly masqueraded in the streets.[45] Appeals were made to the buccaneering spirit of the Elizabethan era and to Cromwell's proclamation of England's commercial and Protestant destiny in 1655 during a former conflict with Spain over reciprocal rights in the Caribbean. Spanish settlements in the New World were said to be founded on genocide, as the massacre of the Incas at Cholula illustrated, while England's dominions overseas were 'established

---

[42] BL, Add. MS 35,883, fos. 198–217; Cobbett, *The Parliamentary History of England*, x. 666–76, 857; *Craftsman*, 23 Sept. 1738; *Daily Gazetteer*, 13, 15 Dec. 1738, 4 Jan. 1739.

[43] Richard Glover, *London, or The Progress of Commerce*, 2nd edn. (London, 1739), p. 27; *London Evening Post*, 14–16 Mar., 30 Mar.–1 Apr. 1738.

[44] [Richard Copithorne], *The English Cotejo, or The Cruelties, Depredations and Illicit Trade Charg'd upon the English in a Spanish Libel lately Published* (London, 1739); *London Evening Post*, 20–2 Feb. 1739; *Craftsman*, 24 Feb. 1739; *Commons Journals*, 23, pp. 249–50.

[45] *London Evening Post*, 8–10 Feb. 1739.

by the FREE CONSENT of the natives'.[46] The comparison between arbitrary imprisonment under absolutism and fair trials under limited monarchy was also emphasized, and 'No Search', the popular abridgement of freedom of navigation, became an affirmation of English liberty against Catholic despotism.[47] 'The general cry is War', proclaimed the *Post*, 'Revenge on the Spaniards, Restitution for past losses, Satisfaction to our National Honour, and above all, ample security to our future trade and navigation.'[48]

As the spirit of bellicose mercantilism swept the metropolis, the opposition intensified their attack upon Walpole. They condemned his disregard for British liberties, his 'mercenary, low way of thinking', and the general drift of his foreign policy which placed Hanoverian security above British commerce. The government, in reply, emphasized that it alone took the wide view. Walpole's policy of peace and retrenchment, its spokesman insisted, had brought prosperity. War with Spain would injure Mediterranean traffic, and while it might 'acquire the Hearts of the undeserving Commonalty', it would 'never secure the confidence of the money'd part of the subject'.[49] At the same time the government attempted to assuage popular bellicosity by retaining Admiral Haddock in the Caribbean and offering letters of reprisal to injured merchants.[50] But the main card that the government played was the Convention of El Pardo. Government supporters declared it a prelude to a more comprehensive treaty which would settle mercantile grievances without the burden of war or the dislocation of trade. It was a promising start, they said, because the Spanish recognized that major revisions of the 1670 treaty were necessary.[51]

---

[46] Anon., *The British Sailor's Discovery, or The Spanish Pretensions Confuted* (London, 1739).

[47] *London Evening Post*, 30 Mar.–1 Apr. 1738, 22–4 Feb. 1739; *Craftsman*, 6 Jan. 1739; [George Lyttelton], *Further Considerations on the Present State of our Affairs at Home and Abroad in a Letter to a Member of Parliament from a Friend in the Country* (London, 1739), pp. 14–19; G. B. Hertz, *British Imperialism in the 18th century* (London, 1908), pp. 34–7.

[48] Quote from *London Evening Post*, 17–19 Aug.; cf. 28–31 Oct. 1738.

[49] *Daily Gazetteer*, 13 Nov. 1738.

[50] *Craftsman*, 18 Mar. 1738; McLachlan, *Trade and Peace with Old Spain*, p. 110.

[51] Thomas Gordon, *An Appeal to the Unprejudiced concerning the Present*

The opposition, by contrast, focused upon the limitations of the agreement. In its eyes the right to freedom of navigation remained unrecognized, as did other issues such as logwood rights in Honduras and salt rights in Tortuga. Moreover, merchant claims had been reduced from £340,000 to £95,000 on account of the Spanish crown's claim against the South Sea Company. These accommodations led William Wyndham to denigrate the Convention as the 'coup de grace to that miserable lingering state which our navigation and commerce have long been in'. Micajah Perry concurred, demanding a general inquiry 'in which the whole body of our merchants, planters and sailors are plaintiffs, and our ministers and negotiators defendants'.[52] Faced with a hostile Commons, Walpole's majority sank to 30. As the division list revealed, 200 of the government's 262 supporters were placemen or pensioners of the Court. Even within this group confidence waned, for, as the Reverend Henry Etough observed, 'many of the majority in private conversation wished for war, and reproached the Minister for want of courage.'[53]

Outside Parliament, Walpole's agreement was strongly censured. As the earl of Marchmont told Montrose, the 'city is in a flame and almost nobody pleased'. According to one account, the populace attacked a man outside the Commons for crying out 'No Merchants, No Merchants, but Conventions and Treaties for ever.'[54] Indeed, the Convention did little to abate popular passions; scepticism about government policy gave way to outright denunciation. One ballad portrayed Walpole bribing the Spanish for hollow concessions. It ironically told merchants and sailors to 'banish their Fears',

Discontents Occasion'd by the Late Convention with Spain (London, 1739), pp. 13, 32; Anon., *Popular Prejudices against the Convention and Treaty with Spain Examined and Answer'd* (London, 1739), pp. 6–7; Horace Walpole, *The Convention Vindicated from the Misrepresentations of the Enemies of our Peace* (London, 1739), p. 20.

[52] Quotes are from Cobbett, *The Parliamentary History of England*, x. 1059, 1309; cf. *Commons Journals*, 23, p. 277.
[53] BL, Add. ms 9200, fo. 63; for the annotated division list see *Gentleman's Magazine*, 9 (1739), 304–10.
[54] *A Selection from the Papers of the Earls of Marchmont in the Possession of the Rt. Hon. Sir George Rose* (3 vols.; London, 1831), ii. 111; *London Evening Post*, 22–4 Feb. 1739.

Nor mourn for lost Liberty, Riches, or *Ears*;
Since *Blue-string* the Great,
To better their Fate,
Once more has determin'd he will *Negotiate*.[55]

By early 1739, then, the opposition was in full cry against
Walpole's Spanish policy. The anti-ministerial newspaper,
Common Sense, singled out the hardening of mercantile
opinion against Walpole. 'Things seem to be come to a Kind of
Crisis betwixt him and the merchants,' it surmised, 'and either
He or They must fall.'[56] It was at this point that the City of
London formally lent its weight to the campaign. On 20
February 1739, the Common Council drew up a petition to
Parliament against the Convention, one that the pro-
ministerial aldermen attempted but failed to veto.[57] The Court
party counteracted this move by publishing a list of the Common Council along with their occupations, in an attempt to
prove that the civic assembly was unqualified to comment on
the merits of the Convention. But few citizens were impressed
with this action, remembering Walpole's derogatory comments about the City in 1733, and later that year several wards
campaigned among the Livery to oppose the mayoral ambitions of Sir George Champion, one of the two aldermen in
Parliament who had voted for the Convention.[58] Since Champion was next in line for mayoral office, these initiatives
entailed a dramatic departure from the usual custom of nominating the two most senior aldermen below the chair as prospective candidates. Sir George argued that this was irregular and
that he was not accountable as a member of the Corporation
for his actions as MP for Aylesbury. But the opposition retorted
that he 'deserved to be so stigmatiz'd for having espoused in
P—l——t what he had agreed to remonstrate against in
Common Council'.[59]

---

[55] Anon., *The Negotiators, or Don Diego brought to Reason* (London, 1739),
p. 5.
[56] *Common Sense*, 17 Feb. 1739.
[57] John Almon, *The Debates and Proceedings of the British House of
Commons . . . 1743–6* (2 vols.; London, 1764), ii. 131.
[58] Journals of Common Council (hereafter Council Journals), 58, fos. 121–2;
Daily Gazetteer, Mar. 1739; *London Evening Post*, 13–15 Sept. 1739.
[59] Quote is from *London Evening Post* 25–7 Sept. 1739; cf. *Daily Advertiser*,
24 Sept. 1739; *Champion*, 9 Oct. 1739.

The mayoral election of September 1739 emerged as a trial of strength between the Court and opposition in city politics. The government issued 4,000 circulars to the liverymen on behalf of Champion and canvassed the Post Office, the Customs and Excise, and even the liveried tradesmen in Clare Market, part of the Duke of Newcastle's franchise. At Common Hall, where over 3,000 liverymen assembled, the ministerial party soon abandoned their sponsorship of Champion. The other candidates, Sir John Salter, a ministerial Whig, and Sir Robert Godschall, brother-in-law to Sir John Barnard, were returned to the Court of Aldermen, where the former was elected.[60]

After the successful campaign against Sir George Champion, several leading oppositionists took the opportunity to put other issues before the electorate. Richard Glover, a Hamburgh merchant and poet associated with Leicester House, proposed that a motion of thanks be sent to the City members for opposing the Convention. Seconded by William Benn of Bishopsgate ward, this motion was accepted by the Livery.[61] Alderman and Sheriff, George Heathcote, the returning officer, added that Common Hall should also recommend the repeal of the aldermanic veto, but he was prevailed upon to postpone his motion until the following day, when the aldermanic bench would appear in its official capacity to proclaim the new Mayor. On that occasion Heathcote admitted that the Court of Aldermen had not so far exploited its power as it might have, but to await abuses was 'shutting the Stable door when the Steed is stolen'.[62] Repeal of the veto was the City's only security against ministerial domination. This speech was warmly applauded, but the lord mayor, Micajah Perry, refused to put the question on account of its irregularity, and similarly rejected a motion calling for a Common Council meeting on the state of the nation. Active in the opposition to the excise and the Convention, Perry was uneasy about a more open,

[60] CLRO, Book of Common Hall, vii, fo. 277; Boyer, *Political State of Great Britain*, lviii (1739), 310; *London Evening Post*, 25–7 Sept. 1739; [Benjamin Robins], *A Narrative of what Passed in the Common Hall of the Citizens of London Assembled for the Election of a Lord Mayor* (London, 1739), p. 3.

[61] *A Narrative*, pp. 6–7; *Daily Post*, 5 Oct. 1739.

[62] Quote is from *Gentleman's Magazine*, 9 (1739), 550; cf. William Maitland, *The History of London from its Foundation by the Romans to the Present Time* (2 vols.; London, 1756), i. 601–2.

participatory system of city politics. But he placated the rank and file by recognizing the popularity of Heathcote's motion, and declared that as an MP for London, he felt bound by their sentiments and 'doubted not but the other City members would be of the same opinion'.[63]

The mayoral election of 1739 was thus the occasion of a more searching critique of city government. Profiting from the unpopularity of the Convention, radicals like Heathcote sought a more active role for the Livery in City politics and a restoration of Common Council's autonomy, an issue which had smouldered since 1725. Predictably, the ensuing City elections proved a trial of strength between the two parties. In the annual Common Council elections at the end of the year, the Court launched a counter-offensive in several wards, arguing that the Tory-Patriot caucus was guilty of exploiting civic patronage in a manner that hardly squared with its professions of civic virtue and governmental purity. There was some substance to the charge, for crucial building-contracts had been distributed in a partisan manner to opposition councillors; but the electorate continued to find the Convention a more appealing issue.[64] In Bishopsgate, where a stream of electoral propaganda condemning the Spanish Convention and Whig corruption flooded the hustings, the opposition successfully repulsed the efforts of Sir John Eyles to capture the ward. In Vintry they ousted many Whig members. And early the following year, the opposition maintained its hold on Farringdon Without, where the local banker, Richard Hoare, son of the well-known Tory alderman and former London MP, was returned to the Upper Court. Finally, as a strategic move in preparation for the next mayoral contest, the opposition installed two of its members as sheriffs.[65]

In the next mayoral election, the two anti-ministerialists who had played a conspicuous role in the rejection of Champion in 1739, Sir Robert Godschall and George

---

[63] Quote is from *A Narrative*, pp. 17–18; Maitland, *London*, i. 601–2; *The Proceedings of the Court of Hustings and Common Hall of the Livery of the City of London at the late election for Lord Mayor* (London, 1739), pp. 20–8.

[64] On the question of partisan contracts see Anon., *City Corruption Display'd* (London, 1739).

[65] *London Evening Post*, 20–2 Dec. 1739, 23 Apr. 1740; CLRO, Small box 36/21; *A Journal of the Shrievalty of Richard Hoare* (London, 1815).

Heathcote, were nominated by Common Hall. The Livery clearly intended that Godschall, the senior alderman, should be Mayor, but the ministerialists mustered in strength in the Court of Aldermen and rejected this proposal by 11 : 8. Heathcote sought to frustrate this decision by claiming that his health had been impaired while carrying out the duties of Sheriff the previous year. Sir John Eyles and the Court supporters rejected this supplication, but Heathcote was excused without a fine at the Common Council meeting of 10 October.[66] A further election was called. Champion's candidature was advertised, to no avail. The next alderman in line, Sir John Lesquesne, refused to stand unless the Court of Aldermen explained its rejection of Godschall; and so the Livery nominated as their second candidate the former mayor and Tory-Jacobite, Humphrey Parsons.

Despite the fact that Parsons was a *bête noire* of the Whigs, the Court of Aldermen again rejected Godschall, this time by a single vote, 12 : 11. The opposition press was enraged by the decision, but the Tory-Patriots eventually decided that Parsons should stand. However, their supporters on Common Council did thank Parsons 'for restoring the Peace and Tranquility of this City, which has been greatly disturbed by the late extraordinary and uncommon proceeding'. This language was too provocative for the ministerial aldermen, who used their veto to block the motion. But the Patriots gained their revenge at the next Council meeting when it was resolved that the 1725 Act applied only to acts and ordinances and not to questions.[67]

Parsons's death in March 1741 precipitated yet another mayoral election, and again Godschall was passed over, this time in favour of the opposition wine merchant, Daniel Lambert. Godschall's exclusion for the third time in six months underscored the continued domination of the Court of Aldermen by the government Whigs. As the division lists

[66] CLRO, Repertories of the Court of Aldermen, cxliv. 389–90, 400; Council Journals, lviii. 182; *London Evening Post*, 27–30 Sept. 1740; *Journal of Richard Hoare*, p. 20; *An Impartial Relation of the Proceedings of the Common Hall and the Court of Aldermen* (London, 1740), pp. 12–13.

[67] Council Journals, lxiii, fos. 191–2; *London Evening Post*, 11–13 Nov. 1740; *Journal of Richard Hoare*, p. 28.

show, throughout the crisis the ministerialists managed to retain a hard core of eleven supporters to exclude Godschall, eight of whom were linked to the major moneyed companies.[68] By contrast, the opposition could only rely upon seven, although by March 1741 the advent of younger opposition members upon the bench—such as William Benn and Robert Ladbroke—gave them a better chance to challenge the Whig supremacy. Indeed, it was only the continued support of moderates like Micajah Perry and the former Tory, Sir John Williams, that gave the Court party the ability to ostracize Godschall for the earlier humiliation of Sir George Champion. The Spanish crisis and the revival of the veto, which had once more emerged as a crucial issue in City politics as the ministerial aldermen became the butt of rank-and-file frustration and hostility, had pushed Court resources to the limit. Already a minority at Common Hall and in Common Council, where the opposition were able to muster 110 supporters to the Court's 71, the ministerial party held on to their aldermanic majority by a very narrow margin.[69]

The parlous state of the Court party became eminently clear in the general election of May 1741. The opposition had drawn up its list of candidates as early as the previous November. It included Sir John Barnard, Sir Robert Godschall, George Heathcote (hitherto MP for Southwark), and Humphrey Parsons—in effect, three opposition Whigs and one Tory. Upon Parsons's death in March 1741, the in-coming mayor and prominent wine merchant, Daniel Lambert, who had been active in both the Excise and Spanish crises, was chosen in his stead. The ministerial party, by contrast, was by no means as well organized or as confident of victory. Initially the Court Whigs proposed a 'merchants'' list in an attempt to rally the

---

[68] These were William Baker (EI), Robert Baylis (EI), Sir William Billers (EI), Sir John Eyles (SS), Sir Harcourt Master (former SS), Sir William Rous (EI), Sir John Thompson (B). Two other Court aldermen who voted against Godschall were directors of the moneyed companies, namely Sir Edward Bellamy (B) and Sir John Slater (EI). (B) = Bank of England; (EI) = East India Company; (SS) = South Sea Company. The division lists were printed in Maitland, *London*, i. 609–18.

[69] The relative strength of Common Council has been gauged from the 1739 lists, using the Chamberlain's poll of 1734 and contemporary comments in the newspapers. By 1741, when the opposition began to penetrate the inner-city wards, its majority was greater still.

support of moderate as well as ministerial opinion. This included two aldermen: William Baker, a well-known American merchant with contacts in the textile and fur trade; and Micajah Perry, the Virginia merchant and former London MP who had opposed the Excise and the Convention, but had identified with the Court as the radical line of Common Hall had become more pronounced. These two were joined by men not active in City politics, Kenelm Faulkner, a Turkey merchant, and Roger Drake, a West India merchant with affiliations in both camps.[70] But this list of candidates was eventually abandoned in favour of another drawn up under the chairmanship of Sir Joseph Hankey at Merchant Taylors' Hall. It featured Sir Edward Bellamy, London's foremost fish importer, a Bank director and ministerial alderman who had retained a relatively low profile during the mayoral contests of 1739–41; Aldermen Micajah Perry and Sir John Barnard; and Admiral Vernon.

This list was clearly promoted to win over the middle ground. It was specifically pitched to those liverymen who had opposed the Excise and the Spanish Convention, and had welcomed the government's subsequent declaration of war against Spain, but were unhappy about the increasingly radical tone of Common Hall and Council. The nomination of Admiral Edward Vernon, in particular, whose exploits against Spain in the Caribbean had been celebrated throughout the metropolis, was an attempt to capitalize upon war fever. The opposition press thought Vernon's candidature 'a shallow artifice', and while it championed his victories it urged the Livery to reject this ruse 'with a becoming scorn and contempt'.[71] These words were heeded. While Vernon fared well in neighbouring Westminster against the Court, the City poll in his name was virtually abandoned after the fourth day, as it was for Bellamy and Perry. From the beginning the election of the opposition slate was never seriously in doubt.

[70] *London Daily Post*, 27 Apr. 1741; *London and Country Journal*, 28 Apr. 1741.

[71] Quotes are from *London Evening Post*, 30 Apr., 1–2 May 1741; cf. *London Daily Post*, 27 Apr. 1741; *Daily Gazetteer*, 29 Apr. 1741; Anon., *Considerations Humbly Offered, First, to the Inhabitants of the City and Liberty of Westminster, Secondly to the Worthy Liverymen of the City of London, with Regard to the Nomination of Admiral Vernon to be their Representative in Parliament* (London, 1741), p. 29.

The 1741 general election was a clear demonstration of the anti-ministerial sympathies of the Livery. The Court's attempt to divide the Patriot interest and win over the allegiance of moderate voters was decisively rejected. Even Godschall, who came bottom of the poll in 1734, received over 3,000 votes, approximately 100 more than the votes of Bellamy and Perry combined.[72] The dominant temper of Common Hall was re-emphasized in the post-electoral Instructions to the new members. On this occasion the voters came out in support of a fully-fledged Country programme.[73] They demanded a Place Bill, advocated a return to triennial parliaments, and raised the old issue of standing armies in peacetime. They revealed their hostility to Walpole in their opposition to an extension of all excise laws, and defended the imperatives of bellicose mercantilism in their hopes for a 'glorious' peace. The liverymen also condemned the use of military force by the returning officer in Westminster, where, for the first time in almost twenty years, the opposition challenged Court power in what was commonly regarded as a royal constituency.[74] Finally, they hoped their members would make every effort to repeal the aldermanic veto, the predictable conclusion to the widespread opposition to the Court which had mounted in intensity since 1733. Faced with this clear confirmation of anti-ministerialism, the Court party lost its nerve. In September it capitulated to popular pressures and allowed Sir Robert Godschall to assume mayoral office.[75]

In the aftermath of the election, in which the administration experienced serious losses, the parliamentary opposition concentrated their efforts on Walpole's overthrow. During the stormy session of 1741–2 the City of London played a conspicuous role in sustaining the relentless pressure against the first minister. The newly elected Sir Robert Godschall presented a petition drawn up by Richard Glover and signed by 300 merchants criticizing the Admiralty for failing to provide sufficient convoys to protect commercial shipping.[76] The

---

[72] For details of the voting see the *Journal of Richard Hoare*, pp. 79–84. Godschall received 3143 votes, Bellamy 1311, Perry 1710.

[73] *London Evening Post*, 12–14 May 1741.

[74] See ch. 5.

[75] *London Evening Post*, 26–9 Sept., 27–9 Oct. 1741; *Craftsman*, 3 Oct. 1741.

[76] *Commons Journals*, 24, pp. 49, 93. For the importance of the merchants'

Common Council renewed their complaints against Spanish *guardacostas*. In February the assembly drew up further Instructions to London's Members, calling for a change of men and measures, and by inference the impeachment of Walpole for 'past mismanagement'.[77] This representation was followed in the next three months by similar Instructions from no fewer than twenty-nine constituencies, including Bristol, Coventry, Edinburgh, and York.[78]

Seven defeats in the Commons brought the administration to its knees. Yet Walpole's fall from power in February 1742 did not lead to a purification of political life. William Pulteney tried to placate public opinion with a modest Place Bill which debarred all minor civil servants from sitting in the Commons.[79] But this was a token gesture to public opinion amid the regrouping of the Old Corps. From early on it was apparent that the aspirations of London and other large cities were likely to fail. ' 'Tis but a melancholy consideration', wrote James Ralph in February, 'that the disposition of power seems to be, even now, more the subject of inquiry than the redress of grievances, or Ways and Means to secure us from the artifices of wiccked ministers for the future.'[80] Few politicians were prepared to testify against Walpole, and so the secret committee set up to investigate his conduct fizzled out in the summer. By the autumn the general feeling in the City was one of frustration and resentment. Court power had been broken in the City; Walpole had fallen; but reform seemed as elusive as ever. In its Instructions to the London members, the fifth in three years, the City stated that it was astonished to find politicians

who, under the mask of integrity, and by dissembling a zeal for their country, had long acquired the largest share of its confidence, should, without the least hesitation or seeming remorse, greedily embrace the first occasion to disgrace all their former conduct.[81]

petition in the final attack upon Walpole see John Owen, *The Rise of the Pelhams* (London, 1957), p. 31.

[77] Council Journals, lviii, fos. 222v, 225–6.
[78] See ch. 7.
[79] *Commons Journals*, 24, p. 348; Betty Kemp, *King and Commons* (London, 1956), p. 57.
[80] *Champion*, 13 Feb. 1742.
[81] *London Evening Post*, 21–3 Oct. 1742.

London's alienation from the government did not, then, end with the defeat of Walpole. The reconciliation of the leading opposition Whigs with the Court was regarded as apostasy in City circles, and deepened popular scepticism of high politics. After Walpole, City discontent quickly focused upon the government's continentalism, which raised fears about the subordination of British to Hanoverian interests. In October 1742 the Common Council had condemned 'the parade of Land Armies and the Hire of Foreign Forces', and contrasted the lavish commitment to European alliances with the poor protection of British dominions overseas. Two months later five of the six City aldermen in Parliament joined forces with the Tories and a rump of Patriot Whigs to oppose the hiring of 16,000 Hanoverian troops.[82] The inactivity of the Pragmatic army during the winter and the clear partiality of George II towards the Hanoverian troops at Dettingen brought a fresh surge of anti-Hanoverianism. Prints and ballads exposed the neglect of British troops. According to one bookseller's servant, 11,000 copies of a dialogue between two troopers, recounting the king's behaviour at Dettingen, was distributed from Paternoster Row.[83] In March two leading opposition aldermen, George Heathcote and William Calvert, attended a Tory rally at the Fountain Tavern on the Strand where toasts were drank to 'the promotion of true interest in H.M.'s BRITISH DO-MINIONS'. A few months later the Common Council deliberately snubbed George II by ignoring his victory at Dettingen in its summer Address.[84] Jacobite observers were elated by these events. Thomas Carte was so overwhelmed by the ferment against the Court that he believed the 'only distinction left' was that of 'Englishmen or Britons, and Hanoverians'. 'Were you in London to hear what is said there openly every day and in the most public places', he reported in July, 'you would not think there was a man for the present Government.'[85]

Even allowing for Jacobite optimism, there is little doubt

---

[82] Council Journals, lviii, fos. 254–6; Cobbett, *The Parliament History of England*, xii. 1053–8.

[83] M. Dorothy George, *English Political Caricature* (2 vols.; Oxford, 1959), i. 94–5; Anon., *The Yellow Sash; or H———R BESHIT*; Anon., *Old England's Te Deum*, PRO, TS 11/982/3625.

[84] Council Journals, lviii, fo. 286; *London Evening Post*, 15–17 Mar. 1743.

[85] RA, Stuart MSS 249/113b and 251/30.

that the conduct of the war on the continent had angered a wide section of metropolitan opinion. Henry Fox told Ilchester in October 1743 that the ferment against Hanover had grown so serious as 'to disturb as sanguine a Politician as I am'.[86] The threat of a Jacobite invasion in 1744 inevitably silenced anti-Hanoverian protest; the suspension of Habeas Corpus pushed it underground. The City aldermen in Parliament continued to oppose British subsidies to Hanover, although there was less consensus on other issues: for example, Sir John Barnard, William Calvert, and Daniel Lambert opposed Dodington's motion for a naval inquiry in February 1744.[87] None the less, relations between the government and the City remained strained, and Pelham's willingness to modify Cartaret's pro-Hanoverian foreign policy did not inaugurate a new climate of reconciliation. In fact, the government's continued opposition to the repeal of the aldermanic veto, which had been the subject of concerted petitioning since December 1743, thwarted even the possibility of a *rapprochement* with City moderates.[88] The defeat of a motion on repeal in January 1745 by the relatively narrow majority of 117 : 90—largely on the grounds that without some check upon demotic politics London would become 'more seditious and more licentious than ever'—did little to reconcile the City to the government's new leaders.

At the outbreak of the 1745 rebellion the Court was seriously isolated from the mainstream of City opinion. Unpopular with the majority of Common Hall, its support on Common Council had dwindled to less than 50 out of a total of 236 as the opposition took over many of the inner-city wards hitherto under the sway of the big merchants and financiers. What was particularly disconcerting was that since 1743 the government had lost its majority on the Court of Aldermen so that it could not exercise any veto over Council petitions and remonstrances. Not that the Council gave any particular cause

[86] BL, Add. ms 51,417, fo. 105.

[87] Owen, *Rise of the Pelhams*, p. 213; Anon., *The Lord's Protest, to which is Added a List of the MPs who Voted for and against the Hanoverian Troops in British Pay, January 18 1743/4* (London, 1744).

[88] Council Journals, lviii, fos. 284, 295–6, 302, 354–5, 361–2; CLRO, Misc. ms 288.4; John Almon, *Debates and Proceedings*, ii. 97–140.

for alarm. As in 1744, so the following year the Court of Common Council professed loyalty to the Crown.[89] But the government could not afford to take any chances and did all it could to mobilize its supporters and bolster loyalism in the metropolis. With the blessing of the bishop of London the pulpit reasserted the traditional arguments of Whig orthodoxy, the threats which a Stuart restoration posed to commerce, credit, and liberty.[90] Cheap tracts revived fears of a Catholic persecution and a country sunk in French vassalage, oppressed by arbitrary law. Pope-burnings and anti-Catholic plays saw a new lease of life. The War Office staged a series of military parades as the troops returned to Flanders, and local militia regiments were quickly if ineffectually mobilized.

Within the City itself, government supporters ensured that the City lieutenancy remained firmly in loyal hands. The committee set up to reorganize the trained bands was packed with courtiers.[91] It included four directors of the East India and South Sea Companies; William Selwin, the Receiver-General of the Land Tax and the unsuccessful candidate in the Chamberlain's contest of 1734; and a number of prominent merchants and insurers who had stood in the Court interest in local elections. Control of the city's internal security was also supplemented by loyalist associations and volunteer regiments. Their organization and management was also masterminded by notable government supporters such as Sir William Baker, who acted as an intermediary between the duke of Newcastle and the Spitalfields volunteer regiments. To these enterprises the merchants and cosmopolitan plutocracy of London lent éclat and money: they outshone the Common Council in their professions of loyalty, mustering 140 coaches in procession to St James; they supported the public credit at a time when the progress of the rebel army prompted a financial crisis; and they gave freely to the various subscription funds for government troops in the North.[92] Most sectors of overseas

[89] Council Journals, lviii, fos. 307, 378.

[90] See my 'Popular Disaffection in London during the Forty-Five', *London Journal*, i/1 (May 1975), 23–4.

[91] CLRO, Court of Lieutenancy Minute Book (1744–9), fos. 44–5.

[92] *London Magazine* (1747), 463; *London Gazette*, 10–14, 24–8 Sept. 1745; CLRO, Alchin Box D, no. 32; *A List of Subscribers to the Veterans Scheme* (London, 1748), ed. Samuel Smith; PRO, SP 36/67/169–72, 241, 36/69/76. See

trade were represented in these enterprises, but the core
support came predictably from the bastions of high finance:
the directors and big stockholders of the major moneyed
companies; the Dutch, Huguenot, and Jewish financiers; and
the traders in the most prestigious companies such as the
Russia and the Levant.[93]

How did the City of London respond to these initiatives?
What, in particular, was the reaction of the City opposition to
loyalist ventures? All the evidence suggests that the City was
divided over strategy. Whereas many in the opposition camp
were prepared to shelve their political grievances during the
crisis, some radicals made co-operation contingent upon
political concessions. National harmony, they argued, could
best be fostered by some gesture towards the political demands
set down in 1742, by popular remedies designed to break the
sinews of Court influence and to arrest the anti-libertarian
tendencies of thirty years of Whig rule. These remedies did not
only include the conventional reforms of the Country programme: Place and Pension Bills; the restoration of triennial
parliaments; heavier penalties against electoral bribery, and so
forth; they also included the repeal of the Riot Act, the Black
Act, the elimination of the National Debt, the abolition of
standing armies, and a reduction in indirect taxation. These
grievances were set out in the rejoinders to the earl of Egmont's
Faction Detected, a pamphlet which defended the reconciliation of the opposition Whigs with the Court and condemned
the activities of the London and Westminster radicals who were
propelling the state towards popular anarchy and Jacobitism.[94]

also my 'Resistance to Oligarchy: The City Opposition to Walpole and his
Successors, 1725–47', in John Stevenson (ed.), *London in the Age of Reform*
(Oxford, 1977), p. 15.

[93] These conclusions are based on an analysis of the 256 merchants and
financiers who signed the 1744 loyalist Address and supported at least two of
the four loyalist ventures in 1745.

[94] John Perceval, *Faction Detected by the Evidence of Facts*, 2nd edn.
(London, 1743); Anon., *The Groans of Britons at the Gloomy Prospect of the
Present Precarious State of their Liberties and Properties, Compared with
what it Has Been* (London, 1743); Anon., *Public Discontent Accounted for
from the Conduct of our Ministers in the Cabinet and our Generals in the
Field* (London, 1743); Anon., *Opposition not Faction, or The Rectitude of the
Present Parliamentary Opposition to the Present Expensive Measures*
(London, 1743).

At the outbreak of the Jacobite rebellion in 1745 they were restated both in the City and Parliament, where Sir Francis Dashwood pressed for further safeguards against corruption to bolster popular loyalism.

The first signs of a division within the opposition camp came in early September when the news of the rebellion reached London. Even before the City had received official confirmation of the uprising, the Lord Mayor, Sir Henry Marshall, and Sir John Barnard prepared a loyalist Address from the opposition-dominated Court of Aldermen, assuring the king of their 'Zeal and Readiness to Oppose his Enemies and every attempt against the Rights of his Crown and our present happy Constitution'. Three days later, when a similar Address was proposed in Common Council, the radicals raised objections. George Heathcote, in particular, refused to support any motion that omitted popular grievances and the obligations of the king to his people.[95] His objections were overruled and a conciliatory, uncontroversial motion was passed. Heathcote claimed that the motion was not an accurate reflection of Council sentiment, as so many members were out of town. This is conceivable, but it was significant that several of the commoners responsible for the Address had also framed the Instructions of February and October 1742 and had been actively campaigning for the repeal of the veto. They included Richard Sclater, a druggist and deputy of the stridently anti-ministerial ward of Farringdon Without; Robert Henshaw, an attorney from Aldersgate; James Heywood, a prominent linen-draper and opposition Whig who was closely associated with the Half-Moon Club, the headquarters of the opposition caucus; and James Hodges, a bookseller from Bridge ward who as Town Clerk became a prominent supporter of William Pitt. Clearly, the leading members of the City opposition were divided in their response to the Forty-Five, and not along party lines. Tories and opposition Whigs were to be found in both camps.

A further division within the opposition occurred over the loyalist associations and subscription funds to aid the government's military effort against the rebels. These schemes were

---

[95] CLRO, Repertories of the Court of Aldermen, cxlix. 386–7; *Papers of the Earls of Marchmont*, ii. 346–7.

ostensibly for local defence or as a supplement to the regular troops. In practice, their military importance was less significant than their political. Avidly promoted in the early months of the crisis, no fewer than twenty-five counties and twelve provincial towns established loyalist organizations, their main role was to boost allegiance to the Crown and immobilize dissent. Many Tories and Independents none the less had qualms about them. Some, like Sir George Savile, objected to swearing personal allegiance to the Crown rather than to the laws of the realm. Others believed that the associations thwarted the creation of a militia, a truly constitutional army. Others still were unhappy that such associations were created by royal warrant rather than by Parliament.[96]

Similar objections were raised about subscriptions. In the Commons Tory radicals denounced them as an illegal tax, subverting the House's right to scrutinize supply and denying them the opportunity to comment upon the government's defence policy, which, as the rebel army defeated General Cope and troops were rushed back from Flanders, appeared to border on incompetence. Thomas Carew and George Heathcote even compared subscriptions to the benevolences of Charles I's reign, and emphasized that they infringed 'the most sacred privilege of parliament, the power of granting money'. The Welsh Tory, Sir Watkin Williams Wynn, concurred with this view. According to William Ellis, he 'did not speak but on the Topic of subscriptions cried Hear & gave hint to some of his people to do the like'.[97]

Opposition to the loyalist associations and the subscriptions was stronger in the City of London than it was in Parliament. The Corporation was noticeably lethargic about setting up a subscription fund and it was not until November that it finally established one in conjunction with earlier projects at Jonathan's and Garraway's begun by Alderman Sir Joseph

---

[96] Sheffield City Library, Wentworth Woodhouse Muniments, M1, fo. 309. I am indebted to Dr Gordon Elliot for this reference. John Debrett, *The History, Debates, Proceedings of Both Houses of Parliament* (London, 1792), ii. 64–7; Rupert C. Jarvis, *Collected Papers on the Jacobite Risings* (2 vols.; Manchester, 1971–2), ii. 313.

[97] P. C. Yorke, *Life of Lord Chancellor Hardwicke* (2 vols.; Cambridge, 1913), i. 478; Chatsworth House, Derbyshire, Devonshire MS 335/0.

Hankey and the Broad Street financier, James Colebrooke.[98]
Similarly, the City's loyalist association took some time to
germinate, in spite of the early declaration of intent and
pointed exhortations from London preachers. Hardwicke confided to the archbishop of York in mid-October that he could
not say that 'the Association and Subscription in the City of
London has made all the progress that one would wish'.[99]

Nevertheless, when the loyalist associations and subscriptions did finally get under way, a substantial section of the
London opposition did support them. Nineteen aldermen,
including eleven members of the anti-Walpolean coalition,
signed the declaration of 4 October pledging their support for
'our Present Happy Constitution'. Twelve contributed to the
Guildhall fund to aid government troops in the north, among
them three City MPs, Sir John Barnard, Sir Daniel Lambert,
and Sir William Calvert. Conspicuous by their absence from
these lists were the Tory aldermen Robert Alsop and William
Benn, a soap-maker who had risen to prominence as a
councillor in Bishopsgate ward in the mayoral controversy of
1739. They were joined by the opposition Whig aldermen
Samuel Pennant of Bishopsgate ward, a Jamaica merchant, and
the firebrand George Heathcote, another West India merchant,
regarded by the sugar planters as 'forty-one Heathcott' for his
intrepid radicalism and continued hostility to the Court.[100]

Of the Common Councilmen, 92 out of a total of 236
supported the loyalist declaration. Approximately half were
affiliated to the opposition, including several important committee men. Few Common Councillors tendered individual

---

[98] A history of the City subscription scheme can be found in Samuel Smith
(ed.), *Veterans Scheme*, pp. 1–2. Smith thought the subscriptions were opened
on 20 Nov., but this date appears to have been for the amalgamated scheme.
The subscription at Garraway's began in Oct., and Hankey's scheme sometime
before mid-Nov. See CLRO, Repertories of the Court of Aldermen, clix. 1463,
and MS 186.7.

[99] Quote from BL, Add. MS 35,568, fo. 93; cf. J. J. Majende, *A Sermon
Preach'd at the Cathedral Church of St. Paul, London, On Sunday Morning
the 10th of November 1745* (London, 1745).

[100] On Heathcote's nickname see L. M. Penson, *The Colonial Agents of the
British West Indies* (London, 1924), pp. 282–3. The other alderman who did not
sign was Micajah Perry, but his absence can be explained by his financial
difficulties. He was forced to wind up his business in the mid-1740s and
resigned his aldermanic gown in 1746. See Guildhall Library, MS 8728/6,
fos. 5–6, and Jacob Price, 'The Excise Affair Revisited', pp. 301–2.

contributions to the Guildhall fund (the Council itself donated £1,000), but of those who did, opposition sympathizers featured as prominently as ministerialists. Significant contributions also came from two leading opposition livery companies, the Goldsmiths and the Vintners; from Cordwainer, a ward which had swung over to the Patriots since the Spanish crisis; and from St Bride's, Fleet Street, a parish in the traditionally Tory ward of Farringdon Without and a former stumping-ground of Francis Atterbury. So the Guildhall subscription fund, like the loyalist declaration, was never monopolized by the ministerial Whigs. Although the financial and mercantile bourgeoisie outside the City political élite provided the impetus for the project, it was organized with the help of moderate Patriots such as Sir Richard Hoare, the lord mayor and a banker of Tory lineage, who was later thanked for his efforts.[101]

The political crisis of 1745 thus divided the City opposition. Even the members of the same political clubs sometimes disagreed about their response to the rebellion, for a survey of the Centenary Club, a key organization for the opposition in the western wards, reveals no consensus of opinion about the subscription fund or the loyalist declaration.[102] While many Patriots agreed to support the administration in buttressing loyalism, the more radical or intransigently anti-ministerial members eschewed all contact with a government insensitive to their political demands. Such behaviour inevitably opened them to the charge of Jacobitism. Was it in any way justified? Recent commentators, following in the tradition of Lord Mahon and eighteenth-century histories of London by John Northouck and Henry Chamberlain, have suggested that it was. On the evidence in the Stuart papers, Eveline Cruickshanks has reaffirmed the spectre of a disaffected capital. George Rudé, too, has claimed that while many city politicians

---

[101] Essex RO, D/DM Z 2.

[102] Three of the members in 1745 refused to co-operate with the various loyalist schemes: Robert Pycroft of Portsoken, brewer; Henry Sisson, Farringdon Within, druggist; Richard Skinner, Farringdon Within, linen-draper. Three others, Aldermen William Calvert and Richard Hoare, and James Heywood, supported both the subscription and the loyalist declaration. The other ten members supported one of these ventures. For the club members see Guildhall Lib., MS 544/1. See also my 'Clubs and Politics in Eighteenth-Century London: the Centenary of Cheapside', the *London Journal*, 11/1 (summer 1985), 51–8.

behaved with considerable circumspection during the Forty-Five, 'their Jacobite sympathies were hardly in doubt'. Taken together with the 'considerable Jacobite undercurrents in the ale-houses and beer-shops', this ferment could have reached insurrectionary proportions.[103]

Several observations must be made about this interpretation. In the first place, one must question the possible convergence of popular and City Jacobitism tentatively advanced by Rudé and even more emphatically by A. A. Mitchell. What evidence there is of Jacobitism in the Quarter Sessions indictments and recognizances suggests that it had a distinct ethno-religious character. The majority of defendants hailed from the predominantly Catholic areas of the metropolis. At least five were professed Catholics; a further three appeared in the papist returns for London and Middlesex; and others like Alice Woodward, the wife of a Holborn weaver who blessed 'Johnny the Pretender' and hoped that mass would soon be read in St Paul's, hardly left their religious sympathies in doubt.[104] What is also striking is the high incidence of Irish Catholic names among the accused, which suggests that Jacobitism had strong roots in the Catholic immigrant community, or, in a crisis which created a Catholic *peur*, with rumours of an imminent papist rising against Protestants, dark conspiracies led by Romish priests, and Catholic-inspired arson, that they were a predictable target population.[105] Whichever explanation we adopt it is clear that London Jacobitism, while not insignificant, was not part of the mainstream. Comparatively few prosecutions came from those populous outer parishes where there had been a strong tradition of militant Toryism and

[103] George Rudé, *Hanoverian London 1714–1808* (London, 1971), pp. 154–7, 208–9; Eveline Cruickshanks, *Political Untouchables, passim*; see also A. A. Mitchell, 'London and the Forty-Five', *History Today*, 15/10 (Oct. 1965), 719–26. For earlier reflections on London's Jacobitism see John Northouck, *A New History of London* (London, 1773), p. 356; Henry Chamberlain, *A New and Complete History and Survey of the Cities of London and Westminster* (London, 1770), p. 321; Lord Mahon, *History of England* (7 vols.; London, 1858), iii. 275.

[104] For an extensive analysis of popular Jacobitism in 1745 see my 'Popular Disaffection', *London Journal* (1975), 5–27.

[105] On the rumours see *London Evening Post*, 19–22 Oct. 1745; *Morning Advertiser*, 19–21 Oct., 11–13 Nov. 1745; *St James Evening Post*, 9–12 Nov. 1745; SP 36/72/56; Bedfordshire RO, HW 87/124, Richard How to his son, London, 20 Oct. 1745.

considerable disaffection in 1715–17. This cannot be attributed to local tolerance of disaffection, for the militia and watch had been primed for action; in some areas, such as Spitalfields, masters and journeymen stepped up vigilance.[106] Rather, it suggests that loyalism struck a responsive chord in the London population. Guy Fawkes's day was celebrated with gusto, with the 'pope and pretender burnt in many places'.[107] Such was the strength of anti-Catholic, libertarian sentiment that quite humble men and women were prepared to prosecute cases of seditious oaths and words. Indeed, the prosecutions for disaffection reveal a strong aversion to Jacobite sentiment among the rank and file as much as they do an official policing of a factious, plebeian population. To be sure, victuallers and soldiers feature prominently as prosecuting witnesses, and there was a predictable crop of office-holders and gentlemanly retainers; but in a third of all cases the social standing of the prosecutors, men and women from all walks of life, was little different from the accused. In the popular mind in London (although not necessarily elsewhere), the Jacobite cause had come to symbolize the return of absolutism and Catholic bigotry and a denial of national identity.[108]

This still leaves the question of Jacobitism within the City's official assemblies. Here the evidence is more ambiguous. Without doubt the exiled Court had high hopes of sympathetic response from the City, largely on the basis of reports of the political temper of the Common Council and Court of Aldermen in the summer of 1743. According to a list drawn up for the Jacobite emissary James Butler, the equerry of the king of France, 11 aldermen and 178 Common Councilmen were Jacobite sympathizers, 'headed and led on by men of spirit, honour and firmness'.[109] But the list must be handled with care. Several of the aldermen from whom the Jacobites had high hopes of support subscribed to the fund for military aid

[106] Lieutenancy Minutes (1744–9), fos. 124–5; *St James's Evening Post*, 19–21 Oct. 1745.

[107] *Gentleman's Magazine*, 15 (1745), 609.

[108] I have emphasized the uneven survival of popular Jacobitism in my 'Popular Jacobitism in Provincial Context: Eighteenth-Century Bristol and Norwich', in Eveline Cruickshanks and J. Black (eds.), *The Jacobite Challenge* (Edinburgh, 1988), pp. 123–41. For the evidence about the prosecuting witnesses see my 'Popular Disaffection', *London Journal* (1975), 19–21.

[109] William Balhady's copy of this list is to be found in the Stuart papers,

against the rebels, Daniel Lambert and Robert Willimot among them. Various ministerial supporters, such as John Day, the deputy of Cordwainer, were classified as oppositionists. Moreover, the attributions used on the list, 'Jacobite/Patriot', 'Whig', and 'Hanoverian', were very ambiguous. Save in the case of the aldermen, about whom more was known, all signs of anti-ministerialism were read as Jacobitism, a highly problematic interpretation given the heterogeneous nature of the City opposition, the clear hostility to Jacobite candidates at the hustings (even to the anti-Excise hero, John Barber), and the actual *behaviour* of London's more prominent citizens and councillors during the Forty-Five. After all, potential Jacobites had viable constitutional arguments for refusing to join loyalist associations and to contribute to subscription funds. Why then, in a constituency not known for its political timidity, did they not follow their inclinations? A plausible explanation must be that they were not really Jacobites at all.

I do not wish to rest my case on the known behaviour of City politicians. But I want to suggest that the 1743 list wildly exaggerated and distorted the true nature of London's antipathy to the government. A number of London aldermen had flirted with Jacobitism in the early Hanoverian era, Barber and Humphrey Parsons especially. And one suspects that some of the duke of Wharton's circle, men such as Colonel Samuel Robinson, had contacts with the exiled house as well. But the bleak political climate of the 1720s, in which opposition to Whiggery seemed such a formidable task, brightened after the Excise crisis. From 1734 onwards the City opposition was in the ascendant. It monopolized the parliamentary representation. It had captured the Court of Aldermen, effectively nullifying the veto. To be sure, the prospect of further reform had eluded the City in 1742, but this was not necessarily irrevocable. Despite the frustrations of the mid-1740s, there were compensations and possibilities for change without courting the Pretender. In any case, many City politicans had a lot to lose from such a desperate recourse. A review of stock and bond holdings during the period 1747–50 suggests that

---

Stuart MS 254/154. The list is reprinted in Cruickshanks, *Political Untouchables*, app: II, with annotations showing who supported the subscriptions and/ or the loyalist association.

about a quarter of the Common Councilmen invested substantial sums in long- or short-term annuities. Insurance valuations also disclose that many had stock-in-trade worth £1,000 or more and owned houses worth £500. The Common Councilmen were hardly the petty shopkeepers of ministerial propaganda. They were solid citizens, as or more mobile than their fathers, with a real stake in the City.[110] This hardly disposed them to risky Jacobite ventures.

A few aldermen may have inclined towards Jacobitism in 1745. During his visit to London in the summer of 1743 Butler had purportedly a number of private talks with six members of the Upper Court.[111] Of these potential recruits, Westley died before the outbreak of the Forty-Five and Edward Gibbon had lost interest in London politics, resigning his gown that summer. Of the other four, Willimot and Lambert were unlikely converts, too active in the loyalist ventures to be reckoned committed Jacobites. This left William Benn, who broke his leg while falling from his horse in September 1745 and was reported to be 'in a dangerous way'.[112] And George Heathcote. The latter had not been initially regarded as a Jacobite sympathizer, but he was in touch with some leading conspirators during the crucial months of the crisis. According to Lord Sempill, Heathcote 'opened himself' to Sir John Hinde Cotton in September 1745, saying he 'did what he could without formally despising the established laws to force the Court to persecute him, by which he hoped to drive things to the utmost extremity'.[113] How reliable a report this was and whether any other aldermen were implicated in Jacobite plans it is impossible to say. In the early 1750s Jacobite sources were linking Heathcote with Benn and also with Matthew Blakiston, a wealthy grocer on the Strand and a member of the

[110] Of the 65 mid-century councillors whose fathers were liverymen before them, 51% joined the same company, 26% joined a company of equivalent status, 19% joined a company of higher status and 4% of lower status. The evidence about the wealth of councillors is derived from wills, insurance registers (Hand-in-Hand and Sun Fire) in the Guildhall Library. MSS 8,674 and 11.936, and stock and bond purchases in 1750.

[111] Cruickshanks, *Political Untouchables*, p. 40.

[112] *London Evening Post*, 17–19 Sept. 1745.

[113] Cited by James Browne, *A History of the Highlands and the Highland Clans* (Glasgow, 1840), app. III, p. 437.

Independent Electors of Westminster, who became an alderman in May 1750.[114] Other disaffected aldermen included John Blachford, who is said to have attended a Jacobite club in Fenchurch Street in 1751 and the following year presented the Goldsmiths' Company with a portrait of himself and five other aldermen from the Company drinking dubious healths at his house in Bowcombe on the Isle of Wight.[115] But there is no evidence that any of these men were party to Heathcote's desperate flirtations in the final months of 1745. And judging from the subscriptions to Thomas Carte's *History of England*, neither they nor Heathcote were ideologically-committed Jacobites, for having agreed to contribute, all quickly fell in arrears. The overall impression is that Jacobitism was very much a marginal force in city politics, not part of the opposition mainstream. The notion that the Pretender had 'a great party in the city',[116] to use John Murray's words, was the product of Jacobite optimism and the self-aggrandizement of spies and conspirators who turned King's evidence. It is from such sensational and ambiguous evidence that the myth of a disaffected capital has been constructed.

Rumours of disaffection during the Forty-Five none the less circulated, and the radicals who objected to the loyalist ventures predictably received the butt of criticism. 'Did not the Common Language and Behaviour of too many of our own Countrymen', asked one pamphleteer, encourage the Pretender and the French 'to hope for that success from a murmuring, discontented, and divided nation?'[117] In this manner the Whigs prepared the way for the next general election. Public interest in the rebellion, and particularly in Tory-radical prevarications, was maintained at fever pitch by a few well-executed scenarios. At the impeachment of Lord Lovat a few months

[114] Lord Mahon, *History of England*, iii. 275n; Andrew Lang, *Pickle the Spy* (London, 1897), pp. 178, 192.

[115] John J. Baddeley, *The Aldermen of Cripplegate Ward 1276–1900* (London, 1900), pp. 94–5; Nottingham Univ. Lib., Newcastle papers, NeC 2091. See also entry for Blachford in the Guildhall Lib., Stocken MSS.

[116] Robert Fitzroy Bell (ed.), *Memorials of John Murray of Broughton 1740–47* (Scottish History Soc., 27; Edinburgh, 1898), p. 465. On the subscription to Carte's *History*, see Bodleian Lib., Carte MS 175, fos. 61–74.

[117] *A Letter to a TORY FRIEND upon the Present Critical Situation of our Affairs* (London, 1746), p. 13.

before the election, the former secretary of the Pretender, John Murray, disclosed that a number of Tories well-entrenched in Westminster radical circles had communicated with the Jacobite agent, Lord Traquair. The Tories derided the accusation and the government never followed it up, but it had the desired effect. 'You may easily imagine that Murray's evidence makes a great noise,' wrote Elizabeth Yorke to her brother, 'and it is not unlikely but it may have further consequences.'[118]

Two further incidents helped to maintain public interest in the trial and emblazon the standard of patriotic Whiggery. On 24 March 1747, the Commons ordered an investigation into the conduct of the Westminster Independents at their annual dinner at Vintners' Hall, where the landlord of the White Horn, Piccadilly, had apparently been assaulted for harbouring one of the leading prosecuting witnesses in the Lovat trial.[119] Nothing came of the incident, but it did little to dissociate the Independent Electors and their city allies from Jacobitism, an association first raised during the trial and execution of Counsellor David Morgan, one of several Welsh dissidents active in Westminster politics.[120] The final attempt to exploit the trial for political purposes came in early April, when Newcastle directed the London sheriffs to hold up the head of Lord Lovat after his execution. Since the practice had died out, the request had very obvious political overtones, and the sheriffs pleaded with Newcastle that 'the Clamour against them for doing it would be very disagreeable'. Robert Alsop protested that 'he had always behaved with the greatest Moderation, and had the highest Opinion and Esteem for his Grace, and was much concerned that such a difficulty as this should be thrown upon him'.[121] On the day of the execution he refused to carry out the order without written confirmation, whilst his colleague, Thomas Winterbottom, a government supporter, judiciously absented himself.

---

[118] David N. MacKay (ed.), *Trial of Simon, Lord Lovat of the '45* (Edinburgh and Glasgow, 1911), p. 127; P. C. Yorke, *Hardwicke*, i. 583–4.
[119] *Commons Journals*, 25 p. 326; W. S. Lewis (ed.), *The Yale Edition of Horace Walpole's Correspondence* (34 vols; New Haven, 1937–70), xix. 387–8.
[120] Philip Jenkins, *The Making of a Ruling Class: The Glamorgan gentry 1640–1790* (Cambridge, 1983), pp. 166, 173–4.
[121] SP 36/96/59, 62.

In these circumstances it was hardly surprising that the 1747 elections in the metropolis should be fought against the background of the Forty-Five. In Westminster, where the Independent Electors were deluged with anti-Jacobite propaganda and were heavily censured for their refusal to support the subscriptions and loyalist associations, the opposition had great difficulty finding someone to stand. Eventually the Tory Sir Thomas Dyke came forward, but he proved no match for the combined forces of the Court and Bedford House.[122] In Middlesex the opposition committed political suicide by publicly disowning all subscribers. Even the support of the returning officers, Lord Mayor William Benn, and several other aldermen proved of little avail against two candidates representing 'the Protestant Interest against the Pretender and all his adherents'.[123]

Such a rapid reversal of anti-ministerial fortunes was less likely in the City where the opposition party was more firmly entrenched. But the ministerial Whigs had carefully paved the way to win over the moderates. Henry Pelham agreed to the repeal of the aldermanic veto in March 1746 and placated the small creditor in the City by raising the government loan of 1747 by open subscription.[124] Together these actions isolated the radicals and left them vulnerable to the full force of anti-Jacobitism. Henry Fielding portrayed the extremists as a group of malcontents who 'openly drew their Corks in the Pretender's favour' when the rebels reached Derby. Another writer reminded his readers that 'the too free and immoderate exercise of Liberty did not a little contribute to the fomenting and raising the late pernicious Rebellion'.[125] Trouble-makers, especially those who had opposed subscriptions and associations, were to be vilified.

---

[122] Salop RO, James Bonnell papers, 22 Oct. 1747. I am indebted to Dr Linda Colley of Yale University for this reference. For more details on the mid-century Westminster elections see ch. 5.

[123] *Felix Farley's Bristol Journal*, 27 June 1747; Greater London RO, CRO 136/Mx F.P.2 Acc/1085 (the election diary of Sir Roger Newdigate, 1747).

[124] Council Journals, lix, fos. 13–14, 29–30; *Commons Journals*, 25, pp. 62–3, 78, 92; Dickson, *The Financial Revolution*, pp. 223–7.

[125] [Henry Fielding], *A Dialogue between a Gentleman of London, Agent for Two Court Candidates and an Honest Alderman of the Court Party* (London, 1747), p. 8; *General Advertiser*, 19 June 1747. See also *General Evening Post*, 30 June–2 July 1747.

The Patriots tried hard to settle their differences and present a united front to the electorate. The two leading radicals, Benn and Heathcote, were dropped from the opposition slate. So, too, was Edward Ironside, a Lombard Street banker who had signed the loyalist declaration of October 1745 but had failed to subscribe to the Guildhall fund. They were replaced by three moderate aldermen: Henry Marshall, the former MP for Agmondesham and sponsor of the loyalist Address of September 1745; Robert Ladbroke, a distiller with considerable local influence in both Castle Baynard and Spitalfields; and Danial Lambert, a familar figure in City circles who had worked his way up from the ranks and had represented London in the previous Parliament. The Half-Moon Club hoped that these candidates, alongside Sir John Barnard, would be preferable to the rival Merchants' list on account of their long-standing association with the Corporation. But this attempt to promote a moderate image and press the claims of seasoned politicians with local roots proved unsuccessful. The current of anti-Jacobitism proved too strong. Even the moderates failed to avoid the taint of treason levelled at their more radical associates. The Merchants' list was returned *in toto*. It included Sir John Barnard, whose political reputation placed him in an unassailable position; Sir William Calvert, a renegade Patriot and avid supporter of the loyalist ventures of 1745; and two prominent City merchants, Slingsby Bethell and Stephen Theodore Janssen, whose Whig ancestry blended well with the political mood of Common Hall.[126] In fact, here the Court Whigs successfully appropriated the radical heritage from the Tory-Patriots, for both of these eminently respectable and loyalist merchants could claim a republican genealogy to garnish their conservatism. None of these candidates were out-and-out courtiers. That would have stuck in the Livery's throat. But they were men whose allegiance to Hanover was unquestioned. As Henry Pelham recognized, the metropolitan elections were 'comfortable declarations of the anti-jacobitism of this part of the world'.[127]

[126] *General Evening Post*, 4–7 July 1747. Bethell was the great nephew of the Whig republican, Slingsby Bethell; and Janssen, whose father had been associated with Robert Harley, was the grandson on his mother's side of the anti-Catholic crusader, Henry Cornish, executed for his complicity in the Rye House plot.

[127] Pelham to Horace Walpole, 4 July 1747, BL, Add. MS 9186, fo. 105.

The 1747 elections revealed, once again, the Whig trump card. Whenever the Whig party was able to pose as the only real alternative to a Jacobite restoration, and by implication the defender of British liberties against foreign oppression, its electoral popularity soared. Despite the fact that large sections of the London opposition were impeccably loyal in 1745, the suspicions which surrounded the radical elements in the City, both in terms of policy and affiliation, were sufficient to sully its reputation among a hitherto resolutely anti-ministerial citizenry. Shaken by the memory of the rebel army encamped outside Derby and the ensuing financial panic, Londoners played safe. Placated by a government willing to address local grievances, they put loyalism before structural reform.

The half-decade after Walpole's fall also underscored the contrariety of the forces which opposed him and the difficulties of maintaining the unity and momentum of the Country platform once his colourful and controversial personality left the political scene. This was not immediately obvious within London, where the aldermanic veto and the Court's continentalist foreign policy continued to embitter the wide sections of the citizenry. But even within London the particular alliance of mercantile and civic interests that gave the Country platform such vitality began to dissolve by 1745. Many of the merchants who had supported the opposition during the Excise and Spanish crises, veered to the Court during the rebellion. Whatever the deficiencies of Whig statecraft, dynastic stability was an essential precondition of commercial prosperity. At the same time radical objections to the loyalist initiatives were regarded as irresponsible and opportunistic by moderate elements in the City. It only required Pelham's repeal of the aldermanic veto and gestures towards small creditors to win the middle ground for the Court.

At the same time, the politics of the 1730s revealed that the government could not ignore the growing demand for a more bellicose mercantilism in the West. Nor could it disparage the voice of trade without alienating important sections of urban opinion. 1747 may have been a dramatic reversal of opposition fortunes, but it was itself not irreversible. The particular mix of patriotism, trade, and empire which bedevilled Walpole could quite easily resume under his successors. The dramatic expansion of the transatlantic economy after 1740 meant that imperial strategy and blue-water policies would remain high on the political agenda. Precisely how the politics of trade and empire intersected with the political aspirations of the City during the following decade or so forms the subject of my next chapter.

3
London, Patriotism, and Empire
1747–1763

AFTER the general election of 1747, City politics entered a new era. The failure of the opposition to adopt a common front over the Forty-Five irrevocably splintered the alliance of Tories and independent Whigs that had shaped the politics of the previous two decades. Confronted with a vociferously loyal electorate in 1747, opposition politicians modulated their anti-ministerialism, a shift that led George Heathcote to resign his gown in January 1749 and to retire to Bath a disillusioned man.[1] At the same time, the reversal of opposition fortunes in 1747 did not inaugurate a new epoch of ministerialism in City politics. Although the Court party recovered Walbrook on Heathcote's departure and won over Sir William Calvert to its camp, it did not make any inroads in ward politics. Nor was it strong enough to resist the election of the Westminster Independent, Matthew Blakiston, as Alderman of Bishopsgate in June 1750.[2] Indeed, the support that aldermen like Sir Henry Marshall and Stephen Theodore Janssen gave to the anti-Court candidate, Sir George Vandeput, in the Westminster by-election of 1749 revealed that official party labels were an imperfect guide to political behaviour, especially on the question of Court interference in metropolitan elections. The prevailing trend, in fact, was towards an abatement of party strife and a more pragmatic approach to local and national politics. There were few contests at the ward level along party lines, and although four candidates were put up for the vacant post of City Chamberlain in May 1751, the election aroused little interest beyond

---

[1] Heathcote explained his resignation in a letter printed in the *London Evening Post*, 26 Jan. 1749. In the Court of Aldermen, Heathcote was thanked for his 'disinterested conduct' during his years of service, but the motion was contentiously debated; see *Gentleman's Magazine*, 9 (1749), 43.
[2] *Gentleman's Magazine*, 20 (1750), 280.

some speculation that Heathcote might stand.[3] The fluidity
of the situation was underscored by the fact that several
oppositionists, including Richard Glover, competed for the
chamberlainship, and that few of the incoming aldermen were
identified closely with any one party. Even the wealthy sugar-
planter, William Beckford, who became Alderman of Billingsgate in 1752, cast his net wide. Entering Parliament on the
Shaftesbury interest in 1747 and closely allied with a number
of West Country Tories, Beckford was soliciting the support of
Bedford, Fox, and Leicester House in his efforts to carve out a
political career for himself and his brothers.[4] 'Upon the whole
nobody could be more extraordinarily civil than Mr. Beckford
was in his dealing with me this morning', wrote Henry Fox to
Ilchester less than a month after Beckford's election as
Alderman of Billingsgate, 'Do you think him a Jacobite as by
his City Friends He should seem to be, & many tell me he is?'[5]

So the politics of the Forty-Five and the entry of new men
combined to produce a change in the political temper of the
Corporation. Pelham's accommodating attitude to City interests also facilitated this process. Having repealed the
aldermanic veto, he sought to placate the small creditor in City
circles by agreeing to raise government loans by open subscription and by reducing the National Debt. These issues had been
vigorously advocated by Sir John Barnard in the late 1730s and
1740s, and they were taken up by Pelham at the end of the War
of Austrian Succession as the Debt soared to over £68 million.
In 1747 and 1748 he raised two loans by open subscription
along lines set down by Barnard. In the following three years he
forced a reduction of the Debt on the · major moneyed
companies.[6] In so doing he not only removed some of the sting
out of a long-standing grievance in City politics, he also won
the confidence of Barnard, a very influential figure, who even

---

[3] *Whitehall Evening Post*, 25–7 Apr., 4–7 May 1751; *London Evening Post*,
23–5 Apr., 2–4 May 1751; Maitland, *History of London*, i. 687–8.

[4] Linda Colley, *In Defiance of Oligarchy*, p. 258; Sir Lewis Namier and John
Brooke, *History of Parliament: Commons 1754–1790* (3 vols.; London, 1964),
i. 329–30, ii. 75.

[5] BL, Add. MS 51,419, fo. 156; see also PRO, 30/24/28, fos. 349–50, and
Bedford Estate Office, Bedford MS xxx, fo. 48.

[6] Dickson, *The Financial Revolution*, pp. 212–14, 220–3, 234–40; Lucy
Sutherland, 'Samson Gideon, 18th. c. Jewish Financier', *Trans. Jewish
Historical Society*, 17 (1951–2), 79–80.

after Pelham's death in 1754 continued to collaborate with his brother on problems of Treasury finance.

The shifting temper of City politics was even seen in the agitation against the Jewish Naturalization Bill in 1753. Conventionally, the Jew Bill has been highlighted as an exemplary episode in party politics; at the very least, as a sign of the lingering vitality of Toryism in the country at large.[7] Without doubt, there is a good deal of truth to this reasoning. Naturalization Bills had been the bane of the Tories since the 1690s, and the modest dispensations which were offered to wealthy Jews, particularly those of the Sephardic community, were no exception to the rule.[8] When the terms of the 1753 Bill became public, the bishops found themselves confronted with recalcitrant clergymen in their dioceses, especially in Tory-dominated sees such as Oxford and Norfolk. Similarly, politicians in Tory counties such as Gloucestershire and Cornwall and cities like Exeter faced a rough ride from their constituents.[9] In these circumstances it was not surprising that the Tory heartlands of the South-West and the Midlands featured quite prominently in the volley of Instructions against the Bill.[10]

In the provinces these protests were fuelled with fears for the security of church advowsons as well as an ingrained anti-semitism and xenophobia. In London and the Home Counties they were also directed at the Jewish merchants and financiers who formed part of the metropolitan plutocracy, whose

[7] T. W. Perry, *Public Opinion, Propaganda and Politics in Eighteenth-Century England* (Cambridge, Mass., 1962).

[8] Under the terms of the Bill, Jews were no longer obliged to take the Anglican sacrament under a private naturalization, simply the Oaths of Supremacy and Allegiance. This had already been granted in the colonies under the Plantation Act of 1740: see Perry, *Public Opinion*, pp. 16–21, 47. On the general hostility to Naturalization Bills see H. T. Dickinson, 'The Tory Party's Attitude to Foreigners: A Note on Party Principles in the Age of Anne', *Bull. Institute Historical Research*, 40 (1967), 153–63. For opposition in the City see Council Journals, lix, fos. 105 ff., 331.

[9] BL, Add. MS 35,398, fos. 84, 102, 120, 125, 128, 151, 166.

[10] In the South-West, instructions were drawn up in Bristol, Devizes, Exeter, Gloucester, and Wiltshire; in the Midlands, in Coventry, Cheshire, and Warwickshire; in the South-East, in London, Reading, Essex, Kent, Middlesex, and Suffolk; and in the North, in York: see *London Evening Post*, 7–9, 23–5 Aug., 20–3 Oct., 3–6, 8–10, 15–17, 17–20 Nov. 1753; *Read's Weekly Journal*, 27 Oct. 1753; *Public Advertiser*, 7, 19 Nov. 1753; *Jackson's Oxford Journal*, 29 Sept., 17 Nov. 1753.

speculative deals on behalf of foreign fund-holders troubled merchants and tradesmen of different political colours, particularly those who hoped to share in the profits of high finance.[11] These anxieties were addressed in the *London Evening Post*, where the Jew Bill was portrayed as a fillip to financiers expert in 'the Mysteries and Iniquities of Stock-Jobbing', to men who had purportedly acquired 'Vast Estates by plundering the publick'.[12] In other words, the agitation touched raw nerves about the potentially corrosive influence of the moneyed interest in society and politics and the likely increase of Jewish participation in the funds as a result of Naturalization. 'When the M—r has the riches of the Jews always at hand,' declared one writer, 'he is deliver'd from all dependence upon the Commons, and can, as he likes, either buy a Majority in the House, or send them to their homes, and order Jewish Centinels to keep Watch over them.'[13] To this fear was added another which accompanied every public debate against naturalization, namely, the notion that a massive immigration of foreign traffickers would prejudice the trade of the local shopkeeper. Not surprisingly, Samuel Martin reported to Thomas Birch that 'the Clamour against the Jew Bill is much greater in London than amongst the Gross of the people whom he had met with in his Journey to Cornwall'.[14]

Even so, the City of London took some time to mobilize its forces against the Bill. It was only when the merchants in the Portugal trade signed a petition against the measure that the Common Council took up the issue in earnest, and then at a meeting attended by only 9 aldermen and 125 commoners. This proved something of an embarrassment to anti-ministerialists. They explained the City's tardy response to the bill by emphasizing the underhand way in which it had been

[11] My research on the consolidation of East India stock and the purchase of bonds in 1750/1 reveals a broadening of the investor constituency, particularly among those middling tradesmen who sat on the London Common Council: see the ledgers, East India House, L/AG/14/5/328.

[12] *London Evening Post*, 28–30 June 1753.

[13] *London Evening Post*, 22–4 May 1753.

[14] BL, Add. MS 35,398, fo. 178; on the threat to the ordinary trader see *Gray's Inn Journal*, 9 June 1753; *London Evening Post*, 21–3 Aug. 1753; Anon., *A Letter to the Worshipful Sir John Barnard . . . on the Act of Parliament for Naturalizing the Jews* (London, 1753), p. 11.

promoted late in the parliamentary session.[15] Yet this was only
a partial explanation. The City's lack of preparation was also a
symptom of its own disunity, a point implicitly recognized by
Horace Walpole, who denigrated the protest as the act of 'a
worthless set of Jacobites in the Common Council'.[16] It was
not until September, in fact, that the City's agitation to the Bill
gathered momentum, its instructions setting precedents for
other large towns.

Once set in motion, however, the London opposition to the
Jew Bill proved difficult to deflect. Pelham managed to
minimize its political impact in many other constituencies by
tactically withdrawing the Bill, but in London it resonated
through the hustings in the general election of 1754. Here
opposition focused upon Sir William Calvert, who had supported Jewish Naturalization in Parliament and Common
Council. Initially the Court was optimistic about Calvert's re-
election, calculating that the fluidity of political alignments
and the conflicting claims of several opposition candidates
would secure this Court-sponsored candidate a place in the
final four.[17] Calvert, too, expected victory. 'I saw Mr. [*sic*]
William Calvert last night,' wrote the duke of Newcastle to the
king on the eve of the election, 'who told me he had the
greatest appearance of merchants for him yesterday upon
the Exchange that ever was known. He seems confident of
success.'[18]

In an election that was fought principally on the question of
Jewish Naturalization this was not to be. Throughout the
campaign broadsides and prints blazoned Calvert's sympathy
for Jew and jobber. One satire depicted the wealthy brewer
receiving £100,000 as a bribe for voting for the Jew Bill.
Another had as its central figure the financier Samson Gideon,
with a demon on his back and a hatful of money, declaring that
he would freely distribute the profits of his last lottery if Sir
William was returned.[19] As the electioneering battle neared its

---

[15] *London Evening Post*, 19–22 May 1753.
[16] BL, Add. MS 35,606, fo. 79.
[17] BL, Add. MS 35,398, fo. 165v.
[18] BL, Add. MS 32,735, fo. 48.
[19] Israel Solomans' 'Satirical and Political Prints on the Jews' Naturalization Bill 1753', *Trans. Jewish Historical Society*, 6 (1908–10), 205–33.

close, so the attack upon Calvert broadened to embrace
his subservience to the Court and 'the mercenary Tools of
Power'.[20] One pamphleteer saw the election as a trial of
London's independence and of its status as a beacon of liberty.
'On all occasions of speculation, on all dubious events and
proceedings of P–rl–ment,' he declared, 'all Men look up to
the Metropolis and observe and enquire how the City of
London takes such and such a measure, and how they act in
Relation to it.'[21]

The 1754 election turned out to be a signal defeat for the
ministerial interest in the City. In spite of the support Calvert
received from the Court, the East India Company, and the
Dissenters, he came bottom of the poll. In a lively election in
which approximately 6,000 of the 8,600 liverymen (70 per cent)
participated, Calvert received 2,650 votes, 5 fewer than Sir
Richard Glyn, and some 900 fewer than the two leading
contenders.[22] At the same time, Calvert's defeat did not revive
the Patriot coalition of the late Walpolean era. In fact there was
no attempt to promote party or caucus slates of any kind, a
dramatic departure from earlier London elections. Nor did the
election substantially boost City Toryism. The most outspoken anti-ministerialist of the six, William Beckford, who
secured the help of Alderman Benn during the election and had
strong links with the Tories, as well as contacts with Bedford
and Holland House, scrambled home by less than 300 votes.
The real favourites of the Livery were Barnard, Bethell, and
Ladbroke, who each obtained over 3,000 supporters. The first
two were pre-eminently City representatives, whose political
ambitions in Parliament were secondary: the urban counterpart of the independent country gentlemen, they regarded their
prime function in the Lower House to be the protection of the
City's privileges and liberty. The latter candidate, Sir Robert
Ladbroke, managed to straddle rival parliamentary factions in
1754, soliciting the favour of both Bedford and Newcastle.[23]

---

[20] *London Evening Post*, 25–7 Apr. 1754; see also Anon., *An Address to the
Livery of the City of London* (London, 1754), and Anon., *Address to the
Worthy Liverymen of the Free City of London* (London, 1754).

[21] *An Address to the Livery of the City of London*, p. 7.

[22] *London Evening Post*, 7–9 May 1754; *Read's Weekly Journal*, 11 May
1754; *Gazetteer and London Daily Advertiser*, 25 Apr. 1754; *Public Advertiser*, 30 Apr. 1754; BL, Add. MS 32,735, fos. 268–72.

[23] BL, Add. MS 32,735, fo. 48; Bedford Estate Office, Bedford MS xxx, fo. 44.

Whether his overtures to the Court through the medium of the bishop of Peterborough were successful or not, it is difficult to say. Certainly the *London Evening Post* suspected that he had gained ministerial support.[24] Even so, it seems likely that the less partisan citizenry would have found him a more experienced and arguably less opportunistic candidate than Beckford, whose civic and parliamentary ambitions were thought to be self-serving. Although Beckford could claim some London lineage through his uncle, a former Alderman for Aldgate, his meteoric rise in City circles and his high politicking led many to suspect that his principal objective was to consolidate his family's social standing and to strengthen the West Indian interest in the Commons.[25]

The Jewish Naturalization Bill signalled the limits of Pelham's politics of consensus in London. The prospect of a fresh intrusion of Jewish money in the funds angered those who hoped to dabble in high finance and raised the spectre of an augmentation of moneyed power and influence. It converged with a residual Toryism to produce a substantial opposition to the Court and a new humiliation for the City's ministerial supporters. None the less, the lasting impact of the agitation was negligible. It did not generate another round of confrontations between Court and City. That only emerged with Minorca.

The fall of Port Mahon in Minorca in May 1756 came in the context of deteriorating relations between Britain and France, particularly over trade and territory in the New World. The rising tension between the two nations and the drift in Dutch policy to a position of strict neutrality led the duke of Newcastle to pursue a series of subsidy agreements in Europe in an attempt to contain French influence. He sought to bolster good relations with Austria by promoting Maria Theresa's son as the King of the Romans, and he agreed to a new four-year subsidy to the Landgrave of Hesse-Cassel, hiring 8,000 local troops at a cost of over £36,000 per annum. In addition he purchased the aid of 30,000 Russian troops in Livonia to

---

[24] *London Evening Post*, 2–4 May 1754.
[25] *Gazetteer*, 25 Apr. 1754; see also *Public Advertiser*, 23 Apr. 1754, where Beckford's lack of experience in City government is held against him.

dampen Prussian ambitions in Central Europe, particularly towards Hanover.[26]

Newcastle's new interventions in Europe met with a mixed reception in parliamentary and City circles, where the old fears of partiality towards Hanover and the neglect of a more aggressive naval policy were revived. 'I have not told you half what you will find about *Subsidy* and *Continent*,' he lamented to Hardwicke in July 1755, '*Cabals, Combinations* too strong to be resisted are formed upon that very point. They have blown up the City against it, and it is not in the power of men to contain them.'[27] This reaction was somewhat alarmist, for Alderman William Baker subsequently assured the administration that the City was well aware of the delicate diplomatic situation.[28] But there were rumblings of discontent from the opposition camp in London, especially from the *Monitor*, a new weekly sponsored by William Beckford's brother, Richard, and written by authors with close links to the Common Council.[29] These struck a chord in City circles because of the increasingly precarious record of the government in America, where the French reinforced their position in Acadia and came close to taking Ohio. The measures that were eventually taken to relieve Ohio and to frustrate French plans for a series of forts from New Orleans to Montreal were welcomed in the City. In September 1755 the Common Council thanked the king 'for the vigorous measures that have been taken to protect our Commerce and Colonies from all Encroachment of the French', assuring his Majesty that it would 'cheerfully con-

---

[26] C. W. Eldon, *England's Subsidy Policy Toward the Continent during the Seven Years War* (Philadelphia, 1938), *passim*; see also D. B. Horn, *Great Britain and Europe in the Eighteenth Century* (Oxford, 1967), chs. 6, 7.

[27] BL, Add. MS 32,858, fo. 332.

[28] BL, Add. MS 35,415, fo. 105.

[29] *Monitor*, 6, 27 Sept., 18 Oct., 8 Nov., 6 Dec. 1755. On the origins of the *Monitor* see Marie Peters, *Pitt and Popularity: The Patriot Minister and London Opinion during the Seven Years War* (Oxford, 1980), pp. 13–14. Richard Beckford became Alderman of Farringdon Without in Oct. 1754. The other pioneer of the *Monitor* with formal City links was Arthur Beardmore, William Beckford's attorney and Common Councilman for Walbrook. The two principal writers for the paper were Dr John Shebbeare and Rev. John Entick. Shebbeare did not remain with the paper very long, quarrelling over the financial arrangements. See Guildhall MS 214/3, fos. 291–6 (the information of Jonathan Scott in 1762 about the paper's origins).

tribute' to further ventures.[30] The Address was conciliatory, but its fulsome language was also somewhat ironic. The City's support for the government clearly depended upon a vigorous American policy.

Despite William Pitt's call for a more enterprising strategy to protect 'the long injured, long neglected, long forgotten people of America',[31] the government easily fended off criticism of its foreign policy during the parliamentary session of 1755/6. The loss of Minorca, however, disrupted its equanimity. Situated on the main maritime route to Italy and the Levant, the island was strategically important for the protection of England's commercial interests in the Mediterranean. Minorca had also proved an invaluable base in the war with Spain. Its loss was a strain on British prestige, sufficient confirmation to many of Newcastle's unimaginative and incompetent conduct of foreign affairs.

The administration quickly recognized the potentially serious nature of the defeat. As soon as it received official confirmation of the capture of the island's fortress, Port Mahon, it sought to lay the blame upon Admiral John Byng, the naval commander who was belatedly sent out to counter French advances in the Mediterranean. Carefully edited extracts of Byng's correspondence were published in the *Gazette* suggesting that the fall of the island was his sole responsibility, omitting such evidence as might have exonerated Byng's actions by showing the difficulties which he encountered. Such disinformation had its effect. After some initial confusion public opinion swung against Byng. In mid-July the populace burnt his effigy before his country mansion in Hertfordshire and in the following month similar demonstrations were staged elsewhere. In London,

an Effigy dressed in the uniform of an Officer in the Navy was hung on a Gibbet on Great Tower Hill, near Postern Row, which was to represent A—— B——. There were near 10,000 people present at the sight who used the Effigy with the greatest contempt by firing of Musketts, throwing stones, Mud &c till about seven o'clock, when Fire was set to a load of faggots and some tar barrels that were piled

[30] Council Journals, lxi, fos. 1–2.
[31] Basil Williams, *The Life of William Pitt, Earl of Chatham* (2 vols.; London, 1913), i. 269.

round the Gibbet, which soon set fire to it, and consumed that and the Effigy among'st the repeated Shouts of the Populace.[32]

The popular vilification of Byng boosted government fortunes in the early months following Minorca, but it was not to last. The opposition press had remained sceptical of the government's account of the capture of Minorca and in July the first major defence of Byng appeared.[33] Penned by Samuel Johnson at the instigation of the former Westminster Independent, Paul Whitehead, it exposed the ministry's misrepresentation of Byng's engagement with the French. Byng, Johnson argued, had observed the letter of his instructions from the Admiralty, and, handicapped by sickness and poor supplies, had done all that could be expected of him. These revelations were quickly picked up in the opposition press. In his letters to the 'People of England', John Shebbeare amplified the theme of ministerial culpability, while in the *London Evening Post* and the *Monitor*, Minorca was coupled with the defeat of Oswego in America in a pitch for a change of measures and men.[34] Newcastle considered silencing them with a few well-organized prosecutions, but Sharpe deterred him from that course. 'I am much apprehensive there is little prospect indeed of a London jury convicting the printers', he opined.[35] In the event only one arrest was made, probably without government direction. On 14 August a Southwark magistrate arraigned John Siswick for posting a scurrilous handbill on the pillars of St Saviour's, St Margaret Hill. The paper, a mock auction of Minorca 'By Order of Thomas Holles of Newcastle', had done the rounds in the City before ending in the company of waggoners south of the river.[36] Within the month another was widely distributed near the Exchange. 'The Paper', the duke of Newcastle was informed,

was a passionate, factious, violent and inflammatory Manifesto,

---

[32] *Whitehall Evening Post*, 26–8 Aug. 1756.

[33] Brian Tunstall, *Admiral Byng and the Loss of Minorca* (London, 1928), pp. 163 ff.

[34] [John Shebbeare], *A Fourth Letter to the People of England* (London, 1756), p. 97; *London Evening Post*, 24–7 June, 29 June–1 July, 24–6 Aug. 1756; *Monitor*, 17, 31 July, 4 Sept. 1756.

[35] BL, Add. MS 32,867, fo. 136.

[36] SP 36/135/242–52; for a copy of the broadside, see BL, Add. MS 35,594, fo. 148.

Addressed to the Citizens of London, exciting them to demand Justice from his Majesty upon the M——rs, who had barely betrayed their country, and sold it to France for 300,000 £, exhorting them at the same time to do themselves Justice if it was denied them from the Throne.[37]

Against this background the London Common Council drew up an Address to the Crown urging an enquiry into the loss of Minorca. The action did not take the Court by surprise, and it had already primed its supporters for the approaching meeting.[38] It had also solicited the advice of Sir John Barnard, who was personally against the drafting of a motion, believing that 'Parliament was the proper place for those things'. If there was an Address, Sir John continued, 'he should advise a mild and gracious answer, for he never remembered an instance of popular discontent, whether ill or well founded, that was either shifted or prevented by an angry return from the Crown.'[39]

The government paid heed to Barnard's advice. Although one of its intermediaries, George Bellas, was appointed to the drafting committee, he was unable to prevent a few barbed references to ministerial policy. Moved by deputy James Hodges and seconded by the West India merchant, Samuel Turner, the Address drew attention to the delays in the defence of North America, and deplored the loss of Minorca 'without any attempt by timely or effectual Succours to prevent an attack after such early Notice of the Enemy's intentions'. It was also critical of the Lords' rejection of the Militia Bill, a popular opposition issue in 1756, and ended by pressing for an inquiry into 'the Authors of our late Losses and Disappointments'. To this representation Hardwicke drew up a conciliatory reply.[40] Even the king played his part, showing no impatience or uneasiness during the formalities.[41]

At this stage, then, the government sought to avoid a direct confrontation with the City, even to the point of dissuading

---

[37] BL, Add. MS 32,866, fos. 488–9; cf. fos. 275–6.
[38] BL, Add. MS 32,997, fo. 20.
[39] BL, Add. MS 32,866, fos. 448–9.
[40] Council Journals, 61, fos. 80–2; BL, Add. MS 35,594, fos. 158–9, for the reply.
[41] BL, Add. MS 32,866, fos. 492–3.

some of its financial supporters from mounting a counter-Address. James West thought 'it happy the address is worded in the violent way it is, for it now begins and every day will more and more open the eyes of the people to penetrate into the views of the Jacobites that began, of the discontented ones that approved, and of the party in, that hoped to avail themselves of it'.[42] He hoped the agitation would 'die of itself' and predicted that Barnard's opposition to the Address would divert attention away from the ministry. For a time this appeared to be the case. Barnard became the butt of opposition invectives in the City; and the efforts of the *Monitor* to challenge Marshe Dickenson's mayoral candidature in September 1756, on the grounds that he had supported the parliamentary motion to bring Hanoverian troops into the country rather than espouse the City's own campaign for a militia, fell flat on the ground. Although there were some murmurings against Dickenson at Common Hall, only the confirmed Tory John Blachford opposed his elevation to the Chair in the Court of Aldermen in early October.[43] The customary promotion by seniority was upheld.

But while the Livery appeared reluctant to adopt an anti-ministerialist stance, the Common Council was not prepared to let the government off the hook. In strident and unequivocal terms—what Walpole described as 'in the style of 1641, and really in the spirit of 1715 and 1745'—the assembly bolstered its Address with a series of Instructions to its Members.[44] Led by Alderman John Blachford, the Council called for a 'strict and impartial Parliamentary Inquiry into the causes of these National Calamities' and made it quite clear that a simple condemnation of Byng was unacceptable. Since the preparations of the French Fleet at Toulon were so widely known, the Instructions argued, 'we cannot impute these fatal events to Neglect alone, and therefore conjure you to inquire why a respectable Fleet was not immediately sent from hence, and why so small a Squadron was ordered upon this important

---

[42] BL, Add. MS 32, 866, fo. 496.

[43] *Monitor*, 25 Sept. 1756; Guildhall MS 100, fo. 11; *Public Advertiser*, 8 Oct. 1756.

[44] Lewis, *Walpole's Correspondence*, xxi. 12–13, and Council Journals, lxi, fos. 113–15, for quotes in this paragraph. On Blachford's role in promoting the instructions see BL, Add. MS 32,868, fo. 451.

Service'. The Council also called for an end to 'all unnatural Connections on the Continent' and an inquiry into Britain's American policy and the misappropriation of public funds. It also renewed the demand for a militia as an alternative to the introduction of foreign mercenaries in Britain. The highly publicized Maidstone affair, in which the Court had shielded a Hanoverian soldier from the full force of English law, drew the Council's ire.[45] It was nothing less than a violation of the Bill of Rights. Finally, the Common Council resurrected the Country proposals to limit placemen and pensioners and to restore triennial parliaments as 'the only means to obtain a free Representative of the People'.

The City Instructions of October 1756 were a strategic intervention, designed to boost the campaign in the country at large for a strict inquiry into the defeat of Minorca and by extension a change of measures as well as men. Contrary to recent interpretations,[46] the government had been very pre-occupied with the public response to the Minorca affair. As county grand juries began to table Instructions to their members urging an inquiry into Minorca, the ministry was not idle. The duke of Newcastle had consulted Hardwicke about how the government should respond to the Buckinghamshire Instructions of August 1756, and he was soon rallying his supporters to head off similar initiatives elsewhere. In Sussex, he warned Major Battine that 'possibly somebody may be mad and malicious enough to propose one at our Assizes. I must therefore depend upon you being there; and hope all our Friends will attend to prevent any such step as that, which surely cannot be carried at Horesham.'[47] At the same time, ministerial supporters were advising counter-Addresses to turn back the tide of opposition that was swelling up in the

---

[45] On the Maidstone affair, where William Shroeder stole two handkerchiefs from a local shop and was committed to jail, much to the dismay of the Hanoverian officers, who wished to try him in a military court, see BL, Egerton MS 3440, fos. 80, 184–94, and *London Evening Post*, 30 Sept.–2 Oct. 1756. The earl of Holdernesse ordered the mayor of Maidstone to proceed with the prosecution, but urged the Hanoverians to lay their case before the king.

[46] J. C. D. Clark, *The Dynamics of Change: The Crisis of the 1750s and the English Party System* (Cambridge, 1982), *passim*.

[47] BL, Add. MS 32,866, fo. 432; cf. fo. 462; Add. MS 35,415, fo. 245.

provinces, especially in areas experiencing a poor harvest and food riots.[48] In Bristol, Robert Nugent and Josiah Tucker organized two Addresses, one from the Corporation and the other from the gentlemen, clergy, and merchants, both of which expressed confidence in the ministry and doubted not that the king would promote 'a free and constitutional inquiry' into Minorca.[49] In fact the Corporation's Address, which declared it a 'high presumption to dictate measures to his Majesty at this juncture', was an explicit rejoinder to the Common Council of London's Address in August.

As ministry and opposition jockeyed for popularity in the initial aftermath of Minorca, so the City of London raised the stakes. The early Addresses and Instructions from the counties had tended to concentrate upon the demand for an inquiry into Minorca and a militia bill, the latter to counteract the baleful influence of foreign mercenaries on English soil and free money for a blue-water policy. Only Somerset had advocated political reform as a solution to the crisis, and then its programme was restricted to a reduction of 'unnecessary' placemen and pensioners.[50] The City put reform on the agenda and brought the towns into the campaign. Cities such as Coventry, Ipswich, Lichfield, Nottingham, Salisbury, and Wells, and counties like Kent and Staffordshire emulated London in their call for triennial parliaments, coupled in some instances with calls for place and pension bills.[51] In these places in particular, the Minorca crisis was symptomatic of a deeper malaise in British politics, a pervasive corruption that could only be rectified by reducing executive influence in the Commons, by reanimating the public spirit through a militia, and by making the House itself more accountable to the electorate.

In the final five months of 1756 some thirty-six constituencies issued Instructions or Addresses demanding an inquiry

---

[48] For accounts of anti-government feeling in the riot-prone Midlands see BL, Add. MS 32,867, fos. 1, 117, 298–9; Add. MS 35,594, fos. 164–8.

[49] *London Evening Post*, 16–18 Sept. 1756.

[50] Ibid., 16–19 Oct. 1756. The militia could be regarded as a reformist measure, in that it was a means to invigorating civic virtue.

[51] Ibid., 16–18 Nov. (Nottingham), 18–20 Nov. (Salisbury), 25–7 Nov. (Ipswich, Kent), 9–11 Dec, 1756 (Staffordshire, Wells), 15–18 Jan. 1757 (Coventry); *Public Advertiser*, 24 Nov. 1756 (Lichfield).

into the loss of Minorca. As Table 3.1 reveals, the English counties were extremely well represented, some sixteen of them participating in the quest for a parliamentary inquiry. Strongly Tory counties were predictably high on the list, mobilizing their grand juries at the local assizes, and very occasionally, as in the case of Devon and Breconshire, at specially convened meetings of the shire.[52] But when one includes the boroughs, one discovers that the Tory-dominated constituencies constituted a minority. Even with the addition of York and Bristol, where one of the Addresses was put up by the Tories in opposition to the Corporation and the merchants, the Tories were responsible for just under half of the remonstrances. The broadly based character of these public Addresses and Instructions is further underscored by the fact that in some Tory counties it was the Patriots rather than the stalwarts of the party who made the running. This was the case in Devon where the bishop of Exeter reported that 'clamours are great & there is no stopping people's mouths'.[53] The bi-partisan nature of the Instructions is also evident in the strong representation of the South-East and East Anglia. This was the area where the Country platform made substantial gains in the agitation against Walpole.[54]

The protests against Minorca were not, then, simply party-inspired. Nor were they superficially representative. Admittedly, a few owed something to the territorial influence of aristocratic grandees, or to the active canvassing of politicians like George Townsend, one of the main promoters of the militia, who sent circulars to all the towns urging them to send petitions to Parliament.[55] The Bedford interest, for example, almost certainly engineered the Tavistock Address that was signed by fifty-four inhabitants. William Pitt's ally, Thomas Potter, laid the groundwork for the one in Bedfordshire. Together with John Wilkes he organized the nomination of a favourable grand jury at the assizes, and assured his mentor that he 'had taken all possible Care wh[ich] so few Hours

[52] Lucy Sutherland, 'The City of London and the Devonshire–Pitt Administration 1756–7', *Proceedings of the British Academy*, 46 (1960), 147–93. Lincolnshire also held a special meeting to draw up instructions.
[53] BL, Add. MS 35,594, fo. 156.
[54] See ch. 7.
[55] BL, Add. MS 32,867, fos. 72–3.

TABLE 3.1. *Instructions and Addresses on Minorca 1756*

	West/South-West	North/Midlands	East/South-East
Counties	i Brecon (T)	a Cheshire (T)	a Bedfordshire (T)
	i Devon (T)	i Lancashire (T)	i Buckinghamshire
	a Dorset (T)	i Shropshire	i Essex
	i Hereford (T)	i Staffs (T)	i Hunts
	ai Somerset (T)		i Kent
			i Lincolnshire
			a Norfolk
			i Suffolk (T)
Boroughs	a Bath	a Bolton	i Ipswich
	ai Bristol	a Chester (T)	ai Lincoln
	a Exeter (T)	i Coventry	ai London
	i Leominster	ai Lichfield (T)	i Maidstone
	ai Salisbury	a Nottingham	ai Southwark
	a Tavistock	ai York (T)	
	i Wells	i Oxford	

a   Addresses
i   Instructions
(T) Tory constituencies

Sources: London Evening Post, Public Advertiser

warning w[oul]d allow, not to be defeated by *any* Opposition'.[56] The Yorkshire Instructions, moreover, were never formally endorsed and may even have been fictional. When they first appeared in the press, they so astounded the earl of Holdernesse that he could not persuade himself that 'a production of that Sort can really have come from a Part of the Kingdom famous for their dutiful Affection to the King'.[57]

Even so, Instructions and Addresses frequently required some rudimentary organization; drafts, circulars, canvassing, signatures, procedures which brought the political nation into orbit. The two Bristol Addresses from outside the Corporation were widely circulated and signed by a significant proportion of the electorate. In the case of the Tory Address, which Tucker suspected had been framed by the well-known London writer, John Shebbeare, it also engendered considerable controversy, for the local Tory MP, Jarrit Smith, protested 'with great Warmth against every part of ye proceeding'.[58] The Southwark Address, by contrast, contained fewer signatures, only 262. Even so, because it echoed a Surrey Address that the ministry had successfully scotched, it inevitably raised passions to a high pitch.[59] Political passions also ran high in Norfolk, where Horace Walpole failed to prevent a grand jury Address. 'Nothing therefore could be obtained', he confessed to the duke of Newcastle, 'but to reduce it to more temperate language.' Such a stratagem was not even possible in Dorset where Shaftesbury's amendments to the Address were rejected.[60]

Local dignitaries were thus sometimes unable to influence the drafting of Instructions and Addresses in the summer of 1756. Indeed, the Newcastle and Hardwicke papers suggest

---

[56] PRO, 30/8/53, fo. 49, cited in Paul Langford, 'William Pitt and Public Opinion, 1757', *English Historical Review*, 88 (Jan. 1973), 71. The Tavistock address, signed by 54 inhabitants, can be found in SP 36/136/185.
[57] BL, Egerton MS 3,436, fos. 97–8; see also Langford, 'Pitt and Public Opinion', *English Historical Review* (1973), 71.
[58] BL, Add. MS 32,867, fo. 127; see also fos. 193–4, 208.
[59] Ibid., fo. 175; *London Evening Post*, 2–4 Nov. 1756; *Public Advertiser*, 3 Nov. 1756.
[60] BL, Add. MS 32,867, fo. 262; cf. also fos. 482–3; Add. MS. 32,866, fo. 401. In Norfolk, Sir William Harcourt was forced to sign the address, fearing that his son's popularity in the forthcoming Norwich by-election depended upon it.

that the remonstrances accurately reflected the sentiments of substantial sections of the political nation, many of whom were profoundly unhappy with Newcastle's policy towards France. To be sure, the dimensions of the agitation for an inquiry into Minorca were not as significant as those which had confronted Walpole in 1741, nor did the alienation from the Whig regime run so deep. Relatively few constituencies actually advocated structural change. In most of the counties, where rival Whig and Tory factions had reached some compromise over political representation, dissatisfaction centred upon a change of ministry and a militia rather than upon parliamentary reform. It was principally in the larger towns and cities, following London's lead, that the call for a Country programme was heard. At the same time, many Addresses and Instructions emphasized the threat to American trade posed by Minorca, especially those that hailed from the ports, the textile districts of the West Country and Yorkshire, and the burgeoning industries of the West Midlands. Here one finds a renewed insistence upon a vigorous blue-water policy to safeguard expanding markets central to the country's prosperity, even to the point of invoking the memory of Admiral Vernon.[61] It was an issue that had compromised Walpole in his final years, as contemporaries were fully aware. It remained to be seen how his successors would placate the bellicose mercantilism that continued to resonate in the country at large.

The rise of William Pitt to a position of political prominence offered the hope that these demands would be heard. Before Minorca Pitt had established a reputation for putting principles before political advancement and those principles included a commitment to a more vigorous interventionist policy in the New World and a strident anti-Hanoverianism. In 1756, however, Pitt was hampered by the realities of power. The Pitt–Devonshire administration was heavily reliant upon the support of the country gentlemen in Parliament and against it were ranged the superior battalions of the Old Corps and the Cumberland–Fox phalanx.

Outnumbered in the Commons, Pitt none the less emerged

---

[61] *London Evening Post*, 10–12 Aug. 1756.

with some credit during his brief ministry. He attacked Holdernesse for his part in the Maidstone affair and insisted that the Hanoverian soldier, William Shroeder, face the full rigour of the law. He also enhanced his popularity by quashing a clause that had been inserted into the reply to the King's Speech in the Lords, thanking the monarch for bringing foreign mercenaries into England. On the subject of Britain's future financial and military commitment in Europe, he even managed to merge the popular suspicion of continental entanglements with existing diplomatic commitments, putting arguments for the need for a diversionary war in Europe that would bottle up French forces. Horace Walpole's prediction that Pitt would lose popularity 'if he 'Hanoverises' did not materialize.[62] Indeed, he convinced the more intransigent opponents of continentalism in the City that a further Prussian subsidy was necessary.[63]

The question of Minorca none the less remained the most pressing issue. Pitt recognized that he could not abandon his pledge for a parliamentary inquiry, however intractable the political situation. According to Hardwicke, he 'talked of the enquiry as a thing that would ruin him, if he attempted to stop it at the outset, after what he had formally declared'.[64] In the circumstances he did all that could be expected of him, short of resignation. As far as the court martial went, the cards were stacked against Byng, who was denied crucial witnesses at his trial. But Pitt and his colleague at the Admiralty, Lord Temple, did seize upon the ambivalent verdict of the court martial which sentenced Byng to death for neglect of duty, rather than cowardice or treasonable conduct, and at the same time recommended mercy. Pitt pressured the king for a pardon and attempted to push a special act through Parliament which would release the members of the court martial from their oaths of secrecy.[65] But neither of these overtures proved successful. Nor were the efforts of the London Common

[62] Lewis, *Walpole's Correspondence*, xxi. 17.

[63] Cobbett, *The Parliamentary History of England*, xv. 788; Eldon, *England's Subsidy Policy*, pp. 90–1; *Monitor*, 11 Dec. 1756, 19 Mar. 1757.

[64] *The Life and Correspondence of Philip Yorke, Earl of Hardwicke*, ed. Philip C. Yorke (3 vols.; Cambridge, 1913), ii. 376.

[65] Horace Walpole, *Memoirs of the . . . Reign of George II* (2 vols.; London, 1822), ii. 318–50, 358–65.

Council to secure Byng a royal pardon. Launched by Aldermen Blakiston and Scott in conjunction with Paul Whitehead, this move was blocked by the pro-Newcastle lord mayor, Marshe Dickenson, who refused to call a Common Council meeting without knowing the terms of the motion for royal mercy.[66] With the failure of this eleventh-hour intercession, Byng's execution was inevitable. It seriously compromised the possibility of an open parliamentary inquiry. Pitt's dismissal less than a month later completely frustrated it.

Pitt none the less emerged with some honour from his period of office. On 12 April, ten commoners led by George Bellas of Castle Baynard and George Wylde of Bishopsgate asked the Lord Mayor to convene a Common Council to confer the freedom of the city upon Pitt and the chancellor of the exchequer, Henry Legge, who had attempted to raise a loan by open subscription. Dickenson again prevaricated, but this time he was only able to moderate the terms of the motion. It praised Pitt and Legge's 'loyal and Disinterested Conduct during their truly Honourable tho' short administration', their efforts at 'public economy', and their attempt to 'stem the General Torrent of Corruption' in mid-century politics. Finally, the motion emphasized 'their zeal to promote a full and impartial inquiry into the real causes of our late losses and disgrace in America and the Mediterranean'.[67]

The Common Council motion of April 1757 was London's first commendation of an administration for over half a century. It did not imply a major departure from the City's former political stance, for the motion was a further endorsement of Patriotism and consequentially a critique of orthodox Whiggery. To the middling tradesmen and merchants on Common Council, Pitt's political style and gestures offered an alternative to the myopic and corrupt politics of clientage practised by his successors, a system of politics that ignored popular aspirations, and privileged a narrow circle of aristocrats, financiers, and careerists to the detriment of emergent commercial interests. Such a populist stance struck a chord in

---

[66] BL, Add. MS 32,870 fo. 260; Guildhall MS 100 (Marshe Dickenson's diary), entries for 9, 11 Mar. 1757.

[67] Council Journals, lxii, fo. 158; Guildhall MS 100, entries for 12, 14, 15 Apr. 1757.

some of the provincial centres such as Newcastle and Worcester that had hitherto sympathized with the Country platform in Walpole's final years. It also drew support from those who had hoped Pitt's accession to power might boost American trade and facilitate a closer scrutiny of public expenditure and military commitments. It is no accident that the merchant society of Anti-Gallicans thanked Pitt for his services, as did the Whig corporation of Norwich, where the American market in textiles was becoming increasingly important.[68] Pitt, in other words, could appeal to a broad spectrum of interests, on pragmatic as well as ideological grounds. In the spring of 1757, however, Pitt's popularity remained fragile. As Paul Langford has shown, the campaign of the gold boxes was a largely partisan affair perpetrated by Pitt's foremost supporters in Tory circles and puffed up in the Patriot press.[69] Although some contemporaries believed that Pitt's popularity in the country was formidable—one pamphleteer claimed that his ministry had been supported 'by every independent Man of Consequence in the Nation'[70]—it remained to be seen whether public opinion would coalesce behind London leadership. Here at least, as the election of James Hodges to the position of Town Clerk revealed, Pitt's support on Common Council was firmly entrenched.[71]

Despite the euphoria of early 1757, the willingness of Pitt to serve with Newcastle in the reconstituted ministry of May 1757 was viewed with misgivings in the City. The *Monitor* thought Pitt had 'veered about'. Raking up memories of Pulteney's apostasy in 1742, it feared that Pitt too had 'deserted the cause of his country', and began to question Pitt's

---

[68] *Public Advertiser*, 25 Apr. 1757.

[69] Langford, 'Pitt and Popular Opinion', *English Historical Review* (1973), 58–71.

[70] Anon., *An Appeal to the People: Part the Second* (London, 1757), p. 61. See also James, Earl Waldegrave, *Memoirs from 1754 to 1758* (London, 1821), pp. 61, 129–30. Waldegrave thought that the addresses to Pitt were factional, but he also thought that 'the popular cry without doors was violent in favour of Mr. Pitt'.

[71] *London Evening Post*, 7–10 May 1757; *Con-Test*, 14 May 1757. Hodges had moved that Pitt be given the freedom: see Guildhall MS 100, for 15 Apr. 1757.

sincerity about an inquiry into Minorca.[72] The *Con-Test*, another journal which had hitherto favoured Pitt, brushed aside these allegations and argued that Pitt's reconciliation with the old guard was not inconsistent with his former conduct, which had been directed at the 'measures' not the 'members of an ill conducted administration'. Only future events, it surmised, could place his conduct in proper perspective, and all suspicions should be suspended 'till we have facts to ground them upon'.[73]

But events boded ill for the coalition. No sooner had it taken office but Frederick of Prussia was defeated at Kolin and was forced to evacuate Bohemia. The army of observation, composed of those foreign mercenaries who had attracted such unpopularity in Britain a year before, failed to provide timely reinforcements and was in its turn beaten at Hastenback. These setbacks threatened to wreck the subsidy policy which both Newcastle and Pitt had supported and to aggravate old political divisions; for it was feared Brunswick and Hesse would recall their troops and leave the British no alternative but to send their own, an action which Pitt had persistently renounced. To further confuse the situation, the duke of Cumberland, whose command of the army of observation had never been accepted by the Pittites, signed a separate peace between Hanover and France. This agreement, the Convention of Closterseven, so incensed Pitt that he refused to give Cumberland's army another penny until the treaty was rescinded.[74] After four months in office, the political leaders of the new administration were bickering over subsidies and the Hanoverian connection. The general drift of British continental policy threatened to undermine Pitt's reputation and confirm his subservience to pro-Hanoverian interests at Court.

The Rochefort expedition raised this issue. The first coastal raid upon France proved a dismal failure, with the navy and the landing force showing a lamentable lack of co-ordination. It inevitably raised demands for a public inquiry. Horace Walpole informed Conway on 13 October that 'the City of London talk

[72] *Monitor*, 2 July 1757.
[73] *Con-Test*, 29 June, 9, 23 July 1757.
[74] Eldon, *England's Subsidy Policy*, pp. 96–106; Williams, *Life of Pitt*, i. 311; BL, Add. MS 32,893, fo. 264.

very treason, and connecting the suspension at Stade with this disappointment, cry out that the general had positive orders to do nothing in order to obtain gentle treatment of Hanover'.[75] Two weeks later, a Patriot delegation headed by Deputy Thomas Long and George Wylde, both of Bishopsgate ward, requested that the Lord Mayor call a Council meeting for an enquiry. Dickenson stalled them and alerted the ministry. Hardwicke hoped that Pitt would intervene 'to prevent his friends in that body from going into it'. But Pitt does not appear to have done so.[76] Instead, the ministry tactically pre-empted the address by agreeing to a commission of inquiry. This hardly satisfied the Patriots in the City, who continued to demand a full parliamentary inquiry into the affair and angrily protested at Sir John Mordaunt's acquittal before a court martial.[77]

Military and naval victories quickly assuaged whatever misgivings the City may have had about the coalition. In November 1757 Frederick scored a success at Rossbach, and the following year at Crevelt won two victories that enabled Pitt to ease massive Prussian subsidies through the Commons with virtually no opposition. Pitt even agreed to send British reinforcements to the continent as the public was swept up with war fever. In the summer of 1757 he sent 12,000 troops to the army of observation, an action that was warmly commended by William Beckford and well received in the City.[78] Ironically the few doubts that were voiced were laid at Newcastle's door, even though, as Newcastle testified to White, Pitt was 'the person who first formally proposed it'.[79]

Pitt's ability to win public support for military expenditures none the less depended upon the way in which he integrated them with imperial strategies. He constantly emphasized the primacy of colonial campaigns over European, which he regarded as diversionary, intended to stretch France to her

---

[75] Mrs Paget Toynbee (ed.), *The Letters of Horace Walpole, Fourth Earl of Orford* (16 vols.; London, 1903–5), iv. 105.

[76] Guildhall MS 100, 26 Oct. 1757; BL, Add. MS 32,875, fos. 255–6, 318, 394.

[77] Peters, *Pitt and Popularity*, pp. 94–102.

[78] William Stanhope Taylor and John Henry Pringle (eds.), *Correspondence of William Pitt, Earl of Chatham* (4 vols.; London, 1838–40), i. 327, 330: Toynbee (ed.), *Letter of Walpole*, iv. 184.

[79] BL, Add. MS 32,882, fo. 95; see the *Monitor*, 28 July 1758, where there is an amusing dialogue between 'continental Harry' and 'colonial Will'.

limits. In November 1758 he warmly commended Beckford's speech in the Commons advocating the primacy of American over German operations and assured his ally that the American theatre was 'the primary consideration of every Man in his Majesty's Counsells & equally so of the King himself'. He admitted that 'in point of expense the dearness of provisions & other Incidents might make the War in Germany the primary consideration and that he was afraid in that respect It came too near the American expense,' but what, he asked, 'could be done if necessity made it so?'[80]

This was a clever line because it was the colonial victories which truly captured the popular imagination. Louisburg, Quebec, Goree, Guadaloupe, Niagara, and Ticonderoga—these were the events that were eagerly seized upon in the press. Only Frederick's victory at Minden in 1759 achieved comparable publicity. In August 1758 the City of London congratulated the king on the conquest of Louisburg and the islands of Cape Breton and St John, and their Address was quickly followed by others from Exeter, Newcastle, and Norwich.[81] The year 1759 saw a series of victories on the American front and the capture of the valuable sugar island of Guadaloupe. The fall of Quebec was celebrated wildly in London. Horace Walpole thought 'our bells are worn threadbare with ringing for victories' in this 'glorious and ever-memorable year', and commented wryly that the king would be so overwhelmed with Addresses that 'he will have enough to paper his palace'.[82] Amid the general elation Pitt inevitably attracted popular attention, and all the military and naval successes were attributed to him alone. In December 1758 a Newcastle supporter noted that 'Mr P continued to be favour'd with the common approbation' and that 'the number of his snarlers is found to increase'. Hardwicke asserted in October the following year that there was no 'stripping him of his Popularity, which is now greater than ever'.[83] The duke of Newcastle

---

[80] BL, Add. MS 32,885, fos. 524–6.

[81] *London Evening Post*, 24–6 Aug., 5–7 Sept. 1758; *Gentleman's Magazine*, 25 (1758), 28, 243.

[82] Toynbee (ed.), *Letters of Walpole*, iv. 314; *London Evening Post*, 30 Oct.– 1 Nov. 1759.

[83] BL, Add. MS 32,886, fo. 201; Add. MS 32,897, fo. 442 (Hardwicke); ibid., fo. 373 (Newcastle).

flatly told the king they could not do without him. When the king rebuked Newcastle in September 1759 for allying with Pitt over the issue of a Garter for Lord Temple, Newcastle asked him

whether he thought that this War, at this Immense Expense, could have been carried on without the Unanimity of the People; The Popularity; the Common Council &c; which was entirely owing to Mr. Pitt; so that It could not have been done without Him—To which I had no answer.

Within two years of Rochefort the wartime coalition had attained a popularity unknown that century. Both in Parliament and without, concord appeared to prevail, and the press, overwhelmed by the run of spectacular victories, made a great play upon national unanimity. Even in the City of London political differences were shelved as tradesmen and merchants busied themselves with the economic windfalls of military and naval success. All sectors of the mercantile bourgeoisie appear to have profited from the war, at least until the acute credit shortage of 1759 presented difficulties for the over-extended trader. War finance presented the major public creditors with a field day, especially those who were able to stay the course to reap the very favourable loans of the last years of war. Extensive campaigns in Germany and along the American and Caribbean littoral swelled the ranks of government contractors and subcontractors. No fewer than twenty-seven found their way into Parliament in 1761, including three aldermen, Sir William Baker, Samuel Fludyer, and Thomas Harley.[84] Moreover, virtually every sector of the London business community appears to have speculated in privateering. One finds, among those presenting letters of marque to the High Court of Admiralty in 1756 and 1757, big public creditors, directors of the major insurance and moneyed companies, Portugal, West India, and America merchants, Lombard Street bankers, and an impressive array of mariners, rope-makers, cheesemongers, warehousemen, linen-drapers, goldsmiths, and distillers.[85]

[84] Namier and Brooke, *History of Parliament: Commons 1754–90*, i. 131–8. Namier's figures in *The Structure of Politics, at the Accession of George III*, 2nd edn. (London, 1957), 48–9, are somewhat different: he then claimed there were 50 merchants in the 1761 Parliament, of whom 37 had contracts with the government. [85] PRO, HCA, 26/5-7.

Among those in City politics who speculated in privateering were the aldermen William Arnold, William Baker, William Beckford, Samuel Fludyer, and Edward Ironside. They were joined by twelve Common Councilmen, including three linen-drapers, a wine-merchant, Richard Munday of Bishopsgate Street, and Richard Molineux, an ironmonger from Cateaton Street who was the sole owner of a 200-ton sloop. As the list reveals, privateering was a popular pastime for many trades-men and merchants with a little venture capital, and spanned the political spectrum.

Of course, the privateers and the financial plutocracy were not the only beneficiaries of war. The successful drive for empire, anchored on British naval supremacy and the capture of important French trading posts, boosted the Atlantic economy; British convoys protected the sugar consignments of West Indian planters and afforded them a protected market in England where demand persistently outstripped supply. Prize sugars complicated the picture a little, as did the flood of French sugars on the market after the capture of Guadaloupe and Martinique. But the half-refined sugar from Guadaloupe soon lost its reputation, and prize sugars only marginally impaired the high prices that planters enjoyed. Moreover, these two contingencies were more than offset by the prohibition of corn spirit distillation from 1756–9, which forced distillers to use molasses or brown sugar as substitutes.[86]

Other advantages to the sugar trade also accrued from the war. The dislocation of the French sugar economy enabled the British West Indians to increase their proportion of world sugar-production and compete favourably in those markets, such as North America, where the French had successfully continued a lucrative clandestine trade in rum and molasses. Rum production also received a fillip from the presence of the British navy in Caribbean waters. To be sure, the West Indian sugar economy was beset by long-term problems such as soil-exhaustion and cost-inflation which made London factors wary of extending lengthy credits to planters. But even the

[86] Pares, *War and Trade*, ch. 10. See also his 'London Sugar Market 1740–69', *Economic History Review*[2], 9/2 (1956), 254–70.

great merchant house of Lascelles and Maxwell looked back in later years upon the Seven Years War with nostalgia.[87]

The West India sugar trade undoubtedly prospered from the war. So too did other sectors of the Atlantic economy. The British capture of the principal sugar islands, its blockade of Nantes and capture of Goree, gave the slavers a splendid opportunity to advance their miserable trade. The tobacco trade expanded rapidly, although the heavy issue of paper money in the colonies created an inflationary situation which deepened the planters' indebtedness to the export merchants. The import trade to America developed in leaps and bounds, and the colonies quickly became the principal market for British manufactured goods.[88] The war also gave the Portugal trade a new lease of life. In this case, the disruption of French sugar-production aided the expansion of Brazilian sugar, and this prosperity was transferred back to Portugal, increasing Portuguese purchasing power and hence textile imports from Britain.[89] The British also took over several valuable trades from the French—the gum trade of Senegal, for instance, and the fur trade of the Canadian frontier—while the victories in the East enabled them to capture the Chinese tea trade.

A successful war against Britain's principal commercial rival, France, under the deft leadership of William Pitt thus inaugurated a new era of harmony between Court and City. Articulate mercantile interests entrenched in city government reaped the windfalls of imperial victories while the moneyed élite busily engaged themselves in war finance and other speculative sidelines. Pitt's willingness to promote a number of domestic issues also endeared him to City circles. He

[87] Richard Pares, 'A London West-India Merchant House 1740–69', in Pares and Taylor, *Essays presented to Namier*, 75–107; Richard B. Sheridan, *Chapters in Caribbean History* (London, 1970), i. 22–3.

[88] Jacob M. Price, 'Capital and Credit in the British Chesapeake Trade, 1750–1775', in Virginia B. Platt and David C. Skaggs (eds.), *Of Mother Country and Plantations* (Proceedings, 27th Conference in Early American History; Ohio, 1971), pp. 9–10; Ralph Davis, 'English Overseas Trade 1700–1774', *Economic History Review*[2], 15 (Dec. 1962), 285–303.

[89] H. E. S. Fisher, *The Portugal Trade: A Study in Anglo-Portuguese Commerce 1700–1770* (London, 1971), p. 39. For a general view of the economic benefits of war, see A. H. John, 'War and the English Economy 1700–1763', *Economic History Review*[2], 7 (1954–5), 329–44.

strongly defended the Habeas Corpus Bill of 1758, which would have extended its writ to impressment and other cases of confinement for non-criminal matters, declaring 'that an honest heart for Liberty in a Judge was with him as good a character as the most shining talents' and that 'he would oppose all arbitrary discretionary government whether in Black Gowns or Red Coats.'[90] Pitt also supported the county militia, an important issue for Tories and Patriots, and gave his blessing to the demand, which gathered momentum in 1760, that the City control their own trained bands.[91] Finally, he welcomed the Qualification Bill by which parliamentarians were obliged to take their property oaths when they took their seats as well as at the hustings.[92] On this issue, as on the county militia, he did not go as far as his Tory supporters would have desired, but his gestures certainly forestalled any back-bench revolt against the ministry.[93]

Good relations between the government and the City of London nevertheless depended upon Pitt's continuance in office and his ability successfully to sustain the overall strategy of his war campaign. From 1759 onwards doubts about the practicability of that policy threatened to create serious divisions within the ministry and to undo the *rapprochement* between London and the Court. Newcastle had never been an enthusiast for ambitious colonial schemes and had always accepted Pitt's policies grudgingly. In 1758 he feared that Britain would not be able to withstand the financial burdens of an extensive war. In July of that year he described the idea of long-term hostilities as 'visionary and impracticable' and hoped for peace the following winter.[94] In 1759, as credit tightened, he was forced to rake the City for an £8m. loan and to allow lenders very favourable terms in order to attract

[90] BL, Add. MS 32,879, fo. 276. The Bill would also have made it easier to secure a writ of Habeas Corpus during the legal vacation. The Bill failed in the Lords. The City of London considered taking the issue up but eventually the Half-Moon caucus declined to do so: see Add. MS 32,879, fo. 224.

[91] PRO, 30/8/6/19/1, fos. 87, 184; 30/8/6/40, fo. 134; BL, Add. MS 32,918, fo. 117; Add. MS 35,420, fo. 188.

[92] Devonshire House, Chatsworth MS 260/265.

[93] Pitt was not prepared to risk his relationship with Newcastle by advocating a perpetual militia. Nor was he adamant about the Qualification Bill: see Chatsworth MS 260/265, 283, 286; BL, Add. MS 32,903, fo. 82.

[94] BL, Add. MS 32,882, fo. 95.

Dutch capital. The year was a bleak one for the Treasury. The prospect of falling stocks, additional taxes to meet the interest on heavy loans, and general financial exhaustion at home alarmed both Newcastle and Legge, the chancellor of the exchequer, and made them eager to conclude the war.[95] In October 1759 Newcastle consoled himself that this was Pitt's wish also. But the war continued, and when Newcastle broached the question of financial difficulties with Pitt and the impossibility of sustaining the war effort for another year, Pitt flew into a rage and claimed 'that was the way to make Peace impracticable & to encourage Our Enemy'.[96]

The financial strain of the war thus engendered a division in government circles between the hawks and the doves. To some extent, the division was there from the beginning, for the Whig magnates, true to the policy that Walpole had bequeathed them, had never relished the prospect of an extensive war which stretched British resources, and had always been far more accommodating to Hanoverian interests on the continent, even to the extent of sacrificing colonial acquisitions for a satisfactory European settlement. The debate on the peace terms inevitably brought these tensions into high relief. From 1759 onwards the ministerial phalanx under Newcastle's leadership viewed Pitt's ambitious expeditions with increasing unease. In their eyes there was a point at which further British victories could only prove an embarrassment, a hindrance to smooth and rapid peace negotiations.

The reservations of the Whig leaders and their financial associates made little impact in the City of London. Here Pitt's ambitious projects and his leadership of the war were enthusiastically acclaimed. The Common Council never failed to congratulate the king on the military and naval victories of the war, particularly those in the New World. At the same time its Patriots pushed hard for the retention of British acquisitions, so much so that Pitt had to temper the Address on Louisburg because the City threatened to mobilize the nation in favour of its permanent annexation. Even then the message came

[95] BL, Add. MS 32,887, fos. 107 ff.; 32,888, fo. 318; 32,889, fo. 96; 32,893, fo. 481; 32,895, fo. 295; 32,901, fo. 238.
[96] BL, Add. MS 32,897, fos. 494, 514, 520; 32,904, fos. 278–9; Chatsworth MS, 260/261.

through, for Newcastle noted a hint of *'Take* and *Hold'*. Its general tone, he pointed out to Hardwicke, was 'calculated to recommend Expeditions & Naval Operations'.[97]

While the war fever continued and the treasury managed to surmount the financial problems of funding the war effort, the congratulatory Addresses of the City were publicly tolerated by the Newcastle faction. But as the prospect of a settlement came into view, the increasingly strident tone of the City Addresses, buttressed by an even more hawkish press, began to disrupt the political equipoise of the previous few years. In November 1759 the *London Evening Post* brushed aside all fears of financial exhaustion and demanded the mobilization of capital for the final assault. Britain could recoup her losses, it claimed, by a punitive peace.[98] Early the next year the newspaper ran a series of issues on the necessity of retaining Guadaloupe and Marie Galante and the importance of British control of America; 'such a Source of trade and Commerce that would be sufficient of itself to employ all our trading and Commercial People, and find a Vent or constant consumption for all the Goods, Products and Manufacturers of Great Britain'.[99] If France refused to accept British terms, it continued, we should take retributive action in the Caribbean, particularly in Martinique. The *Monitor* agreed with these sentiments and the London Address of October 1760 was in harmony with them.[100] It emphasized the economic importance of retaining North America and hoped that the king would 'effectually' prosecute 'the various and extensive services of this just and necessary war' until, as Newcastle noted, 'His Majesty shall be able to *dictate the Terms of Peace'*.[101] Hardwicke thought this Address 'more zealous' than the others and marvelled that Pitt had let the City 'speak so loudly about *Preserving'*.[102] Newcastle feared that it would injure the public credit, since investors were anticipating a rise in

[97] BL, Add. ms 32,884, fo. 100; see also 32,882, fo. 118; 32,883, fos. 160, 182–3.

[98] *London Evening Post*, 13–15 Nov. 1759.

[99] Ibid., 3–5, 5–8, 12–15 Jan. 1760 (quote from the first).

[100] Ibid., 4–6 Mar. 1760; *Monitor*, 2 Feb., 6 Sept. 1760; Council Journals, lxii, fo. 140.

[101] BL, Add. ms 32,913, fo. 162.

[102] Ibid., fos. 208–10.

securities with the coming of peace, and were reluctant to subscribe to new loans while the war dragged on. When Pitt told him that 'every word in the address was worth £100,000' the duke replied 'that those Gentlemen were not the persons who would furnish the Government with money'. Indeed, he doubted that the aldermen and Common Councillors who attended the king would subscribe £200,000 to the next loan. The Address 'will do good Abroad', he concluded, 'but the Contrary at Home'.[103]

A new dimension was added to the debate on the war with France in the following month with the publication of Israel Maudit's *Considerations On The Present German War*. Developing the traditional line about Britain's continental connections, Maudit questioned the current involvement in Germany and the huge deployment and abuse of funds which it had squandered. Appropriating one of the main planks of the Patriot programme, the pamphlet was a roaring success; it went through no less than five editions in three months, reaching a total printing of 5,750.[104] Although Maudit emphasized the importance of naval power and a vigorous prosecution of the war by sea, his pamphlet did put Pitt's hawkish allies in the City on the defensive. They recognized that it boosted the fortunes of anti-war factions, including George III and his Court circle, and threatened to undermine the unity of European and colonial theatres which had been the hallmark of Pitt's policy since 1757.

It was against this background that a new general election was held in March 1761. In the City Richard Glover, the Hamburg merchant now allied to Leicester House, attempted to organize opposition against Pitt, whom he dubbed the 'German Minister'. Along with several other merchants, he promoted the candidature of Thomas Harley, an American merchant and government contractor, soon to become the new Alderman for Portsoken ward.[105] At the livery meeting on 4 March, where official nominations were put to Common Hall, Glover tried to have Beckford ousted from the City list. Beckford told his mentor how he 'had the honour to have those

[103] Ibid., fos. 186–7.
[104] Peters, *Pitt and Popularity*, pp. 182–90.
[105] BL, Add. MS 32,920, fo. 26; *London Evening Post*, 26–8 Feb. 1761.

for enemies who are not well wishers to Mr. Pitt, who tryed every method in their power to defeat my being nominated one of the four'.[106]

None the less William Beckford was nominated as one of the official livery candidates, along with Harley, Sir Richard Glyn, a Lombard Street banker and Pittite,[107] and the Newcastle client Sir Samuel Fludyer. Marshe Dickenson and Barlow Trecothick, who at the time was not a freeman of London, decided not to stand once they had failed to win places on the City list. But Sir Robert Ladbroke had his name put forward, running as an Independent in the style of Sir John Barnard, a true City man above factionalism.[108] This gambit proved successful. Labroke's long-standing experience in City politics won him the public support of no fewer than eight aldermen, and his ability to profit from the rivalry of the other candidates took him to the top of the poll. Harley came second with 3,983 votes, and Beckford third with 3,663. The prominent Pittite was still regarded in some quarters as a carpet-bagger in City politics, and he had to answer for his inattention to City affairs.[109] Consequently, he was forced to rake the London areas for votes. He attempted to solicit the favour of Bedford, who replied that he had 'given the interest I had with the liverymen of London in favor of Sir Robert Ladbroke & Mr. Harley but with no negative to any one of the candidates'.[110] He also solicited the interest of the Ordnance Department and the Board of Works, a somewhat impudent action which startled Newcastle's supporters. Kinnoul complained to Newcastle that it was 'not unreasonable to ask that they should be for Fludyer, *not exclusive of Beckford*, surely that cannot give offence anywhere'.[111]

The fourth City seat fell unexpectedly to Glyn rather than Fludyer, who continued to represent Chippenham. It was only on the final day of the poll that Glyn edged ahead of the

---

[106] PRO, 30/8/6/19, fo. 103.

[107] For Glyn's Pittite sympathies see *Whitehall Evening Post*, 30 Nov.–2 Dec. 1758; PRO, 30/8/6/40, fo. 141.

[108] *London Evening Post*, 3–5, 5–7, 21–4 Mar. 1761. For Newcastle's link with Fludyer see BL, Add. MS 32,913, fo. 251.

[109] *London Evening Post*, 3–5 Mar. 1761.

[110] Bedford MS xvii, fo. 108.

[111] BL, Add. MS 32,921, fo. 184.

Treasury candidate to win by ninety-two votes. Fludyer's defeat was the product of emergent divisions within the ministerial camp between Newcastle and Bute, divisions that were engendered in part by the continuing debate on the conduct of the war and the need for a peace settlement. Kinnoul reported that 'the Whigs seem to be cutting one another's Throats' and that some of the Dissenters, including Dr Chandler, who later came out strongly in favour of the Peace of Paris, had voted against Fludyer.[112] Even so, the relatively modest showing of the Pittite candidates, Beckford and Glyn, was an ominous sign. It revealed that the Livery did not entirely share the Common Council's acclaim for the Patriot minister, and, amid high freight and insurance rates, tight credit, and a flush of bankruptcies, that anti-war feeling was gaining ground.

Pitt's resignation in October 1761 over the British response to the Family Compact between France and Spain brought the bristling tensions about the war into the open. Bute learnt that the 'storm runs high' in the City and that some were 'rash enough to say they will have their master again'. Joseph Yorke, too, claimed that the first letters which he had received from the Hague 'were filled with lamentations and violence, & it was said the popular Cry would force him in again'. On the other hand, Newcastle heard from the governor of the Bank that 'things go on well in the City if not better now that Pitt was out'. Everyone wanted peace, he claimed, only 'the mob of the City may think or talk otherwise'.[113] This view was shared by Alderman Sir William Baker. He thought that few were uneasy about Pitt's resignation, 'except the worst of the Common Council', and urged that the English offers to the French should be published to show that Pitt's views were in harmony with the rest of the cabinet. But Thomas Walpole thought such action unnecessary. In his view, the resignation 'might have an effect on a Lord Mayor's show but nothing else'.[114]

Even so, the ministry did take steps to avert a political crisis

---

[112] Ibid.
[113] BL, Add. MS 32,929, fos. 74, 834; see also fo. 387; and Chatsworth MS 260/347.
[114] BL, Add. MS 32,929, fos. 83–4; Chatsworth MS 260/347.

over Pitt's resignation. They offered him a £3,000 annuity for three lives out of the plantation duties, and his wife a barony. This was an astute move, for Pitt's reputation had been partially built upon his political integrity, particularly his refusal to profit from the perquisites of office while Paymaster-General of the forces. His acceptance of a pension and a lesser peerage for his wife arguably sullied an otherwise untarnished career. Bedford believed that Pitt had been eliminated 'in a way which must entirely cut up . . . [his] ill-gotten popularity by the roots'.[115]

And so it seemed. The *London Evening Post* had difficulty explaining away Pitt's preferment and prophesied that the 'idol of the People' would likely become 'the Object of their Execration'. Richard Rigby reported to Bedford that 'The City and the People are outragious about Lady Cheat-em as they call Her, and her husband's pension' and fully expected Pitt to be burnt in effigy.[116] The dismay even penetrated the Common Council, for Beckford had to abandon a meeting scheduled to thank Pitt for his services. In the provinces too, there was consternation about the pension. In a tradesman's club in Chichester, one of Newcastle's clients reported, 'some of them say, he is gone off at last, after making a great Noise, like Lord B—h'.[117]

Pitt's open letter to Beckford, emphasizing that the pension and peerage were 'unmerited and unsolicited', did not silence the gibes about the 'Patriot–Pensioner', but it did enable his friends in the City to launch a counter-attack. At a meeting at the Half-Moon tavern on 21 October his supporters proposed Instructions for a punitive peace settlement, a war with Spain, and an inquiry into Pitt's resignation.[118] The following day, at a meeting of the Common Council, they pushed through more modestly phrased Instructions urging an inquiry into the administration of the war under Treasury auspices, and demanded that their representatives oppose all attempts to give up acquisitions that might injure British security and

---

[115] BL, Add. MS 32,929, fo. 192.
[116] *London Evening Post*, 13–15 Oct. 1761; Bedford MS xliv, fo. 208.
[117] *London Evening Post*, 8–10, 13–15 Oct. 1761; BL, Add. MS 32,929, fos. 235, 239 (quote from this last).
[118] Chatsworth MS 182/206; BL, Add. MS 32,939, fos. 402, 437.

restore French naval power. They insisted that North America and the Newfoundland fisheries remain in British hands and pressed their Members to support supplies for a continuation of the war so that a 'safe and honourable' peace might be secured. These Instructions were less confrontational than the Half-Moon resolutions, but they were hawkish enough.[119]

The City Instructions were also accompanied by a number of resolutions relating to Pitt. Beckford rejected a strong motion asking Pitt to take the seals of office whenever he should be offered them again, but he supported two others. The first, thanking Pitt 'for the many and important Services rendered to his King and Country', passed unanimously. The second, lamenting his resignation and the ill consequences of the 'loss of so able and upright a Minister at this critical juncture', provoked a division. Two aldermen, Sir Robert Ladbroke and the banker and Butite, Francis Gosling, opposed this resolution along with 13 councillors. Nine aldermen, including Beckford and his parliamentary colleague, Sir Richard Glyn, together with 100 councillors supported it.[120] In the half-filled assembly, only a fraction declined to identify themselves with Pitt.

The ministry was outraged by the City Instructions and several of its leading members, Fox and Bedford especially, urged retributive action along the lines of another aldermanic veto.[121] In the end, it was decided to placate City opinion by agreeing to an inquiry into the expenses of the German war and at the same time to run a paper campaign against the Patriots. With government backing to the tune of £100,000, a flurry of pamphlets attacked Pitt's overbearing arrogance and the hypocrisy of his acceptance of a pension, and questioned whether the successes of the war could be attributed to him alone.[122] Several put forward the thesis that Pitt had only resigned because he feared the odium of a peace where some concessions were inevitable, and queried the constitutionality

[119] *London Evening Post,* 22–4 Oct. 1761; Council Journals, lxii, fo. 298.

[120] BL, Add. MS 32,929, fo. 442. The nine aldermen were Beckford, Glyn, Stephenson, Bridgen, Martin, Cartwright, Gascoyne, Chaloner, Rawlinson.

[121] BL, Add. MSS 32,929, fos. 11, 476; 32,930, fo. 132; Chatsworth MS 182/206, 207.

[122] Williams, *Life of Pitt,* ii. 119 ff. Anon., *A Letter to the Rt Hon Author of a Letter to a Citizen* (London, 1762); Anon., *The Case of a Late Resignation Set in a True Light* (London, 1761).

of his open letter to Beckford, which had divulged cabinet business. They also projected the populist image of an industrious nation burdened by war and bedevilled by profiteers and hawkish tribunes. In one, the Common Council was described as a 'set of idle drones, who, from behind their counters sell the labours of other men's hands' and 'care little what taxes are imposed on the industrious people, since they only add the tax to the commodity'.[123] With a vested interest in war, it had abrogated to itself the right of instructing the City representatives, a right which officially belonged to the Livery.

Amid this barrage of criticism, support for the Patriots continued to come in. The boroughs of Bath, Cork, Norwich, and Stirling, and the merchants of Dublin drew up Addresses lamenting Pitt's departure. The Common Council of Chester praised the London resolutions, as did York's, notwithstanding Rockingham's efforts to restrain them. The Corporation of Exeter even recommended its members to follow the London Instructions to the letter.[124] Adding to this provincial chorus, the Patriots reaffirmed Pitt's popularity with a dash of civic display. Beckford personally pressed Pitt to attend the civic banquet on the Lord Mayor's day, emphasizing that 'a refusal at this critical juncture would damp the ardour & public spirit of every well wisher to this Country'.[125] Pitt reluctantly obliged and he was fêted all the way. 'At every stop the Mob clung about every part of the Vehicle,' the *St James's Chronicle* reported, 'hung about the Wheels, hugged his Footmen, and even kissed his Horses.' As he entered the banquet with Lord Temple, 'there was a loud and universal Clap which was continued for some time'.[126] So overwhelming was Pitt's reception that it incensed two of the other notable guests, the king and Lord Bute.

Pitt's restoration to favour in the City was a carefully orchestrated affair and the Addresses in his favour were arguably disappointing, in view of the rain of gold boxes which had greeted his dismissal in 1757.[127] Yet the acrimonious pitch

---

[123] *A Letter to the Rt Hon Author*, p. 67.
[124] Williams, *Life of Pitt*, ii. 121; PRO 30/8/6/17, fo. 12; *London Evening Post*, 17–19, 21–4 Nov., 10–12 Dec, 1761; Add. MSS 32,929, fos. 444–5; 32,930 fos. 158–9; 32,931, fo. 51; Peters, *Pitt and Popularity*, p. 212.
[125] *Correspondence of Pitt*, ii. 65; PRO, 30/8/6/19, fo. 110.
[126] *St James's Chronicle*, 12–14 Nov. 1761.
[127] Peters, *Pitt and Popularity*, p. 212.

of Patriot rhetoric continued to trouble some ministerial supporters in 1762. Rigby, for example, thought the country was 'reverting very fast into the situation of that in ye year 1756, which made Mr. Pitt's spirit and activity necessary to be called into it'.[128] But, despite the heated debates in Parliament for an inquiry into the Treasury's administration of the war on the continent and a war with Spain, the government continued to scale down its commitments in Europe and brazened out the demands for Pitt's return and a punitive peace. War with Spain was declared, but within months peace negotiations with France were resumed.

The publication of the preliminary articles of the Peace of Paris in late November 1762 confirmed the worst fears of the London Patriots. England retained Canada and Senegal, St Vincent, Tobago, Dominica, and the Grenadines. Minorca was exchanged for Bellisle, and Spain gave up all claims to Florida and accepted British logwood rights in Honduras in return for Havannah. France agreed once more to demolish the fortifications at Dunkirk and continued to occupy the Indian factories which she held before 1749. But the most notable concessions which she won, and the ones which provoked most criticism, were the retention of Goree and the sugar islands of Guadaloupe, Marie Galante, and St Louis. In addition, she secured fishing rights in Newfoundland.

This settlement was clearly unacceptable to London's Patriots. The prospect of a French presence in Newfoundland had always been contested. While Beckford had adopted a conciliatory position over the secession of Guadaloupe and Martinique, the Patriot press had generally taken a tougher line. In mid-December the *Monitor* again demanded the retention of the sugar islands and deprecated the concessions which France and Spain had received. The *London Evening Post* summed up the preliminaries with the remark that England had always been 'famous for extreme generosity to its allies', but this time 'we are about to out-do our usual outdoings'.[129]

When Parliament reconvened after the summer recess the peace proposals were met by a storm of protest which

---

[128] Bedford MS xliv, fo. 300.
[129] BL, Add. MS 32,935, fos. 310–11; *A Letter to the Rt Hon Author*, p. 70; *Monitor*, 18 Dec. 1762; *London Evening Post*, 30 Nov.–2 Dec. 1762.

underlined the convergence of Patriot and plebeian opinion in London and the mounting opposition to Lord Bute. Since Pitt's resignation in October 1761 the king's favourite had endured the abuse of the opposition press in print, poem, and ballad. His Scottish heritage, with its Jacobite overtones, was crudely caricatured. His devious dealings at Court were magnified to promote the spectre of a Caledonian takeover of the state and an impending despotism. And the anti-Catholic sympathies of the British were once more inculcated to project the fear of underhand dealing with the French.[130] On the first day of the session the new courtier faced the humours of the London crowd. Rigby recalled how 'Lord Bute was very much insulted, hiss'd and abused in every gross manner, and a little pelted' on his way to Westminster, and how, on his return, 'the Mob discovered him, follow'd him, broke the glasses of ye Chair, and in short, by threats and menaces put him very reasonably in great fear'.[131] By contrast, a fortnight later Pitt was cheered all the way to the Commons for the debate on the preliminaries. Rigby told Bedford that the Patriot ex-minister 'was huzzaed to the very door of the House in the lobby by a Mob . . . who attended also his going out & paid the like compliment'.[132]

The criticism which beset Bute in London did little to impair the government's peace settlement, which passed the Commons by comfortable majorities. But it remained to be seen whether the solid endorsement of the peace preliminaries in the Commons would alter the balance of forces in London. Things did not look promising for the Court. Bute's unpopularity intensified as a result of the cider tax, which was strongly opposed by the Common Council, and Beckford used the agitation to rally support for Pitt. On 22 April nearly 200 councilmen and twelve aldermen attended a reception hosted by the sugar planter where toasts were drank to Pitt and to 'Liberty, Property and No Excise'.[133] The following month Sir

---

[130] On the propaganda against Bute see John Brewer, 'The Misfortunes of Lord Bute: A Case Study in Eighteenth-Century Political Argument and Public Opinion', *Historical Journal*, 16 (Mar. 1973), 7–43.
[131] Bedford MS xlvi, fos. 140 ff.
[132] Ibid., fo. 170; see also *HMC Lothian*, v. 245.
[133] *London Evening Post*, 21–3 Apr. 1763. For the Common Council's petition against the cider tax see Council Journals, lxiii, fos. 72–6.

Charles Asgill attempted to mobilize support for the ministry on the Court of Aldermen by moving an Address congratulating the king on an 'honourable' peace settlement, but Beckford, together with seven or eight aldermen, objected to the phrasing of the motion. In the end, an Address thanking the king for concluding 'a very just and expensive War by a necessary and advantageous Peace' passed by one vote. It was a significant victory for the Court, for three of the aldermen who voted for the Address had eighteen months earlier lamented Pitt's departure from office. At the same time, the Address did not meet with the approval of the crowd, for its supporters faced a barrage of hissing and catcalls on their way to St James's.[134]

Bute's supporters followed this up with an Address from the merchant community. According to Newcastle's sources, the principal sponsors of this move were all subscribers to Bute's loan of 1762: George Amyand, Peregrine Cust, Samuel Touchet, and Richard Glover, the merchant who had opposed Beckford's parliamentary candidature in 1761. On 10 May they attempted to win the support of the West India interest, but that group voted 14 : 9 against an Address.[135] A meeting chaired by Edmund Boehm was none the less held three days later at the King's Arms Tavern, Cornhill, and on 18 May, 400 merchants joined the cavalcade of 133 coaches and chariots to present a laudatory Address at St James's. The crowd, it was reported, watched the procession without enthusiasm.

Newcastle's supporters denigrated the Address, claiming that its principal promoters were 'not of the first Credit in the City' and that many of its signatories were 'low Tradesmen who had been press'd into service by all possible means'.[136] But the list of 920 signatories in the *St James's Chronicle* did little to

[134] The three aldermen who defected from Pittite ranks over the peace were Sir Richard Glyn, Sir Thomas Chaloner, and Sir Thomas Rawlinson. On the motion and division see Rep. Court of Aldermen, clxvii, 280, 286; BL, Add. MS 32,948, fos. 269–70; *St James's Chronicle*, 10–12, 12–14 May 1763; *Gazetteer and London Daily Advertiser*, 16 May 1763; *London Evening Post*, 14–17 May 1763.

[135] BL, Add. MS 32,948, fos. 269–70, 281; *London Evening Post*, 10–12, 12–14, 14–17 May 1763.

[136] BL, Add. MS 32,948, fos. 281, 316; see also *Gazetteer and London Daily Advertiser*, 30 May 1763, which believed that the address had been hatched by Bute's creditors, 'aided and assisted by the Jews, Apprentices, Clerks, and all the dross of Merchandize'.

confirm these impressions.[137] To be sure some of Newcastle's greatest financial associates—Vanneck, Honeywood, Martin, Mellish, Gore, Sir George Colebrooke, and Bartholomew Barton—did refuse to support the Address. But some of those whom Newcastle hoped to dissuade from signing, such as Philip Zachary Fonnereau, Arnold Nesbit, and Henry Muilman, did endorse it. Together with Joseph Salvador, the most important Jewish financier to follow Sampson Gideon, and Nicholas Magens, one of the principal Dutch underwriters, they were not prepared to allow political divisions at Court to frustrate their commendation of the peace.

These plutocrats were joined by a substantial section of the moneyed élite. At least 28 leading subscribers to the 1757, 1759, and 1761 loans signed the Address. So, too, did 100 past, present, and future directors of the major moneyed companies. Among the rank and file, over 60 per cent can be identified in contemporary directories as 'merchants'. About 150 were indisputably engaged in overseas commerce, encompassing all sectors, even the American, African, and Caribbean, although these were perhaps not as well represented as the Baltic, North European, Levantine, and Mediterranean trades. Other Addressers were part of the financial and service economy of overseas commerce. They included attorneys, Fenchurch Street bankers, warehousemen, and Blackwell Hall factors. By contrast, comparatively few Addressers were engaged in domestic industry, save for the silk and linen manufacturers. There were few brewers and distillers and even fewer outfitting and provision traders. In sum, the Address which supported the Peace of Paris emanated from the mercantile community as a whole, Newcastle's innermost circle of public creditors and Pitt's most hawkish merchants excepted.

The merchants' Address underscored what Newcastle's informants had been telling him all along; that since the beginning of the new reign anti-war feeling was gaining ground among powerful sections of the London bourgeoisie. It also highlighted the limits of Pitt's popularity.[138] As long as Pitt

---

[137] *St James's Chronicle*, 21–4 May 1763. I have used all the available London directories to locate the 'merchant' addressers.

[138] For some important reflections on Pitt's popularity see Brewer, *Party Ideology*, ch. 6, and Peters, *Pitt and Popularity*, ch. 9.

conformed to the Patriot ideal and was identified with Britain's naval and military victories, his popularity was assured. But from 1760 onwards events conspired to undermine his support. The credit shortage and high interest rates prompted misgivings within the merchant community about continuing the war. The advent of a British monarch critical of continental subsidies removed one of the major planks of the Patriot programme, criticism of the Court's Hanoverian bias, and prompted some Tories to gravitate towards the ministry. Moreover, Pitt's acceptance of a pension inevitably impugned his reputation as the great Patriot. By 1762–3, Pitt was only able to avail himself of his solid, though never unquestioning, base of support on the London Common Council, of his still considerable reputation in the opposition press, and of whatever popularity he might attain with the plebs, as a counterpoise to the Scottish favourite Lord Bute. The notion that he represented the interests of trade and commerce was no longer tenable.

From a somewhat different perspective Pitt's popularity underlined the tremendous importance of the City of London as a forum for public opinion and political change. Throughout the Seven Years War, the springboard to Pitt's popularity had been the City of London, especially the middling citizens of the Common Council and the journals and weeklies which brought their views and activities to a wider audience. This was not, of course, his only source of support, for it is clear that he did appeal to that broad, heterogenous constituency which admired patriotism, disliked the politics of dependency and preferment, and identified with the quest for empire. But the City remained his principal institutional base, whose Addresses and Instructions were closely watched in the provinces, especially in those towns and densely industrial villages whose economic prosperity was increasingly linked with America. The result was that, even in an era of electoral ossification, the City of London remained a vibrant force whose running commentary on government necessarily punctuated the world of high politics and affected its policies. The Newcastle and Bedford papers leave us in no doubt that City politics absorbed the attention of the élite. Indeed, in an era of party fragmentation, the City's remonstrances made the leading politicians increasingly aware of the relative autonomy and complexity of public opinion and of the need to woo and manage it more successfully. That lesson was brought home especially to the Pelhamite Old Corps in the wake of Minorca. It constituted part of its political education.

Did the growing visibility of the City in the political discourse of the 1750s signal any great change in its political temper? The late Lucy Sutherland once suggested that it did, seeing the mid-1750s as the birth of London radicalism and a middling class consciousness.[139] But such an argument seems suspect. The emergence of the City as a quasi-autonomous force in English politics dates back to the Civil War, and its independence from major opposition groups—which Dame Lucy regarded as a precondition for its class character—is quite evident in the Walpolean era. Moreover, the radical stance of the City was tempered rather than advanced in the 1750s by the paradox of having a Patriot in power. The crisis of Minorca, after all, saw the last campaign for parliamentary reform for almost twenty years, and this hiatus may in part be attributed to Pitt, who ironically instilled new life into Whig oligarchy and assuaged the passions of anti-ministerialism with the peals of victory and the cannons of Cherbourg. (And, of course, by espousing libertarian causes such as the Habeas Corpus and Militia Bills, and championing a blue-water policy which had been a hallmark of Patriot ideology and an accompaniment to political reform in the Walpolean era.) In this sense, in combining patriotism and empire, Pitt followed in the wake of Admiral Vernon and those earlier countrymen who pursued Walpole in his final years.

Lucy Sutherland was none the less correct in recognizing that a sense of class did inform London politics during this era; although again I would argue that it was a long-term development and not a specific product of the 1750s. It had its roots in the struggle between the two 'Cities', the Corporation and the financial plutocracy, whose interests and political sympathies had begun to diverge in the Williamite era and were increasingly polarized by the City Elections Act of 1725 and the structures of Hanoverian politics, in which the moneyed men

[139] Lucy Sutherland, 'The City of London', 60–7, and *Opposition to Government*, pp. 31–6.

were the clients of government and of aristocratic patronage. Growing out of London's strong corporate tradition and privileged status within the realm, which officially gave the City a special voice in the varied communities that made up the commonwealth, it was fuelled by those oligarchical developments which marginalized popular aspirations and left the City of London as the pre-eminent spokesman of the excluded. As an obvious focus of anti-ministerial sentiment and an exemplar of open, participatory politics, tetchily independent of aristocratic authority, the City took on the mantle of articulating the interests of trade and independency. Social developments within the City aided this role, for as we shall see in the next Chapter, the principal assembly of mid-century London politics, the Common Council, became increasingly representative of domestic trade and manufacture and distanced from the world of overseas commerce and high finance with which it was formerly linked. At the same time, the class notations of London politics were complex. The City was not stridently anti-aristocratic. But it would not brook aristocratic hauteur, condescension, or lackeydom, and it nurtured a residual contempt for aristocratic degeneracy that was later to inform middle-class definitions of the 'unproductive classes'. Aristocratic leadership was accepted within limits, and those limits were predicated upon the values of patriotism and independency which gave appropriate weight to those solid citizens who constituted the central constituency of the 'People'. As the *Protester* advised politicians in 1753, their 'most solid recourse' in a crisis 'would be in a Gentry, the liberal professions, the whole mercantile interest and in short all who had any pretense to be comprehended in the middle rank of people'.[140] In staking out this ground, and in amplifying those values of civic responsibility and commercial probity upon which the good sense of the 'People' was said to be grounded, the City of London had played a major role.

[140] *Protester*, 9 June 1753.

PART II
The Social Configurations of Metropolitan Politics

4

The City of London

HISTORIANS have for a long time recognized the important role that the City of London played in the opposition to Walpole and his successors, but they have been rather less specific about the depth of that opposition and the countervailing forces that the government was able to muster in its favour. Generally speaking, they have tended to see the emergence of the City opposition as a rather contingent affair, a cumulative alienation of different segments of London society, all of which had particular grievances with the ministry. This view has something to commend it, for it is clear that the tempo of protest changed at critical junctures and threw up a different set of leaders. Yet such a perspective elides long-term developments in London society and the foundations upon which successive campaigns were built.

Fortunately, we can approach this subject by building upon the analysis that Gary De Krey has advanced for Augustan London. In his study of City politics in the first age of party, De Krey emphasized the extent to which London was divided by religion and wealth. He not only showed the close association between nonconformity and Whiggery—what might be taken to be a truism—but he went on to show the critical salience of Dissent in London politics.[1] In the period 1685–1715 nonconformists were well grounded in City politics, with as many as sixty-five sitting on Common Council and some twenty-five holding senior City offices. Dissenters were also especially visible in overseas commerce, especially in the colonial, silk, and Iberian wine trades, and they played a critical role in the financial revolution. It was hardly surprising that the 'politics of belief', as De Krey describes it, should resonate through City circles during these years.

It is sometimes argued that after the Hanoverian succession nonconformity entered a period of stasis. The doctrinal

---

[1] De Krey, *A Fractured Society*, ch. 3.

divisions over the growth of Arianism, which surfaced in 1718 and led to a dramatic meeting of London ministers at Salters' Hall, are attributed in part to this decline in growth. So, too, are the long-term effects of Occasional Conformity, which led younger generations to abandon the denominations for the Church of England. These issues certainly troubled the nonconformist community and made the question of decline a very topical issue in the early 1730s.[2] Men like Strickland Gough feared that doctrinal disputes would unsettle the relations between ministers and congregations and encourage the already perceptible migration of gentlemen from the nonconformist fold. Even so, the numerical strength of Dissent in the large commercial centres and cities was still considerable. In the greater London area the number of Dissenting congregations arguably expanded in the first four decades of the eighteenth century. As Table 4.1 shows, there was a perceptible rise in the number of congregations within the bills of mortality. At the turn of the century there were eighty meeting-houses in the greater London area, the majority of them within the city walls. By 1715 this number had increased to eighty-nine, most of the expansion occurring in the suburbs, especially among the Presbyterians. In the next two decades the proliferation of congregations in the outlying parishes continued, although by 1738 the decline in the number of Dissenting meetings within the jurisdiction of the City was quite evident. Even so, the City itself fielded some quite formidable congregations. The Reverend Samuel Palmer in 1731 described the Crosby Hall Congregation in Bishopsgate Street as 'now very large and rich', making 'the largest annual congregation of any Presbyterian Church', and commended the New Broad Street congregation for its wealth and respectability. Surveying the Dissenting interest as a whole, he noted that fourteen congregations in London and Westminster had increased in size since 1695, while fifteen had disappeared and twenty-two remained as they were.[3] What decline had taken place remained proportionate to London growth, although he did stress that Occasional Conformity and Arminianism had bled

[2] On these issues see Michael Watts, *The Dissenters* (Oxford, 1978), ch. 4.
[3] Dr Williams' Lib., MS 38.18.

TABLE 4.1. *Nonconformist Meetings in the London Area*

	Presbyterian	Independent	Baptist	Quaker	Unknown	TOTAL
1682–1702						
City within	13	12	6	2	—	33
City without	4	5	6	2	—	17
Other	4	11	12	3	—	30
TOTAL	21	28	24	7	—	80
1715						
City within	12	5	4	2	1	24
City without	3	7	9	2	1	22
Other	13	11	14	3	2	43
TOTAL	28	23	27	7	4	89
1738						
City within	10	4	3	2	—	19
City without	3	5	3	1	—	12
Other	14	13	19	9	—	55
TOTAL	27	22	25	12	—	86

Sources: Gary S. De Krey, 'Trade, Religion and Politics in London in the Reign of William III', Ph.D. thesis (Princeton University, 1978), p. 124; id., *A Fractured Society*, p. 85, E. S. de Beer, 'Places of Worship in London about 1738', in A. E. J. Hollander and W. Kellaway (eds.), *Studies in London History* (London, 1969), pp. 393–402.

the community of some of its wealthier members and ministers.

The Dissenters, then, were a far from insignificant force in London society in the 1730s. Politically they were as well organized as at any time since the Revolution. In the early decades of the century the ministers of the three denominations had combined to press for political concessions and to consolidate their group interests. In 1717, for example, they presented a joint address to the Crown congratulating the king on the suppression of the rebellion, adding that 'some were for having us Speak plainly of the hardships The Dissenters lay under and of the little regard that was had to them notwithstanding their Stedfast Loyalty to his Majesty'.[4] Within fifteen years their lay brethren had created a nation-wide caucus to agitate for the repeal of the Test and Corporation Acts. Not content to deploy the services of prominent Dissenters already well-placed in the Whig hierarchy, such as Shute Barrington and Sir Joseph Jekyll, the Dissenters mobilized their big merchants and financiers to solicit concessions from Walpole. The first committee of the Protestant Dissenting Deputies included no fewer than six directors of the Bank of England, one South Sea director, a Hamburg merchant who was soon to become a Bank director, and a lawyer who was appointed Attorney-General of the Duchy of Lancaster within a year.[5] Far from being a marginal force, the Dissenters were well placed in high political circles.

Yet, despite the strategic position of Dissent in Hanoverian politics, there was a perceptible decline of its visibility in City government. Few nonconformists emerged to take the place of prominent aldermen such as Sir William Ashurst or Sir John Fryer, the strenuous advocate of the Protestant Succession.[6] Those Dissenting merchants with parliamentary ambitions evaded the hurly-burly of London elections for safer seats and facilitated the development of pressure-group politics which the commercial success of nonconformity had made possible. The result was that City politics ceased to be a battleground for religious rights and sectarian recognition. Even the 'Sherrifs'

---

[4] Hunt, *Early Political Associations*, p. 155.
[5] Ibid., 168 and app. E.
[6] De Krey, *A Fractured Society*, pp. 89–91.

Cause', by which the City deliberately exploited the reluctance of conscientious Dissenters to hold civic office in order
to finance the new Mansion House, was fought through the
courts rather than the hustings.[7] By the late 1730s the only
staunch Whigs of nonconformist origin left on the Aldermanic
Court were the Eyles brothers, both active supporters of
Walpole. Significantly, their opponents in City politics included two men of Quaker origin: George Heathcote, linked to
the Eyles by marriage but irrevocably opposed to Court
Whiggery, even to the point of befriending High Church cum
Jacobite dissidents; and Sir John Barnard, who was baptized
into the Anglican church by Bishop Compton in 1703.

Heathcote and Barnard's careers were unusual, for the
fragmentary evidence that we have of nonconformist voting
patterns suggests that all denominations voted consistently for
official Whig candidates throughout the early Hanoverian era.
Of the Dissenters listed in the parishes of St Mary Aldermanry
and St Thomas the Apostle in 1733, all who were liverymen
voted for the Court candidate, William Selwin, in the Chamberlain's election the following spring.[8] The same was true of the
General Baptists at the Barbican, the Independent congregation
at Girdler's Hall, and the Dissenting Deputies. Indeed, of the
forty-six nonconformist liverymen I have been able to locate,
thirty-nine voted for Selwin, six abstained, and only one,
Richard Jackson, a Baptist from White's Alley, Moorfields,
voted for his opponent.[9] The nonconformists, in other words,
continued to provide the Whig party with a solid phalanx of
supporters in London elections, at least until 1734. Later that
decade they may not have presented such a united front, for
some Dissenters were bitterly disappointed by the government's refusal to push for full religious toleration in 1736 and
1739. Even so, the economic success of many Dissenting

---

[7] On this issue see Bernard Lord Manning, *The Protestant Dissenting Deputies* (Cambridge, 1952), pp. 119–29.

[8] The Dissenters are listed in Guildhall MS 8991. I have used the 1734 livery list, *An Alphabetical List of the Livery 1733*, to locate those eligible to vote in the Chamberlain's election the following year. For the poll see the *Daily Post Extraordinary* and the *Daily Journal*, 9 Apr. 1734.

[9] For the nonconformist congregations and the Dissenting Deputies see Guildhall Lib., MS 3083/1, 592/4; Dr Williams' Lib., MS 73; Great London RO, N/C/32/1.

leaders and their close involvement in government finance and commercial policy inhibited any venturesome alternative. In 1740 the London committee of the Dissenting Deputies considered raising the stakes by organizing the Dissenting vote in the forthcoming general election.[10] But it ultimately declined to do so. Walpole correctly calculated that the memory of the High Church assault upon nonconformity and its close association with Whig finance would temper any wholesale desertion of government ranks. Too many leading nonconformists had too great a stake in the Hanoverian regime to abandon orthodox Whiggery.

The declining visibility of Dissenters in City government and the ministry's refusal to grant the denominations full toleration reduced the importance of religion in London politics. Anglicans no longer seemed so threatened by the rise of Dissent and occasional conformity, and indeed the parish ceased to be the battleground or focus of party conflict. In fact, by 1734, many churchwardens could agree to disagree about their politics, a position that was rare twenty years earlier.[11] However vibrant political divisions over religion appeared in other towns—and I shall stress their importance in Bristol and Norwich later in this study—they had lost much of their intensity in London.

If religion ceased to animate City politics to the same degree as in the Sacheverell era, the divisions over high finance continued to resonate in the wards and Common Hall. The plutocracy's basic commitment to Whiggery was apparent from the foundation of the Bank of England, but after 1714, when the Tories were proscribed from office, it became emphatically clear. In fact, the financial community as a whole, including many of the merchants associated with the older 'royalist' companies, proved to be ministerial devotees in City politics, ready to lend their weight to curb dissonant voices which might unsettle the new economic order. The City Election Act of 1725, in particular, confirmed the alliance

---

[10] Hunt, *Early Political Associations*, p. 161.

[11] Of the churchwardens who voted in the Chamberlain's election of 1734, 32 voted for Selwin and 45 for Bosworth, with 7 abstaining. Of the 26 churchwardens whose brother-officers also voted, 16 voted in unison and 10 for opposing candidates. The names of the churchwardens are to be found in the visitation books, Guildhall ms 9537/33.

of Whiggery and big business in the interests of strong oligarchical government. It also nullified the efforts of the small merchants and traders formally to question the economic ramifications of high finance. Since the beginning of the century it had been argued that the new money-market would undermine traditional trading enterprise, tempting industrious merchants to invest in speculative and inherently unproductive ventures. In 1715, for example, a pamphleteer mourned that 'the very Men who were bred up merchants and were considerable in the Profession have neglected and almost left off Foreign Trade, and fallen into this New and much more profitable way of Dealing'.[12] This was clearly alarmist, but the disastrous effects of over-speculation reverberated through London in 1720 when the South Sea Bubble ruined many small creditors and lent considerable credibility to the notion that high finance was inimical to trade, as well as sharpening the unpopularity of the plutocrats who rode high upon public gullibility and misfortune. In the shrieval election of 1721, for example, hundreds of voters assailed the two Whig moneyed candidates to the cry of 'No Courtiers! No South Sea!'[13] This suspicion of the great financial syndicates was sustained by the subsequent activities of the South Sea Company, whose exploitation of the Assiento beyond the terms laid down in the Treaty of Utrecht soured Anglo-Spanish relations and disrupted transatlantic commerce. The pernicious influence of high finance upon trade and private credit was raised by the Common Council in its opening Address to George II. But the Whig financiers on the aldermanic bench, unable to eliminate the offending clauses about the decline of 'real Credit' and the current hazards to trade, promptly vetoed the whole draft.[14]

By the 1720s the debate over high finance had entered the political discourse of the day. But before we can highlight this critical division within the bourgeoisie, we need to explore its socio-political configurations in more detail. Certainly at first sight it would seem that there was little to choose between the financial commitments of Whig and Tory-Patriot aldermen. As

---

[12] John Holland, *The Directors of the Bank of England; Enemies to the Great Interests of the Kingdom* (London, 1715), p. 4.
[13] *Norwich Gazette*, 24 June–1 July 1721.
[14] Henderson, *London and the National Government*, pp. 117–18.

rich merchants and manufacturers who were prepared to devote a considerable amount of their time in civic service, one would expect them to invest some of their fortune in the funds. Thus the private account books of Hoare's bank reveal a fairly brisk trade in government annuities among opposition aldermen such as Sir Robert Ladbroke, Sir William Calvert, Sir Robert Godschall, and George Heathcote. The latter, for example, received dividends in December 1725 on £6,000 Orphans stock, £10,745 Bank stock, £3,215 India stock and two blocks of South Sea stock valued at £6,370 and £3,000.[15] Despite the political animus against the moneyed interest, these men were not exactly foreigners to Exchange Alley.

Yet such piecemeal information ignores the extent to which Whig rather than Tory-opposition aldermen had their fortunes bound up in high finance. Of the thirty-three opposition aldermen of the Walpolean era (1720–42), only eight, or 24 per cent, had held major directorships. These had normally been held before the Hanoverian accession and usually for a small number of years. By contrast, some twenty-five of the thirty-six Court aldermen, or 69 per cent, sat on the boards of the three major moneyed companies and their tenure was far more substantial. Together they chalked up no less than 369 years of office in the various companies, an average of 14.7 years each compared to 5.3 for their opponents.[16] Several of the Whig aldermen, moreover, had played important roles in their foundation or reconstitution. Sir Gilbert Heathcote, for instance, was one of the founding members of the Bank of England, as well as a promoter of the new East India Company. Sir John Eyles, the son of a Baptist clothier from Chippenham, was a sub-governor of the South Sea Company for over a decade and was primarily responsible for the financial rehabilitation of the company after the Bubble. Even those not formally affiliated to the great moneyed syndicates were sometimes heavily committed to their operations. They included Sir John Tash, a close colleague of Sir Gilbert, who left £22,500 in stock and bonds to his heirs out of a fortune of £103,000, and Joseph

---

[15] This information is derived from the private account books, organized alphabetically, at Hoare's Bank, Fleet Street.

[16] These calculations are derived from Beaven, *The Aldermen of the City of London*, ii. 118–28.

and Henry Hankey, bankers in the mercantile quarter of Fenchurch Street.[17] Thus to all intents and purposes 78 per cent of the Whig aldermen in the Walpolean years appear to have been strongly implicated in high finance.

The opposition aldermen, on the other hand, were a more diverse breed. By the 1730s they included John Barber, the Queen's Printer from 1710–14, a close friend of Bolingbroke, Pope, and Swift to whom he left small legacies in his will. They also featured some of the richer manufacturers of the metropolis: William Benn, a Bishopsgate soap-maker, who owned freeholds in urban Middlesex as well as Hertfordshire; William Calvert, the leading porter-brewer in London, producing 55,700 barrels annually by 1748; and Humphrey Parsons, Horace Walpole's 'Jacobite brewer', whose Red Lion brewery was built up by his grandfather and consolidated by his father, MP for Reigate for 1685–1717, tax-farmer and victualler to the navy.[18] Merchants, however, dominated the opposition bench, but unlike their Whig counterparts, who were clustered in the more established trading companies, they tended to be active in the more dynamic and open sectors of overseas commerce such as America and the West Indies, or alternatively in the wine trade of the Iberian peninsula. These were trades which felt the pinch of Walpole's commercial policies during the 1730s. In addition the opposition won the support of merchant-insurers outside the institutional insurance market, from private underwriters who were perturbed by the growing interference of Spanish *guardacostas* as well as by the closed, privileged world of high finance. Sir John Barnard is the best representative of this point of view, campaigning in print and Parliament against the more speculative activities of the financial world, for greater access to government loans, and, in the case of the Sugar Colony Bill of 1732, for freer colonial commerce.[19] Finally, there were the bankers. These men

[17] For Sir John Tash see CLRO, Court of Orphans, inventory exhibited 9 Mar. 1735. For the Hankeys, India Office, L/AG/14/5/329, p. 129.

[18] (Barber) *London Evening Post*, 1–3 Jan. 1741; (Benn) PROB 11/817/211; (Calvert and Parsons) Peter Mathias, *The Brewing Industry in England 1700–1830* (Cambridge, 1959), *passim*; (Parsons) B. D. Henning (ed.), *The History of Parliament: The House of Commons 1660–1690* (3 vols.; London, 1983), iii. 208–9; Sedgwick (ed.), *Commons 1715–54*, ii. 326–7.

[19] *Gentleman's Magazine*, 3 (1733), 198; Sedgwick (ed.), *Commons 1715–54*, i. 435–7.

sometimes hailed from old goldsmith families and were not intimately connected with the 'City' in the modern sense of the term. The Hoare family, for example, catered principally to the gentry, while the Childs, whose political affiliations were never extreme, had a very mixed clientele. In sum, the opposition aldermen were rarely closely associated with high finance, despite the odd director like Sir John Lesquesne, who represented the mercantile ward of Broad Street, first as a Common Councilman and then briefly as its Alderman. Rather, they represented a broader range of business beyond the inner circle of the Exchange and the boardrooms of the major moneyed and mercantile companies.

If the social divisions in City politics are fairly explicit at the aldermanic level, they are also among Common Councilmen, with some qualifications. Stuart assemblies had always drawn a substantial proportion of their members from the overseas merchant community and the joint-stock companies which constituted the embryo of the financial establishment.

TABLE 4.2. *The Social Composition of the London Common Council in the Late Seventeenth and Eighteenth Centuries* (%)

	1660	1676	1682	1689	1738	1748	1761
Overseas commerce	35.2	27.5	23.9	33.0	15.3	18.4	22.4
Professions	7.4	11.3	17.3	13.1	9.8	8.4	12.8
Wholesale/retail	38.7	39.5	42.1	35.7	45.5	42.6	40.8
Manufacturers	7.3	10.2	6.6	7.7	14.5	15.8	13.8
Craftsmen	9.5	12.0	9.6	9.9	14.9	14.7	10.2
Total found (out of 234)[a]	137	167	197	182	235[a]	190[a]	196[a]

[a] In the eighteenth century there were 236 seats.

As Table 4.2 shows, over a quarter and sometimes a third of the 234 seats came from this sector. Together with the wholesalers and larger retailers, the other dominant group on Common Council, they made up approximately 65–70 per cent of the assembly. By the Hanoverian era, however, mercantile representation was on the decline, replaced by a growing number of master craftsmen and manufacturers. The basic trend was towards diversity; a greater variety of retailers and wholesalers in the provisioning trades, more domestic suppliers and craftsmen, and a rising number of industrialists, as dyers, soap-makers, and sugar-refiners set their sights on municipal politics in a sustained fashion.

TABLE 4.3. *The Partisanship of the London Common Council 1738–1745* (%)

	Whig	Tory-Patriot	TOTAL
Overseas commerce	35.1	14.2	21.8
Professions	8.2	9.5	9.0
Wholesalers/retailers	35.1	37.3	36.4
Manufacturers	12.4	20.1	17.2
Craftsmen	9.3	18.3	15.0
Total found	97	169	266

These changes were not evenly distributed between the two parties. An analysis of the more partisan Common Council-men in the years 1738–45 (Table 4.3) reveals that the ministerial Whigs were disproportionately represented in overseas commerce and banking. If one includes the factors, packers, and warehousemen within this category then it constituted 35 per cent of the Whig councilmen. The Court party also made headway in the textile trades, a familiar line of business for Dissenters and one with which the Whigs had traditionally been associated since 1713. In contrast the opposition drew much of its support from the industrial trades, among brewers, coopers, soap-makers, and sugar-refiners, in particular. Together with the builders and craftsmen in silver, gold, and pewter, they constituted 38 per cent of the opposition group. Save for the merchants, packers, and bankers, in fact, the opposition party reflected the growing heterogeneity of Hanoverian councils more accurately than their opponents.

This emerges quite clearly if we look at their livery affiliations. The Court Whigs were recruited primarily from the Great Twelve Companies, those dominated by the greater merchants and financiers. In 1734, in the aftermath of the Excise crisis, 67 per cent of the pro-ministerial councillors belonged to this privileged stratum; in the early 1740s, as many as 80 per cent. On the other hand, roughly a third of the opposition frequented the same halls, 37 per cent in 1734 and

33 per cent in the years 1739–45.[20] This did not mean that the ministerial Councilmen were necessarily richer than their opponents, although a survey of their propertied wealth is instructive. As Table 4.4 reveals, both courtiers and anti-ministerialists had proportionately the same number of rich tradesmen and merchants. But the opposition drew more of its members from the trading rank and file. In other words, the Court Councilmen had greater access to the world of big business and were more likely to have identified with its priorities. The opposition men, by contrast, were more firmly rooted in the lesser companies: in the case of native Londoners those of their fathers; in the case of the manufacturers, those that reflected their craft.

TABLE 4.4. *The Propertied Wealth of Common Councilmen 1739*

Rateable value of business premises	Court Whig (%)[a]	Opposition (%)[b]
£10 or under	2.8	13.3
£20 or under	15.4	22.8
£50 or under	64.7	70.4
£100 or under	75.0	82.8

[a] Total of 71.
[b] Total of 105.

Sources: Land tax 1738 (Guildhall MS 11,316/117); Chamberlain's poll 1734; Butler's list of Common Council affiliations 1743 (Stuart MS 254/154)

The pattern that is revealed from a social anatomy of the Courts of Aldermen and Common Council is that the ministerial Whigs were very much the party of high finance and the more established sectors of overseas trade closely connected to it. They were also strongly represented in textile manufacture and were able, through the privileged world of the livery companies, to command the vote of status-conscious councilmen. Conversely, their opponents were more solidly rooted in the middling trades, particularly the industrialists of the riverside and the outwards of the City. They were altogether

---

[20] These conclusions are based on an examination of the registers of the livery companies and the freedom admissions of the City of London. I located 168 in 1734 (66 Whig, 102 Tory-Patriot) and 141 in the period 1739–45 (56 Whig, 85 Tory-Patriot).

more heterogeneous in their occupational composition, reflecting the broad changes that had taken place in Common
Council membership since 1688. The Tory-Patriots were not
without mercantile support. They were always able to count
upon a vocal and influential minority of merchants outside the
establishment who, for a variety of reasons, were alienated
from government policy. In sum, the Tory-Patriots on Council
had a following which accurately reflected their populist
ideology: they drew on tradesmen and merchants outside the
clientage of the state and high finance, upon men who had a
stake in an independent City and cherished its open, political
traditions and sense of civic responsibility. It remains to be
seen whether these divisions extended to the broader electorates of City politics and what further qualifications are in
order.

FREEMAN POLITICS

We may begin with the freemen: the resident '£10' citizen-
householders, paying scot and bearing lot, who elected representatives to the Courts of Aldermen and Common Council.
Unfortunately, no manuscript scrutiny-books or petition-lists
at the ward level have survived for the middle decades of the
century, and so a comprehensive examination of freemen
politics is impossible. One can, however, take 'snapshots' of the
political affiliations of the councillors over a period of twenty
years. Two surveys were drawn up by Jacobite agents in 1722
and 1743. I have checked their results against other fragmentary information and also, where possible, against poll-book
data; and they appear reasonably accurate, except for the
continual confusion between anti-ministerialism and crypto-
Jacobitism. I have also used the 1734 Chamberlain's poll which
was published in the newspapers to determine the political
allegiance of the Common Council in the immediate aftermath of the Excise crisis.[21] Together they form a useful series
at important junctures in the political history of the City:
1722, on the eve of Layer's rebellion and but a few years from

---

[21] The 1722 and 1743 lists are to be found in PRO, SP Dom 35/39/298 ff. and
Stuart MS 254/154. The Chamberlain's poll is to be found in *Daily Journal
Extraordinary*, 9 Apr. 1734, and *Daily Post Extraordinary*, 9 Apr. 1734.

the Election Act; 1734, the beginnings of a resurgence of popular anti-ministerialism; and 1743, the aftermath of Walpole's fall, when the Court party in London was at the nadir of its fortunes. Assuming the sympathies of ward voters were broadly reflected in the returns and were not continually obstructed by vestry oligarchies or by the returning officer, one can investigate the electoral geography of freemen politics and arrive at general conclusions about the nature of grass-roots Tory-Patriotism and Whiggery.

TABLE 4.5. *The Electoral Geography of the Wards 1722–1743*

	1722	1734	1739	1743
Inner city wards (%)				
Court	30	41	47	35
Tory-Patriot	38	38	28	62
Neutral/Unknown	32	21	24	3
Middle city wards (%)				
Court	14	24	20	17
Tory-Patriot	67	50	60	83
Neutral/Unknown	19	26	20	0
Outer wards (%)				
Court	0	9	6	0
Tory-Patriot	94	64	76	100
Neutral/Unknown	6	27	18	0

Table 4.5 provides an immediate impression of the changing political temper of the wards over these two critical decades. As it reveals, the Court party was best represented in the inner core of the city.[22] The wards within this area were clustered around Cheapside, a street well known for its 'Goldsmiths, Linen Drapers, Haberdashers, and other great Dealers'.[23] In those precincts, dominated by Norwich and Blackwell Hall factors—especially those of a Dissenting persuasion—Whig support was well based. Coleman Street ward, for instance,

---

[22] The division of the 25 wards into three categories (inner, middle, and outer) follows De Krey, *A Fractured Society*, pp. 171–2.
[23] Maitland, *London*, ii. 880–92; Hermione Hobhouse, *The Ward of Cheap in the City of London* (London, 1963), pp. 94–104.

inhabited by merchants and wholesale dealers, remained a virtually impregnable ministerial stronghold, even in the heyday of anti-Walpolean agitation. And Bassishaw, whose 105 freeman-householders in 1721 included 12 merchants, 13 factors, 5 packers, 3 tailors, 2 clothworkers, 2 warehousemen, a woolman, and an upholsterer, reversed the dominant trend in City politics by ousting an anti-Excise deputy in 1736, and electing a confirmed courtier as alderman in January 1739.[24] Cheap ward, too, closely associated with the woollen industry, was predominantly Whig, although its situation at the focal point of urban electoral activity made it extremely vulnerable to outside pressures. Finally, Bread Street and Vintry where Low-Church vestries were reinforced by Dissenting minorities, maintained a consistently Whig record.[25]

The Court party also made significant gains in the pre-eminently financial wards near the Exchange. Langbourn, the bankers' ward of Lombard and Fenchurch Street, returned Whig majorities in 1734 and 1743, while ministerial supremacy in Broad Street, dominated by the Bank of England, South Sea House, and the commercial quarter of Threadneedle Street, was only checked in the final phase of popular anti-ministerialism in 1742. However, Cornhill ward was never dominated by the Court faction, in spite of the fact it was the centre of metropolitan finance and marine insurance. Throughout the twenties and thirties it appears to have remained doggedly neutral, shifting its support to the Patriots in the early forties, a bewildering pattern in view of the political proclivities of the neighbouring wards.

None the less, the broad trend is clear. The commercial and financial wards within the inner area of the City showed a general tendency to vote for the Court party rather than the opposition, a pattern that was only arrested in the final tide of protest which swept Walpole from power. The opposition strongholds, by contrast, included the bank-side wards of Dowgate and London Bridge, the inner western wards surrounding St Paul's, Castle Baynard, and Farringdon Within, and most significant of all, the populous wards outside the walls.

---

[24] CLRO, MS 83.3, 1721/2, returns listing potential jurors with occupations.

[25] Bread Street's principal householders were engaged in the cloth trade, haberdashery, or the professions; Vintry's were wholesale provisioners, dyers, coopers, and builders. See CLRO, MS 83.3.

To the west was Farringdon Without, embracing not only Fleet Ditch and the main arterial road to Westminster, inhabited by builders and artisans in the decorative crafts as well as a few lawyers and gentleman-bankers, but the alleys and courts of the meaner craftsmen bordering Smithfield, Hatton Garden, and Lower Holborn. To the north lay Aldersgate and Cripplegate, lowly suburbs of smiths, weavers, carters, and poor watchmakers. These districts were infamous for their robust Toryism, prompted, no doubt, by the presence of several Dissenting chapels. Further afield, to the east of Moorfields, was Bishopsgate ward, where mercantile enclaves like Great St Helen's and Devonshire Square were matched by squalid tenements on the periphery of Spitalfields.

This ward contained a sizeable and influential nonconformist population and was only held with difficulty. Finally, in the region of Houndsditch, Petticoat Lane, and the Minories was Portsoken, whose southerly precincts were 'taken up by butchers, who deal in the wholesale way, selling carcases of veal, mutton and lamb to the town butchers'.[26] This East-End ward was only marginally Tory in 1734, and does not appear to have been a notorious opposition division, for two of its five Common Councillors joined the loyalist association during the Forty-Five. None the less, it was never contested by the Whigs in the decade 1733–43, and continued to return men broadly sympathetic to the anti-ministerial coalition.

Thus, whereas the Whigs dominated the Exchange and wards closely linked to the cloth trade and non-conformity, the Tory-Patriots were consistently strong in wards beyond the walls and around St Paul's, and made considerable headway along the riverside. Not that the opposition wards lacked wealthy, even eminent, citizens. Castle Baynard and Farringdon Within, for example, were chiefly inhabited by substantial provision-merchants, builders, timber-merchants, booksellers, cutlers, caterers, and a sprinkling of clerks, lawyers, and goldsmiths.[27] Queenhithe, the great wholesale corn market serving the Thames hinterland with its factors and wharfingers, returned at least five opposition Common Councillors out of a possible six after 1722; while the predominantly

[26] Don Manoel Gonzales, *London in 1731* (n.d.), p. 32.
[27] For the jurors' occupations in these wards see CLRO, MS 83.3.

commercial ward of Walbrook, to the south of Cheapside, in close proximity to the Exchange, shifted from the Tories in 1722 to the Whigs during the 1730s and back again to the opposition in 1743. Judging from an earlier scrutiny, the skinners, leathersellers, and goldsmiths were fairly evenly distributed between the two parties, while the merchants, factors, and packers opted for the Court by a ratio of 4 : 1.[28] Clearly the opposition party were able to harness the support of a significant proportion of the middling tradesmen of the metropolis, particularly in the High Church parishes around St Paul's and Fleet Street. But the broad social pattern revealed in this preliminary survey is a division between the richer, compact, pro-ministerial wards of the commercial world and the more extensive, diverse districts on the periphery of the city, the purlieu of the meaner trades, where Tory radicalism was firmly rooted.

Table 4.6 illustrates this pattern in greater detail. The average annual rental in the predominantly Whig wards was

TABLE 4.6. *Property Ratings in Whig and Tory-Patriot wards*

	Average rental (£ p.a.)	Substantial dwellings (%)	Active freeman	Livery in 1751 resident in ward
Whig Wards				
Bassishaw	30.0	11.2	78	49
Bread Street	32.0	17.0	187	117
Cheap	45.8	36.6	241	224
Coleman Street	22.3	9.4	224	126
Langbourn	40.1	27.2	306	231
Vintry	19.9	6.9	111	56
Tory-Patriot Wards				
Aldersgate	18.0	1.0	—	156
Bishopsgate	24.3	8.5	690	401
Castle Baynard	26.0	9.6	200	133
Cripplegate	12.9	2.3	1,220	352
Dowgate	24.7	10.0	—	63
Farringdon Wn	24.5	11.8	710	270
Farringdon Wt	19.2	5.5	1,092	776
Bridge	35.0	17.0	166	159

[28] The Walbrook scrutiny for 1714 is included in the 1721 returns, ibid.

never less than £19.9. In four of the seven wards property rates were assessed at a mean of £30 or over. And the percentage of substantial dwellings (assessed at £50 p.a. or over) was in two instances extremely high, 27.2 per cent in Langbourn and 36.6 per cent in Cheap. The opposition wards, on the other hand, were conspicuously poorer. Property rates ranged on average from £12.9 in Cripplegate Within and Without to £35 in Bridge ward. The proportion of substantial dwellings was never more than 17 per cent; in Cripplegate and Aldersgate it was as little as 2.3 and 1 per cent respectively.

The number of active voters in these wards can also be significantly contrasted. In Farringdon Within and Bishopsgate approximately 700 voters participated in the ward elections of 1737 and 1739. Over 1,000 polled at a Smithfield precinct contest in 1739 in Farringdon Without, and as many as 1,220 in the tumultuous aldermanic contest of 1723 in Cripplegate, where the exclusively freeman electors swamped the potential livery vote in the locality.[29] The proportion of liverymen in the freemen electorate of the pro-ministerial wards was usually higher; the electorate itself more compact. Langbourn was the only Court division which appears to have had more than 300 active freemen, and one may presume that a fair number of these were liverymen as well. There were admittedly a number of opposition wards with a sizeable middling electorate, and at least two divisions, Farringdon Without and Bishopsgate, were dominated by local liverymen of some substance. (Indeed these are the Tory areas where Whig campaigning was most evident.) Nevertheless, the general pattern is clear. The emphatically Tory-radical wards were drawn principally from the poor populous suburbs; the Court wards from the compact and conspicuously financial thoroughfares. Only in the final stages of the clamour against Walpole was Court hegemony in these wealthy districts impaired.

THE POLITICS OF COMMON HALL

The electoral geography of ward politics revealed a clear congruence between London Whiggery and financial capital. The poll-books of the Livery outline this relationship in greater

---

[29] *London Evening Post*, 22–5 Dec. 1739; Henderson, *London and the National Government*, p. 102.

detail. In the five elections between 1722 and 1734 for which information has survived,[30] the more prestigious companies, which became increasingly divorced from the technical pre-occupations of their crafts and emerged as wealthy pro-prietorial fellowships, showed a marked sympathy for the Court faction in city politics.

TABLE 4.7. *The Political Disposition of the Livery 1722–1734*

	1722	1724	1727	1734
Whig majorities				
Substantial companies	14	11	14	12
Other companies	7	13	9	6
Tory-Patriot majorities				
Substantial companies	1	3	3	3
Other companies	28	20	25	27
Divided				
Substantial companies	4	4	2	4
Other companies	7	10	8	9

Note: the substantial companies are defined as the Great Twelve, plus the Apothecaries, Brewers, Dyers, Leathersellers, Pewterers, Scrivenors, and Stationers. Companies are considered to have a Whig or Tory-Patriot majority if 55% or more voted for the party slate (or, in the case of the 1722 election, the three-candidate slate plus one other). The exception to the rule is the 1727 election, where the creation of the first Country slate resulted in substantial cross-voting. In this instance, a majority is secured by one of the parties obtaining 40% of the total vote. The 1724 figures refer to the parliamentary by-election of Nov. of that year.

As Table 4.7 reveals, the Whigs generally secured more majorities among the nineteen substantial companies than they did among the remaining forty-one. In terms of absolute numbers, they secured 43–50 per cent of their total vote in the

[30] The relevant polls can be found in *A handlist of poll books and registers of electors in Guildhall Library* (London, 1970), pp. 37–8. To this list should be added the *Daily Journal*, 20 Mar. 1724 (the poll of Sir John Williams), and *Daily Journal Extraordinary*, 9 Apr. 1734 (the poll for John Bosworth). The five polls are Apr. 1722 (parliamentary), Mar. 1724 (shrieval), Dec. 1724 (parliamentary by-election), Oct. 1727 (parliamentary), and Apr. 1734 (for Chamberlain).

1722, 1724, and 1734 contests from the more prestigious companies, compared to 40–2 per cent among their opponents. More dramatically, we find that among the Great Twelve livery fraternities, whose high entry-fines were but one reflection of their social eminence, seven voted consistently for the Whigs. The Clothworkers, Drapers, Fishmongers, Haberdashers, Mercers, Merchant Taylors, and Salters all provided the ministerialists with a solid core of supporters. In most contests, over two-thirds of their members opted for the Whig list; among the Mercers and Drapers the proportion of loyalists was often much higher. As many as 127 liverymen of the former company rallied to the ministerial list in 1722, as opposed to 47 against. In 1734 the ratio was 150 : 43.

Outside the Great Twelve there were other companies noted for their commercial affiliations which allied themselves to the Court faction. Whiggery prevailed among the Leather-sellers, for example, a company in which guild regulation had been abandoned in favour of closer contacts with the mercantile community. This transition was well under way by the mid-seventeenth century when wool-merchants, clothiers, and Merchant Adventurers joined the livery. Indeed, the decision to adopt a property qualification of £1,000 for all applicants to the cloth of the company virtually excluded all the practising leathersellers and reinforced the tradition of open trade within the trade. Similarly, Glovers, a company divorced from its craft, was solidly Whig, as were the Apothecaries, 'that damned squirting set', as Charles Churchill later dubbed them,[31] who aspired to professional status and instituted a £16 livery fine to exclude middling chemists and druggists from their ranks. While they still retained contact with their trade, they also attracted mercantile clientele to their fraternity.

However, not all prestigious companies were Whig. The Grocers, Skinners, and Ironmongers, for example, all of whom retained close links with the mercantile community, were politically divided. And two of the Great Twelve were avowedly Tory-Patriot. The Vintners, intimately associated with the wine trade which experienced some lean years in the

---

[31] Guildhall MS 214/3, fo. 305. Information on the Leathersellers was taken from Richard Grassby's talk to the London seminar at the Institute of Historical Research, London, in the spring of 1971.

1720s, retained clear-cut opposition sympathies. So did the Goldsmiths, a company which had traditionally combined their formal trade with private banking, and, along with the Corporation itself, had been largely ousted from the profitable world of government credit by the development of Revolution finance. Nor should it be assumed that every Whig company was firmly associated with the mercantile plutocracy. The Glass-sellers and Wax-chandlers generally adhered to the Court party. So did one conspicuously industrial company, the Weavers, which was dominated by Huguenot capitalists, profited from the fiscal protection of the state, and harboured close links with the Levant and East India trades.[32] Nevertheless, the correspondence between the Court faction and merchant capital was marked. Of the twelve companies who formed the backbone of ministerial support, eight retained intimate contact with merchant-financier interests.

While the mercantile companies tended to sympathize with the Court faction, the smaller fraternities showed a willingness to side with the opposition. Of the eleven companies outside the Great Twelve whose livery fees did not exceed £5, five voted consistently for Tory-Patriot candidates and two only deviated in one of the five elections between 1722 and 1734.[33] More important still were the political affiliations of those companies whose economic survival and social standing were threatened by the expansion of the London domestic market and the breakdown of guild regulation and control. This applied particularly to the food trades whose formal economic functions were undermined by the increasing complexity of the metropolitan market attendant upon the growth of London's population after the Great Fire, and the emergence of powerful intermediaries in the network of distribution and exchange.

Take the grain trade for example. During the late seventeenth century, the paternalistic regulations governing the sale and marketing of bread by which the Corporation professed to

---

[32] G. B. Hertz, 'The English Silk Industry in the Eighteenth Century', *English Historical Review*, 24 (Oct. 1909), p. 714.

[33] The five who voted consistently were the Butchers, the Farriers, the Fruiterers, the Musicians and the Scrivenors. The Broiderers and Glaziers returned Tory–opposition candidates in four of the five elections. The Glass-

protect the consumer underwent fundamental transform-
ations. While the city continued to administer the assize of
bread, fixing the size, weight, quality, and price of the loaf
according to the market price of wheat and flour in nearby
granaries, the actual network of commodity exchange became
increasingly specialized. The general retail markets of the
metropolis were overshadowed by the growth of the two great
wholesale markets at Bear Key and Queenhithe; and the grain
trade was largely monopolized by London-based factors and
corn-merchants, who sometimes sold for provincial farmers on
commission, but more frequently dealt on their own account
for either the domestic or export market. By the mid-
eighteenth century, when a new corn exchange was established at Mark Lane, all but the most powerful provincial
middlemen, the Kentish hoymen, had been eliminated from
the central markets. A small clique of fourteen factors
dominated the exchange. Together with the urban corn-
chandlers, who not only supplied flour to the bakers and local
consumers but also acted as distributing agents for the
Queenhithe wholesalers, and the jobbers, described in a 1774
Commons committee as those 'who attend the Market for the
express purpose of buying Grain to resell on the same market
day, or within a day or two afterwards', the factors exercised a
preponderant influence on the distribution and marketing of
grain in the metropolis.[34] Although the traditional sanctions of
the 'open market' were designed to eliminate the forestalling
and engrossing of grain, in practice the trade was vulnerable to
such abuses.

For the London bakers these developments were ominous. In
the seventeenth century the City had attempted to harmonize
the demands of the company with those of the consumer by
delegating the supervision of the assize regulations to them. By
the eighteenth century this arrangement was rapidly becoming
inoperable. The expansion of the metropolitan suburbs made
formal guild-supervision impossible. The right to search each

sellers and the Wax-chandlers were predominantly Whiggish in temper. The
Masons and Upholders were politically divided. For information about livery
fees see R. Campbell, *The London Tradesman* (London, 1747), pp. 306–8.

[34] Ray B. Westerfield, *Middlemen in English Business* (New Haven, Conn.,
1915), pp. 154–6.

shop and the attempt to compel all bakers within twelve miles of the capital to join the company became difficult to enforce. A mid-century account of the company's finances reveals declining membership at all degrees in the guild hierarchy, and a levelling of fraternal fines and dues.[35] Livery admissions dropped from 75 to 35 in the period 1720–7 to 1742–9. The number of freemen joining the company slumped from 162 to 120 and the total number of presentments from 391 to 180. Although the Company managed to maintain its income by the energetic enforcement of the rights of quarterage and search, it clearly sensed its demise in status with the Corporate hierarchy. As early as 1707 the master warden and assistants complained that the Bakers 'have always given their Attendence on the Lord Mayor's Day at their stand which used to be about Bread streete or Friday streete in Cheapside. But of late yor Petitioners Stand has been in St. Paul's Church yard and many Companys Inferior to yor Petitioners placed before them'.[36]

The Bakers' inability to maintain a monopoly over the trade was compounded by their increasing dependency on the middlemen. In the late seventeenth century the company vigorously protested against the activities of the provincial mealmen who were selling small peck and half-peck loaves in central and surburban markets. 'Divers mealmen in & about London', ran one order in 1683, 'do cause great quantity of their own meale to bee made into severall sorts of cursized bread by divers bakers.' Nine years later the Company complained that 'above a hundred Mealmen were sett up within this Citty and Suburbs who had gott the major part of the Bakers trade into their hands.'[37] Thereafter they focused their attention on the corn-chandlers who were charged with selling poor quality flour at high prices. In 1735 the Bakers demanded a modification of the assize regulations to align these with the varied quality of flour used in bread production. The current conditions, they asserted, were detrimental to the trade. 'A Baker of strict virtue', the *Gentleman's Magazine* reported, 'declares

[35] CLRO, Companies 1.37.

[36] Quoted in Sylvia Thrupp, *A Short History of the Worshipful Company of Bakers of London* (London, 1933), p. 68.

[37] CLRO, Companies 1.11.

he could not from the profits of a large Trade, get a competent maintenance for his Family.'[38] How reasonable these claims were it is difficult to determine. But there is little doubt that the smaller and middling bakers affiliated to the Company sensed the erosion of their vested privileges before the forces of market capitalism. On several occasions in the first half century the Bakers petitioned the Corporation for statutory enforcement of their guild regulations to resuscitate their flagging fortunes, and in 1753 their efforts were rewarded. An Act of Common Council that year decreed that all individuals practising the trade outside the company should be fined £10 in any London court, and that henceforth the Chamberlain would refuse to admit a baker to one of the other livery companies.[39]

The Bakers were simply one of a series of livery companies which sought to uphold their customary rights before the advance of the free-market economy. The Butchers and Poulterers, confronted with similar problems, also hoped to. Both resented the appearance of interlopers in the suburban food markets, attempted to attract renegade tradesmen to their own fraternities, and complained about the forestalling of goods and the absorption of the trade by the larger capitalists.[40] In each case the companies fought an uphill battle, for the traditional machinery of guild enforcement could not keep pace with rapid expansion of the capital, nor was it equipped to deal effectively with the changing complexities of the processes of distribution and exchange. For a time the carcass-butchers were able to maintain a monopoly over the wholesale meat trade at Smithfield and to deal with the provincial drovers on their own terms, although the emergence of forestallers' markets at Mile End, Islington, Knightsbridge, Stoke Newington, and further afield at Potters Bar, Hounslow, Hayes, and Southwell, inevitably circumscribed their control.[41] For the city retailers, however, the butchers of Newgate, Leadenhall, and the Honey Lane market and the rise of the

---

[38] Thrupp, *Bakers*, p. 30; Guildhall broadsides, 7:138.

[39] CLRO, Companies 1.37.

[40] CLRO, Companies 1.29; P. E. Jones, *The Worshipful Company of Poulterers of the City of London* (London, 1965), pp. 55–70.

[41] A. B. Robertson, 'The Smithfield Cattle Market', *East London Papers*, 4/2 (Oct. 1961), pp. 80–7, and 'The Suburban Food Markets of 18th Century London', *East London Papers*, 2/1 (Apr. 1959), pp. 21–6.

West End markets, Bloomsbury, Carnaby Street, St James's, Oxford Street, Clare, and Hungerford prejudiced their monopoly from the beginning. In this way, the demands of the greater households, the development of the London season, and the commercial penetration of metropolitan capital, combined to bring about the final breakdown of customary guild-regulation within the trade.

Companies like the Butchers, Bakers, and Poulterers, whose economic fortunes and standing within the London commonalty were adversely affected by the changing pattern of distribution and exchange and the rapid expansion of the metropolitan population without the walls, showed a marked tendency to align themselves with the Tory-Patriot opposition in city politics. Other companies who faced similar difficulties did the same. The Innholders for example, who were unable to attract tapsters and stable-keepers into their company, and who also lost the right to control innholders and victuallers within a three-mile radius of the capital in 1757, voted consistently for the opposition throughout the 1720s and 1730s. In this case the government's fiscal policy added a further grievance, for the 1729 duty on compound waters and spirits and the 1736 duty on gin-shops only encouraged the clandestine trade and exacerbated the company's difficulties. By 1771 the fraternity found itself in such desperate straits that it decided to open its doors to all comers and renounced its traditional *raison d'être* altogether. Not surprisingly, the company showed a warm sympathy for Wilkes, the hero of the little man in City Politics. In 1776 it agreed to open its Hall to treat the radical supporters in the Chamberlain's election, though not at the company's expense.[42]

There seems therefore to have been a rough congruence between the lesser trading companies and Tory-Patriotism. Companies who genuinely represented their trade, sought to regulate the internal London market, and found it difficult to attract wealthy clientele outside their own sphere of activity, identified with the City opposition. To the food-retailing fraternities we must add the Blacksmiths, Feltmakers, Painter-Stainers, and Barbers, who resented the competition of the fashionable wig-makers of the West End and lost the wealthy

---

[42] Oliver Warner, *The Innholders Company* (London, 1962), pp. 51–8; CLRO, Companies 3.17.

patronage of the Surgeons in 1745. One should also include the Joiners and Plasterers, who sought to control their trades more closely, and experienced fierce competition from building speculators and fashionable furniture manufacturers in the West End. All these companies, in contrast to the prestigious mercantile companies, showed a consistent bias towards City 'Toryism' in the five elections which I have reviewed.

So far I have tried to outline the more obvious political divisions within the Livery and relate them to a wider economic context. The central weakness of such a survey is that some of the livery companies were no longer associated with their specific trades, and that, by examining the companies as coherent units, we can only deal with the broader social configurations. We cannot ascertain whether the mercantile community was in any way divided, nor whether certain wholesale trades and professions had firm political loyalties. A more detailed analysis of livery politics according to wealth and occupation is therefore necessary. For this purpose I have concentrated upon the Chamberlain's election of 1734, one of the most controversial contests of the mid-century, in which the anti-Excise candidate John Bosworth narrowly defeated the ministerial representative William Selwin.

One of the most interesting revelations of the election is the degree to which the mercantile élite rallied to the Court. Of the 336 electors listed in Henry Kent's directory of merchants and eminent tradesmen, 248 (i.e. 74 per cent), voted for Selwin. Prominent among them were the directors of the major joint-stock companies of the metropolis. Nine directors of the Bank of England (eleven, if one includes a former associate, Sir John Eyles, and a future director, Alexander Sheafe) supported the ministerial candidate. So too did seven South Sea directors, plus one of the principal directors during the South Sea Bubble, Sir Harcourt Master, and a merchant-financier of Hackney and Katherine Court, Tower Hill, namely Jonathan Collyer, who joined the company in 1739. Six directors of the East India Company (including four aldermen—Sir William Billers, Sir John Salter, Sir Robert Baylis, and Sir Francis Child) were also among Selwin's supporters; as were twelve members of the major insurance companies and two prominent insurers, James

Porten of Lime Street and Alderman Robert Willimot of Mincing Lane. Only one representative from the mercantile directorate of the metropolis, John Hyde of Charterhouse Square, the deputy-governor of the London Assurance company, voted for Bosworth: he was a prominent tobacco-merchant trading in Maryland, and his opposition to Walpole's candidate was predictable.[43]

A similar, though more complex, pattern emerges among the bankers. Of the fourteen private bankers listed in the directory, ten voted for Selwin and four for Bosworth. Two of the four Patriots, representatives of the Fleet Street firm of Arnold and Hoare, catered predominantly for the gentry, lending money on mortgage or bond, receiving rents, and collecting dividends on stock investments. Although the partnership did not eschew mercantile dealings—indeed, during the 1730s several important opposition aldermen and Common Councillors were among its customers—the bulk of its business was with landed society.[44] By contrast, the Lombard Street bankers associated with the mercantile world were solidly Whig. They included John Freame of Freame and Barclay, Nathaniel Brassey, William Knight, James Martin, Richard Morson, and Joseph Vere of Glegg and Vere. Together with the odd firm in Change Alley and Fenchurch Street, these pro-ministerial bankers issued loans to City men, and, unlike their West End counterparts, concentrated on the discount of bills and the purchase of stocks or securities.

Equally conspicuous among the devotees of the Court were the Turkey merchants. The statutory regulations governing entry into the Levant Company, which exercised a formal monopoly over the trade, meant that a disproportionate number of Turkey merchants within the whole metropolitan commercial community joined the London livery. There were perhaps eighty members in the company during the 1730s, forty-one of whom were active traders. Thirty-five of them participated in the 1734 election for a new City Chamberlain,

---

[43] For his Maryland interests see the brief reference in Price, 'Capital and Credit', in Platt and Skaggs (eds.), *Of Mother Country and Plantations*, pp. 7–36. I would like to thank Joe Ernst of York University, Toronto, for this reference.

[44] D. M. Joslin, 'London Private Bankers 1720–1785', *Economic History Review*, 7 (1954), pp. 175–9.

and all but two, Bartholemew Clarke of Garlick Hill and Thomas Carew of Size Lane, voted for Selwin. Among the more prominent were representatives of the Radcliffe family of Devonshire Square, whose recorded imports of silk, cotton, mohair, dyestuffs, and other miscellaneous products from Syria and Persia averaged between £14,000–15,000 in the period 1731–6, and whose partnership capital in 1755 exceeded £34,000. Together with the family firms of Lock and Bosanquet, and the Broad Street partnership of Snelling and Fawkener, they were responsible for 37.6 per cent of all silk imports from Aleppo during the 1730s, and a somewhat higher share of other imports from the Levant.[45]

The Turkey merchants were not the only overseas traders who supported the Court candidate in 1734. Three of the four directors of the Royal Africa Company who participated in the Chamberlain's contest voted for the ministerialist; so too did thirty-two of the forty-two electors loosely classified as 'merchants' in Henry Kent's Directory. They included two Italian merchants, Peter Gaussen of Great St Helen's, and Thomas Godfrey of Crutched Friars; one Hamburg merchant, Peter Devisme of Throgmorton Street, and two London Huguenots who acted as agents for Amsterdam investors; one North American trader, Thomas Trueman of Broad Street; one West India factor, Metcalfe Lascelles; and two important metropolitan financiers, Benjamin Mee of Gracechurch Street, and Nathaniel Newnham of Swithin's Lane, who both subscribed £10,000 or more to the 3 per cent loan of 1742.[46]

Selwin, therefore, attracted the support of influential sectors of the financial and mercantile plutocracy. The small minority of opposition merchants, by contrast, were either drawn from specialized sectors of the overseas-trading market which felt imperilled by government policy, or alternatively, from the more dynamic sectors of the mercantilist system which pressed for political recognition commensurate with their economic power. Among the first one may cite the wine-importers who canvassed vigorously against the Excise in 1733.[47] They

[45] For the comments on the Levant merchants see Ralph Davis, *Aleppo and Devonshire Square: English Traders in the Levant in the 18th Century* (London, 1967), pp. 58–70.
[46] Dickson, *The Financial Revolution*, p. 288.
[47] *Daily Post*, 14 Mar. 1733; *Daily Journal*, 15 Mar. 1733.

included leading members of the City's political community: men like Sir John Barnard; Daniel Lambert, Common Councillor for Aldgate 1732–7, and Alderman for Tower ward 1737–50; William Cleaver, a wine-cooper of St Dunstan's Lane, Deputy of Tower ward; and James Razer of Lawrence Poultney Lane, Common Councillor of Dowgate. Among their allies were the London tobacco-importers, Alderman Micajah Perry of St Mary Ax, Joseph Dash of London Bridge, Samuel Palmer of Fountain Court, Aldermanbury, and Charles Blandy of Bread Street Hill, Common Councillor for Queenhithe. During the 1730s these merchants were attempting to reassert their control over the colonial markets in the face of Scottish competition and planter intransigence, a battle in which the proposed excise duty was but one aspect of deteriorating metropolitan-colonial relations.[48] Together they sought to mobilize the London consumer and retailer against Walpole's economic policies, and were among John Bosworth's most conspicuous supporters in 1734.

The political affiliations of the mercantile élite, then, reveal patterns that were quite explicit within the court of Aldermen. The established sectors of overseas trade and the great financial syndicates remained solidly Whig in 1734; only the wine trade and a medley of merchants in the expanding economy of the West voted for the opposition. But what of the other liverymen, especially those of the middling trades? How did they vote in 1734? In order to determine their political preferences in some detail, I have taken two soundings of the poll for the election of Chamberlain. From jury lists I located the occupational status of approximately 500 middling-to-substantial liverymen who voted in 1734. I have also been able to trace the rateable value of 592 liverymen, a 10 per cent sample of the total poll. Both of these samples are geographically unrepresentative in the sense that they do not include voters from Southwark or the Home Counties; nor do they give a very precise measure of wealth or occupational status; but they do offer some very rough guides.

The results of these surveys are laid out in Tables 4.8 and 4.9. They corroborate, in the first instance, what we have

---

[48] David Alan Williams, 'Anglo-Virginia Politics 1690–1735', in Alison G. Olson and Richard M. Brown (eds.), *Anglo-American Relations 1675–1775* (New York, 1970), pp. 89–91.

already established: that the richer liverymen, especially those in overseas trade, showed a clear preference for the Court party; that the textile trades were predominantly Whig; that those who might have been subject to an excise tax in 1734

TABLE 4.8. *Occupational Survey: The Chamberlain's Election 1734*

	Bosworth/opposition	Selwin/Court
Gentlemen/merchants	7	32
Cloth trade	13	24
Silk/fine fabric trades	7	13
Book trade	8	19
Leather trades	1	6
Professions	2	3
Outfitters	23	26
Provisioners	41	48
Building trades	23	22
Household crafts	17	17
Miscellaneous trades	11	11
Wine trade	15	3
Druggists/chemists	7	0
Goldsmiths/silversmiths	10	6
Domestic suppliers/ cheap-metal trades	27	23
Liquor/riverside trades	23	18
TOTAL	235	271

Source: I have used the 585 liverymen whose occupational status was mentioned in the jurors' lists of 1732–4. (79 liverymen did not vote.)

were predictably oppositionist. Table 4.9 also shows that the opposition made most headway among the small-to-middling liverymen, whereas the Whigs fared better at the top of the scale. But the figures also reveal that the Court party secured the support of many lesser liverymen. Nearly 24 per cent of the Whig vote was rated at under £20, compared to nearly 27 per cent among their opponents. In fact there were areas of the City where its social penetration was substantially deeper than might be expected. In the eastern wards of Bishopsgate, Portsoken, Aldgate, and Lime Street, and in the suburban parishes of Westminster, Finsbury, and the East End, the

TABLE 4.9. *Frequency Distribution of the Properties of Liverymen who Voted in 1734*

Annual value (£)	0–19	20–39	40–59	60–79	80–99	100+	150+	(no.)
Court voters	23.9	33.3	19.8	9.7	4.5	6.6	2.1	(288)
Patriot voters	26.9	40.5	17.8	8.6	1.7	3.6	1.3	(305)

Source: Land Tax and poor rate assessments for the City, Westminster, and the Tower and Holborn divisions of Middlesex.

opposition voters were on average richer than those of the Court. Even in the solidly anti-ministerial wards of Aldersgate, Cripplegate, and Farringdon Without, the contrasts are not as glaring as one would expect. While the residences of the opposition voters were assessed at an average of £28.8 per annum, those of the Court were only marginally higher, £35.5 per annum. Here, as in the East End and eastern wards, the Court party was able to attract the support of a substantial number of small-to-middling liverymen as well as the big fry. How can we account for these geographical disparities, and indeed of the Whig party's ability to command the allegiance of the very modest liveryman?

Part of the answer for this seemingly incongruous pattern lies with Nonconformity, a still considerable if declining force in City politics. Solidly Whig, the Dissenters and Quakers were well represented in the eastern wards of Portsoken and Bishopsgate as well as in the East End suburbs of Stepney and Bethnal Green, particularly among the textile trades. There were also some thriving meeting-houses in Cripplegate and Aldersgate and at least three in the extensive ward of Farringdon Without: at the Old Bailey, in Leather Lane, Holborn; and in Nevil's Alley, Fetter Lane. In spite of the doctrinal disputes which raged within their ranks these congregations provided the Whigs with a sizeable phalanx of supporters, one which certainly extended beyond the merchant élite to the trading rank and file.

Needless to say, the electoral presence of Nonconformity cannot completely explain the Whig following among the small-to-middling liverymen. What also has to be taken into account is the depth of its clientage, both personal and institutional. As the minutes of the Whig caucus in the early

Hanoverian era reveal, this could be considerable. The party was able to avail itself of the patronage of many government departments, the Post Office, Ordnance, Excise, Customs, Pay Office, and Victualling Office, as well as those of the moneyed companies. Office-holders in these departments who happened to be liverymen were expected to vote for the ministerial party, and those who did not, such as Mr Davis, the partner to Sir Joshua Sharpe, who served 'the Customs but votes contra' could find their positions threatened. The same was true of the tradesmen of the great joint-stock enterprises like the East India Company, some of whom were said to have been dismissed for voting against the Court candidate, Sir George Champion, in the Mayoral election of 1740. In addition to this patronage, the Whig party could also call upon the personal influence of its foremost merchants, which in a heavily residential city, could extend beyond the routine business networks. The chance survival of an electoral survey for Walbrook ward in 1714, for example, shows that the leading merchant of the neighbourhood, Sir Gilbert Heathcote, was prepared to pressure apothecaries and blacksmiths to vote Whig, and that merchants from outside, such as Benjamin Mee of Threadneedle Street, were called in to work on other dependent tradesmen.[49]

Just what the cumulative impact of this patronage was one can only guess. The *Craftsman* calculated in 1727 that the client economy brought the ministerial party some 1,500 votes, roughly a quarter of those who normally voted at Common Hall.[50] This was probably an exaggeration, but the barbed references in the opposition press do suggest that a formidable battery of patronage was mobilized at critical junctures in the service of the Whig party. In 1734 this included not only the more obvious office-holders, merchants, and financiers, but a number of minor officials in the Customs: King's waiters, land-waiters, tide surveyors, and jerquers. It also included several contractors of the Royal Household and the Board of Works: Henry Flitcroft, the master carpenter and clerk of the works at Whitechapel; John Smallwell, the master joiner; Andrew Jelf, the King's mason, and Thomas Kynaston,

[49] Horwitz (ed.), *London Politics*, p. 141. For the Walbrook list see CLRO, MS 83.3.
[50] *Craftsman*, 28 Oct. 1727.

the clerk to the controller and paymaster of the artificers. No doubt these men were able to enlist the votes of needy artisans who aspired to some of the plumb jobs in urban construction, widening the ambit of Whig patronage beyond commercial circles.

I do not wish to make too much of government patronage in London politics. It was clearly not as crucial as it was in Admiralty boroughs, nor as extensive as in Westminster, where many tradesmen were dependent upon the custom of the Court and its allies. In fact heavy-handed pressure upon petty office holders and tradesmen could be counter-productive, for there was a strong tradition of independence in City politics which could be mobilized against it. Not only did the opposition complain of indiscreet electoral influence, bribery, and intimidation, but it campaigned continually against the very structure of influence that the Whigs could utilize. Thus in 1727 the *Craftsman* wondered 'whether all overgrown Companies are not prejudicial to and, in some measure, inconsistent with the Liberties of a Free people, as well as a True Interest of a Trading Nation, with regard to the Influence which they have in the Election of Members of Parliament, particularly for this great and honourable City'.[51] Even so, state and moneyed patronage did provide the Court party with a firm base of support, more extensive than that of the opposition, which was largely confined to City contractors and to appointments at Tory-dominated hospitals such as Bethlem, Bridewell, and St Bartholemew's. It seems very likely that this patronage extended to the smaller liveryman, swelling the lower ranks of the Whig Party and moderating the social disparities which separated Court from opposition.

CONCLUSION

Historians have often noted the opposition of London's middling citizens to the dominant Whig order. They have been less successful in explaining why. Those who have concentrated upon the unpopularity of the moneyed interest have been rather ambivalent about its social permeation, concentrating their attention upon the infighting with the mercantile

---

[51] Ibid., 7 Oct. 1727.

élite rather than on its wider ramifications. Such a focus has at times lent itself to a Namierization of City politics, a battle between ins and outs, with those excluded from favour profiting from the accumulated grievances of twenty years of Walpolean rule.

This type of interpretation has something to commend it, for it is clear that political and economic proscription did fuel the City opposition. Some of its leaders had enjoyed better fortunes before 1714. Closely identified with the Tory party, by birth, kinship, or religious persuasion, they resented the sharp turn of events which accompanied the Hanoverian accession; so much so that they sometimes espoused a whimsical Jacobitism, as did Aldermen John Barber and Humphrey Parsons. Others rode on the back of City agitations simply to frustrate government policy or to gatecrash the inner circle of government creditors. It would be wrong to see the opposition to the Excise or to the Spanish Convention as devoid of self-interest. Yet the City's antipathy to the Walpolean regime was based on more than sheer opportunism, or indeed residual party prejudice. It had its foundations in the long-standing distrust of the financial plutocracy, whose privileged place within the new order threatened the political independence of the City and the economic security of its middling traders. This hostility to Revolution finance shaped City politics until the mid-century. It was only with Pelham's financial reforms and the growing acceptability of government credit that its political salience diminished. Even so, the influence of the great financiers upon foreign and commercial policy could still fan the fires of City anti-ministerialism, as the London support for John Wilkes testified. Like his Patriot predecessors he could appeal to the political reservations of the middling trader as well as the adventurous Atlantic merchant concerning the great men of the Exchange.

To argue that the development of Revolution finance shaped the social configurations of City politics is not to argue that other factors were inconsequential. In an age when kin and apprenticeship could strongly influence political choice it is not surprising to discover continuities across generations and some remarkably stable voting-patterns among older livery-men. Nor is it surprising to find religious differences informing political allegiance. Sermons continually reminded congregations of their political heritage, recalling as a consequence the old Augustan party battles and discriminating religious policies of the past. Among the Dissenters, in particular, the memory of former persecutions died hard, so that, despite Walpole's refusal to grant them full citizenship, the nonconformists remained resolutely committed to successive Whig governments. Not until the 1760s, when a more radical Whiggism began to make headway among Dissenting congregations, did the dissidence of Dissent add a new dimension to City politics.

Throughout the Walpolean era the Dissenters provided the Court party with a solid phalanx of supporters, broadening the boundaries of Whiggism beyond its immediate economic beneficiaries. Yet religion did not animate City politics as formerly. The language of politics was more secular; the role of the clergy, incidental. Even the churchwardens of the same City parishes could differ in their politics, as a review of their voting behaviour in 1734 reveals. In this more secular world, politics revolved around the fiscal policies of the state and the challenge to the political independence of the City by the combined forces of Court and moneyed power. As we have seen, that combination could muster a sizeable dependent vote in its favour, perhaps a quarter of the Livery. That it was unable to dominate City affairs was a testimony to the strong tradition of independence in this exceptional national constituency and to the resolution of its middling electors.

5

The City of Westminster

In contrast to the City of London, a political community with a long-standing tradition of independence of Crown and government, Westminster politics were conducted under the shadow of the Court. With its two royal residences, Parliament, and the main government departments, Westminster lay at the very centre of national politics. The playground of fashionable society as well as the politicians' London, it was the headquarters of the social and political élite; a world of *beaux quartiers* not counting-houses, a *Residenzstadt* and a political capital combined. Scions of the aristocracy, country gentlemen, lawyers, and Court hangers-on embellished its electorate, adding a touch of 'quality'—some might say 'dignity'—to the activities of the hustings.

For such an eminent constituency, Westminster's franchise was remarkably wide. Drawn primarily from the resident householders paying scot and bearing lot, it numbered 9,000 in 1750, rising to around 12,000 at the turn of the century. Social heterogeneity was its hallmark. Apart from the gentry and their army of retainers, there were the artisans, inn-keepers, and traders of a burgeoning luxury-economy, even a few unskilled labourers who had established semi-permanent moorings in its poorer courts and alley-ways. Concentrated in the eastern parishes of the West End, but clustered also in the passages and back-streets of the more fashionable suburbs and administrative precincts, their overwhelming presence gave Westminster politics a popular character. The sheer size of the electorate did not of itself inhibit the aristocratic domination of the constituency, although it did necessitate elaborate controls. But the strategic location of Westminster, its close liaison with the City of London,[1] and the development of the

[1] Anon., *Number of Liverymen in London Wards and Neighbouring Counties 1751* ([1751]; available in the Bodleian Library Collection, Gough London 40). According to this list, 528 liverymen lived in Westminster, 463 in Middlesex, and 277 in Southwark. The total livery was calculated at 6,535 strong, a conservative estimate (c. 7,500 would be a more accurate figure).

coffee-house and tavern as the breeding-grounds for debate and discussion, rendered it vulnerable to shifts in national politics and to confrontations between the Court and dissident elements both in and outside high society. Amid the wealth and influence of the 'quality', London's royal constituency was always vulnerable to popular pressures that could engulf the metropolis as a whole.

Indeed, by the mid-eighteenth century Westminster elections had become notorious for their violence. During the scrutiny of the 1749 poll, Thomas Hawkins, a 77-year-old resident of Strutton Grounds was asked by the High Bailiff whether he remembered any contests in the constituency. 'No, I never heard of anything,' he answered, 'only of disturbances, of beating one another.'[2] There was some truth in this pert reply. West End elections were frequently punctuated by pitched battles at the hustings. In 1698 three hundred horsemen at the service of James Vernon and Charles Montague ran down their opponents in Tothill Fields and cudgelled them into nearby ditches.[3] During the aftermath of the Sacheverell trial in 1710, the High Church mob 'committed great Disorders in buffetting and abusing many Housekeepers' who voted for the Whigs. Westminster elections were the cockpits of party strife during the Augustan era. There were massive turn-outs at the poll, over 7,000 in 1708.[4] The Hanoverian succession did not radically change this state of affairs. While both parties averted a contest in 1715, the second election of the new reign was fought with renewed acrimony. The Court cavalcade 'consisting partly of Troopers, Horse-Grenadiers and Footsoldiers' was insulted in the streets. At Tothill Fields, one journal reported, 'The Rumpers lost their Colours, and the Troopers made a pitiful Retreat, stealing off by sixes and sevens.'[5] The Tories, led by Francis Atterbury, won the election, but it was subsequently annulled. The Jacobite plot in the summer of 1722 marred their hopes of another victory in

[2] 'The whole Proceedings on the Scrutiny of Pollers at the contested Westminster Election, Anno 1749, between Sir George Vandeput and Lord Trentham', BL, Lansdowne MS 509a, fo. 39b. I am greatly indebted to Michael Mendle for bringing my attention to this invaluable source.

[3] Thomas Carew, *Historical Account of the Right of Elections* (2 vols.; London, 1755), ii. 235.

[4] 'Election papers', Univ. College, London, Parkes MS 29.

[5] *Daily Post*, 27 Mar. 1722; *The Weekly Journal, or Saturday's Post*, 24 Mar. 1722.

the December re-election, and thereafter they fell into disarray. In 1727 and again in 1734, the Court Whigs were returned without a contest.

However, the 1740s witnessed a resurgence of opposition to the Court party. The mounting attack upon Walpole's accommodating policy towards Spanish privateering in the Caribbean crystallized around the figure of Admiral Vernon, whose victory at Porto Bello and (later) at Cartagena highlighted the inadequacies of the Court's earlier diplomacy. In his early parliamentary career Vernon had gained a reputation as an outspoken critic of the government, opposing the Excise Bill in 1733 and making continual demands for more adequate provisions for British tars. Now he was acknowledged as the very epitome of patriotism and liberty. Popular demonstrations were held in his honour in November 1740, and the London Corporation offered him the freedom of the City. In the general election of 1741 he was nominated in six constituencies, including London and Westminster. In the City, the ministerial party promoted his candidature in an attempt to divide the opposition, but in Westminster he was put up with Charles Edwin against the Court interest a mere two days before the election. This action took the Court by surprise. Sir Charles Wager, one of their candidates, the man who, ironically, was responsible for Vernon's promotion, gave an account of the contest to the admiral, still in the Caribbean. 'Two days before the election', he wrote, 'when Lord Sundon and I dreamed of no opposition, you and Edwin [were] set up for the City of Westminster and at the election, a poll demanded for you both, which continued six days, with such mobs and riots as never was seen before, tho' there have been considerable ones I believe within your memory.'[6] According to one witness, the trouble began the second day when one of Edwin's managers assembled a mob at the hustings in Covent Garden to intimidate the Court voters. By one o'clock he recalled, the mob had become 'quite outrageous and threw into the Portico, Dirt, Stones, Sticks, Dead Catts and Dogs, so that the Candidates, High Bailiff, Clerks and Inspectors were obliged to retire into the Church, and the poll to be stopt above an Hour'

---

[6] 'The Vernon Papers', ed. B. McL. Ranft, *Pub. Navy Records Society* 99 (1958), 237.

[7] BL, Stowe MS 354, fos. 244–5.

The violence continued and on the sixth day, the High Bailiff John Lever—who, it was later revealed, received £1,500 from the secret service fund for his trouble[8]—peremptorily shut the poll. This action so antagonized the crowd that they stormed the hustings, forcing Lever and Lord Sundon to seek refuge in St Paul's, Covent Garden, from where they summoned the Horse Guards to protect them. On the arrival of the troops, the Earl of Egmont recounted, Sundon

ventured to go out at the other end of the church, and crept into Sir Jo. Cross's coach, driving a full gallop home to his house near St. James' Palace, the mob in great numbers following, hooping and hallowing, cursing and flinging stones, by which the windows were broke, plenty of dirt thrown into him, one of his footmen's skull cracked by a brick bat thrown at his head and his Lordship wounded in the hand. As soon as he passed by the Palace the Guard drew out loaded with ball and prevented the mob from pursuing him . . . in Cleveland Row with design to pull down his house.[9]

Within the month the Grand Jury of Middlesex placed a writ at King's Bench complaining of Lever's partiality to the Court party and his use of military power to terminate the election. They also condemned the activities of the High Constable, Arthur Rawlinson, who hired a gang of bruisers under the leadership of John Broughton, 'a profest Boxer', to browbeat the opposition.[10] A parliamentary petition from the burgesses and inhabitants of Westminster followed, and in December 1741, in the final concerted campaign in the Commons to oust Walpole from power, the election was annulled. In the subsequent re-election, two opposition candidates, Charles Edwin and Lord Perceval (for Vernon was by then a member for Ipswich), were unanimously returned.

However, the Court party had their revenge in the general election of 1747, in which, as I have already mentioned, the Jacobite rebellion emerged as the central and overriding issue. In the months before the election the Whigs exploited the Jacobite bogey to their advantage, levelling accusations of

---

[8] Francis Gashry, an MP and a member of the Navy Board admitted before the select committee to enquire into Walpole's administration that Lever had been given £1,500 (3 June 1742), *Commons Journals*, 24, p. 331.

[9] 'Egmont Diary III, 1739–1747', HMC lxiii. D.3, p. 220.

[10] Anon., *Proceedings of the General Meeting of the Electors of Westminster in the Interest of Admiral Vernon and Charles Edwin Esq.* (London, 1741), pp. 2–3.

treason at several prominent members of the opposition organization, the Independent Electors of Westminster, first formed to co-ordinate the petition against Lever's return in 1741. In addition, a Whig-dominated Commons ordered an enquiry into the activities of that society itself.[11] Nothing came of this, but its propaganda value was nevertheless considerable. A flurry of prints and broadsides portrayed the Independents as a rump of Jacobite malcontents. As in London and Middlesex, the Westminster election was a disaster for the opposition. A discredited and disorganized faction had little chance against Bedford's brother-in-law, Lord Trentham, and the popular admiral Sir Peter Warren. In fact Sir Thomas Dyke and a local JP, Sir Thomas Clarges, secured only 500 votes apiece and soon abandoned the poll. 'The elections for London, Westminster, Southwark and the county of Middlesex have all gone for Whigs,' commented Dudley Ryder in July, 'The eyes of people are much opened by rebellion.'[12]

Although the Court won such a resounding victory in 1747, they were confronted with the possibility of another contest in Westminster two years later, for Lord Trentham was forced to present himself for re-election on his appointment to the Admiralty. As in 1741, the Court faction did not anticipate any difficulties. Writing to Lord Gower, Trentham's father in August 1749, Henry Pelham recounted, 'I did privately mention to the Duke of Bedford the public expense and trouble of a Westminster election, which His Grace seem'd to hearken to, but upon an answer which he had from Lord Trentham I find that has no weight in their consideration.'[13]

But events proved otherwise. Gower, by his defection to the Court, had incurred the hatred of his former Tory allies. And his son did not observe the customary procedure of presenting himself for renomination before a general meeting of the inhabitants. One handbill questioned whether this 'did not imply a sovereign sufficiency in himself as well as Contempt of his Electors' and wondered whether 'the Admiral can

[11] See ch. 2.
[12] Harrowby MS 21, pt. 2 (Lincoln's Inn), quoted in Sedgwick (ed.), *Commons 1715–1754*, i. 57.
[13] PRO 30/29/1/11, Granville papers, no. 21, fo. 318.

command what the Lord formerly condescended to solicit'.[14] Finally two local issues, the hostile reception to a French comedy troupe which both Gower and Trentham had patronized, and the uproar over the government's decision to hang one of the six men apprehended in a bawdy-house riot on the Strand in July, provoked a formidable opposition to the Court. One campaigner feared that Trentham's contest against a rather insignificant opponent, Sir George Vandeput, would 'cost him 15 years purchase for the neat income of his Employment'.[15]

The 1749 election turned out to be one of the most violent and vituperative struggles of the first half-century, and it is surprising that historians, with the exception of George Rudé, have paid so little attention to it.[16] As a result of a protracted scrutiny and a parliamentary inquiry the ferment continued for as long as two years, and bore some striking similarities to the Wilkite agitation twenty years later. Nearly 9,500 inhabitants voted in the contest, and even when this number was whittled down to just over 8,000, Lord Trentham emerged with a slender majority of 170. Two petitions were drawn up in protest, both alluding to the returning officer's partiality towards the Court, but neither won a hearing before a hostile Commons. Instead, the Lower House elected to hear the High Bailiff's complaints of intimidation by the Independents, and effectively frustrated an inquiry into his conduct. In the ensuing investigation, Richard Crowle, one of Vandeput's counsel, was found guilty of prolonging the scrutiny; and two other Independents, John Gibson an upholsterer of Covent Garden, and Alexander Murray, brother to Lord Elibank, were charged with using threatening language towards the High Bailiff and with high contempt of the House.[17] Only Murray defiantly resisted the Commons' censure. When he refused to hear his sentence on his knees, Walpole recalled, 'the Speaker stormed, and the House and its honour grew outrageous at the dilemma they were got into'. 'If he gets the better,' he continued in his letter to Horace Mann, 'he will indeed be a

---

[14] West Sussex RO, Goodwood MS 51, fo. 13.
[15] Ibid., fo. 66.
[16] Rudé, *Hanoverian London*, pp. 158–61.
[17] *Commons Journals*, 26, pp. 18–21, 26–7, 31–3, 60–2.

meritorious martyr for the cause.'[18] And that indeed was what
he became; for when the London sheriffs released him from
Newgate during the parliamentary recess, the mob accompanied him to his brother's house in Henrietta Street to the cry
of 'Murray and Liberty'.[19] When Parliament returned in the
autumn of 1751, the Commons hounded Murray out of English
political society by stamping a £500 reward on his recapture.
They also urged the government to prosecute the authors,
publishers, and printers of a pamphlet in his defence. The
administration hardly needed encouragement. They had already arrested the printer and publisher of the tract, one
William Owen of Homer's Head, Temple Bar. A year later he
was acquitted after a seven-hour trial at the Middlesex
Guildhall, a decision in full defiance of all attempts by the
Crown prosecution to restrict the jury's deliberations to the
simple issue of publication alone.[20]

So much then for the broad narrative of events. Throughout
the 1740s, after twenty years of Whig domination, the
Westminster Independents were able to mount a sustained
opposition to the Court, and at a time when the parliamentary
supremacy of the Newcastle Whigs and their allies was at its
zenith, almost managed to defeat one of their prime candidates
on home ground. But what was the social character of this
opposition? Is it possible to find any distinct pattern of
political affiliation among the many social groups in Westminster's wide electorate? Do the elections reveal, as George
Rudé has suggested, a clear correspondence between trade and
independency, with a collateral tendency to vote according to
class and occupation? And if so, in what way did these factors
combine with opinion, influence and corrupt practices in
determining the outcome?

A consistent pattern emerges in the first place from a
geographical analysis of the poll.[21] As Table 5.1 illustrates, in

---

[18] *Walpole Correspondence*, xx. 224 (Walpole to Mann, 6 Feb. 1751).
[19] *Westminster Evening Post*, 25–7 June 1751; *London Evening Post*, 25–7
June 1751.
[20] *Gentleman's Magazine* 22 (1752), 333; *A Complete Collection of State
Trials and Proceedings for High Treason*, 4th edn. (10 vols.; London, 1778),
app. xxiii. 195–208.
[21] The original poll-books for 1749 can be found in Middlesex Rec. Off.
Useful summaries before and after the scrutiny can be found in the *London*

TABLE 5.1. *The Poll for the Westminster Elections 1741 and 1749*

| | 1741 | | | | 1749[a] | |
| | Court | | Independent | | Court | Independent |
	Sundon	Wager	Edwin	Vernon	Trentham	Vandeput
St Margaret/St John	913	958	167	195	1,313 (943)	550 (357)
St George, Hanover Square	569	548	308	334	937 (856)	520 (452)
St James, Piccadilly	844	875	610	632	1,113 (985)	991 (823)
St Anne, Soho	225	240	374	387	342 (322)	366 (345)
St Paul, Covent Garden/ St Martin le Grand	95	104	220	226	204 (186)	264 (238)
St Martin's	728	783	866	894	694 (620)	1,267 (1,145)
St Clement Danes/St Mary le Strand	159	178	616	631	198 (181)[b]	686 (563)[b]
TOTAL	3,533	3,686	3,161	3,299	4,811[b] (4,103)	4,654[b] (3,933)

[a] Figures in parentheses give the final poll after the scrutiny.
[b] 10 votes cast on the first day.

both 1741 and 1749 the Court won a solid majority in four of the nine Westminster parishes. In the fashionable suburbs of St George, Hanover Square, and St James, Piccadilly, they gained a comfortable victory, but it was in St Margaret, Westminster, and St John the Evangelist that their superiority was unsurpassed. Dominated by the deanery of Westminster and the main administrative departments, this electoral parish was very much a Court Preserve. As the opposition press fully realized, it was of decisive importance. Without this overwhelming majority, the Court candidates would have been defeated in both elections.

Whereas 65 per cent of the Court electors came from the four western parishes of the city, the distribution of votes for the Independents was more diffuse. The majority of them, about 45 per cent of the total, came from the commercial parishes of St Martin-in-the-Fields, St Clement Danes, and St Mary le Strand. It was in these three areas, stretching from Temple Bar to Charing Cross, and northwards along Drury Lane and St Martin's Lane to Long Acre, that much of the political activity of the opposition was concentrated. Of the twenty-one taverns opened for Edwin and Vernon in 1741, fifteen were situated in these parishes alone, including seven on the Strand, three at Temple Bar, with the headquarters at the Cross Keys tavern, Charing Cross.[22] The Independents also secured a marginal victory in St Anne, Soho, in both elections, but there were other districts, outside the City precincts, where their interest was strong. In 1741 and again in 1749, they attempted to admit the inhabitants of the Savoy and Cold Bath Fields, Clerkenwell, to the poll. On the sixth day of the first contest huge crowds arrived from Clerkenwell to vote for Vernon and Edwin, only to be rejected by the high bailiff. Both parties agreed to refuse votes from these neighbourhoods in 1749, but the Independents later renounced this understanding and, as Sir Thomas Robinson stated, 'were for opening this channel which might in its consequences pour in a thousand new voters to the Westminster election'.[23] Of the extramural

Evening Post, 7–9 Dec. 1749, and *Whitehall Evening Post*, 14–17 May 1750. See also BL, Lansdowne MS 509B, fo. 562. The parish totals for 1741 are cited in *Westminster Elections 1741–1751* (n.d.), a collection of printed ephemera in the British Library.

[22] Parkes MS 29.   [23] Goodwood MS 51, fo. 60.

inhabitants, only those in St Martin le Grand, a liberty attached to the deanery of Westminster within the City of London, were formally eligible to vote in West End contests. A sanctuary for foreign artisans who wished to evade the trading regulations of the Corporation, the liberty appears to have been dominated by the neighbouring wards of Aldersgate and Farringdon Within, and provided the Independent faction with a phalanx of about a hundred supporters in 1749.[24]

The Court strongholds were therefore in the residential western parishes of Westminster, and as one moves eastwards, away from the great squares and fashionable streets to the more populous and less salubrious districts of the city, and out into the Middlesex parishes of Clerkenwell, so the support for the Independents becomes more pronounced. But does a closer analysis of the 1749 poll confirm this trend? The rough equation between the gentility of the Court vote and the trading character of the Independent was certainly not lost on contemporaries. At the introduction of the Westminster petition of 1741 for example, one commentator noticed that the 3,000 subscribers 'were in general persons of somewhat lower than middling fortunes'. And in 1749, while the Court pamphleteers glossed over the broad social divisions between the two camps, the Independents relished the distinction. 'Do you think these jambefouttres of Tradesmen, Shopkeepers, Tories, Jacobites', one satirically declared, 'can defeat us at the Election! The Impudence of these Bourgeois! To set themselves in Opposition to such a Number of Quality and Distinction.'[25] However, the social gulf that separated the two parties was more than propaganda. It was reflected in the poll. Although there were a number of well-known parliamentarians, magistrates, and lawyers at the forefront of the opposition, the gentry in the main rallied to Lord Trentham in 1749. In the parishes of St Margaret Westminster, Hanover Square, and St James, Piccadilly, the allegiance of the esquire

---

[24] In 1749 30 inhabitants of St Martin le Grand voted for Trentham, 95 for Vandeput. For further information on the liberty see Alfred V. Kempe, *Historical Notes of the Collegiate College of St. Martin le Grand* (London, 1825).

[25] Anon., *The Two Candidates, or Charge and Discharge* [1749], p. 9; Anon., *A true and Impartial Collection of Pieces in Prose and Verse . . . Written and Published on Both Sides . . . during the Contest for the Westminster Election* (London, 1749), p. 22.

and gentleman was overwhelmingly in favour of the Court—as high as 5 : 1 in the first and 3 : 1 in the others.[26] Even in Soho, where Trentham failed to secure an overall majority, eighty-three of the gentry polled in his favour as opposed to twenty-four against. Among the members of Parliament who participated in the contest, moreover, almost 80 per cent sided with the Court. Only a handful of independents—men such as James Peachey, whom Egmont described as 'naturally a republican Whig of levelling and wild notions of government', Country Tories such as the Dashwoods, and allies of the Leicester House coterie—gave their votes and interest to Vandeput.[27] On the commission of the peace too, the pattern was much the same. Seventy-six of the eighty-three magistrates whose names have been traced on the poll opted for Trentham. While some of them lacked the social standing of the parliamentarians, their influence was of equal importance. As the dignitaries of local government they were capable of exerting considerable influence on the Westminster rank and file. There is ample evidence from the pamphlet literature, the Bedford papers, and judicial records, for example, that the more active members of the bench played a partisan role in curtailing the activities of rival mobs at the hustings, arresting their opponent's ringleaders, and countersigning affidavits against injured parties.[28]

While the wealth, social standing, and influence of the gentry provided the Court with a firm base of electoral support,

---

[26] The actual numbers were as follows: St Margaret's (incl. military officers)—Trentham 291, Vandeput 55; St George—Trentham 258, Vandeput 84; St James—Trentham 230, Vandeput 76.

[27] 88 of the 109 parliamentarians sided with the Court. The opposition faction included 10 supporters of Leicester House and 9 Tories.

[28] In 1747 and 1749, two Independent magistrates, Sir Thomas Clarges and John Upton, were involved in legal battles over the arrest of Bedford's bruisers. See [Paul Whitehead], *The Case of the Hon. Alexander Murray Esq.* (London, 1751), pp. 6–12; the *London Evening Post*, 7–10 July 1750. Among the Court faction Henry Fielding appears to have been the most active Justice in 1749. The accounts and expenses bundle of Bedford's election papers, deposited in the Bedford Estate Office reveals that Fielding heard the testimony of several Court voters who claimed that they had been assaulted at the hustings. He also issued a recognizance for Robert Tracey of St Martin's, whom John Moss, a constable of St Paul, Covent Garden, accused of 'assaulting and beating him in the execution of his office'. On 18 Apr. 1750 Tracey's escheat was respited until further notice: Middlesex RO, SR 2832, rec. 205; sessions book 1069/36.

TABLE 5.2. *An Occupational Analysis of the Independent Vote in Seven of the Sixteen Opposition Wards in the 1749 Election.*

	1	2	3	4	5	6	7	TOTAL	%	Independent vote in total vote (%)
Catering trades	27	17	18	11	17	13	17	120	11.6	78
Provision merchants	75	29	14	17	12	7	39	193	18.6	78
Domestic suppliers	11	7	6	9	3	6	10	52	5.0	76
Outfitters	39	43	26	30	44	38	23	243	23.4	78
Liquor trades	10	10	5	1	4	6	5	41	4.0	72
Building trades	31	3	14	13	7	8	8	84	8.1	67
Silk/Cloth trades	3	4	3	2	2	3	9	27	2.6	66
Carrying trades	5	3	1	4	1	1	1	16	1.5	64
Luxury trades										
domestic	12	9	15	3	2	2	–	43	4.1	69
equestrian	5	–	10	1	1	–	–	17	1.6	65
high class	12	8	13	3	7	4	3	50	4.8	77
Book trade	1	3	1	4	1	–	4	14	1.4	54
Leather trade	–	5	2	–	1	–	1	9	0.9	90
Professions	17	–	4	3	3	3	2	32	3.1	60
Gentlemen	16	10	6	10	5	2	2	51	4.9	34
Miscellaneous	21	9	3	1	2	7	2	45	4.3	66

1 St James, Golden Square
2 St Anne's, Leicester Fields
3 St Martin's, New Street
4 St Martin's, Strand
5 St Martin's, Drury Lane
6 St Mary le Strand
7 St Clement Danes, Hollywell

the backbone of the Independent party was trade. With the exception of St George, Hanover Square, well over 90 per cent of the Independent voters in each parish were tradesmen and shopkeepers. As the sample in Table 5.2 shows, the outfitters of Westminster—the tailors, shoemakers, the peruke-makers in particular—constituted the largest single conglomerate of allied trades. Together with the victuallers, innholders, and provision-merchants, they made up over 50 per cent of the rank and file in the Independent strongholds. More important still, these groups showed a marked tendency to vote for Sir George Vandeput rather than Trentham. So too did the liquor trades, the domestic suppliers and curiously enough, the luxury craftsmen, the jewellers, carvers, cabinet-makers, and upholsterers who lived off Golden Square and St Martin's Lane. In fact, aside from the printers and booksellers, the Independents made substantial gains throughout the trading population. Only the gentlemen displayed a firm inclination to support the Court faction in these seven opposition wards.

Moreover, the preponderance of voters for the Independent candidate increases as we move further down the social scale. Of the nine wards in St Martin's only the wealthiest, Charing Cross, with an average annual rental of £34, emerged with a majority for Trentham. In Suffolk Street, Spur Alley, and Exchange, three wards where the average rent ranged between £25 and £30, Vandeput gained a clear victory. But it was in the poor precincts that the support for the Independent was most convincing. In New Street (average annual rental £24.2) 142 votes were cast for Vandeput as opposed to 31 against; in Bedfordbury, a ward in which only 3.2 per cent of the houses could be considered substantial, with a mean rental of under £22, the Independent received 166 votes, the Court candidate 54. And the pattern continues along Long Acre, Drury Lane, and the Strand.[29] Even in the marginal parishes a similar trend is evident. In St Anne's, Soho, for example, the richer ward, King's Square, sided with the Court; the poorer, Leicester

[29] The proportion of Court votes to Independent was as follows: Charing Cross, 166 : 88; Suffolk St., 80 : 92; Exchange, 47 : 88; Spur Alley, 75 : 84; Strand (av. rent £20.9), 33 : 112; Drury Lane (£19.7), 30 : 122; St Mary le Strand (£23.5), 21 : 100; Sheer Lane (£26.4), 50 : 119; Drury Lane (£21.5), 39 : 120; Hollywell Ward (£21.1), 23 : 126; Temple Bar (£15.8), 24 : 62. These figures are only approximate. I have calculated the average rental from the poor-rate

Fields, with the Independent. And in St James, where the Court interest gained an overall majority, the less fashionable wards of Golden Square and Marlborough Street gave Vandeput a victory by 285 : 196 and 231 : 205 respectively.

Quite clearly, then, it was the lower-to-middling tradesmen of Westminster who were the ardent supporters of the Independent cause, and a rough correlation can be made between the genteel character of the Court vote and the *petit-bourgeois* character of their opponents. Such a skeletal analysis however leaves many questions unanswered, and it would be wrong to infer from these trends that the Westminster electorate showed a marked tendency to vote according to class and occupation. In themselves they tell us very little about the operative alignments within the political structure—about the social homogeneity of the trading population, for example, and the complex web of client-relationships which kept the trading population divided amongst itself. Such problems are particularly important for an understanding of the electoral sociology of mid-century Westminster, since the consumer economy of the West End fostered ties of dependency between the 'quality' and the tradesman, and developed the already fine distinctions of status and social esteem within the artisan body. Westminster lacked the large cohesive workforce which was attracted to the wharf-sides of the City of London and to the populous out-parishes to the north and east of the metropolis. Trade within its boundaries was largely created and conditioned by the home market, and judging from the high incidence of casual labour, by the vagaries and vicissitudes of the London season. 'What a swarm of Gardeners, Poulterers, Pastry-Cooks, Eating houses', Defoe exclaimed in 1727, 'are supported by the mere Extraordinaries of Eating.'[30] And he went on to comment, as did his contemporaries, on the astounding development of the luxury trade, and the importance of fashion in its promotion. The whole thrust of the Westminster economy meant that there was a regular

books for the whole ward. When I failed to locate the residence of each voter, I omitted his name from the survey. The poor-rate books are in Westminster Public Library.

[30] Daniel Defoe, *The Compleat Tradesmen* 3rd edn. (2 vols; London, 1732), i. 106; see also 107 ff.

intercourse between the worlds of the gentry and the trader, and this was not without its political repercussions. The economic dependence of the urban tradesman on the profitable custom of the gentleman can, of course, be exaggerated. The demand for luxury goods of all kinds was remarkably pervasive, and it was possible for the small tradesman to build up a solid clientele from the lower-to-middling ranks of urban society. Campbell in his survey of London trades in 1747 cited jewellers who 'work only for the Shopkeepers'.[31] But the very character of Westminster's socio-economic structure, the presence of a fashionable gentry, the lavish expenditure of aristocratic households, not to mention the wide matrix of Court patronage, had a decisive impact on West End politics. If one examines the social permeation of Court and aristocratic clientage, it should be possible to modify, or at any rate complement, Rudé's tentative equation between trade and Independency.

The presence of the main government departments and the royal household within Westminster gave the Court party a ready-made source of electoral influence. The streets and alleys around Whitehall, the royal mews, and the stable yard at St James's were emphatically pro-ministerial precincts. The inhabitants of Scotland Yard, for example, were described in 1749 as 'all Gentlemen that belong to the Court, to the Board of Works . . . all the three yards were Inhabited by people that had places'.[32] It was customary to admit all householders from these areas to the poll, in spite of the fact they were technically non-ratepaying citizens. Vandeput's scrutineers contested this right without success, and had to resign themselves to the disqualification of a few minor Court dependents who lodged elsewhere, or who, as 'the King's menial servants', were excluded from this dispensation.[33] They took exception to

---

[31] Campbell, *London Tradesmen*, p. 143.

[32] Lansdowne MS 509a, fo. 37b.

[33] Ibid., fos. 268–71; Goodwood MS 51, fos. 49, 74. On 5 Jan. 1750, the High Bailiff declared that the franchise fell on the ratepaying householders, the occupiers of Chambers in the Chancery Inns of Court, the watermen of St Margaret and St John, and the inhabitant householders in Whitehall, Scotland Yard, the Royal Mews, and stable yard, St James, 'not being the King's menial servants'. The vote of the inhabitants of St Martin's le Grand was 'left open to future consideration', but they were ultimately admitted.

John Tucker, the admiralty gardener, and to Thomas Lawrence, whose job was 'to look after the Coals and Timber belonging to his Majesty'. And among the other Whitehall residents whose eligibility to vote was questioned we find a handful who considered themselves 'gentlemen' but on closer examination turned out to be a doorman at the admiralty, a 'clerk in the Treasurer of the Chambers Office', a labourers' foreman connected to the Board of Works, some soldiers, and the king's glazier.[34]

Petty officials such as those could generally be relied upon to give their votes to the Court candidates without prior solicitation, and indeed, it was generally assumed that they were under some obligation to do so. Although the main task of co-ordinating the ministerial interest in 1747 and 1749 fell to Bedford House, the Court grandees and their immediate associates nevertheless ensured that their minions fulfilled their obligations to the letter. In 1749 in particular, a close watch was kept on potential backsliders, and concerted attempts were made to ensure that the electoral machine ran smoothly. On 29 November for example, Lord Trentham wrote to the Master of Horse, the duke of Richmond, requesting his services in mobilizing the Royal Mews vote, 'it being infinitely material to us', he added, 'to get a head of the Poll today if possible'. Two days later he begged 'the favour of yr Grace's influence over Greening the King's Corn Chandler in St. James's market who refused to vote'.[35] In cases where more lowly dependents proved recalcitrant, they were blatantly bullied into submission. During the scrutiny, for instance, it was disclosed that John Reddesford, a shoemaker and Chelsea Pensioner who lived in a garret in Green Alley, St Margaret's, 'was taken away by three or 4 gentlemen in a Hackney Coach to Poll and they said if he would not Poll for Lord Trentham they threatened him he should be turned out of his Pension'.[36] More conspicuous retainers might not be badgered in this way, but their insubordination would not escape notice. A 'memorandum of Voters who had not polled'

---

[34] Lansdowne mss 509a, fos. 468b, 521, 554b; 509b, fos. 25–6, 50–3, 466, 509, 524b, 525, 533.
[35] Goodwood ms 51, fos. 51–2, 55.
[36] Lansdowne ms 509b, fo. 39b.

in the Bedford papers shows how intricate the web of Court and aristocratic clientage could be, and how closely it was examined. It contained, among others, the following entries:[37]

Revd Mr. Butler Jnr North St Westr by ye Bishop of Norwich
Mr Hartley King's Messenger Jermyn St to be influenced by Coll Pelham
Mr Cornwall who shows ye Tombs at Westr Abbey—the Bishop of Rochester
William Goodwin Butcher St James's Market by Lady Georgina Spenser & Lord Granville
Charles Light Butcher St James's Markt to be influenced by Lord London (polled).
Mr Blundell a carpenter in the Pay'd Alley by St James Market to be influenced by his Honr Vane & the Duke of Cleveland
Mr Hancock, shoemaker Tothill St by Coll Rossell of 1st Regiment.

Finally a note was made 'to write to Mr Calcraft in Jermyn St over against St James's Church about any business relating to Mr Fox'.

Yet the network of administrative and aristocratic patronage was never simply confined to the more immediate dependents. It reached out, beyond the petty contractors, purveyors, and subalterns of the Court, to envelop a much wider section of the electorate. The local influence of the Treasury, the Horse Guards, and Royal Mews, for example, was powerful enough to mobilize the inhabitants of Charing Cross in favour of Trentham, in marked contrast to the eight other parish precincts in St Martin's, who voted decisively for Vandeput. The tradesmen associated with the royal stables secured 250 votes in their interest alone.[38] The more prominent retainers included Galfridus Mann, a draper on the Strand and a local vestryman; Richard Buckner, the official purveyor of the Stables and the page of the Back Stairs; and Henry Godde, the esquire saddler. The duke of Bedford thought Godde was a little 'cold in ye cause', but with a little goading from Richmond, he ultimately proved faithful to his masters, and brought in some forty electors. A list of his supporters reveals that he could command votes in Clare Market, Covent Garden, and Soho, as

---

[37] Bedford Estate Off., box of election papers for the 1749 election (hereafter Bedford Election Papers), accounts and expenses bundle.
[38] Goodwood MS 51, fo. 39.

well as in the area around Charing Cross. They were drawn moreover from a fairly representative sample of local trades, featuring food retailers, carpenters, bricklayers, as well as watchmakers and high-class saddlers.[39] The web of Court clientage, permeating the lower and middling strata of Westminster society, could prove a remarkably potent political force. The earl of Egmont put its 'dead influence' at 2,000.[40]

Perhaps the best illustration of how extensive such patronage could be was in St Margaret and St John. Court hegemony in this electoral division transformed the parish bureaucracy into a vigorous party machine. In 1741 the vestrymen formally declared their support for the government candidates Sundon and Wager, and distributed 2,000 copies of their resolution throughout the neighbourhood. They also requisitioned the watermen of the parish chest as an ancillary bruising-brigade.[41] In 1749 their activities were even more impressive. As the groundswell of opposition to Trentham reached alarming proportions the Court urged their vestry agents to create hundreds of new voters within the two parishes. They had ample opportunity to do so. It was estimated there were as many as 424 empty houses in the area, and over 1,000 tenants who did not pay the rates.[42] On 4 December Sir Thomas Robinson informed Richmond that it was 'difficult to say when Germination will stop, as an instance 600 more on the Close of Saturday's poll had voted for St Margaret's and St John alone than even polled before', and in another of his dispatches confessed he wished that 'some Supernatural power (for nothing else can) could against the time of the scrutiny conjure up houses for the Nos who have polled without'. But with the help of the overseers the Court brought the situation under

---

[39] There are two lists of Godde's supporters. In the Goodwood list (MS 51, fo. 28) 40 names are mentioned; in the Bedford Election Papers, 62. 42 dependents have been traced on the poll, of whom 38 voted for Trentham. The list included 12 outfitters, 11 food-retailers, and 7 artisans in the luxury trades, principally saddlers.

[40] BL, Add. MS 47098 (F).

[41] Lansdowne MS 509a, fos. 131–3; Stowe MS 354, fo. 244. Westminster Pub. Lib., E 2420, fos. 66–7, 195. Lord Trentham was introduced to the St Margaret's Vestry on 17 June 1747. The assembly promised to promote his and Sir Peter Warren's interest at the general election.

[42] Bedford Election Papers, estimate of Thomas Woodward, General Surveyor of the duty on Horses, 29 Nov. 1749; see also *Remembrancer*, 24 Feb. 1750.

control. Within the month Robinson was able to report that there were only 142 Court supporters not on the parish books and added that 'before the scrutineers get to the Vestry I believe we shall find good reasons to support their votes'.[43]

If the influence of the Court and the main government departments was a significant factor in determining the allegiance of the smaller as well as the more prosperous tradesmen, the power of the aristocratic households was also important. Although many of the nobility preferred to rent fairly modest apartments for the London season rather than build lavish town residences as their Parisian contemporaries did, some aristocratic estates were quite extensive. The Portland property in Soho embraced half the parish in St Anne's; and St Paul, Covent Garden, was quite simply a Bedford domain. The degree of naked coercion, the active intimidation of tenants by the great landlords, was small, even negligible. The structure of urban tenure did not make it a profitable assignment: the estate rentals of Bedford and Portland show that long leases were the norm not the exception, with a high incidence of sub-tenantry. Indeed, the Bedfords sold many of their peripheral properties for a fixed annual rent, a 'fee-farm' as it was called, and had therefore relinquished any general control over them.[44] Of the seventy-two tenants-at-will on the Covent Garden estate, only thirty-two seem to have voted in the 1749 election. Sixteen of them were bold enough to vote for the Independent candidate rather than Bedford's brother-in-law, apparently without receiving eviction orders—with one or two notable exceptions. The only tenant who clearly was penalized for his political affiliations appears to have been Matthew Creighton, an upholsterer on Bedford Street, who actively canvassed for the opposition in Covent Garden, and even testified for them at the scrutiny.[45] The charges that were bandied about the press concerning

---

[43] Goodwood MS 51, fos. 60, 66, 75.

[44] F. H. W. Sheppard (ed.), *Survey of London*, 42 vols. (London, 1900–86), xxxvi. 33.

[45] Greater London RO, E/BER/CG/E/6/2/3-5, Covent Garden Estate Rental 1749–1751. For Creighton's activities during the scrutiny see Lansdowne MS 509b, fo. 278. He was also present at a meeting of the Independent caucus at the Sun tavern, 12 Dec. 1749, according to a report in the Bedford Election Papers, account and expenses bundle.

Bedford's intimidation of his tenants were, therefore, exaggerated. In other neighbourhoods, however, a different picture emerges. A Kensington tailor for example informed Vandeput's election committee 'that he went away at the time of the Election, that he deemed himself a Lodger but he said that his Landlord called and insisted upon his polling & his wife sent for him upon that & he came back & polled'.[46] Similarly, one Daniel Chapman, a broker in Warwick Street, testified that his 'Landlords came to me and insisted upon my going with him & some others to poll'. He 'did the same the Last Election', he added, 'but he slipt away from him then as he had . . . a good many People with him'.[47] So one cannot entirely rule out the direct pressures of landlords upon the humbler voters of Westminster, although, among the more aristocratic property-owners, it does not appear to have been a formidable instrument of control.

But there were other ways of bringing pressure to bear on the West End tradesmen. The most important avenue was custom. The burgeoning luxury-consumption economy of the metropolis, invigorated by the rise of a pseudo-gentry and the pressures of social emulation, bound the urban shopkeepers and craftsmen to the beau monde in a complex system of parasitism and dependency. The gentry were able to exploit such patron–client relationships to advantage. The duke of Richmond for example, compiled a draft letter to his genteel acquaintances, as well as asking his own associates to speak to their tradesmen. 'If you are only a Lodger', he claimed, 'you still must have some interest in Westminster, & your exerting it upon this Occasion will extremely oblige.'[48] Trentham and Bedford, on the other hand, used their servants to rally their dependents. A haberdasher at the King's Arms round Court recalled that 'Mr Mawley came to me yesterday as from my Lord Trentham & asked me if I had polled & about my Vote & he say'd my Lord would be glad to know that I might not give him nor his Friends much trouble'. And William Joyce, a painter in Broad Court, St Martin's, admitted 'that in the time of Polling he thought he had no right to Poll but he was

[46] Lansdowne MS 509a, fos. 528–9.
[47] Lansdowne MS 509b, fo. 375b.
[48] Goodwood MS 51, fo. 41.

solicited to do it & he refused it but he say'd the Duke of Bedford's Steward came & say'd he insisted upon it'.[49] Tradesmen might profess abstinence to escape such pressures—Lord Egmont even mentioned some 'who out of Policy will vote on no side to oblige no Party'[50]—but there is little doubt such pressures were applied.

Patron–client relations might of course involve a reciprocal exchange of goods and services where such manipulation, however implicit, was unnecessary. Many of the more prosperous tradesmen of the West End, the principal beneficiaries of the gentry élite, freely adopted the life-style and political stance of their social superiors. Edward Lyde, for example, an oilman on the Strand who catered for the royal household and nobles such as Earl Fitzwalter, proved a useful ally of the Court in 1749. He was one of the vestrymen in the parish of St Martin's who Bedford's steward thought 'may be depended upon for Lord Trentham'.[51] The influence of such men, the products of aristocratic clientage, was considerable. Take for instance the case of John Phillips, a carpenter in Brook Street, Hanover Square. He inherited from his father a number of long leases from aristocratic landowners, renovating the properties for a peppercorn rent. Throughout the 1740s he received the most renumerative building contracts on Bedford's Covent Garden estate.[52] When he put his interest at the service of Lord Trentham in 1749, he claimed to command the allegiance of almost a hundred voters, though the poll-books suggest it was nearer fifty.[53] Drawn almost totally from the parishes of St

---

[49] Lansdowne MS 509b, fos. 516, 521b.

[50] BL, Add. MS 47098 (F).

[51] 'List of gentlemen of the vestry of St. Martins who may be depended upon for Lord Trentham', Bedford Election Papers, PRO, LS 8/88; Earl Fitzwalter's household accounts in London, Essex RO, D/DM A7, Dec. 1748–Dec. 1749.

[52] Greater London RO, E/BER/CO/E7/2/42, and 45. A general bill for repairs on the estate (Apr. 1746–Nov. 1748) totalled £806. 18s. 0d. Phillips was also paid £634. 3s. 5d. for demolishing and rebuilding the north range of shops in Covent Garden during the summer of 1748.

[53] Bedford Election Papers. 29 of Phillips's men do not appear to have voted in the 1749 election; 43 polled for Trentham; and 15 for Vandeput. James Richardson, a glazier in Little Marlborough St., appears to have been a less flamboyant client of the Bedford household: 18 of his 24 'dependents' voted for the Court; only 2 deserted the ranks for the opposition. His list again included a fairly diverse medley of trades, and all his retainers were drawn from the locality.

James Piccadilly and St George, Hanover Square, his local influence was not simply confined to the building trade and the fifteen householders in his own yard. It included food-retailers of every description—victuallers, butchers, bakers, and greengrocers; several outfitters; a yeoman, Jee Lee of Paradise Row; and several gentlemen.

Wealthy tradesmen such as Phillips were key men in the Court's electoral organization. Thirty-six of the fifty managers whom Bedford hired in 1749 came from this social group.[54] Some were building contractors in the highly profitable urban market, but the majority were in high-class trades for high-class clientele; saddlers, silversmiths, upholsterers, cutlers, and coachmakers. Nathaniel Jeffreys, for example, a manager in St Martin's, was Sword-Cutter to His Majesty.[55] His associate Benjamin Goodison supplied furniture for the royal palaces during 1727–67, and furbished the stately homes of the nobility with the latest London styles.[56] Whatever their rank, there is little doubt that these officers wielded considerable local influence, as employers perhaps, or as vestrymen. Through their mediation the Court faction were able to penetrate the parish assemblies and requalify a markedly higher percentage of contested votes than the opposition, who had singularly few contacts on the vestry floor.[57] Responsive to the commands of the genteel patrons, upon whose custom they relied, they were able to supplement the institutional channels of political influence and extend the web of informal dependence.

One of the managers' prime functions was to supervise the tavern entertainment during the days of the poll. Treating was a customary event in mid-century Westminster elections, and it was practised by both parties. It was one aspect of the Court campaign to which contemporaries did not take exception. The tavern bills in the Bedford papers suggest that it was carried out with a good deal of discrimination. For one thing, it was an expensive business. The duke of Bedford opened 222

[54] Bedford Election Papers, accounts and expenses bundle.
[55] Frederick A. Pottle (ed.), *Boswell's London Journal 1762–63* (London, 1950), p. 60.
[56] Anthony Coleridge, *Chippendale Furniture* (London, 1968), pp. 133–5.
[57] Lansdowne MS 509b, fo. 562.

taverns and coffee houses for his brother-in-law in 1749 at a cost of just under £4,900. In association with Sir Peter Warren, he spent £4,400 in 1747.[58] Not surprisingly, the managers and their subordinates were cautious of the way in which they deployed their master's money. They not only made a concerted effort to bring their 'guests' to poll the following morning—one agent stated he 'had been up Several Nights . . . in order to keep the People together & prepare them for the ensuing day'—but they affixed a list of voters to the tavern bills.[59] A letter from one manager, a timber merchant in Berwick Street, Piccadilly, illustrates the calculating and punctilious spirit in which such transactions were conducted. He told Bedford's steward that he had informed William Rackstraw at the Ham in Wardour Street that he

might open his house to treat those in the interest of Lord Trentham that had not poll'd, and that you'd poll for Lord Trentham, and that he treated no others by my express orders. And for all such as he got, I gave him this liberty, that he might treat them to 3, 4 or not exceeding 5/-a piece, and I would see him paid. The bearer heard me give these orders to Rackstraw, and I believe he got near Twenty votes.[60]

The Court managers allowed generosity to obscure the real purpose of such hospitality. Treating was undoubtedly a reward for unsolicited loyalty. The Court faction spent around £1,800 in 1734 and £500 in 1762 entertaining their stalwarts, even though their candidates were returned unopposed.[61] But these were trifling amounts compared to the sums expended during the 1740s when the ministerial party hoped to enlist many uncommitted voters. It was left to the managers to transform convention into a profitable enterprise.

The activities of the Court managers were never wholly

---

[58] Bedford Election Papers; BL, Add. mss 15, 955, fo. 149, and 15, 957b, fo. 222. The general abstract of electoral expenses in the Bedford papers suggest that with incidental expenses, over £5,000 was spent entertaining the electors in 1747.

[59] Bedford Election Papers: see for example, the list of Noah Cusons at the 'Half Moon', Seven Stairs, in Park St., Grosvenor Square, in the St George bundle; or that of Otmann Muller at the King's Head, Downing St., among the St Margaret's bills. The agent's (Michael Mullwainly) letter is in the inspector's bundle.

[60] Bedford Election Papers, accounts and expenses bundle.

[61] BL, Add. ms 32995, fos. 174–5; Bodleian Lib., Dashwood, 62/2/1-11.

confined to the tavern. They employed more direct methods of enticing individuals to the hustings. In the aftermath of the election it was revealed that a Dutchman from the Hague had been persuaded to vote by the principal manager of St Margaret's, Henry Cheere, a statuary in Old Palace yard. He confessed that 'he was sorry he polled' but 'Mr Chear told him there wod be no Scrutiny'. Similarly, the Knightsbridge agent deluded a local labourer into believing 'that all the people tho' they were Lodgers if their Rent was 40s a year had a Right to poll'.[62] Many of the unsavoury incidents that were revealed during the scrutiny, moreover—the threats, the browbeating, and the ruthless manipulation of the plebeian voters of the West End—were conducted under their aegis. It was the Court praetorians in St Martin's for example, who took hold of a wig-maker from Duke's Court and 'threatened to put him in the Roundhouse for not polling & at last they brought him to Poll Nolens Volens'. And we find that two of the Soho managers themselves were responsible for forcing a journeyman coach-harness-maker to vote against his will, first plying him with drink and then bringing pressure to bear on his master, while two of their colleagues in St Margaret's threatened a cow-keeper and former Chelsea pensioner in Pye Street 'that if he did not poll he should be sent to Guarrison'.[63] These were the henchmen whose activities ultimately determined the strength of the Court vote. Some of them even provided special services. The regular contractors on the Covent Garden estate—Edward Ives, plumber; John Spinnage, painter; William Perrit, carpenter; and Richard Norris, bricklayer and brazier—transformed their work-force into an electoral militia in 1749. From their bills in the Bedford papers it appears that, during the eleven days of the poll, they furnished the Court party with at least 150 bruisers to carry on the battle at the foot of the hustings.[64]

We have seen something of the way in which administrative and aristocratic patronage could be mobilized in the Court

[62] Lansdowne MS 509a, fos. 374b, 526–7.

[63] Lansdowne MSS 509a, fos. 332–3; 509b, fos. 13, 459. The Soho managers were Grandey Hooper, gent., Wardour St., and Thomas Chamberlain, a pewterer in Greek St. In St Margaret's, they were John Jackson, of Tothill St., gent., and Thomas Smith, Esq., of New Palace Yard.

[64] Bedford Election Papers, inspectors bundle.

interest in 1749, and how pervasive this web of influence really was. The power of the political and social élite, the gentry, the Justices, the MPs, the vestry oligarchies, the interest of the royal household, the government departments, and Bedford House—all were at the service of Lord Trentham in 1749. More important still, the network of client-relations which this galaxy of powers could utilize was exceedingly complex. Through the agency of the large urban contractors, the purveyors, and genteel tradesmen of the commercial thorough-fares and *beaux quartiers*, the political influence of the Court penetrated the middling and lower ranks of Westminster society. The vigorous and often ruthless exploitation of clientage by these individuals in particular transformed the servant-economy into a formidable electoral machine.

In view of this it is difficult to make a rigid equation between trade and Independency and the genteel character of the Court vote. Over 70 per cent of Trentham's supporters were drawn from the artisan and shopkeeping class. Certain sectors of the luxury trades, the equestrian crafts in particular, showed a marked tendency to support the Court; but among the others we find that the linen-drapers, whose wealth and polite education entitled them 'to the first Rank of Tradesmen', distributed their votes fairly evenly among the two candidates, while the upholsterers sided emphatically with the Independents.[65] A taxonomy of the urban populace along these lines yields a bewildering picture. Not only is it on occasion misleading—many a pampered servant and liveried guardsman dignified himself with the status of gentleman—but it does not tap the real interplay of social forces at the electoral base. In a constituency such as Westminster, dominated by the gentry and conditioned by the existence of a luxury-consumption economy, the web of political influence cut across trade and occupation. The butchers and poulterers of the two major flesh-markets in the City, for example, showed a sturdy independence to the Court and their market-managers, where-as their companions in Piccadilly, catering to a select clientele,

[65] The totals of Court votes to Independents were as follows: saddlers, 23 : 13; linen-drapers, 33 : 27; cutlers, 11 : 17; upholsterers, 25 : 45; jewellers, 9 : 35.

were more subservient, and were requisitioned by Edward Ives for Bedford's vigilantes.[66]

When we consider the armoury of interest at the Court's disposal it is surprising that their opponents made any showing at all. How then are we to explain the tremendous resurgence of opposition to the government during this decade? Historians have tended to discount the idea that the rank and file were a political force in their own right, and have sought to interpret major electoral contests in terms of intrigue and divisions within the gentlemanly hierarchy. Such a view will not bear examination in mid-century Westminster. There were of course a number of noblemen and local gentry who did lend their services to the anti-ministerial faction during the 1740s. The Prince of Wales, for example, summoned his chairmen to defy Bedford's bruisers at the hustings in 1749, and his Leicester House coterie gave considerable financial support to Sir George Vandeput during the scrutiny which dragged on for six months or so.[67] But the depth of influence, interest, and patronage which these men could mobilize to the advantage of the Independents was minimal, and meagre compared to the clientage of the Court grandees. Their leadership of the Westminster opposition, moreover, was desultory, devious, and not always welcomed. They do not appear to have played a formidable role in the 1741 contest, for Charles Edwin bore the brunt of his own electoral expenses;[68] nor were they assured of an obsequious reception among the lawyers and tradesmen of the Westminster Independents. In 1741, for instance, the Leicester House group under the direction of William Pulteney attempted to cajole the organization into nominating Charles Wyndham as a suitable successor to Admiral Vernon in the Westminster re-election, but the tradesmen on the body resented this intervention and approached Viscount Perceval

---

[66] Bedford Election Papers, inspectors bundle. Edward Ives gave the Piccadilly butchers a total of £14 'for their attendance at the election'. The Clare and Newport Market butchers voted 57 : 14 and 13 : 4 in favour of Vandeput.

[67] Ibid., accounts and expenses bundle, John Becuda's bill; Sedgwick (ed.), *Commons 1715–1754*, i. 287; John Carswell and Lewis A. Dralle (eds.), *The Political Journal of George Bubb Doddington* (Oxford, 1965), p. 31.

[68] BL, Add. MS 47091, fos. 4–5.

instead. 'I found these Men really my Friends', the young nobleman recalled, 'from a kind of freedom wch I had accostumed myself to in dealing with my Inferiors wch being different from ye Insolence generally practiced by Persons of my Rank to that Class of men has upon many occasions done me good service.' Although Leicester House opposed this venture, '& all ye Great Men of the Party did their utmost to prevent it', he continued, 'I was elected one of ye Committee by a considerable majority and leader of the Westminster opposition'.[69] The tradesmen among the Independents, there-fore, were not prepared to relinquish their organization to gentry control. Nor were they blithely deferential to their nominal leaders. They firmly renounced Perceval on his desertion to the Court the following year; and in the bitter factionalism which plagued the pressure-group in 1749 and 1750, during the scrutiny and its aftermath, showed how sensitive they were to manipulation from above.[70]

The reversionary interest and the loose parliamentary con-federation of inveterate Tories and Independents played an incidental role in co-ordinating the activities of the West-minster opposition. As stewards of the Independent Associ-ation, they graced its annual gatherings at Vintner's Hall and periodically supplied it with funds. But they left the running of the society to lesser partisans. From the few reports we have of the Independents it appears that the principal activists were the prominent tradesmen and lawyers of the Strand and the nearby Inns of Court; men such as Matthew Blackiston, a well-known grocer who subsequently pursued a chequered career in City politics; or Samuel Johns, an attorney at Lyons Inn and the Six Clerks Office, regarded by Robinson in December 1749 as 'the Field Marshal & Commander in Chief'.[71] In the event of a fiercely contested election, these men could be relied

---

[69] BL, Add. MS 47091, fos. 4–5.
[70] Maitland, *London*, i. 623–30; Goodwood MS 51, fo. 72. The Independent electors issued three sets of instructions in 1742, in Jan., Feb., and again in Oct.: all demanded à vigorous enquiry into Walpole's misconduct and a Country programme to curtail ministerial influence in the Commons and make it more responsive to the electorate; the October terms were an implicit condem-nation of Perceval's reconciliation with the Court. Perceval replied in *Faction Detected* and there were subsequent rejoinders from the opposition.
[71] Goodwood MS 51, fo. 72.

upon to offer their professional services—drafting petitions, gathering signatures, marshalling evidence of electoral mal-practices. They were joined by a few magistrates with a Tory lineage, and a number of other local dignitaries out of place in Court society. Together they formed an alienated band in a gentlemanly world dominated by Whig orthodoxy. It is not surprising to find they had established links with the anti-Court patriciate in the City of London. As the mainstay of the Independent interest they kept the spirit of opposition alive in Westminster. On three occasions in 1742 they urged their representatives to press for a repeal of the Septennial Act and the reduction of placemen and pensioners within Parliament, and in the final set of Instructions condemned the Commons' lassitude in pursuing an inquiry into Walpole's misconduct.[72] Not an annual meeting passed, moreover, without some reference to the electoral victory of 1741.[73]

The Independent Electors provided an element of continuity to the sustained opposition of the Court in this period. The society functioned principally as an organ of redress, waiting upon events, capitalizing upon electoral irregularities. And it also performed a significant role as the vanguard of the anti-Court interest providing the disparate social groups within the opposition with leadership and unity of purpose. For the artisanate, the independent craftsmen and tradesmen of the eastern parishes, the same hard core which made up the radical rank and file during the seventies, had yet to play an independent role in Westminster elections.[74] We find no evidence of men like Francis Place and his compatriots deliberately pitting their energies and organizational abilities

---

[72] Maitland, *London*, i. 623–30.

[73] Goodwood MS 51, fo. 72; see also *Daily Post*, 5 Nov. 1742; *Westminster Elections 1741–1751*, BL, Add. MSS 32704, fos. 75–6; *Gentleman's Magazine* 17 (1747), 150.

[74] BL, Add. MS 33123, fos. 88–9, 101. Of the 258 radical petitioners of 1774 whose occupational status was known, 93 were classified under trades 'dependant upon the consumption of provisions', 128 were tradesmen 'of the lower class', 22 'of a higher class', and 12 'of the Addition of Gentlemen'. The supplementary lists, however, included only 233 tradesmen and 11 gentlemen. According to my estimate, 54 were provision-merchants, 50 were in the catering or liquor trades, 40 were outfitters, and 29 were in building and its associated crafts.

against wealth, name, and influence. That decisive development, the genesis of a *petit-bourgeois* political consciousness, did not occur until the very end of the century. Instead we detect, within the ebb and flow of events, a congruence of dissimilar and wide-ranging groups, merging together in a chorus of protest to the Whig regime—out-of-place aristocrats, ambitious lawyers, wealthy tradesmen, dissident journalists, independent artisans, and the plebeian rank and file. It was a defensive alliance, a common front against the arbitrary implementation of ministerial power backed by law and privilege, a configuration comparable to the one which rallied to Wilkes, popularly based but 'patrician' or at least professionally dominated. Only in the early nineteenth century do we uncover a greater sensitivity to the authority of the political élite, a suspicion of high-society dissidents, and a higher degree of conscious leadership from within artisan ranks.

This did not mean, of course, that the activities of the subaltern groups within the anti-Court coalition were unimportant. No opposition could have been mounted against such a powerful galaxy of aristocratic powers without the resilient support of the independent craftsmen and the robust advocacy of the plebeian crowd. The spontaneous activities of the latter were indeed decisive. Their rumbustious espousal of Vernon and Murray, their intermittent protest for 'liberty', their defiant stand against the remorseless exploitation of clientage sustained the momentum of protest, indeed determined its intensity. Their participation provoked increasingly aggressive reprisals from the Establishment—troops, organized bullying, electoral chicanery in the vestries—tactics which conceivably opened the door to legal redress and exposed, in its transparency, the brutal logic of patron–client relations in the luxury economy of the West End. Without a militant crowd and a pervasive climate of protest, opposition dissolved (as it did during the 1750s), and the bonds of Court and aristocratic clientage, obfuscating class allegiances, inhibiting their articulation, accentuating deference and dependence, once more prescribed the electoral destiny of Westminster.

6

Urban Surrey and Middlesex

IN early 1742, within two months of the triumph of the
Westminster Independents, a by-election was called in the
county of Surrey. Eight years later, in the wake of the controversial by-election in Westminster, when the Independent
Electors struggled once more to wrest the constituency
from the Court and the big urban patrons such as the duke of
Bedford, another by-election was called in the Home Counties,
this time in Middlesex. Fortunately for the historian, manuscript copies of both polls survive. They enable us to gauge the
sensitivity of the county freeholders at critical junctures in
metropolitan politics, and to test the proposition first advanced by George Rudé, that the Wilkite furore heralded the
advent of the small urban-voter and a new age of open,
independent politics. Was Rudé right? Or did the Walpolean
era (and its protracted aftermath) witness developments on a
similar scale? If the social dimensions of Home County
politics were broadly similar, then our conventional chronology of popular politics, with its purported hiatus in the mid-
century and rejuvenation in the reign of George III (or King
Wilkes) will have to be seriously revised.

THE SURREY BY-ELECTION OF MARCH 1742

During the immediate aftermath of the campaign against
Walpole, within weeks of his fall from power, a by-election
was staged in the county that lay south of the River Thames
and took in Southwark and the sprawling conurbation that
stretched from Lambeth to Bermondsey. The occasion of the
election was the appointment of Charles Calvert, Lord
Baltimore, to the Admiralty Board. The proprietor of Maryland
and its governor in 1732, Baltimore had been returned for
Surrey in 1741 as an opposition Whig who had been active in
the campaign against the 'Great Man'. A Gentleman of the

Bedchamber to the Prince of Wales, he had opposed the
Spanish Convention in 1739 and had helped frame the
controversial motion for Walpole's removal in February 1741.[1]
In spite or perhaps because of this, he was one of the
beneficiaries of the negotiations between the two Courts in the
spring of 1742. His advent to office, like that of William
Pulteney, signalled the end of the opposition Whig alliance
with the Tories and the political survival of the Whig Old
Corps. It was also an affront to those voices in the opposition,
strongly represented in the City of London, who had hoped for
a comprehensive dismissal of Walpolean supporters and their
replacement by a ministry committed to 'patriotic' measures.
In fact, the City Instructions calling for parliamentary reform
and an inquiry into 'all persons who in their respective
Imployments have contributed to the complicated Evils who
have so long oppressed and dishonoured this nation' were
published as the electoral writs were drawn up.[2]

The Court opponents in Surrey made no attempt to run on a
Tory ticket in 1742. No established Tory family had contested
the election since 1722, a fact which underlined the limited
appeal of the True Blue Interest in this predominantly Whig
county. As Arthur Onslow noted, 'the Whig cause' in Surrey
was incontestably dominant.[3] In the circumstances, the anti-
Court forces sought to mobilize support on a platform along
the lines of the Westminster Independents, who had successfully defeated the Court in 1741. Indeed the celebrations of
their victory in December 1741, when every West End street
was said to be ablaze with bonfires and illuminations, must
have been fresh in the memory.[4] Calling themselves the
Independent Electors of Surrey in emulation of their fellows in
the West End, the opposition freeholders campaigned for the
'Freedom of Parliaments' and a public enquiry into Walpole's
mismanagement.[5]

[1] Sedgwick (ed.), *Commons 1715–54*, i. 327, 518–19.
[2] *London Evening Post*, 11–13 Feb. 1742.
[3] *HMC 14th Report*, app. ix, p. 519.
[4] *Norwich Gazette*, 26 Dec.–2 Jan. 1742. The original return was declared
void on 23 Dec. 1741. Perceval and Edwin were chosen as opposition
candidates the following night at the Crown and Anchor on the Strand and
were returned uncontested.
[5] *London Evening Post*, 20–3 Mar. 1742; the *Craftsman*, 27 Mar. 1742.

The brief references to the election in even well-informed newspapers like the *London Evening Post* suggest that the opposition to Lord Baltimore had little time to organize. Even so, 'numerous meetings' were held in London, Southwark, and several market towns in the County to muster support for Woodroffe, the independent candidate.[6] Among other things, opposition freeholders resident in London were offered free coach rides to the hustings at Guildford from Jonathan and Will's coffee-houses in Cornhill, in the heart of the banking quarter. This sort of electoral activity was more than matched by Lord Baltimore, whose supporters organized rendezvous in Westminster, Holborn, and Southwark, as well as at Tom's coffee house in Cornhill. Without doubt, Baltimore's purse proved deeper than his opponent and his electoral machine better oiled. None the less, the virtually unknown and inexperienced Thomas Woodroffe put up a remarkably good showing at the polls. At the end of the first day he was well in the lead. 'The general voice of the People', claimed the *London Evening Post*, 'is FREEDOM and INDEPENDENCY, which is a Proof how almost all would vote were they not *influenc'd* by some means or other.'[7] Ultimately, the combined influence of the two Courts and the Onslow interest, the pre-eminent force in the county, engineered Woodroffe's defeat. But only by twenty-four votes. Indeed, it was asserted that his challenge was only defeated because of the abrupt closure of the poll on the second day, and the refusal of the returning officer to allow the Independent Electors time to organize a thorough scrutiny.[8]

The Surrey by-election suggested that a substantial number of voters were deeply dissatisfied with the reversionary interest's betrayal of the anti-Walpolean coalition in the spring of 1742. The very fact that Woodroffe was able to muster some 1,702 votes in a potential electorate of roughly 4,000—and at relatively short notice—was indicative of the strength of popular feeling against Walpolean politics and Court intrigue. Clearly, many could not be persuaded that Sir Robert's dismissal would change very much, as subsequent events

---

[6] *Norwich Gazette*, 20–7 Mar. 1742.

[7] *London Evening Post*, 23–5 Mar. 1742.

[8] Ibid., 25–7, 27–30 Mar., 1–3 Apr. 1742; *Norwich Gazette*, 27 Mar.–3 Apr. 1742.

disclosed. But from what quarters, one must ask, did this opposition emanate? Was it simply from the old Tory constituency? Or can one detect developments that prefigure the radicalism of the Wilkite era, when Sir Joseph Mawbey mobilized the small urban-voter against the territorial authority of great gentry?[9] These questions need to be answered.

As the manuscript poll[10] of the by-election reveals, several leading members of the London opposition answered the call to vote for Woodroffe. They included Alderman Robert Willimot, the merchant-insurer who first rose to prominence during the campaign against the Excise and represented the City from 1734–41; Alderman Daniel Lambert, a wine merchant, who had just been elected MP for the City on an anti-Walpolean ticket; and William Calvert, the Alderman-brewer of Portsoken ward who was soon to replace Sir Robert Godschall as one of the City's parliamentary representatives. The influence which these men exercised was potentially quite considerable, given their high visibility in City politics. Together with a number of Common Councilmen, they were able to give Woodroffe the edge in the City by 79 : 73.[11] But elsewhere in the metropolis, as Table 6.1 shows, Lord Baltimore held sway.

In Westminster the Independent Electors proved no match for the electoral authority of the Court whose voters included

TABLE 6.1. *Affiliations of the Urban Surrey Freeholders*

	Baltimore	Woodroffe
City of London	73	79
City of Westminster	27	7
Urban Middlesex	81	37
Urban Surrey	144	114
TOTAL	325	237

[9] Namier and Brooke (eds.), *Commons 1754–90*, i. 382–3.

[10] Guildhall Lib., 'The poll . . . March 1741/2 . . . ' (photostat of MS 39291 in BL).

[11] Six Common Councilmen voted for Woodroffe. They were William Bedell, merchant (Vintry); Thomas Eden, merchant (Broad Street); Hugh Knowlings, felt-maker (Broad Street); Thomas Northey, apothecary (Queenhithe); William Prowting, apothecary (Tower), and Isaac Scott, dry-salter (Cripplegate). In City politics all voted for the opposition, save for Bedell.

Henry Pelham, France Fane, the merchant-financier John Gore, and Sir Matthew Decker. In the Court-dominated parish of St Margaret's, where many of the freeholders resided, Woodroffe failed to win a single vote. But even in areas outside the immediate purview of Court influence, Woodroffe found himself in a minority. In urban Middlesex, for example, Lord Baltimore's supporters outnumbered the Independent Electors by 2 : 1. More significantly, in the urban area of the South Bank, where Woodroffe secured the allegiance of the Borough MPs and local brewers, Ralph Thrale and Thomas Inwen, not to mention a number of parish officials, the Independent Electors failed to achieve a majority. The thumping victory achieved by the opposition in the Southwark general election was not replicated by the somewhat more substantial residents, the urban freeholders, some ten months later. Although Woodroffe won Southwark by one vote, he lost ground in Rotherhithe, Vauxhall, and Lambeth, where one presumes that the government shipyards and the influence of the Mitre told against him.

The urban freeholders thus failed to rally to the Independent platform despite the flush of opposition victories in London, Westminster, and Southwark. A longer poll may have redressed the disparity between the two parties to some degree, but it is debatable whether Woodroffe could have made up the eighty-eight votes that separated him from Baltimore. Only in the City of London does the opposition's demand for electoral reform and a clean sweep of the Walpolean ministry appear to have made substantial headway. The gross voting figures might, of course, conceal more subtle differentiations, the equation of urban Independency with the small-to-middling freeholder, for example; but the few soundings I have made suggest that this was not the case.

TABLE 6.2. *The Relative Wealth of the Urban Surrey Freeholders*

	£2–9	10–19	20–9	30–9	40–9	50–99	100+	TOTAL
Baltimore	12	14	11	8	3	9	3	60
Woodroffe	8	13	8	7	6	9	2	53

Note: Wealth is determined by the annual value of their urban residences.

As Table 6.2 shows, there was little to choose between the wealth of Court and Independent voters living in the metropolis. Woodroffe's supporters may have included proportionately more freeholders of middling means, for this small sample probably conceals the concentration of wealth and influence of Baltimore's more prestigious voters in the cities of London and Westminster. Even so, it would be inaccurate to suggest that his opponent did not attract men of considerable wealth. Several of Woodroffe's supporters were respectable merchants, listed in Henry Kent's selective directory of 1734. Apart from the aldermen whom I have already mentioned, they included Sir William Chapman, a merchant of Broad Street, who was a member of the committee appointed to oppose the Excise Bill and an aldermanic candidate in Broad Street ward in 1735.[12] Also among the Independent voters was Hugh Knowlings, a Common Councilman and felt-maker whose business premises in Southwark were insured for £625; Isaac Scott, a dry-salter in Thames Street, whose counting-house, warehouse, and sheds were insured for £1,000; and Thomas Eden, a merchant of Broad Street, who owned tenements in Wandsworth, St Martin-in-the Fields, Shoreditch, and Bishopsgate.[13] Woodroffe may not have gained the allegiance of as many political patrons, financiers, and urban gentry as his opponent, but he was not without men of substance.

What Table 6.2 suggests is that the Surrey by-election of 1742 did not herald a revolt of the small-to-middling urban freeholders against the dominant forces at Court and in the country. Rather, the re-election of Lord Baltimore confirmed the traditional dominance of the Whig interest in urban Surrey, re-enforced in this instance by the influence of the Court. Just as the Whigs had usually secured comfortable majorities in Southwark and the neighbouring urban parishes in earlier Surrey elections,[14] even during the Tory landslide of 1710, so

---

[12] Henderson, *London and the National Government*, pp. 141, 169.

[13] Thomas Eden (Guildhall MS 8674/73, fos. 57–8; 8674/74, fos. 128, 341; 8674/92, fo. 76); Hugh Knowlings (Guildhall MS 8674/77, fo. 214; 8674/94, fo. 29; Guildhall MS 11,936/56, fo. 199); Isaac Scott (Guildhall MS 8674/73, fo. 313). These are the records of the Hand-in-Hand and Sun Fire insurance companies.

[14] The urban Surrey vote 1705–19 was as follows: in 1705, 67 voted Whig and 2 Tory; in 1710, 109 and 77, respectively; and in 1719, 72 and 79, respectively (excluding split votes).

they did again in 1742 (and in an urban electorate that had almost doubled since 1710). Where the Whigs lost ground in 1742 was in the rural rather than the urban parishes. Here Woodroffe secured 1,400 votes to Baltimore's 1,296. In view of the fact that this was prime Onslow country, it requires some comment.

The Onslow family never officially endorsed Baltimore's re-election. In a studied deference to the electorate it did not presume to tie up both seats. Yet there is no doubt that Lord Baltimore was favoured by the Onslows and that the family interest was put at the service of the two Courts. Moreover, Speaker Onslow had ample opportunity to mobilize the country gentry in Lord Baltimore's favour, for the 1742 by-election occurred during the spring Assizes, which were briefly adjourned to permit polling.[15] If one judges from the poll, he fulfilled this task. Of the hundred squires who voted in the election, as many as 77 voted for Baltimore. Of those actually resident in the county, twice as many voted for Baltimore as for Woodroffe.[16] Only the older gentry, those whose families are mentioned in the 1664 Hearth Tax returns, showed any reluctance to do so.[17] Onslow was also able to marshal the clerical vote in favour of the Court candidate, and the evidence shows that they overwhelmingly obliged. Yet, despite this battery of influence, organized by the principal magnate of the county, Baltimore failed to trounce his opponent.

Clearly many of the freeholders paid heed to the rhetoric of the Independent Electors and deplored the apostasy of the Whig opposition, whose actions frustrated the prospect of reform. The strong preference for Woodroffe among the freeholders of the London environs might be explained in this way. Living in places like Putney, Clapham, and Dulwich, they were regularly exposed to metropolitan argument. Among the backwoodsmen the vote against Baltimore may also have registered years of resentment against Whig government, just as it had in other southern counties in 1734.[18] But it seems reasonable to speculate that part of the reason for Baltimore's

---

[15] *London Evening Post*, 25–7 Mar. 1742.

[16] The actual figures were 33 for Baltimore and 17 for Woodroffe.

[17] These families were located in C. A. F. Meekings (ed.), *Surrey Hearth Tax 1664* (Surrey Record Society, 17; London, 1940), nos. xli, xlii. Twelve voted for Baltimore and eight for Woodroffe.

[18] Langford, *The Excise Crisis*, pp. 153–4, 169.

modest showing in the rural parishes was that many free-holders feared that his victory would shore up the county for the Court–Onslow interest and deprive them of even a modicum of choice in the future. A vote for Woodroffe thus became something of a protest against the engrossing influence of the leading family in the county to whom the Court would be indebted for Baltimore's re-election. In this instance Independency meant something rather different from that advocated in London; it addressed the tolerable limits of patrician influence rather than a fulsome freedom of choice. It was not until Sir Joseph Mawbey contested Surrey in the 1770s that the more radical notion of Independence would make real headway, and then with the backing of a more militant body of urban freeholders. Despite the near success of the Independent Electors in 1742, Surrey was still a local society only partially attuned to the political rhythms and discourse of the metro-polis.

THE MIDDLESEX BY-ELECTION OF MARCH 1750

During the protracted scrutiny of the Westminster contest of 1749, a by-election was called in neighbouring Middle-sex. Algernon Seymour, earl of Somerset, died of gout of the stomach in early February 1750, and the earldom of Northumberland fell to his son-in-law, Sir Hugh Smithson, the MP for Middlesex. Sir Hugh's promotion to the Lords meant a fresh election in the county, one which the Court party were optimistic of winning after the resounding defeat of the Tories in 1747. Writing to Bedford three days after Seymour's death, Henry Pelham informed him that Smithson had recommended as a suitable replacement one Fraser Honeywood, a London banker of Presbyterian origin. 'He has a very good estate', Pelham remarked, 'and is a very active Whig . . . I doubt not but with clarity and spirit we shall be able to carry the election.'[19]

Contrary to Pelham's expectations, the city financier failed to win the seat, his second unsuccessful bid to enter the Commons in three years.[20] In a relatively small poll, he

---

[19] Bedford Estate Office, Bedford MS XXV, fo. 69.
[20] Anon., *A Collection of Papers Pro and Con Which have been Published*

secured 1,201 votes out of a total of 2,818. His opponent was George Cooke, a local Middlesex gentleman and Justice of the Peace, one of the more moderate leaders of the Westminster Independents. Cooke had stood for the county in the general election of 1747 but had failed to disassociate himself from those Tory-radicals suspected of Jacobite sympathies. In November 1749 he had initially been proposed as a potential candidate against Lord Trentham in Westminster, but he had declined to stand, presumably in preparation for the impending Middlesex election.[21] His electoral prospects in Middlesex were undoubtedly better, for there he was able to combine local contacts with London affiliations, his association with both Westminster Independents and Leicester House. The Prince of Wales even gave Cooke his public blessing: according to Horace Walpole, Prince Frederick 'sat under the park in his chair', dressed in 'a green frock (and I won't swear but in a Scotch plaid waistcoat)', and 'hallowed the voters to Brentford'.[22] Falling in the wake of the Westminster election of 1749, the Middlesex contest was therefore more than a local affair. It was bound up with the general drift of metropolitan politics since the Forty-Five. From an analysis of a manuscript copy of the poll,[23] together with rate-books, directories, and other records, it is possible to probe the social character of Cooke's support and the sensitivity of the Middlesex freeholders to popular politics in the metropolis. In view of the great appeal John Wilkes made among the smaller freeholders eighteen years later, these questions are of considerable importance.

during the Election of a Knight for the Shire for the County of Middlesex 1750 (London, 1750), p. 22. Honeywood had earlier attempted to buy himself a seat at Shaftesbury.

[21] Anon., *A True and Impartial Collection of Pieces in Prose and Verse Written and Published on Both Sides . . . during the Contest for the Westminster Election 1749*, pp. 2–5.

[22] Walpole to Horace Mann, 11 Mar.1750, *Walpole's Correspondence*, 20. 131. See also Caswell and Dralle (eds.), *Political Journal of Doddington*, pp. 60–1. Doddington reported in his diary that he met Sir Francis Dashwood, Henry Furnese, and Elias Breton at Cooke's house in Lincoln's Inn Fields on the day of the election. They set out together for Brentford via Stanwell Heath, where a general rendezvous of the opposition was made. The Prince of Wales went to Lord Middlesex's at Walton to await the result.

[23] Greater London RO, Acc. 790/81.

A close relationship between Middlesex and London politics was, of course, hardly new. Many of the major figures in the county had intimate contacts in the City, and some of the parliamentary candidates for the county were firmly rooted in the urban milieu. William Withers, for example, an opposition aspirant in 1722, was the son of a former Tory alderman and lord mayor, and the grandson of a long-standing Common Councilman.[24] Sir Francis Child, the London banker and owner of Osterley Park, successfully stood for the county in 1727 and again in 1734. He was the grandson of the lord mayor of 1698/9, had succeeded his brother as Alderman of Farringdon Without, and had himself represented the City from 1722–7. His son was considered as a possible candidate for Middlesex in 1747.[25]

The intimate link between the two constituencies was not solely dependent on such personal associations. The City Sheriffs, annually elected by the Livery, were *ex officio* Sheriffs of Middlesex, and as returning officers could exercise considerable influence in county politics. In 1747, for example, sheriffs Alsop and Winterbottom actively promoted the candidature of Sir Roger Newdigate and kept their friends in close touch with the temper of opinion on the grand jury.[26] Overtures were made among the Tory and independent MPs whose freeholds lay in the West End, and among the Independent Electors of Westminster, for both Matthew Blackiston and his father were listed as certain Tory supporters.[27] Sir Roger also went to Vintners' Hall to enlist the aid of Lord Mayor William Benn, who promised he 'wd do all he cd'.[28] His friends canvassed for

[24] Beaven, *Aldermen*, ii. 119; J. R. Woodhead, *Rulers of London 1660–1689* (London, 1965), p. 179. William Withers's father was alderman of Farringdon Within 1689–1721; mayor 1707/8; and MP for London in 1701, 1707–15. He also stood in 1705 and 1715. Withers's grandfather had been a linen-draper on Cheapside and a Tory Common Councilman for Cheap ward 1660–89.

[25] Greater London RO, Acc. 1085 (the election diary of Sir Roger Newdigate, 14 May 1747).

[26] Ibid. On 25 May 1747, Thomas Carew reported that Winterbottom had informed him that Sir Hugh Smithson was to be nominated as foreman of the grand jury. Winterbottom, Newdigate noted, 'desired I wd engage my Friends & serve ye next term'. On 9 June 1747, however, Sir Roger declined to stand.

[27] Warwickshire RO, CR 136/A 253 (a fragment of the Middlesex poll 1747). The poll lists only three of the four candidates in the election (Smithson, Newdigate, and Cooke, but not Beauchamp Proctor): it is probably a canvasser's electoral forecast, listing pledged votes.

[28] Greater London RO, Acc. 1085, entry for 14 May 1747.

votes among other City dignitaries: Aldermen Francis
Cockayne and Crisp Gascoyne; bankers Richard and Henry
Hoare of Fleet Street; financiers Roger Drake and the
Lethieullier brothers.[29] Indeed Newdigate's diary, from which
this information is derived, reveals in some detail how closely
City sheriffs and other members of the Corporation were
bound up with Middlesex politics. The locus of electoral
activity was centred as much upon the metropolis as the rural
Hundreds.

This was hardly surprising. A good proportion of the
Middlesex freeholds were situated within the London suburbs, in Westminster, Holborn, Finsbury, and the East End. In
the early decades of the century over 50 per cent of the
Middlesex voters came from these areas, and by 1768 the
proportion of urban freeholders had increased to 60 per cent of
the total.[30] Few of these were liverymen, notwithstanding the
well-publicized migration of City tradesmen away from the
inner core of the capital. In 1751 it was estimated that 463
liverymen lived in Middlesex, mainly in Clerkenwell, Shoreditch, and Wapping and the urban hamlets of the east such as
Hackney and Bow.[31] But very few appear to have been
freeholders, and fewer than twenty actually voted in the 1750
by-election. Nevertheless, whether the urban freeholders were
formally associated with the Corporation or not, the close
proximity of such a large body of county voters to the cities of
Westminster and London meant that Middlesex elections were
particularly susceptible to the impact of metropolitan politics.

This is quite evident even in rural Middlesex, for its social
and economic development was heavily shaped by the tremendous expansion of the London consumer-market. To the west
of the City, from Kensington to Hammersmith and out along
the Thames to Chiswick and Twickenham, a surburban fruit-
industry had arisen during the seventeenth century.[32] In the
area between the two great arterial roads of the west, centering
on Heston, Cranford, and Norwood, some 7,000 acres of land

[29] Ibid., entry for 23 May 1747.
[30] The percentage of urban voters was 51.2 in 1705, 54.4 in 1750, and c.61 in
1768. See 1705 and 1750 polls, and Rudé, *Wilkes and Liberty*, p. 80.
[31] Anon., *Number of Liverymen in London Wards and Neighbouring
Countries 1751*, pp. 79–85.
[32] F. J. Fisher, 'The Development of the London Food Market 1540–1640',
Economic History Review[1], 5 (1934–5), 55.

were devoted to wheat cultivation and the production of straw for London stables. Much of the economic activity of the larger towns, suitably situated on the major routes to the capital, was also intimately associated with the metropolitan market. London had few facilities for malting and milling, and so townships such as Brentford, Ealing, and Enfield became distribution centres for corn from the West and the Midlands, with London wholesalers competing with provincial dealers for a share in the trade.[33] The prosperity of these centres on the northern trunk roads certainly impressed Defoe. In his tour of 1725 he commended the new buildings 'belonging to the middle sort of mankind, grown wealthy by trade, who still taste of London'.[34]

It was in settlements such as these that political conflicts generated in the capital had an immediate impact. An analysis of the electoral patterns in 1705 and 1710 confirms this impression.[35] In both these elections Middlesex followed the trend set in the metropolis, electing two Whigs in the first contest and two Tories in the second. The swing towards the Tories in the wake of the Sacheverell trial was approximately the same in the urban and rural areas, but outside the capital the general trend was far more pronounced in the emergent commercial settlements. Thus in the market-gardening region of Kensington and Isleworth, the Whigs secured a majority of votes in 1705, the Tories in 1710. The shift of allegiance from Whig to Tory was even more emphatic in Brentford, where the poll was held, and in the marketing centres of Enfield and Edmonton to the north. In the more rural Hundreds of Spelthorne, Elthorne, and Gore, the pattern was correspondingly more static. In 1705, 1710, and again in 1715, this rustic sub-region provided the Tory candidates with a solid body of supporters.

In the by-election of 1750 the western Hundreds on the periphery of the county once more reaffirmed their allegiance to the Country Tory candidate, George Cooke. The mainstay

[33] Michael Robbins, *Middlesex* (London, 1953), pp. 34–52; Fisher, 'London Food Market', *Economic History Review* (1934–5), 60.

[34] Daniel Defoe, *A Tour through the Whole Island of Great Britain* (London, 1724/5; I refer to the Penguin ed., Harmondsworth, 1971), p. 338.

[35] The following comments are based on an analysis of the 1705 and 1710 polls in Chiswick Public Library.

of Cooke's support lay predictably in the Hundred of Elthorne, where he himself was a prominent landowner. His father, a well-known protonotary of the Court of Common Pleas, had created the Breakspear estate near Harefield in 1713, and his son, in the year of his election to Parliament, added several farms with some 400 acres of land to the family inheritance.[36]

TABLE 6.3. *The Middlesex By-Election of 1750: Aggregate Voting Patterns*

	Cooke	Honeywood
Rural		
Rural Finsbury	19	12
Kensington	132	89
Edmonton	128	83
Isleworth	45	48
Gore	97	48
Elthorne	223	61
Spelthorne	133	115
Rural total	777	456
% of total vote	63	37
% of own vote[a]	48	38
Urban		
Westminster	212	231
Holborn	109	79
Finsbury	99	88
Tower	272	260
Inns of Court	76	54
Urban total	768	712
% of total vote	52	48
% of own vote[a]	48	59
Unlocated	62	33
TOTAL	1,607	1,201

[a] I include the unlocated votes in the total.

[36] William F. Vernon, *Notes on the Parish of Harefield, County of Middlesex* (London, 1872), p. 22. Cooke also purchased some mills on the Colne from Sir Roger Newdigate and in 1758 he bought Evesden farm and fishery from William Ashby of Breakspear.

But Cooke also did well in the districts of Elthorne and Gore, especially among the gentlemen and clergy of the area. Only two of the twelve clergymen who voted in the election sided with the government; only two of the ten Justices resident in the area did so as well. Both of these men, Lewis Way and William Mellish, were financiers with very tenous links in the county. They could not compete with the influence that men like Sir Roger Newdigate, lord of Harefield Manor, could bring to the opposition cause.

Cooke thus emerged with a solid base of support from the rural Hundreds, securing 63 per cent of the vote. His opponent, Fraser Honeywood, gained a marginal victory in Isleworth, where his mentor Smithson wielded considerable power by virtue of his newly acquired inheritance. He also narrowed Cooke's majority in Spelthorne Hundred, where the Somerset interest ran firmly in favour of the Court. But elsewhere Cooke won comfortably. A local man known for his 'Humanity to his Tenants' and his benevolence to the poor, his grass-roots reputation was too solid for Honeywood, whose links with the county were more fragile and selective. As Tables 6.4 and 6.5

TABLE 6.4. *Electoral Majorities in Rural Middlesex (%)*

Parishes	1705		1710		1750	
	Tory	Whig	Tory	Whig	Tory	Whig
0–10 voters	15.4	5.8	19.2	0	10.6	4.3
11–25 voters	21.1	5.8	26.9	5.8	36.2	10.6
26–50 voters	25.0	9.6	21.1	1.9	17.0	6.4
over 50	7.7	7.7	13.5	1.9	8.5	0

TABLE 6.5. *Distribution of Vote in Rural Hundreds 1750*

Parishes	No. votes	Honeywood (%)	Cooke (%)
0–10 voters	57	38.6	61.4
11–25 voters	447	37.1	62.9
26–50 voters	464	40.3	59.7
over 50	265	28.3	71.7

Note: This Table excludes voters from those parishes which did not return a clear majority for one of the parties.

show, Cooke's victory was not confined to any particular sector of the rural population. He secured solid majorities among the smaller villages as well as the market towns. Only in the villages with 26–50 voters did his overall electoral majority fall below 60 per cent, and then by a mere fraction. From the long-term view, in fact, Cooke reaffirmed the traditional Toryism of the Middlesex backwoods. From the short term he broke the spell of anti-Jacobitism which had compromised his candidature three years earlier. Clearly, the freeholders of the larger townships were prepared to forgive Cooke for his refusal to subscribe to the fund for government aid against the rebels in 1745—prepared even to recognize the legitimacy of his stand for a militia 'as the natural and constitutional strength of the Kingdom' rather than some volunteer force led by Court Whigs.[37] However Jacobitical some of his Westminster friends appeared to be, the rural freeholders saw Cooke as a stolid landowner of the county whose moderation had never seriously been in doubt. Certainly, he seemed more suitable than a relatively unknown financier of dubious talents and religion, for whom the courtiers were beating the bushes and pressuring tenants and clients. In this respect, particular exception was taken to Smithson's aggressive canvassing for Honeywood in the metropolis and the market towns. 'What then must be the consequence of a modern Practice,' one pamphleteer asked, 'when no sooner a Seat becomes vacant in *one* House, but some Member of the *other* immediately issued out his Mandamus to supply it according to his good liking, and expects a blind submission should be paid to his *Lordly Conge D'Elire?*'[38] Smithson's conduct transgressed the boundaries of respect that was normally paid to the freeholders of the Home Counties where territorial influence had to be used with circumspection. After the flamboyant display of aristocratic influence in Westminster, where the duke of Bedford had pulled out all the stops to return his son-in-law, it probably strengthened the prevailing mood of popular anti-ministerialism and made the government's Jacobitical jibes and innuendos seem shallow.[39]

---

[37] *A Collection of Papers Pro and Con*, p. 13.
[38] Ibid. 32–3.
[39] Ibid. 12.

Cooke, then, secured a solid foothold in the rural Hundreds of Middlesex. As a respected magistrate, landowner, and familiar figure in the county, he recovered the rural vote from a Whig party which had successfully played the anti-Jacobite card some three years earlier. In the metropolis, too, Cooke clearly recaptured many voters from the Whig fold. In the Tower division, where the Whigs had traditionally done well, Cooke edged ahead of his opponent by a vote of 272 : 260. In the divisions of Finsbury and Holborn, where the electorate had previously been quite volatile, Cooke won easily, winning 208 votes to Honeywood's 167. Only in Westminster, where the Court interest was securely entrenched, did Honeywood emerge with a majority. Cooke, of course, attracted the Independent vote in Westminster. Sir George Vandeput publicly supported Cooke, even though he held no freehold in the county,[40] and among those who actually polled for him were Sir Francis Dashwood, Admiral Vernon, the earl of Egmont (then the leader of the Leicester House coterie), and the flamboyant Alexander Murray, not yet a martyr to liberty. Yet, despite the number of opposition celebrities who rallied to him, Cooke narrowly lost in the West End by a vote of 212 : 231. He repaired the balance, however, by capturing the bulk of the legal profession, those who held offices or owned freeholds within the Inns of Court. Here his family and political contacts—several of his associates among the Westminster Independents were lawyers—held him in good stead.

Yet, from an overall perspective, Cooke did not fare as well in the metropolis as he did among the rural Hundreds and market towns. Although the urban freeholders made up 55 per cent of the 1750 poll, 48 per cent of Cooke's supporters as opposed to 59 per cent of Honeywood's came from the metropolitan area. The size of Cooke's overall majority was not, therefore, entirely sustained in the urban parishes. While he secured 57 per cent of the total vote, he won the support of 52 per cent of the urban freeholders. Even if one concentrates on the suburbs outside Westminster where the Court influence was less pervasive, the general pattern remains the same. As in 1710, so in 1750; the Tory candidate only partially fractured

[40] *A Collection of Papers Pro and Con*, p. 27.

the Court Whig's urban base. The striking polarization of the town–country vote, one of the outstanding features of the Wilkite elections eighteen years later, had yet to emerge.[41]

But if Cooke's victory in urban Middlesex was less than overwhelming, were the social configurations of his support different from those of his opponent's? Did the vigorous campaign of the Westminster Independents, with whom Cooke was implicated, radically affect the political behaviour of the humbler freeholder? The *St James's Chronicle* certainly thought so. Commenting in March 1768 on Wilkes's popularity in the eastern division of the county, it added in retrospect that 'Mr. Cooke, in his former contest with Mr. Honeywood, greatly availed himself of this numerous body of little freeholders'.[42] From the rate-books of the suburban parishes, located in nine different archives, it has been possible to test this hypothesis.

Such an analysis is fraught with difficulties. Multiple-property holders escape note since only one freehold per voter was recorded on the manuscript poll. Furthermore, many urban voters did not reside in their freeholds, and where multiple tenancies existed, their properties often proved difficult to trace. Any survey is therefore skewed against the wealthy proprietor, and, because of the difficulties of tracing names in the poorer, populous parishes, against the minor freeholder. Nevertheless, these biases apply equally to both parties, and as far as possible I have sought to balance my sample according to the actual distribution of votes in each division. From an analysis of the properties of half the urban voters (Table 6.6), some tentative conclusions can be drawn.

The pattern that does emerge contradicts rather than confirms the judgment of the *St James's Chronicle*. If one calculates from the figures in Table 6.6, the average annual value of the property of Whig voters is found to be £35.4; the corresponding figure for the Country Tory voters was £30.9. In Westminster there was little to choose between the two groups, whereas in the liberties and out-parishes of Holborn and Finsbury the mean freehold value for the Court Whigs was significantly

[41] Rudé, *Wilkes and Liberty*, pp. 80–1.
[42] Ibid. 75n.

TABLE 6.6. *Annual Value of Freeholders' Properties 1750*

Division	Honeywood			Cooke		
	Votes	No. fds.	Av. value (£s)	Votes	No. fds.	Av. value (£s)
Westminster	223	135	48.5	212	125	45.3
Holborn	79	35	48.2	109	44	32.0
Finsbury	88	36	29.0	99	46	22.7
Tower	255	114	17.9	257	122	27.3
TOTAL	645	320		677	337	

TABLE 6.7. *Frequency Distribution of the Freeholds of the Urban Voters*

£	0–9	10–19	20–9	30–9	40–9	50–9	60–9	70–9	80–9	90–9	100–49	150
Whig (%)	21.6	26.2	12.5	10.5	9.3	6.4	2.4	3.0	0.9	0.6	3.0	3.0
Tory (%)	19.5	26.2	17.3	10.5	6.8	3.4	2.8	3.1	2.5	0.3	5.2	2.5

higher, £48.2 and £29, as opposed to £32 and £22.7. But this was offset by the wealth of the opposition electors in Tower division. Here the properties of Cooke's supporters averaged £27.3 per annum, Fraser Honeywood's only £17.9.

Table 6.7 shows that all sectors of the urban electorate were evenly dispersed between the two parties. Although a slightly higher proportion of the Whig voters was drawn from the very bottom of the electoral scale, 80 per cent of the Whig freeholds and 73.5 per cent of the Tory freeholds were valued at under £50 per annum. At the very apex of the urban electorate, 6 per cent of Honeywood's supporters and 7.7 per cent of Cooke's owned property assessed at £100 per annum or over. The median freehold values were also very similar, £21.25 for the Court Whigs and £22.9 for the opposition.[43] In other words, there were very few differences between the two parties in the overall distribution of wealth.

Unlike John Wilkes, therefore, George Cooke failed to tap the allegiance of the lesser freeholders of the urban out-parishes. They were not in any case a very significant force in 1750, forming little more than 20 per cent of the urban

[43] Quartile deviation: Whig 22.41; Tory 23.43. Mean deviation: Whig 21.3; Tory 22.1.

electorate as opposed to approximately 57 per cent eighteen years later.[44] Indeed, it seems likely that the tremendously increased fragmentation of suburban freehold properties and their sharp rise in value virtually called the class into existence.[45] At least this seems the logical explanation. What clearly emerges from an analysis of the 1750 poll is that both the humble and middling freeholders of the metropolis showed no preference for Cooke rather than Honeywood. A more selective occupational survey helps to modify, but overall to substantiate, this general conclusion.

Of the 300 urban electors whose social status can be determined from either the 1749 Westminster poll or from the Freeholders' book, over 100 were gentlemen. 40 per cent lived in the fashionable parishes of Westminster and, in an election which they probably regarded as a sequel to the Trentham–Vandeput contest, reaffirmed their allegiance to the Court. Some had even played a significant role in Trentham's victory. Edward Ives, for example, described as an 'esquire' in the Freeholders' book but in reality a prosperous plumber in Bloomsbury market, provided Bedford with a body of hustings-bruisers. Francis Bedwell, a freeholder of St Margaret's, had been a Court manager in his resident parish. With the support of such partisans in the West End and of local neighbours like Sir Dudley Ryder, Stamp Brooksbank, and Peter Muilman in the East, Honeywood emerged with a majority among the urban gentry. He attracted the support of 63 gentlemen, knights, and esquires, 20 more than his opponent. Yet Honeywood never won an outright monopoly of the genteel vote. Local rivals such as Francis Tyssen, a London merchant and lord of Hackney manor, an estate whose rental at the end of the century was assessed at more than £3,000 per annum, gave their interest to Cooke. So, too, did the London liveryman Thomas Foye, whose lands in Whitecross Street and Bunhill

[44] Rudé, *Wilkes and Liberty*, p. 86. Rudé's figures are for the whole county; the percentage in urban Middlesex would undoubtedly have been higher.

[45] This is admittedly guesswork, based on the aggregate totals found in the Freeholder's Books for 1749 and 1768 (Greater London RO, MR/F 8, 12). These list the property-holders liable for jury service, including not only freeholders but copyholders of £10 p.a. and long-lease holders of £20 p.a. In 10 years the number of property holders registered had increased by 66.4%. One would anticipate an even greater expansion of property holdings further down the scale.

Fields, Clerkenwell, were assessed at £108 per annum; not to mention parliamentarians such as Sir Robert Grosvenor, the Tory Member for Chester, and Robert Nugent, the Irish adventurer who sat for St Maws, Cornwall.

Within the legal profession, moreover, Cooke attracted more votes than his opponent. While 22 of the 48 electors associated with the Inns of Court sided with the opposition, support for Cooke among the legal officers themselves, the clerks and notaries of the Court of Exchequer, Chancery, King's Bench, and Common Pleas, was more impressive. Of the 82 lawyers who voted in 1750, as many as 54 gave him their blessing. Cooke also fared well among the county bench and clergy. Twenty-three magistrates out of a sample of 50 rallied to Cooke; so, too, did 24 of the 41 clergymen who participated in the election. In spite of government favour and the influence of the Somerset interest in the Hundreds of Spelthorne and Isleworth, Honeywood never impaired Cooke's standing with many members of the county and legal establishment.

A slightly different voting-pattern appears among the middling ranks of the urban electorate, the merchants, tradesmen, and shopkeepers of the London suburbs. Most of the food retailers, the victuallers, tavern-keepers, butchers, and bakers, voted for Cooke. So, too, did the craftsmen in the more sophisticated trades, the coach-makers of Long Acre and Pall Mall, and the jewellers and watchmakers of Clerkenwell. By contrast, the outfitters, particularly the hatters and haberdashers of the more fashionable areas, favoured the Court. But apart from these occupations, the votes were fairly evenly distributed. Among the medley of artisans in the building trades, for example, 25 voted for Honeywood and 22 for Cooke. The most prestigious member of the group, George Phillips, the well-to-do architect who pulled down Halifax House in 1725 to accommodate two aristocratic mansions in St James's Square, opted predictably for the Court.[46] But in general support for both candidates permeated all sectors of the building industry, even the boat-building business on the eastern banks of the Thames. Here the most prominent shipwrights voted on opposite sides: John Greaves of Lime-

---

[46] E. Beresford Chancellor, *History of the Squares of London* (London, 1907): see under St James's Square.

house, a substantial freeholder with a personal estate of £250, polled for Honeywood; Thomas Horne, whose premises in Broad Street, Ratcliffe Cross, were valued at £120 per annum, opted for Cooke.[47] A similar division of opinion can be detected among the other manufacturers and merchants of the East End. The liquor trade, for example, voted 8 : 9 in favour of the Tory candidate, with the two largest brewers, Daniel Booth of Old Street and Benjamin Trueman of Brick Lane, in opposite camps.[48]

Thus the analysis by occupation confirms and in part complements the general social pattern. Only the small, independent craftsmen in such trades as watchmaking, cabinet-making, and the provision merchants, showed any distinct bias in favour of the opposition. The more prosperous merchants of the liquor trade, the importers, manufacturers, builders, warehousemen, and wharfingers, showed no clear disposition for either party. In fact, in so far as one can determine the social composition of the electorate, there appears to have been a high degree of correspondence between the two parties. Even within the social élite, Cooke's standing in the county and legal communities offset the predictable gains that his opponent made at Court.

The 1750 Middlesex by-election, then, was hardly a prelude to Wilkite radicalism. It saw no substantial mobilization of the small urban-freeholder against the Court and county establishment. In fact in some respects the 1750 by-election reaffirmed old patterns, underscoring the resilient Toryism of the rural villages and hamlets and asserting a preference for the known and the familiar. Cooke's supporters made much of the fact that he was born in the county, was a prominent landowner with a reputation for paternalism, and had served honourably on the bench. They cast his opponent in the role of an ambitious linen-draper turned banker who had married rich and now sought a parliamentary seat to crown his career.[49]

[47] Four of the smaller shipwrights of Poplar, John Pharoah, Simon Rolt, Richard and John Smith, all with freeholds under £10 p.a. voted for Honeywood. Dryden Smith, a ship carpenter from Hermitage, and Jesse Wade of Poplar, both with freeholds under £20 p.a., supported Cooke.

[48] For further information about the more prominent brewers in London see *VCH Middlesex*, i. 169–78.

[49] *A Collection of Papers Pro and Con*, pp. 23, 44.

With superficial links in the county, Honeywood seemed to be the epitome of the modern, moneyed politician, playing the market in a resolutely Whig world.

Orator Henley depicted the Middlesex contest as the struggle between Old and New England.[50] Although he jested, there was an element of truth in his reflections. Cooke's county pedigree and presence were central to his success. At the same time, his victory would not have been possible without substantial support in the metropolis. Judging from the fragmentary evidence in the 1747 poll,[51] Cooke recovered many votes in Westminster, the City, and the East End, doubtless because, rather than in spite of, his affiliation with the Independent Electors. Indeed, one could argue that Cooke's ability to tap the allegiance of the more volatile sections of the electorate—the urban suburbs and commercial townships—overwhelmingly confirmed his victory. Here, at least, the wave of anti-ministerialism which swept the Westminster hustings in 1749 and sullied the nobility's role in metropolitan politics made its impact. Territorial influence and local standing could never determine Middlesex elections by themselves. They could only provide the base—until 1768, a very essential base—for wider appeals.

CONCLUSION

The analysis of the 1750 Middlesex electorate concludes this section on the sociology of metropolitan politics. In the cities of London and Westminster, the class character of urban politics, mediated by clientage and local in dimension, is revealed. Among the mosaic of trades and occupations in these two constituencies, certain striking alignments appear. In Westminster, the upper ranks of the social hierarchy were, subject to the vicissitudes of parliamentary politics, firmly linked to the Court. Through the intricate web of social and economic clientage, these dignitaries, whether aristocratic landlords, or members of the Court, government, bench, or select vestry, were able to muster a vast army of retainers from

---

[50] Guildhall MS 253, fo. 9.
[51] Warwickshire RO, CR 136/A253. The poll suggests that Cooke did well in urban Finsbury, but not in other parts of the metropolis.

the trading world. Yet although the peculiarities of Westminster's luxury economy accentuated the bonds of deference and clientage and militated against the development of an artisan class-consciousness, the subaltern classes of Westminster nurtured a hostility to the Court and aristocracy which prefigured later developments. Led by a small band of alienated professionals and patricians, the independent craftsmen of Westminster fractured the Court's control of this royal constituency for over a decade and laid the foundations for the more autonomous political groupings of later years.

In the City of London the socio-political configuration was of a somewhat different dimension. In this mercantile stronghold the stalwarts of the Court were the plutocratic élite: the financial speculators, merchants, and wealthly middlemen of the interlocking syndicates and directorates of the money-market. A conspicuous minority of these plutocrats were firmly entrenched in the higher echelons of the major livery companies through which they were able to extend their influence. At the same time City politics revealed deep-rooted divisions within the urban bourgeoisie. Against the moneyed interest and their merchant affiliates were ranged a medley of powerful and articulate groups: bankers outside the mainstream of fiscal capitalism, insurance writers outside the great corporations, Atlantic merchants, independent industrialists, tradesmen with long city pedigrees. There was a coherent anti-establishment in the City, a political caucus of seasoned civic activists firmly linked to the electoral rank and file, to the liverymen and freeman voters of the populous wards. These subordinate elements identified with the City caucus because it was a symbol of London's independent status, an affirmation of the political autonomy of the corporation against the powers of high finance. They advocated a civic populism that did not fit with Whig politics.

In urban Middlesex and Surrey, however, there was a greater degree of similarity between the Court and opposition voters. One finds fewer disparities in wealth and social status and a greater persistence of traditional party voting. The ministerial interest could always count upon the allegiance of the wealthy Westminster freeholders and, in the case of Middlesex, upon the urban clergy and Justices of the Peace. But the wealth and connection of the government was to a large extent matched by that of the City of London within the freehold electorate and by the presence of a minority of substantial landowners within anti-ministerial ranks. More importantly, there was little to choose between the two parties within the trading world. Crude measures of wealth revealed a high degree of correspondence between Court and independent or Tory voters at every level and little occupational differentiation. The political weight of the small urban-freeholder, a crucial factor in the success of Wilkite radicalism, had yet to emerge.

Indeed, the numerical strength of the opposition vote in Middlesex and Surrey lay as much with the rural as with the urban freeholder. And local, as opposed to metropolitan or national issues, were of some importance. George Cooke's victory in Middlesex owed much to his local standing in the county and to the parvenu, sectarian status of his opponent, Fraser Honeywood, a Presbyterian banker who had only recently settled there. Similarly, George Woodroffe drew some of his support from freeholders who feared that the Onslow family would wrap up the constituency for the Court. This is not to suggest that the political battles of the metropolis were inconsequential—they were not—rather that the county by-elections depicted a transitional stage in the development of an urban political consciousness which did not reach fruition until the 1760s. Local county preoccupations continued to mediate the appeal of metropolitan-based reform campaigns.

A study of the electoral sociology of mid-century London thus confirms George Rudé's appraisal of Wilkite radicalism as the first metropolitan movement, a movement which harnessed the support of the lowly suburban freeholder, the small tradesman, the professional, and the middling merchant, as well as the plebeian crowd. The popular contests of the 1730s and 1740s were more limited in scope, more transient in duration, although they raised critical issues about the use and abuse of the law and the nature of political governance upon which Wilkites would build. The mid-century contests also gave adequate testimony to the high level of political articulateness among the craftsmen and shopkeepers of the two cities of the metropolis. Some of the predisposing conditions for the growth of extra-parliamentary radicalism had emerged.

PART III

The Provincial Perspective

7

The Provincial Towns and Cities

When you first appeared in this Place, we did believe you
came to ask Forgiveness for your Behaviour in the last
Parliament, rather than Canvass for a Seat in the new One.
When you knew how well you deserved Curses and rotten
Eggs, to push for a triumphal Chair is a Piece of Assurance
we should be surprized at in any Person who had not
pass'd Seven Years in such Company. Pray, sir, give me
leave to ask you, how you would treat a Tenant who had
by Fraud or Forgery enlarged the Term of his Lease from
Three to Seven Years? And after he had kept Possession of
your Tenement for so long, could modestly tell you, he
was the honestest Man in the World, and the only fit
Person to be your Trustee, Executor, and Guardian to your
Children?

The Freeholder's Journal, 23 March 1721.

Sir Courtly Plume, a Borough Town to buy,
A hundred Guineas gives his new Friend Sly:
Sly gives his Promise, but upon the day,
Carries the Poll a quite contrary Way:
The Poll when over, raging, cries the Knight,
You are John Sly, a — Corporation Bite,
— Cries Sly — We still in Politicks are near
Art London you'd bite us, — we've bit you here.

London Evening Post, 18–21 April 1741.

So far we have examined the politics of the City of London and
the larger metropolis. Now we must move further afield, to the
provinces, so that we may be in a position to offer some
broader generalizations about urban politics in the first half of
the eighteenth century. This is not an easy task. The larger
cities and provincial towns are rarely featured in the more
conventional accounts of extra-parliamentary politics under
the first two Georges. It is generally assumed that the big urban
constituencies were less susceptible to management than the

smaller boroughs and that they sometimes followed London's lead in the periodic crises that shook an otherwise stable political world. But just how sensitive the provincial cities were to developments in the metropolis, and how national their orientation was, remains an open question. Historians have tended to interpret the provincial participation in nation-wide agitations as intermittent and pragmatic, governed as likely as not by the economic interests of ruling élites. In other words, they have been sceptical about the meaning of such activity—whether it can be read as an index of an independent, open politics, or of a widespread, popular antipathy to the Whig regime.

This scepticism is deepened by two historiographical perspectives. The more recent, developed by Plumb, Holmes, and Speck, has argued that the political vitality of the post-Revolution era declined quite dramatically after the Hanoverian accession. The proscription of the Tory party from power, the easing if not demise of party tensions, and the rising cost of elections after the Septennial Act, solidified patronage and reduced the capacity of the smaller voter to exercise his franchise and to change the composition of the Commons. Although the growth of political oligarchy had its greatest impact in the smaller boroughs, the large constituencies did not emerge unscathed. Indeed, Plumb sees a growing divorce between the political establishment and the political nation from the second quarter of the century, with an expanding political public, reaching beyond the electorate itself, increasingly unable to influence the course of politics.

The second and older historiographical tradition casts doubt upon the general level of awareness in eighteenth-century England and is more attentive to the sinews and strategies of political management itself. As early as 1903, Edward Porritt argued that the larger boroughs shared many of the characteristics of electoral venality associated with the unreformed era. In his view 'beer and mob rule' obtained in many big towns, including Colchester, Norwich, and Liverpool, while the swamping of the electorate with new freemen in Bristol, Derby, Gloucester, and Northampton undermined older traditions of civic democracy, rendering them vulnerable to mayoral manipulation and aristocratic management. These practices were often so deeply ingrained that large boroughs were as susceptible to nomination and influence as small, although controlling a big electorate was a riskier enterprise. 'There were no election contests which involved more wear and tear on Parliamentary candidates and larger drafts on bank accounts', Porritt opined, 'than those in freeman boroughs in which electors were counted by the thousand.'[1]

This line of argument was taken up by Namier, although he drew somewhat different conclusions from the evidence. Whereas Porritt tended to cast these illegalities as electoral corruption, Namier portrayed them as electoral convention, as anomalies softened by practice and habit. In his eyes, electoral venality was reciprocal, initiated from above to cater to popular expectations, 'a water spout springing from the rock of freedom to meet the demands of the People'.[2] As such, it formed part of a broader structure of client-politics in which patrons were accorded a stake in borough representation in return for regular benefactions. This structure was deferential in the sense that the larger urban constituencies tended to show a preference for the well-born. Apart from London, only the out-ports showed any preference for their own leaders. Elsewhere traditions ran in favour of the neighbouring nobility and gentry, although some provincial towns did periodically return lawyers immersed in civic business and the local economy. The pattern of urban politics was also particularist, with local issues prevailing over national. Namier's selective vignettes of Bristol, Nottingham, Newcastle, and Canterbury were designed to show the irrelevance or superficiality of national issues to an understanding of urban power-struggles and to detonate any notion of urban democracy or advanced political consciousness. Outside the metropolis, there was no sign of radical or reformist fervour and scarcely a flicker of interest in larger, national questions. Grandee patronage and local issues were the order of the day.

Namier's observations pertained largely to the early years of George III, an era of party fragmentation and stable oligarchy in which political tensions had been assuaged by a series of

---

[1] Edward Porritt, *The Unreformed House of Commons* (Cambridge, 1903), p. 77.

[2] Namier, *The Structure of Politics*, p. 104.

spectacular victories over the French and a mood of national confidence. It is thus important to discover whether his generalizations hold for a different political conjuncture. Certainly, one can discover some of the characteristics which he and Porritt detailed as one moves back in time. In the early Hanoverian decades several large boroughs had well-earned reputations for electoral venality. Colchester, for example, proved quite amenable to the coffers of big City merchants and financiers who had purchased Essex estates and angled for a seat on the Commission of the Peace. Hereford, where the country gentlemen were for the most part too poor to stand for election, also welcomed strangers, at a price; although the duke of Chandos, who described the borough as 'extravagantly expensive', probably thought there were too many John Slys for comfort, for by 1734 his interest was said to be 'quite gone'.[3] Canterbury was also a town where it was felt that 'money will do a great deal'. Other towns were dominated by powerful neighbouring families. The Grosvenors ran Chester; the Comptons and Montagus carved up Northampton. The Selwyns and Lord Bathurst retained a powerful interest in Gloucester. The list could be extended.

Of the twenty-eight freemen or inhabitant boroughs whose electorates approached a 1,000 or more in the period 1700–1750, at least seven returned members or nominees of powerful territorial families on a regular basis.[4] A further four were pretty firmly in the grip of closed Corporations whose power of creating freemen allowed them to beat down potential opponents. The High Church Corporation of Exeter, for instance, tolerated only a brief Whig interlude before it

[3] Sedgwick (ed.), *Commons 1715–54*, i. 258.
[4] The 28 are as follows: Reading, Chester, Exeter, Durham, Colchester, Bristol, Gloucester, Hereford, Canterbury, Lancaster, Liverpool, Preston, Leicester, Norwich, Northampton, Newcastle, Nottingham, Oxford, Bridgnorth, Shrewsbury, Taunton, Southwark, Coventry, Worcester, York, London, Westminster, and Hull. My list is derived from the figures given in Speck, *Tory and Whig*, app. and E. Sedgwick (ed.), *Commons 1715–54, passim*. I have assumed that recorded totals probably underestimate the actual electorate by at least 10% — in my view a conservative estimate given the high turnover in urban electorates. The 7 dominated by neighbouring families were Chester, Durham, Gloucester, Newcastle, Northampton, Nottingham, and Shrewsbury. The 4 dominated by closed Corporations were Exeter, Leicester, Liverpool, and Oxford.

created 240 honorary freemen out of 'the most zealous gentlemen, clergy and attorneys of the Tory party'.[5] Similarly, the Leicester Corporation swamped the electorate to frustrate the Whiggish ambitions of its hosiers.[6] Thus, on a conservative count, a third of the larger boroughs were subject to strong territorial and institutional controls. And if one was to include constituencies like Lancaster and Hull where such influences were quite formidable, the proportion would be higher.

This evidence might be seen as lending weight to Namier's thesis. But appearances can be deceptive. An interest in a large borough had to be carefully cultivated. It lacked the security that came with the purchase of burgage tenures and the patronage that might place a small electorate in a dependent situation. The political networks of major urban centres were complex; the lines of patronage often densely mediated. In some cities such as Durham, the Mitre and the Dean and Chapter exerted an influence that might be independent of both government and landed patrons. Even when they converged, misunderstandings could mitigate their effectiveness. The same was true of Corporations. The Nottingham Corporation's willingness to promote two Whigs in the general election of 1747 compromised the duke of Newcastle's private agreement with Lord Middleton and put paid to the chances of the long-standing incumbent, John Plumptre. On the other hand, decisions in high places could meet with local resistance. In early Hanoverian Coventry, for example, where the Whig corporation faced fierce opposition from the freemen rank and file, the earl of Sunderland was told that his nominee for the 1722 election would unsettle the Whig party and undermine local patronage. Consequently, Sunderland decided 'not to intermeddle with this affair', leaving two local Whig candidates to battle it out against a resurgent, vengeful Tory party under Lord Craven.[7]

Overlapping and sometimes competing interests could complicate the exercise of patronage in large towns. Economic developments could increase their fragility. Whereas economic

---

[5] Sedgwick (ed.), *Commons 1715–54*, i. 227.

[6] Ibid. 276; R. W. Greaves, *The Corporation of Leicester 1689–1836*, reprint (Leicester, 1970), ch. 6.

[7] Sedgwick (ed.), *Commons 1715–54*, i. 340.

decline frequently facilitated the growth of patronage, economic expansion sometimes unsettled it. The rise of the hosiery industry in Nottingham, with its concomitant demand for credit, allowed the local banker, Abel Smith, to build up an electoral interest independent of the landed grandees and to sway elections accordingly. By contrast, the debate over the economic future of Chester nearly wrecked the Grosvenors' hold over the town. In the 1730s local Whigs challenged the family's control over the Corporation by launching a campaign to deepen the river Dee in an effort to revive the city's trade. The proposal would have prejudiced the interests of those landowners who owned the salt flats of the Wirral, and when Sir Richard Grosvenor appeared reluctant to move on the issue, his family and the Corporation were 'daily insulted', and his political dominance put to the test. In a violent and raucous contest in which both sides brought in bruisers to intimidate the other, Sir Richard had to lay out £18,000 to retain control of freeman creations.[8] This and his civic benefactions kept his political machine intact, but it was his ultimate willingness to negotiate with local landowners and townsmen over the navigation of the Dee that assured his family's continued supremacy in Chester politics. Patrons had to deliver, and this meant more than festive largesse and annual doles.

The constraints upon the exercise of patronage that I have cited would not have troubled Namier, but they appear to have been more conspicuous in the early Hanoverian era than in the mid-century decades. Gentry control over large boroughs was further limited by the persistence of party strife, especially in towns with a conspicuous nonconformist presence. In Bristol, Newcastle, and Norwich, for example, at least 85 per cent of the electorate voted along party lines during the reigns of George I and II.[9] In Shrewsbury, where a Dissenting meeting-house had been burned down in 1715, less than 3 per cent of a greatly reduced electorate split their votes some thirty-two years later. The same was true of Leicester; 99 per cent of Whig

---

[8] Sedgwick (ed.), *Commons 1715–54*, i. 203–4, 301–2; J. S. Morrill, 'Chester 1660–1832', in *VCH Cheshire* (Oxford, 1979), ii. 127–35.

[9] For Newcastle see Kathleen Wilson, 'The Rejection of Deference: Urban Political Culture in England 1715–1785', Ph.D. thesis (Yale, 1985), p. 208; for Bristol and Norwich see subsequent Chapters.

voters plumped for Mitford in 1754.[10] Such sectarian tensions, heightened by the visibility of Dissent in town politics and scarcely abated by the Whig policy of religious toleration, increased the likelihood of electoral contests and strained the sinews of patronage. So, too, did the sensitivity of the urban electorate to national issues. Contrary to the Namierites, issues did sway voters in the larger towns. Following a rash of Coronation-day riots in some twenty-seven English towns, the first Hanoverian election was fought over the partisan nature of George I's government and the security of the Protestant succession. In 1734, in particular, national issues reverberated through the market squares, taverns, and town halls. At the nomination for the Country-Tory candidates at Preston, it was reported that 'the general cry among the People was Liberty and Property, Triennial Parliaments and No Excise'.[11] A month later the leading Whig, Sir Henry Hoghton, reported to Walpole that he found the town 'in such a high spirit'. He went on to complain that Lord Derby, 'on account of the excise and other unpopular votes this session (which now I feel the weight of)', was now his 'declared enemy'.[12] Similarly, at York the Excise bit into Whig support. Sir John Bland enthusiastically wrote to the Tory Lord Strafford that

We found that Town in generall most Zealously affected towards Us, and the populace so Exasperated against our opponents that it was not in our power to prevent them assembling in a very great Number and shewing their dislike to them. I believe we had hearty promises from at least two thirds of the voters in that City and from almost All the Country votes we met with in the Streets, and many of the principall Citizens offer'd their Services to Sir J. Kaye and Mr. Duncomb, pressing them to offer themselves Candidates for the City at the next general election.[13]

In the event the voters of Preston and York were denied the opportunity of exercising their choice, although their vociferous opposition to the Excise and the continuance of the

[10] J. F. A. Mason, 'Parliamentary Representation', in G. C. Baugh (ed.), *VCH Shropshire* (Oxford, 1979), iii. 268; Greaves, *Corporation of Leicester*, p. 102.

[11] *London Evening Post*, 9–12 Mar. 1734.

[12] Sedgwick (ed.), *Commons 1715–54*, i. 273.

[13] James J. Cartwright (ed.), *The Wentworth Papers 1705–1739* (London, 1883), pp. 489–90. See also J. F. Quinn, 'York Elections in the Age of Walpole', *Northern History*, 22 (1986), 181–2.

Septennial Act undoubtedly affected the nature of the electoral arrangement. But elsewhere, as Paul Langford has shown, the popular voice scored some victories. In the county and urban constituencies with over 1,000 voters, the ministry lost 21 seats.[14] According to the calculations in the *London Evening Post*, the 52 chief towns and cities in England returned 67 opposition members and only 36 ministerial. Together with the county results, the opposition could claim 131 seats, the Walpolean Whigs a mere 52. As the *Craftsman* and other opposition newspapers insisted, the 'Sense of the People' was on their side. It was only the ministry's grip on the 'little beggarly boroughs' that frustrated the wishes of the independent electorate and allowed Walpole's government to survive.[15]

National issues, then, could alter the balance of forces in the large, urban constituencies, and in the early Hanoverian era at least, a divided political élite was prepared to give the freeman and resident householders an opportunity to do so. Contrary to received opinion, which has generalized the electoral experience of the populous constituencies from the county record alone, urban contests actually increased during the Hanoverian era. Among the twenty-eight large urban boroughs, there were 102 contests in the six general elections in the period 1715–47, as opposed to 91 in the period 1722–61. Even if we extend the calculations into the 'Namierite' decades, the same result emerges. In the seven general elections in the period 1722–61 there were 111 contests as opposed to 105 in the elections in the period 1701–15. Whichever comparison we make, it is clear that the big cities were electorally more contentious in the Hanoverian decades than in the Augustan, hitherto enshrined as the great age of political vitality.

Uncontested elections are, of course, an imperfect index of political contention because they could be the result of a very temporary respite from party struggle, brought on by financial exhaustion or disconsolate leadership. The point is nowhere better illustrated than in 1741, when the number of uncontested elections in my urban sample rose from 6 to 13, that is,

[14] Langford, *The Excise Crisis* (Oxford, 1975), pp. 130, 138–9.
[15] The *Craftsman*, 25 May 1734; *London Evening Post*, 30 May–1 June, 6–8 June 1734.

from 21 to 46 per cent.[16] This increase was not, however, a reflection of political stultification, nor of any great disposition to political compromise. In only two, possibly three, cases was there any inclination between rival factions to share the seats. And only in a further four was the constituency sewn up by electoral manipulation or unassailable electoral supremacy. In many cases, the absence of a contest represented a hiatus in political activity brought on by ruinous expenses and electoral setbacks in 1734—compounded, in the case of the ministerial Whigs, by a keen knowledge of Walpole's continuing unpopularity.

A better index of the political vitality of the large urban constituencies would be the relative strength of the parties over time. The general trends can be detected from the psephological profile.[17] The table reveals some interesting fluctuations in party support among the twenty-eight large urban constituencies. It suggests, in fact, that the big towns and cities were a fairly accurate barometer of popular electoral opinion, even allowing for the mediating factors of political patronage and corrupt practice. The Whigs held their own in the first three Hanoverian elections, profiting from the anxieties over the Protestant succession and successive Jacobite scares; although their electoral performance was doubtless improved by the demoralization of the Tory party after the impeachment of its leaders and the banishment of Atterbury, and by what the *Craftsman* aptly referred to as 'Weeding the House', that is, partisan decisions upon controverted elections.

TABLE 7.1. *Seats in Urban Constituencies 1715–1747*

	1715	1722	1727	1734	1741	1747
Whig	35	36	35	27	18	31
Opp. Whig	0	1	5	10	13	7
Tory	23	21	18	21	27	20

[16] The number of uncontested elections during the early Hanoverian era was as follows: 10 in 1715, 5 in 1722, 10 in 1727, 6 in 1734, 13 in 1741, and 16 in 1747.

[17] My calculations are derived from Sedgwick (ed.), *Commons 1715–54*.

As a result of the Excise crisis, however, the party's fortunes began to slip, especially if one adds a record of the medium-sized boroughs to the twenty-eight large ones considered here. By 1741, as Walpole's unpopularity deepened and as opposition confidence grew, urban support for the ministry fell to an all-time low. It took another Jacobite rebellion and divisions within opposition ranks over the price of their collaboration with the Pelhams in 1745 to resuscitate Whig urban representation. As in the early Hanoverian decades, so in 1747, the Whig party fared best when it could pose as the only reliable bulwark of dynastic stability.

Table 7.1 also reveals what has been emphasized by Linda Colley, that the Tory party rode the popular tide during the 1730s and early 1740s.[18] But, in addition, it discloses what she has consistently underplayed, the growing importance of opposition Whig representation in the large towns. Walpole's disregard for talent within his own party, his denial of full civic rights for Dissenters, his dogged defence of measures deemed incompatible with real Whiggery—all combined to raise the dissident Whig presence in large urban constituencies. So, too, did the call for a renunciation of traditional party affiliations in order to build a powerful Country interest in opposition to the Court, one vigorously advocated by opposition newspapers in 1734 and 1741. Without doubt this appeal sometimes meant no more than a tactical alliance of anti-Walpolean forces. Sometimes the Country banner was a catchword. Fielding's Country candidates in *Pasquin*, Sir Henry Fox-Chase and Squire Tankard, were stereotypical Tory country gentlemen. But it did score some notable successes, especially in London and the Home Counties. Drawing upon the political experience of the City, which had successfully run opposition Whig and Tory candidates on the same slate in the 1720s, similar electoral coalitions were organized in Westminster, Middlesex, Canterbury, and Kent. Furthermore, as we have seen, traditional party divisions were bridged in Surrey where a group of 'Independent Electors' challenged Lord Baltimore's re-election in 1742. Similarly, in Hertfordshire the Tory, Charles Caesar, stood successfully as a Country candidate and attracted the

---

[18] Colley, *In Defiance of Oligarchy*, chs. 5, 6.

support of Quakers and dissident Whigs, despite his reputation as a stalwart High Churchman cum Jacobite.[19]

Nor was the promotion of Country candidates solely confined to the South-East. It even penetrated the heartlands of Toryism. At Taunton, where the memory of the Monmouth Rising had sharpened the tensions between a sizeable Dissenting community and the Tory following of the Portman family, the leading patrons and property-owners of the town, a Tory and an Opposition Whig successfully ran against two ministerialists in 1741. In Bristol the Stedfast Society modulated the Tory party's High Church lineage to promote an independent Whig in 1739. At Worcester, another High Church stronghold, the London Tory merchant, Richard Lockwood, was successfully paired with Samuel Sandys. Among those who greeted Lockwood on his initial arrival to the town were members of the Berkeleys, a prominent Gloucestershire family with Tory and Whig supporters, George Dowdeswell, a minor whose father had represented Tewkesbury in the Whig interest, and Sir Herbert Pakington, whose High Church ancestors had sat for Worcester itself.[20] So three western towns with a reputation for strong party rivalries—all had witnessed riots on Coronation day in 1714—went the Country route in the final years of Walpole.

As did Coventry. Here the Tory freemen appealed to William Bromley, MP for Warwick, to stand against the Whig incumbents, especially against John Neale, who had voted for the Excise.[21] But Bromley hesitated and so the freemen pledged their votes to John Bird. One of the leading ribbon manufacturers in Coventry, Bird was a man with a strong Whig pedigree. He was a prominent nonconformist, a member of the principal Presbyterian congregation whose trustees were heavily involved and formally represented in town politics. To boot, Bird was a Walpolean client, holding the profitable post

---

[19] L. M. Munby, 'Politics and Religion in Hertfordshire 1660–1740', in his *East Anglian Studies* (Cambridge, 1968), pp. 117–45.

[20] *London Evening Post*, 27–30 Apr. 1734; on Taunton see James Savage, *The History of Taunton* (Taunton, 1822), pp. 250–2, 315–24; Sedgwick (ed.), *Commons 1715–54*, i. 317–18. For Bristol see next chapter.

[21] *London Evening Post*, 14–16 May 1734. The freemen had earlier written to Bromley urging him to do his utmost to repeal the Septennial Act: see *London Evening Post*, 23–5 Apr. 1734.

of Receiver of the Land Tax for Warwickshire. But Bird's renunciation of his Walpolean affiliations following the Excise crisis won him the assent of the freeman rank and file and ruptured the traditional pattern of Coventry politics. Bird was eventually bought off by Walpole, accepting another post in 1737 'for the peace and quiet of the city'. But the freemen continued to pursue their independent course. A sizeable number plumped for the independent Tory, William Grove, in 1741 and voted for Bird's nephew six years later in an effort to wrest both seats from the Corporation.[22] In the spring of 1742 a gathering of 'independent freemen' demanded a 'strict inquiry into the unhappy state of the nation' and an end of 'all Party Distinctions'.[23] Such were the fruits of Walpolean politics in this haven of nonconformity, this hitherto party-ridden 'fanatick town'.

There was, then, a Country 'moment' in the final years of Walpole's rule, a disposition among Tories and dissident Whigs to shelve their differences and concentrate their energies upon challenging the 'Great Man' and the vested interests which insulated the Court from the popular will. Those historians who have dismissed the Country experiment as the personal project of Bolingbroke, or as a journalistic obsession, have failed to look at the urban record. In roughly half of the large towns and cities there were significant departures from the pattern of party politics which had dominated the urban constituencies since the first decade of the century. These changes were most visible when Tories were paired with opposition Whig candidates. But there were other occasions when anti-Court candidates were promoted by quite broad coalitions, as in Liverpool, where Thomas Bootle gained the support of independent Whig and Jacobite landowners, or when nominal party candidates secured the aid of independents, as in Preston. How Country strategies fared in action depended much on the pool of available talent and the tenacity of party loyalties.

[22] K. J. Allison, 'Parliamentary Representation', in W. B. Stephens (ed.), *VCH Warwickshire* (Oxford, 1969), viii. 248–55, 372–7. Sedgwick (ed.), *Commons 1715–54*, i. 339–41; Coventry poll-books for 1741 and 1747.

[23] *London Evening Post*, 4–6 Mar. 1742. The term 'fanatick town' was employed by Celia Fiennes to denote the high visibility of nonconformity in Coventry: see Christopher Morris (ed.), *The Journeys of Celia Fiennes* (London, 1947), p. 113.

Apart from elections, there were two other focuses for the propagation of Country ideas and associations. The first emerged around the colourful career of Admiral Edward Vernon.[24] The second son of a former secretary of state, Vernon entered the navy as a teenager and was promoted to the rank of Captain in 1706. As a half-pay officer he was returned to Parliament for Penryn in 1722 and quickly made his mark as a vociferous critic of Walpole, opposing the revival of the Salt Tax in 1732, the Excise in the following year, and campaigning hard for a more aggressive policy towards Spain. Dispatched to the West Indies in the summer of 1739 with limited supplies and a small squadron, he distinguished himself by capturing Porto Bello with only six men of war, confirming his belief in the vulnerability of the Spanish colonies to swift, determined naval action. When the news of his victory reached London in March 1740, Vernon became the toast of the town. Both Houses of Parliament congratulated the king on his success. The Common Council of London quickly followed, lacing their address with some barbed references to Walpole's accommodating policy towards Spain. To drive the message home, Londoners offered Vernon the freedom of the city.

Vernon's victory was also commemorated in the North-East, but it was on the occasion of his birthday in November 1740 that his fame was celebrated on a national scale, despite doubts as to whether the anniversary fell on the first or on the twelfth. The *London Evening Post* featured pro-Vernon festivals in Cornwall and the West Country towns of Taunton, Bristol, and Bath, where a correspondent reported that his 'Ears' were 'every minute saluted with the Shouts of the Mob, attended with Well-Wishes to the Immortal Vernon'.[25] Demonstrations of joy were also noted in some of the major Midland centres, at Norwich, Ipswich, and Peterborough, and at York, Leeds, Liverpool, and 'other considerable places in the North'.[26] Although most of the reports emanated from urban centres, several Gloucestershire villages near the Severn also commemorated Vernon's birthday, and doubtless there were

---

[24] For a similar assessment of Vernon's place in mid-century popular politics see Kathleen Wilson, 'Empire, Trade and Popular Politics in Mid-Hanoverian England: The Case of Admiral Vernon', *Past and Present*, 121 (1988), 74–109.

[25] *London Evening Post*, 1–4 Nov. 1740.

[26] Ibid., 6–8 Nov. 1740.

others. A traveller through Essex noted that 'this Joy has so extended itself as to reach even a couple of lonesome Cottages on a Heath, which had club'd together for a few Bushes and a Heap of Fern to make a Bonfire to his Memory'.[27]

Vernon's extraordinary popularity, which did not diminish with the failure of the subsequent expeditions to Cartagena and Cuba, meant that his birthdays were celebrated with more gusto than those of the royal family. It is thus important to capture the admiral's appeal. In the manner of Drake and Raleigh, with whom he was associated, Vernon was the intrepid naval commander of a Protestant island battling the Catholic foe. 'To humble Spain three naval heroes born,' ran one poem, 'DRAKE, RALEIGH, VERNON, Britain's Isle adorn.'[28] By contrast to Admiral Hosier, who had failed to take the galleon station of Porto Bello with a larger squadron in 1727, Vernon was the Heart of Oak who had humiliated the Don and restored Britain's naval prestige in Caribbean waters. British tars would no longer rot in Spanish gaols, Merchantmen would no longer be oppressed by *guardacostas*, nor captains lose their ears. Britannia would rule the waves.

Yet if Vernon was praised for restoring national pride, he also had personal qualities which endeared him to the public at large. In Parliament he had been an outspoken critic of regressive taxation, describing the bill to revive the Salt Tax in 1732 as 'only to ease the rich at the expense of the poor'.[29] He had also campaigned for better pay and sickness amenities for sailors and denounced the sharp practices which had adversely affected the victualling of Hosier's fleet in 1726 and had left the men 'with stinking provision'. These words were matched with deeds. On his own expedition to the Caribbean in 1739, Vernon distributed 10,000 Spanish dollars captured at Porto Bello to his men in order to boost morale.[30] At the same time the sailor's rum allowance was diluted to punch, or grog, and mixed with limes in order to prevent scurvy and to improve the fighting quality of the force. These were the actions of a bluff commander who never allowed the windfalls of war to

[27] *London Evening Post*, 13–15 Nov. 1740.
[28] *Gentleman's Magazine*, 11 (1747), 274.
[29] Sedgwick (ed.), *Commons 1715–54*, ii. 497.
[30] *London Gazette*, 11–15 Mar. 1740.

undermine naval morale and discipline. Vernon never saw naval service as a source of personal, pecuniary advancement or as a social niche for lackadaisical sons of landed families. Predictably, he had a hearty contempt for the foppery and servility of his age. 'Do we think because a Fellow is a Beau and dresses himself up with Powder and Essences that . . . he has more courage than another Man?', he asked the Commons in 1732. 'I suspect there are many of those fine Gentlemen, who are afraid of letting the Wind blow upon them for fear of blowing the Powder out of their Wigs, that could not . . . bear the smell of Gun-Powder.'[31]

So Vernon had the reputation of being a fair-minded, beneficent commander who deplored the profiteering and patronage that undermined naval morale, not to mention the fashionable vices which blunted Britain's fighting spirit. But the context of his victory in 1739 also made him especially noteworthy. For the capture of Porto Bello was not only heroic; it arguably underscored the supine nature of government policy, the extreme reluctance of the Court to take aggressive action against Spain until forced by merchant and popular opinion. As an early poem emphasized, it was Vernon who 'FIRST hath rous'd' Britain 'from her passive Sleep, / And bid her Thunder vindicate the Deep'.[32] It was Vernon who revealed the merits of a vigorous blue-water policy—'They rule the ballanc'd world who rule the Main'—and contradicted the Court claim that diplomacy rather than war would ameliorate Anglo-Spanish relations. Vernon's victory, in other words, was interpreted as a confirmation of opposition argument, highlighting the poverty of Walpole's Eurocentric foreign policy, which many believed catered to Hanoverian rather than strictly British interests. As the *London Evening Post* insisted, 'a certain great Man should interpret all the Applauses heap'd upon Admiral Vernon as so many Satires upon himself', a view that so incensed the 'great Man' himself that it prompted a Crown prosecution.[33]

Vernon's exploits thus served to illustrate the shortcomings of the ministry; even his failures, for it was ultimately felt that

---

[31] Chandler, *Parliamentary Debates*, vii. 166.
[32] *London Evening Post*, 25–7 Mar. 1740.
[33] Ibid., 29 Mar.–1 Apr. 1740; PRO, TS 11/1001/3755.

Cartagena would have fallen had the ministry responded promptly to the admiral's request for reinforcements.[34] In fact Vernon himself was projected as the embodiment of patriotic values: valorous, incorruptible, public-spirited; a counterpoint to Court corruption and timidity. Inevitably, the Court attempted to thwart this juxtaposition, to swim on the national tide and appropriate the credit for Porto Bello. The poet laureate, Colley Cibber, penned an ode on the king's birthday in 1741 which cast George II as the 'Master of the Main' emulating 'Eliza's Glorious Reign'.[35] The promotion of Vernon as·a Court candidate in the City election of 1741 was also intended to emphasize the ministry's own commitment to a more bellicose mercantilism, however belated, and to stress its foresight in bringing Vernon back into active service despite his known antipathy to the ministry. But while Vernon's popularity was open to different political constructions, more often than not it served opposition purposes. In Huntingdon, Peterborough, Taunton, and Southwark, demonstrations of joy for Vernon were occasions for anti-ministerial rallies and pre-electoral canvassing. At Prescott, near Liverpool, Vernon's health was drank in association with the opposition Lords Derby and Strange as well as the Tory candidates for Preston. At Birmingham it was hoped that Vernon would 'frustrate the wicked Designs of those who would infamously betray the Honour of the Country by Scandalously endeavouring to limit the Progress of the Fleet', a reference to the government's laggard follow-up to Porto Bello, well publicized by opposition politicians like Bathurst and Chesterfield.[36] In Wrexham, where a grand Vernon junket was organized by Sir Watkin Williams Wynn, there were healths to 'Church and King, Prosperity to Old England . . . to the Downfall of Corruption, and to a Parliament without a Placeman or a Pensioner'.[37] In those places where Vernon celebrations culminated in effigy-burnings or mock-executions, there was even some ambiguity

[34] On this question and Vernon's subsequent quarrels with the military commander, Major-General Thomas Wentworth, a text-book soldier ill-equipped to deal with Caribbean contingencies, see Cyril H. Hartmann, *The Angry Admiral* (London, 1953), chs. 3–6.

[35] *London Evening Post*, 29–31 Oct. 1741.

[36] Ibid., 4–6 Nov. 1740; Hartmann, *Angry Admiral*, pp. 55–7.

[37] *London Evening Post*, 20–2 Nov. 1740.

as to the identity of the execrable victim. Thus at Stratford, near Bow, in the sprawling parishes of the East End, the Don resembled 'a great fat-gutted Man, with prodigious deep and well-filled Pockets . . . adorned with Ribands and other Trinkets'.[38] The Spanish commander, Don Blas de Lezo? Or the Bob Booty of popular broadside?

In the years 1740 and 1741 at least thirty towns and cities commemorated Vernon's exploits, and a more extensive search into provincial newspapers would doubtless reveal more. Ballads, poems, and prints celebrated his triumphs. Over a hundred medals were struck in honour of the admiral who took Porto Bello, and his head blazoned many an alehouse sign. The first naval hero of the eighteenth century, his tremendous popularity was a symptom of the growing audience for political news in the urban centres and of an emergent imperialism that would resonate through the political order. The euphoria which surrounded Porto Bello, although cleverly orchestrated by the opposition, none the less depicted a new political mood, one better understood by Pitt the Elder than by Walpole, who eschewed adventurous naval interventions to appease Hanover and the landed class. The celebrations in honour of Vernon also anticipated those of Wilkes in their scope and festive display, revealing how sensitive the provinces could be to issues generated in the City and the London press.[39] Like the Excise, the capture of Porto Bello also helped to broaden the base of opposition to Walpolean rule and to refashion the parameters of extra-parliamentary politics. It is surely no coincidence that the large constituencies where Vernon's birthday was observed most vigorously were also those where the Court suffered electoral setbacks; the most striking being in Ipswich, where the admiral of the hour, still in the Caribbean, reversed his defeat of 1734 and picked up no less than 98 per cent of the votes.[40] As a paradigm of patriotism and liberty, a counter-symbol to Walpolean corruption, Vernon lent credibility to the Country cause. His loyalism could not be impugned, nor his motives, while his victories at Porto Bello and Fort Chagre

[38] Ibid., 13–15 Nov. 1740.
[39] On Wilkes see Brewer, *Party Ideology*, ch. 9.
[40] See *The Poll for Members of Parliament for the Borough of Ipswich 8 May 1741* (Ipswich, 1741).

served to keep the memory of the Spanish Convention alive. Together with the Instructions of 1739–1742, Vernon's triumphs helped to focus the political nation's attention upon the deeper implications of Walpolean rule. His popularity was in no sense diversionary.

Like the festivals honouring Admiral Vernon, the Instructions for political reform have rarely been the subject of close scrutiny. Cecil Emden mentioned them in his *The People and the Constitution*, but recent scholars have tended to overlook this brief reference and to assume that there was a hiatus in the practice of sending Instructions to MPs from the Excise Crisis to the Wilkite era.[41] This is incorrect. Following the mayoral contest of 1739, in which Sir George Champion was rejected for voting for the Spanish Convention, the London Livery issued Instructions to its members requiring them to promote a place bill 'in Conjunction with such Patriots as may be willing to join with you'.[42] This initiative was taken up by fifteen constituencies before the motion for a place bill in the Commons in January 1740. Following the Middlesex by-election in the summer of 1740, this campaign was renewed, principally by the counties at their summer assizes. On this occasion sixteen counties (thirteen English, two Scottish, one Welsh) and nine boroughs pressed for a place bill. A further spate of Instructions was launched as Walpole's majorities crumbled in the Commons early in 1742. The first, from Westminster, focused upon its own controverted election and the need to pass legislation on electoral malpractice. But following the City of London's lead in February 1742, there was a more urgent call for a full Country programme and a strict enquiry into Walpolean mismanagement. Twenty-four boroughs and fifteen counties heeded London's call as the enquiry into Walpole's government got under way. And a further fourteen constituencies reaffirmed the need for parliamentary reform and a renewal of the enquiry at the beginning of the next session, when the realignments at Court began to filter through the press. Altogether 100 sets of Instructions were issued from October 1739 until November 1742, by 74

---

[41] Cecil Emden, *The People and the Constitution* (Oxford, 1933), pp. 20–1; Speck, *Tory and Whig*, pp. 30, 149n.

[42] *Gentleman's Magazine*, 9 (1739), 549.

different bodies.[43] By any estimation this was an impressive achievement.

Instructions from constituents were not, of course, a novel strategy. They had been used by the Shaftesbury Whigs during the Exclusion crisis and at various Augustan elections. In the City of London, in particular, they were regularly put before Common Hall after parliamentary contests. But the practice of issuing Instructions between elections was a recent one. It had been first implemented on a large scale during the Excise crisis of 1733, and it was with this successful precedent in mind that the City of London inaugurated another round of Instructions in 1739.

Instructions were intended to convey the sentiments of constituents to MPs on pressing political matters, but there was some debate about their propriety and constitutional status. In 1738 the *Daily Gazetteer* conceded that 'the People may have a right to give Instructions to their members', although it later claimed that there was no legal precedent for them at all.[44] Essentially, the paper felt that Instructions undermined the trinity of powers enshrined in Britain's constitution, setting up a 'Fourth Estate', and it was particularly insistent that Instructions were not binding upon MPs. In fact, the opposition never advanced this claim. When MPs were elected, stated the *Champion*, 'they become Representatives, not of that single borough or corporation for which they are chosen only, but of the whole Nation, and tho' every borough and corporation has afterwards and during the whole sitting of Parliament a right to advise with and convey their sentiments to their members, they have no power to controul or compel them'.[45] None the less, the *Craftsman* and other opposition papers insisted that MPs were 'attorneys of the People' and staunchly defended a delegatory theory of representation that had been part of the radical Whig repertoire and rooted in the myth of Gothic liberty. 'Nothing can be more ridiculous and absurd', maintained the *Craftsman*, 'than to

[43] These calculations are based on an intensive search through the *London Evening Post* and the *Gentleman's Magazine*. Some of the Instructions can be found in *Great Britain's Memorial* (London, 1741).

[44] *Daily Gazetteer*, 6 July 1738; extract from the *Daily Gazetteer* cited in the *Gentleman's Magazine*, 12 (1742), 594–5.

[45] *The Champion*, 23 Sept. 1740.

argue that the Principal, who elects, hath not a right to instruct his deputy, so elected, and to whom He formerly paid Wages for his service; and though that Custom is now discontinued, yet the original design of Representatives still subsists and ought to be observed.'[46] Electors had the right to instruct their members, and not simply on local matters, as Burke later claimed, but on matters of national concern. Despite what has recently been written about Instructions, this advice was taken up.[47] Indeed, contemporaries were very aware that the passage of the Septennial Act, which had weakened the political accountability of MPs, made such interventions more imperative.

Instructions were thus seen as an important constitutional right, alerting MPs to the popular will, and pressuring them to fulfil their trust as representatives. Failure to comply prejudiced an MP's chances of re-election. To what extent Instructions were a genuine expression of popular sentiment was, inevitably, a moot point. Government journalists pointed out that Instructions originated from a variety of sources. 'According to the present Practice,' the *Daily Gazetteer* opined, 'there is very little Certainty as to this Business of instructing. Sometimes it is done by one Set of Men, sometimes by another; in one Place 'tis a solemn Act under a Publick Seal, in another a common Letter written after Dinner.'[48] Predictably, its correspondents were quick to expose irregularities and to cast doubt about the representative nature of specific Addresses. Rumours circulated that the Southwark Instructions of 1742 were the work of a narrow clique which had failed to present them before a general meeting of the electors. The Nottingham Instructions were lampooned in verse as the

[46] The *Craftsman*, 22 Dec. 1739; see also the *Champion*, 4 Nov. 1740. For the radical Whig view, which these writers echoed, see Algernon Sidney, *Discourses concerning Government*, 3rd edn. (London, 1751), s. xliv, pp. 450–4.

[47] See Paul Kelly, 'Constituents Instructions to Members of Parliament in the Eighteenth Century', in Clyve Jones (ed.), *Party and Management in Parliament 1660–1784* (New York, 1984), pp. 169–89. For Burke's views see Lucy S. Sutherland, 'Edmund Burke and the Relations between Members of Parliament and their Constituents', *Studies in Burke and His Time*, 10 (autumn 1968), 1005–21. For the notion that it was crucial for constituents to instruct members on critical national issues see the *Craftsman*, 17 Mar. 1733, 22 Dec. 1739.

[48] Cited in the *Gentleman's Magazine*, 12 (1742), 594–5.

initiative of a boozy, Tory faction which numbered less than 10 per cent of the burgesses. Those from Westminster were said to have been organized by 'few more than a Hundred, and those of the lowest and least Substantial Inhabitants'.[49]

Historians have been understandably sceptical about the representative status of Instructions and this scepticism is not altogether misplaced. Some of the Instructions came from small Cornish boroughs that were firmly under the thumb of patrons in opposition to the Court. This was true of Liskeard, Truro, and St Maws, constituencies dominated by families who in 1740 were linked to the reversionary interest. Similarly, the rash of Instructions from the Scottish shires and burghs, from Angus, Aberdeen, Ayrshire, the Cupar burgh in Fife, and Stirling, were probably associated with Argyll's defection from the Court and the collapse of the Walpole–Ilay connection.[50] In these instances Instructions registered territorial influence and political disputes at the top.

Yet when all these factors are taken into account it may still be argued that Instructions were an important index of popular feeling, of the middling electors especially. As Table 7.2 shows, the constituencies which consistently instructed their Members in the period 1733–56 were not proprietary boroughs. Nor were many dominated by powerful local families. Those that were, such as Chester, Nottingham, and Peterborough, instructed their Members on three occasions only. The more regular practitioners were those with large, independent electorates. Foremost among them were the freeman and inhabitant boroughs which had gravitated to the opposition during the 1730s and had responded to the call for Country coalitions against Walpolean Whiggery. In these constituencies Instructions were promoted by opposition-dominated Corporations in tune with developments in the capital and very willing to follow London's lead. This was true of Canterbury, Worcester, and York. Alternatively, Instructions were promoted by groups in opposition to vested interests in their constituencies. In Westminster, for example, the most radical Instructions came from the Independent Electors, the

---

[49] Ibid., 9 (1739), 650; 12 (1742), 579, 583.
[50] On this web of patronage see John Stuart Shaw, *The Management of Scottish Society 1707–1764* (Edinburgh, 1983), chs. 3, 4.

TABLE 7.2. Constituences which Presented Three or More Sets of Instructions to their Members 1733–1756

	No. electors	1733	1739/40	1740	early 1742	late 1742	1753	1756
Bristol	4,000	X			X	X	X	X
Canterbury	1,000	X			X	X		
Chester	1,000	X	X		X	X	X	X
Coventry	1,500	X			X			
Exeter	1,200	X			X		X	X
Gloucester	2,000	X	X				X	
Lichfield	480		X		X	X		2
London	8,200	X	X		X	X	X	2
Nottingham	1,350	X	X	X				X
Oxford	750	X						X
Peterborough	350	X	X		X			
Reading	600	X			X			
Southwark	3,500	X					X	X
Westminster	8,000	X			2	X		
Worcester	1,500	X	X			X		
York	1,800	X	X		X			X
Cheshire	5,000			X			X	X
Devon	3,000			X	X		X	X
Kent	7,000			X				X
Herefordshire	4,000				X	X		X
Somerset	4,000	X			X		X	X

Sources: the *London Evening Post*, and other London newspapers; Langford, *The Excise Crisis* (Oxford, 1975), app. A; Price, 'The Excise Crisis Revisited', in Baxter (ed.), *England's Rise to Greatness 1600–1763* (Berkeley and Los Angeles, 1983), p. 293; Perry, *Public Opinion, Propaganda, and Politics in Eighteenth-Century England* (Cambridge, Mass., 1962), pp. 111–17.

lawyers and tradesmen who had organized the opposition to the Court and Bedford House during the 1740s and had established strong links with City dissidents. In Coventry the Instructions were organized by the independent freemen of the town who had backed John Bird in 1734 and William Grove in 1741. At Bristol, the Instructions of 1740 and the first set in 1742 were promoted by the Stedfast Society, the Tory caucus of up-and-coming merchants and tradesmen who successfully launched Ned Southwell in Bristol politics (although not before he had pledged himself to a Country programme). As Southwell's own papers reveal, the Instructions calling for Walpole's censure in the spring of 1742 engendered considerable, acrimonious debate—so much so that one member resolved he 'would for the future declare off from having anything to do with public affairs'. They were also widely circulated, for Southwell was told that the original draft had been soiled 'by laying on the table for subscription'.[51]

In the open constituencies, then, Instructions often involved some form of consent; they frequently expressed the dispositions of the more independent sections of the electorate. To be sure, the Instructions did not involve the electorate in so dramatic a manner as the mass-petitioning movements of the Wilkite era. Like those initiatives, we can reasonably predict that they were sometimes co-ordinated by party magnates and their agents. Certainly, the Tories and the opposition Whigs recognized the usefulness of Instructions as a means of mobilizing popular opinion.[52] This was one reason why they were regularly printed in the press—to win converts and instill confidence in the converted. But the popularity of Instructions was not illusory, as T. W. Perry has tended to suggest.[53] In the large constituencies they required organization, planning, persuasion, and agreement. It was difficult to hustle Instructions through a county meeting without affronting the dignities of a grand jury, and indeed grand juries sometimes went

---

[51] Avon Central Lib., Bristol, Southwell Papers, vi. (John Brickdale to Southwell, 15 Feb. 1741/2); vii (Samuel Pye to Southwell, 3 Feb. 1741/2).

[52] See Thomas Carte's 'Scheme for the Counties', Bodleian Lib.. Carte MS 230, fos. 198–9; and *A Selection from the Papers of the Earls of Marchmont in the Possession of the Rt. Hon. Sir George Rose*, 3 vols. (London, 1831), ii. 143–5.

[53] T. W. Perry, *Public Opinion, Propaganda, and Politics in Eighteenth-Century England* (Cambridge, Mass., 1962), pp. 116–17.

out of their way to declare that their Instructions represented county opinion.[54] It was also hazardous to promote Instructions in large towns without some attention to their local reception. Exposures in the press or counter-Instructions were not unknown. The Nottingham Whigs repaid their rivals in kind, lamenting, after Walpole's fall, 'that spirit of jealousy and uneasiness that appears in some of our Countrymen at a time when the strictest Unanimity is so peculiarly necessary'.[55] Similarly, the Bristol Corporation, troubled by the continuing call for a parliamentary enquiry into Walpole's government in the fall of 1742, instructed Southwell to ignore 'popular Clamour' and to vote 'the necessary Supplies for carrying on the war'.[56] Instructions had become too powerful a weapon in the hands of the opposition. 'I am as justly alarmed at the effect the vile instructions that has succeeded those of the City of London may have [upon] the whole nation as any body living,' wrote the earl of Tankerville to Newcastle in November 1742, 'and to speak plainly, if not timely prevented, tend to the destruction of the King and his royal family.'[57] Rather than disparage the existence or question the legitimacy of Instructions, ministerialists began a policy of active intervention, frustrating offensive Addresses and promoting their own.

So far, I have examined some of the organizational and social aspects of Instructions. It is now important to attend to their ideological dimension, for this has some bearing upon our appraisal of parliamentary reform in the first half of the eighteenth century.

It must be admitted that this has not been much of a problem for most historians. Fixated by the inexorable growth of oligarchy, they have been inattentive to the dissident voices of the early Hanoverian era, save for those commonwealthmen studied by Caroline Robbins.[58] Consequently they have tended to marginalize the arguments for reform in the early Han-

[54] Thus the Buckinghamshire grand jury on 17 July 1740 issued Instructions 'at ye Request of great Numbers of Gentlemen, Clergy and Freeholders, our Neighbours': see *Gentleman's Magazine*, 10 (1740), 349.

[55] Ibid. 12 (1742), 580.

[56] Ibid. 595.

[57] BL, Add. MS 32,699, fo. 527.

[58] Caroline Robbins, *The Eighteenth-Century Commonwealthman* (Cambridge, Mass., 1959).

overian era, to dismiss them as 'an archaic, academic Whiggism' advocated, likely as not, by 'bookish radicals with antiquarian tastes'.[59] Alternatively, recognizing the contribution of Bolingbroke and his circle, they have cast reform as quintessentially nostalgic, a response of the declining gentry to the growth of the state and the financial revolution.[60] The only exception to this rule (apart from the present author) has been Linda Colley, who has emphasized the way in which the Tory party 'lent coherent political expression' to 'miscellaneous popular grievances', by 'way of opportunistic sorties into extra-parliamentary politics'.[61]

I have difficulty with all these interpretations. Caroline Robbins commits the cardinal error of assuming that all political dissidence was Whig-based, a view that does not accord at all with the nonconformist record before 1760 and ignores the libertarian contribution of some Tories and Jacobites. Isaac Kramnick, on the other hand, has offered a novel assessment of Bolingbroke which is attentive to crucial socio-economic developments in English politics. But his view tends to narrow the appeal of Country ideas to a declining gentry and to gloss over important changes in commercial society which increased their ideological purchase. In fact some of his presumed equivalences—the quartet of credit, commerce, capitalism, and modernity—oversimplify his insights into the politics of the financial revolution. Colley has been rightly critical of this chain of associations, and of the identification of Toryism *tout court* with economic decline and obsolescent landed values. Yet in her eagerness to repudiate the conventional view of Tory stasis she has exaggerated the Tory sponsorship of reformist ideas and deflated the coherence and political complexity of urban radicalism. In fact the opposition to Walpolean rule was not a

[59] See Lucy Sutherland, 'City of London', in Taylor and Pares (eds.), *Essays to Namier*, pp. 49–74; and Cannon, *Parliamentary Reform*, p. 45.

[60] Kramnick, *Bolingbroke and His Circle*, esp. chs. 2, 3; Daniel Baugh (ed.), *Aristocratic Government and Society in Eighteenth-Century England* (New York, 1975), intro.

[61] Linda Colley, 'Eighteenth-Century English Radicalism Before Wilkes', *Trans. Royal Historical Society*, 31 (1981), 4; see also her *In Defiance Of Oligarchy*, ch. 6. My position is to be found in 'The Urban Opposition to Whig Oligarchy 1720–1760', in Margaret and James Jacob (eds.), *The Origins of Anglo-American Radicalism* (London, 1984), pp. 132–48.

rag-bag of popular grievances rendered coherent by Tory statesmanship. As this study has sought to show, it owed much, in the first instance, to the London experience, to that 'beacon of Liberty' whose politics defy analysis along straightforward party lines. Colley's perspective also presupposes a rather facile provincial public, too preoccupied with local issues and conflicts, too inarticulate to propound a wider view of the political developments around it.

Historians who have examined the arguments for political reform in the first half of the eighteenth century have stressed that the principal objective was to purify Parliament from what one pamphleteer termed 'Anti-constitutional Dependence'.[62] Most reformers accepted the need for some executive influence in the Commons. What distressed them was the proliferation of civil and military officers in the legislature and the abuse of the public purse to a point where unpopular, antilibertarian measures could be passed and their architects defended with impunity. It has sometimes been claimed that this 'insupportable dead weight',[63] as the Nottingham Instructions of 1740 described it, was too insubstantial to shore up ministerial control of the Commons. On a strict count of government placemen and pensioners this may have been the case. But contemporary reformers were also preoccupied with the more subtle arts of pecuniary persuasion, what the *Craftsman* once described as 'Hush Money' and 'Smart Money',[64] and with the activities of 'Borough Jobbers' who fortified the government interest. It took incredible popular pressure (and some defections at Court) to force Walpole to abandon the Excise scheme. Six years later Walpole was again defying popular opinion by advocating a Convention with Spain rather than war. As the well-publicized and annotated division list on the treaty revealed, Walpole pushed it through the Commons with the help of some two hundred dependents of the Court.[65] It was these twin experiences that fuelled the

---

[62] Anon., *The Independent Briton, or Free Thoughts on the Expediency of Gratifying the People's Expectations* (London, 1742), p. 9.

[63] *Gentleman's Magazine*, 9 (1739), 650.

[64] The *Craftsman*, 24 Apr. 1742; for a discussion of Commons patronage in its formal articulations see J. B. Owen, 'Political Patronage in 18th Century England', in Paul Fritz and David Williams (eds.), *The Triumph of Culture: Eighteenth-Century Perspectives* (Toronto, 1972), pp. 369–87.

[65] *Gentleman's Magazine*, 9 (1739), pp. 304–10.

campaign for place and pension bills. Indeed, the Instructions of 1739 and 1740 grew directly out of the opposition to the Convention of El Pardo.

However, the reorganization of the Commons was not the only reformist objective. Equally important was the accountability of the Commons to the electorate and the elimination of corrupt practices that compromised voters' independence. Of critical importance was the demand for frequent parliaments and the repeal of the Septennial Act, a statute which made 'Representatives careless about reconciling their Conduct to the Sentiments of those they represent'[66] and, because of escalating costs, induced electoral compromise. This had been an important issue on the urban hustings since 1722 and was advocated with increased urgency in the Instructions of 1742. It was accompanied with calls for tougher bills against electoral bribery, for greater sanctions against corrupt returning officers and against the swamping of the electorate with new freemen. Very occasionally, as in the Hereford Instructions of 1742,[67] constituents requested the disfranchisement of customs and excise officers. They also resisted acts which would increase those officers' discretionary powers, such as the Gin Act of 1736, and would plausibly extend their political influence.

It is sometimes claimed that this Country programme represented no more than a return to the status quo ante 1714—that it was essentially backward-looking, nostalgic for a bygone era of landed pre-eminence. In fact, this is an oversimplified view. The call for reform came from any quarters, landed paternalists included, but its main impetus derived from the groundswell of commercial opinion which saw legislative change as the only security against a ministry too preoccupied with dynastic stability and its own preferment to protect the expanding sectors of Atlantic trade. Walpole's deference to Hanover, it was claimed, encumbered British foreign policy; his links with the great moneyed companies warped his sense of commercial priorities, privileging the monopolies and inhibiting the development of freer trade.[68]

---

[66] *London Evening Post*, 10–12 Jan. 1745.

[67] Ibid., 16–18 Mar. 1742.

[68] See Anon., *The Independent Briton*, pp. 50–4. Good summaries of the consequences of the Hanoverian connection can be found in the 1743 paper-

Moreover, the misappropriation of public funds and the broadening of tax base hindered industrial enterprise, while the public debt, in the words of one pamphleteer, provided 'a safe and certain Income for the most indolent, and consequently the most useless Part of Society, and a great Discouragement to Industry and Trade'.[69] Political reform, nationalism, industrial and commercial expansion were thus conjoined in Country reasoning. Several sets of Instructions linked the need for reform with the depression in the textile industry. Others saw the Excise and the Spanish Convention as conclusive evidence of the ministry's sinister priorities, its pursuit of preferment and influence at the expense of independent opinion and commercial prosperity.[70] To be sure, Country writers did not offer a sociology of politics, strictly defined. They appealed to all public-spirited individuals with a stake in society and not dependent upon either ministerial favour or day wages for their livelihood.[71] But some journalists did occasionally specify further, invoking the support of farmers and freemen as well as

war over subsidies for Hanoverian troops: see [Stanhope, Lord Chesterfield], *The Interest of Hanover steadily Pursued since the A———n* (London, 1743), and [id. and Waller], *The Case of the Hanover Forces in the Pay of Great Britain* (London, 1743); see also Anon., *Public Discontent Accounted For* (London, 1743).

[69] Anon. *The Independent Briton*, pp. 38–9; see also Anon., *Public Discontent Accounted For*, pp. 31–2.

[70] See the 1742 Instructions from Bath, Bristol, Coventry, Hereford, Lichfield, Minehead, Peterborough, and Staffordshire; *London Evening Post*, 23–5 Feb.; 4–6, 16–18, 18–20 Mar.; 22–4 Apr.; 11–13 May 1742; *Gentleman's Magazine*, 12 (1742), pp. 159, 487.

[71] The social parameters of Independency were not precisely defined. In the *Craftsman*, 10 Jan. 1741, a writer criticized the property qualification for MPs, which cut off 99% of the population, 'including shoreboys, linkmen, ostlers, tinkers, porters, cobblers and several other Englishmen of the same rank, many of whom, though in low stations, may have as clean hands and as honest hearts as some upstart gentlemen, who have long been accustomed to salaries, perquisites and pensions'. This was certainly hyperbolic, but it does suggest that Independency could reach far down the social scale, to the meanest voter. On the other hand, most reformers were sceptical about increasing the franchise because they feared this would simply augment the dependent vote. The *Craftsman* certainly believed that men not engaged in 'honest labour and Industry' were fodder for electoral venality and manipulation, and at one period insinuated that daily labourers were too vulnerable and insecure to warrant the vote: see the issues for 23 May and 14 July 1741. Unlike Colley (in 'English Radicalism', *Trans. Royal Historical Society* (1981), 13–14), I have found no evidence of pre-1750 reformers endorsing universal manhood suffrage: indeed, the pamphlet she cites does not make this claim. It

the gentry. Indeed, *Common Sense*, in one noteworthy edition, saw the freeholders and middling sort as the best defence against Walpolean corruption, a line of argument that was voiced with greater insistency during the 1750s.[72]

Country spokesmen were thus attentive to the political preoccupations of the middling sort and attuned their arguments accordingly. They were also attentive to the recent trends in the electoral structure, recognizing that they lived in the 'golden age' of small boroughs 'whose Poverty easily subjects them to Corruption'.[73] The grand jury of Cornwall was quite emphatic on this point, noting 'the daily instances of an Influence prevailing in our Burroughs in direct Opposition to the Natural Interests of the Gentlemen of this County'.[74] So, too, did the *Craftsman*: 'Nothing can be more ridiculous than to collect the Sense of the People from the Borough Elections', it declared in 1734. Seven years later it asked:

How many Boroughs are there, in which the Right of Election resides in the Mayor, or Bailiff, and a very small number of Burgesses, to say Nothing of the Burgage Tenures and other little Corporations which are absolutely in the nomination of one or two Families? How many Boroughs are there, in which the Majority of Electors are under a commanding Influence by the very Nature of their Places, such as Excisemen, Custom-house Officers of all Ranks and Degrees, Workmen in our Dock Yards, Gunners, Watermen, Innholders, Alehousekeepers, and other Persons who either get their Livelihood by the Government, or lie under the Lash of innumerable Penal Laws?[75]

vindicates, instead, the right of the 'meaner sort' to protest against bad laws and government policies—the 'right to redress'. The pamphleteer's sense of the political nation was certainly socially restrictive. 'All degrees of people', he argued, 'who have leisure and abilities, and a turn to this sort of reading, acquire rational ideas of liberty and submission, of the Rights of the Church, and of the Power of the State, of their Duties as Subjects, and of what they may justly claim as Freemen' (*The Liveryman or Plain Thoughts on Publick Affairs* (London, 1740), p. 9).

[72] *Common Sense*, 28 Nov. 1741; the *Craftsman*, 23 Aug. 1740. See also the *Protester*, 9 June 1753, where it is argued that in times of crisis 'the most solid resource . . . would be in a Gentry, the liberal professions, the whole mercantile interest and, in short, all who had any Pretense to be comprehended in the middle rank of the people'.

[73] The *Craftsman*, 25 May 1734; *London Evening Post*, 23–5 Apr. 1741; see also the *Freeholder's Journal*, 18 Apr. 1722.

[74] *London Evening Post*, 9–12 Aug. 1740.

[75] The *Craftsman*, 25 May 1734, 25 July 1741.

The writer went on to note the political ramifications of this dependency, showing that while the opposition chalked up some spectacular victories in the open constituencies, it failed to capture the boroughs and Cinque Ports. Despite the desertion of some Cornish patrons, the Court emerged with a majority of nearly sixty in the middling and small boroughs of England. Here popular opinion was no match for ministerial patronage.

The fact that unpopular administrations could not be routed through the electoral process became readily apparent in 1734 and 1741. It prompted opposition writers to ponder the inequalities of the system. Had parliamentary representation been calibrated according to land-tax contributions, claimed the *Craftsman*, the South-East and parts of the Midlands and North would have gained more seats and the result of the 1734 election would have been radically different.[76] Had wealth been the criterion, many small boroughs would have been disfranchised in favour of greater county representation. Similar conclusions were reached by a writer in *Common Sense* in January 1741. He noted that 'Several Cornish and Wiltshire boroughs, quite deserted, send two Members each to Parliament; while Birmingham, Leeds, Wakefield, and many other large and populous boroughs don't send one.'[77] He also pointed out that 'a member for York represents ten thousand Freeholders, yet his vote counts for no more than that of a Man who represents twenty'. In other words, the radical blueprint for a redistribution of seats, pressed vigorously after 1770, had been mooted in the campaign against Walpole.

Even so, these observations did not generate any concrete proposal for reform beyond a tentative endorsement of the Cromwellian system or the suggestion that the representation of the smaller boroughs should be organized like the Scottish burghs.[78] And these projects remained the subject of journalist speculation; they were not integrated into the Instructions of 1739–42. Why was this the case?

Part of the reason was clearly tactical. The opposition strove to mobilize as broad a coalition as possible against Walpole and

[76] The *Craftsman*, 27 July 1734.
[77] *Common Sense*, 10 Jan. 1741.
[78] The *Craftsman*, 27 July 1734; *Gentleman's Magazine*, 17 (1747), 331.

had no wish to alienate potential supporters, least of all borough-patrons at odds with the Court. But this taciturnity about redistribution was not entirely self-serving. Not every opposition politician was in favour of the repeal of the Septennial Act, but this issue was not taken off the agenda.[79] Nor were electoral abuses excised from debate lest they affront vested interests. In fact, on the issue of honorary freemen, opposition journalists were as willing to expose Tory chicanery as they were ministerial.[80]

Political opportunism aside, one of the reasons why contemporary reformers hedged on the question of redistribution was that they were not entirely convinced such radical surgery was necessary. Or they were not prepared to endorse such a project if the cancer of corruption could be rooted out by proposals on which there was greater consensus in opposition circles. In their estimation there was enough vitality in the existing system to reverse the oligarchical drift of Hanoverian politics and eliminate Walpolean corruption, provided a comprehensive Country programme, together with the repeal of the Riot and Licensing Acts, was implemented. This optimism was based on the experience of the campaigns against the Excise and the Spanish Convention. Or rather, it was based on an optimistic reading of those campaigns, a prediction that once ministerial influence was reduced and triennial parliaments revived, the power of the People would inevitably prevail. This belief was reinforced by the opposition's strong showing in the open constituencies, particularly in constituencies like Kent, where government influence was formidable, and by its near-victory in 1741. Indeed, the *Craftsman*'s initial calculations on that general election predicted a narrow opposition victory.[81]

It might be argued, in fact, that the opposition's very

[79] On Samuel Sandys's equivocations about the repeal of the Septennial Act see *HMC Egmont Diary*, iii. 256.

[80] The *Craftsman*, 25 May 1734; *London Evening Post*, 9–12 Aug. 1740.

[81] Kent elections became symbolic of popular capabilities in the face of ministerial influence. In this constituency there were 'three Docks, two Episcopal Sees, and four Cinque Ports, besides Multitudes of Revenue Officers who swarm around the whole Coast'. See the *Craftsman*, 25 May 1734; cf. ibid. 23 May. In the *Craftsman*, 25 July 1741, it was calculated that the opposition would gain 285 seats to the Court's 268 (but this was exclusive of double returns).

successes after 1733 partially blinded reformers to the structural, as opposed to contingent, features of Whig oligarchy and led them to exaggerate the prospects for change. In this respect the events of 1742 were a brutal awakening. Walpole was toppled, but basic reforms remained unfulfilled. With the new accommodations at Court the momentum of reform was lost. A few Tory-radicals and urban dissidents continued to demand popular measures. The Westminster Instructions of late 1742 demanded a renewal of the inquiry against Walpole, fearing that 'a precedent of impunity will expose us to the scourge of any future minister'.[82] Like others, they also advocated a fully-fledged Country programme, government economy, and an end to foreign subsidies, and urged that supply be conditional upon such measures. But as the Coventry freemen disconsolately noted, 'the Disposition of Power and Money has been more the Subject of Enquiry than the Redressing of Grievances'.[83] And so it transpired. Early in December a new pensions bill was defeated in the Commons by 221 : 196. 'It seems', wrote Lord Egmont, 'the new Ministry are above regarding the resentment of their old friends and the clamours of the people by their opposing those popular bills which miscarried last year, and which [they] . . . then shewed themselves so eager to obtain.'[84]

The campaign for reform did not entirely die out in 1742. As we have already seen, it continued to be advocated until 1745, when Sir Francis Dashwood and others argued that popular measures were the best guarantee of loyalism in the face of a new Jacobite rebellion. But this line of reasoning badly backfired, with disastrous results at the polls. As Table 7.1 showed, the government regained its majority in the big urban centres in 1747, most notably in London and Westminster. In fact the government showing might well have been greater had not the Tories successfully negotiated electoral compromises at Reading, Nottingham, Newcastle, Coventry, and York.

From the mid-1740s, for two decades, the big urban constituencies enter a period of stasis. Uncontested elections become a typical feature of urban politics. Local oligarchies reassert their

---

[82] *London Evening Post*, 2–4 Nov. 1742.
[83] Ibid., 20–3 Nov. 1742.
[84] *HMC Egmont Diary*, iii. 268.

control. Very occasionally, as in Derby in 1748, the small-to-middling voters revolted against aristocratic dominance; but they usually did so to demarcate the limits of patronage, not to reassert the freedom of elections as did the Gloucester freemen in 1734 and 1741.[85] National crises like the agitation over the Jew Bill in 1753 or the loss of Minorca in 1756 could, of course, see an upsurge in popular activity. Seven of my twenty-eight urban constituencies instructed their members to oppose the Jewish Naturalization Bill; nine called for an inquiry into the government's mismanagement of Minorca. But such flurries of protest rarely had any lasting impact upon electoral politics. Outside of London, where urban radicalism existed on a bedrock of civic democracy, oppositionist voices were muted.

The decline of oppositionist politics at the grass roots cannot be solely explained in terms of the resurgence of loyalism in 1745 and the reassertion of élite control. What also requires emphasis is the degree to which changes in political leadership assuaged the demand for reform. As I suggested in Chapter 3, Henry Pelham's re-organization of the funded debt reconciled many aspiring investors to the financial revolution and removed the stigma of privilege which surrounded the floating of government loans. At the same time the reappointment of Tories to the bench, despite the misgivings of many local Whigs, made government seem less of a Whig monopoly. Upon this revival of confidence in government, William Pitt was able to build. His vision of empire and his reputation for political integrity reconciled many to the Whig regime, and while Britain enjoyed a spectacular series of military and naval victories, patriotism, in both its nationalist and oppositionist guise, marginalized all thought for reform. It was only with his descent from power and the disillusionment with the Peace of Paris that the politics of frustration would resurface. Once again the large towns and cities, and large sections of the professional and commercial middle class, would sound the tocsin of reform.

[85] Sedgwick (ed.), *Commons 1715–54*, 246–7; *London Evening Post*, 3–5 Mar. 1741. The Derby poll for 1748 shows that the stockingers, tailors, and cordwainers voted for the independent, Thomas Rivett. Lord Chesterfield's relative, Thomas Stanhope, secured the vote of the majority of esquires, gentlemen and aldermen.

The history of the large urban constituencies is thus a chequered one. It does not conform to the standard interpretations of the early Hanoverian period. In the era of Walpole's ascendancy urban politics displayed a remarkable vitality. Urban elections were vigorously and frequently contested. They were informed by national issues, to a degree that they constituted a reasonably accurate barometer of public opinion. They were not easily susceptible to political management, and when political passions ran high, the big towns sometimes flouted vested interests and toppled local patrons—as Sir Henry Hoghton, Preston's leading nonconformist and seemingly unassailable representative, discovered in 1741.[86] The big cities were also at the forefront of the opposition to Walpole, rallying to Vernon, instructing members against the Excise, the Septennial Act, advocating place and pension bills and a strict inquiry into the activities of Robinocracy. Contrary to recent interpretations of urban politics, this dissidence was not simply orchestrated from above. Urban politicians forged novel alliances to battle Walpole and his allies, breaking where necessary with conventional party discipline. Tory and opposition Whig magnates were not insensitive to these developments, but they did not mastermind them. Urban electorates were not especially deferential, and they could be downright rebellious if the customary civilities about electoral independence and choice were not observed. As the experience of Gloucester revealed, voters were sometimes very tetchy about their rights to participate in the political process. In 1734 and again in 1741, they reacted strongly against the electoral agreement of Lord Bathurst and the Selwyns of Matson, rival bigshots, Tory and Whig, by promoting a third candidate and plumping for him.[87] As one freeman wrote in an open letter to his brethren, should 'one Man's private or Family Interest' take priority over everything, 'as tho' the essential Difference lay in Persons and not in things?' In his view electoral compromises were unconstitutional. In the context of Gloucester politics it

---

[86] Sedgwick (ed.), *Commons 1715–54*, i. 272–4.

[87] John Cannon, 'The Parliamentary Representation of the City of Gloucester 1727–90', *Trans. Bristol and Gloucestershire Archaeological Society*, 78 (1959), 140. In 1741, 650 out of 854 votes for Hyett (76%) were plumpers.

was also a travesty of past practice, for it was 'notoriously known' that the Bathursts and the Selwyns had 'opposed each other in almost every Proposition'. It also flouted the custom of allowing the freemen a free hand in the selection of one representative, rendering 'this large and populous City . . . of no Weight, of no Consideration or Consequence to the publick Councils or Interests in general'.[88]

The Gloucester case disclosed the limits of deference within a relatively unassuming urban electorate. It also suggests, on the evidence of the open letter, that the immediate post-Excise era saw an increase in voter truculence and a greater willingness to question proprietary politics and conventional venality. 'Can the Friends of Liberty find any Cause to bow the Knee to Baal whilst there are to be found two Honest Men to represent them?', asked the anonymous author. Would subordination be effected by 'even the great, the bugbear argument, the Power of making Hundreds and ten Hundreds of Honorary Freemen . . . ?' This sort of defiance declined after Walpole's fall and from 1745 onwards urban politics begin to conform to the general pattern of oligarchic politics. They begin to take on some of the features described by Namier— although one should not assume, as a corollary, that urban politics were necessarily parochial or unqualifyingly deferential. National issues could still generate passion and argument in urban centres, although they might not transform politics at the hustings as they had done previously. Similarly, the reassertion of political management cannot be read as straightforward deference. Often it was a reflection of élite compromise or of political ennui or exhaustion rather than of voter compliance with local leaders. Namier tended to assume consensus from electoral ossification. As we have seen, the stultification of urban politics in the mid-century decades was the product of a specific conjuncture.

The only way in which the finer points of Namier's argument can be tested is by a detailed case study. For this purpose I have taken Bristol, one of Namier's own examples, to chart the process by which an open constituency was closed down. Bristol is also a useful example in four other respects. It allows one to test current interpretations about the continuity of party politics in large constituencies. It permits, by virtue of its poll-books, tax records, and apprenticeship registers, further reflections on the social bases of urban politics. It also offers some interesting insights into political venality and into the patterns of dependency in a large, mobile electorate. Finally, it provides a unique opportunity for examining the ways in which interest and ideology intersect. This angle, first raised in a systematic way by Namier, has been overlooked in recent literature, yet in constituencies with powerful mercantile or manufacturing lobbies, it remains of crucial importance.

Lastly, as a counter-example to the generalizations I have laid out in this chapter, I shall offer a case study of a quintessentially Whig city, namely Norwich. This important East Anglian textile town had a large, independent electorate, one in close touch with political developments in London. It also sponsored one of the first provincial presses and had one of the most democratic corporate constitutions outside of the City of London. Yet it played no part in the Instructions campaign of 1733 and 1739–42, and while regularly contested, returned Whig after Whig to Parliament. How can we account for this remarkable record? Can it be attributed to its particular locale, to a deep-rooted loyalty to the Norfolk squire who dominated English politics for two decades? Or does it tell us something about the ideological purchase of Whiggery under the first two Georges? These questions will be addressed in a subsequent Chapter. But first we move west, to Bristol.

8

Bristol: The Commerce of Politics and the Politics of Commerce

WELL-TO-DO visitors to Bristol in the early eighteenth century rarely found it a prepossessing city. Travelling down the Great West Road from London they compared it unfavourably to the aristocratic spa of Bath, whose grandeur, space, and symmetry appealed to their own sensibilities. By contrast, Bristol seemed vulgarly commercial, a warren of narrow streets and lanes leading to crowded quays, unrelieved only by the odd monument to mercantile munificence and the steeples of its churches. The Boston loyalist Thomas Hutchinson thought there were few elegant houses 'fit for a first-rate tradesman to live in', a view with which Pope concurred. 'The streets are as crowded as London,' he remarked, 'but the best image I can give of it is, Tis as if Wapping and Southwark were ten-times as big, or all their people run into London.'[1]

The Bristol merchants were not especially offended by these observations and they slowly conformed to the fashionable standards of Georgian taste. Queen Square was not completed until 1727; the Exchange in 1742. Before 1733 they were quite prepared to entertain royalty on pewter plates and to regale polite ears with Bristolese; 'a broad dialect', one visitor noted, 'much worse than the common people in the metropolis, though they are not willing to acknowledge it'.[2] The reason was that merchants put trade before gentility. What would have pleased them most about Pope's description was its commercial prospect. 'Once over the bridge,' he recalled, 'you

---

[1] George Sherburn (ed.), *Correspondence of Alexander Pope* (5 vols.; Oxford, 1956), iv. 204–5, cited by Peter T. Marcy, 'Eighteenth Century Views of Bristol and Bristolians', in Patrick T. McGrath (ed.), *Bristol In The Eighteenth Century* (Newton Abbot, 1972), p. 26.

[2] Marcy, 'Eighteenth Century Views', p. 36. See also Reginald James, 'Bristol Society In the Eighteenth Century', in C. H. MacInnes and W. F. Whittard (eds.), *Bristol and its Adjoining Counties* (Bristol, 1955), p. 236.

come to a quay along the old wall with houses on both sides, and in the middle of the street, as far as you can see, hundreds of ships, their masts as thick as they stand by one another, which is the oddest and most surprising sight imaginable.'[3] As Peter Monamy's painting of Broad Quay revealed, this was a cherished vista.

From the merchants' point of view, eighteenth-century Bristol had entered upon its golden age.[4] Save for London, it was the leading English port and by 1730 the largest town, with a population of approximately 20,000 in 1700 and 64,000 a century later. The root of its prosperity lay in the expanding transatlantic trades. From a well-established base in Irish, French, and Iberian markets, Bristol ventured westwards, building a lucrative commerce in rum, slaves, tobacco, and sugar. From 1670 to 1700, the tonnage of shipping from the West Indies rose from 1,900 to 5,200; over a similar period the number of ships to Virginia doubled; and as the demand for plantation labour increased, so Bristol came to dominate the slave trade, wresting leadership from London around 1730 and yielding to Liverpool some twenty years later. Not that the trade in human cargoes provides us with a reliable index of Bristol's commercial buoyancy, for the crucial factor in the city's prosperity was its ability to serve as both an entrepôt for colonial re-exports to Europe and Ireland and as an outport for manufacturing goods. To boot, there was the local coastal trade of the Severn region. Bristol had a vast hinterland traffic, as Defoe recognized in 1725,[5] distributing agricultural produce from the Midlands, Wales, and the West, and supplying its local industries: sugar-refineries; distilleries; glassworks; iron, copper, and brass works; sail cloth and woollen manufacture. Only with the canal age and the dramatic growth of industry in Lancashire did it cease to be the premier western port.

Bristol's economic importance in the eighteenth century had a number of political ramifications. On matters of transatlantic trade, whether this involved changes in the regulations concerning enumerated products, colonial credit, or

---

[3] *Correspondence of Pope*, iv. 204–5.
[4] See Walter Minchinton, 'The Port of Bristol In The Eighteenth Century', in McGrath (ed.), *Bristol*, 127–60.
[5] Defoe, *A Tour Through the Whole Island*, p. 367.

industrial protection, its opinion was freely given and frequently solicited. Even on broader commercial issues such as
the future of joint-stock monopolies, its petitions and lobbying
had to be reckoned with at Westminster. Yet, because Bristol
had a broad freeman-franchise, with an electorate of over 3,500
in 1700 and 4,500 fifty years later, its contests assumed a wider
significance. Like London, Bristol politics reputedly registered
the pulse of independent, middling opinion, even the passions
of those further down the social scale. Its demonstrations
against the Excise, for example, were gleefully reported in the
London opposition press as indisputable evidence of Walpole's
unpopularity with commercial and popular circles, just as the
Court made ideological capital out of its loyalist effusions in
1745. In political discourse Bristol was frequently privileged as
a bastion of liberty.

Yet it is significant that this image does not square with the
conventional historical verdict. Despite the optimism of the
press, Bristol's reputation as an open, independent constituency remains curiously uneven. While Bristol played a major
contributory role in the popular opposition to Walpole and
instructed its members to support political reforms in 1739,
1742, and 1756, its independence was compromised by mercantile ambition. From 1756 until the American war, Bristol's
political representation was determined by a narrow circle of
merchant politicians without any recourse to electoral choice.
How did this happen? What does the Bristol experience reveal
about the structures of political dominance in early Hanoverian cities?

Perhaps the most influential historian to write about Bristol
politics has been, somewhat paradoxically, Sir Lewis Namier.
For it was he who suggested that the Bristol record repudiated
the assumption that the large urban constituencies were
intrinsically hostile to oligarchy. In his brief sketch in *The
Structure of Politics*,[6] a vignette which set the tone for
subsequent work, Namier emphasized the almost proprietorial
nature of Bristol politics, the degree to which the city was
dominated by rival merchant-groups whose narrow horizons
and petty intrigues reverberated through the constituency.
Despite its wide franchise and anti-ministerial press, Bristol

[6] Namier, *Structure of Politics*, pp. 88–91.

never approximated to London as a centre of demotic politics, let alone urban radicalism. It remained, Namier argued, remarkably parochial and sectionalist in outlook, as solicitous of government favours as any rotten borough and fixated by its own commercial interests. As one recent commentator has summarized: 'Bristol was never a hot-bed of politics; it minded its business, and that business was trade.'[7]

Few would dispute the Bristolian passion for commerce. Visitors to the city thought it almost obsessional. One 'Irish gentleman' considered Bristolians to be 'engrossed by lucre' and 'very expert in affairs of merchandize'. Even 'the very clergy', another observed, 'talk nothing but trade and how to turn a penny.'[8] Certainly, the port-books do little to dispel this impression, for they reveal, conclusively, just how many middling tradesmen, widows, and professional people dabbled in commerce on their own account.[9] Not surprisingly, issues of trade featured prominently on the hustings and prospective candidates were rated for their commercial expertise and connections, whatever their political affiliation. 'Be they who they will, whether Englishmen, Ancient Britons or Hibernians,' advised one electoral broadsheet in 1754, Bristolians ought to return such candidates 'as shall have it most in their Power and Inclination to promote the Merchandize and Trade of this City.'[10] Once elected, MPs were expected to pay unremitting attention to the commercial interests of their constituency and to maintain close contact with the representatives of other ports, especially Liverpool. Edward Southwell was told in 1740 of the 'vast & regular correspondence with ye merchants of this City' that he would be obliged to maintain,[11]

---

[7] Derek Robinson, author of a number of popular books on Bristol, on BBC Radio 4, 16 Jan. 1980.

[8] Marcy, 'Eighteenth Century Views', p. 30.

[9] See PRO, E 190/1215/4.

[10] Anon., *The Bristol Contest* (Bristol, 1754), p. 19.

[11] Avon Central Lib., Bristol, Southwell Papers, v (Isaac Hobhouse to Southwell, 20 Dec. 1740). In a letter to John Berrow, which he composed in December 1741, Southwell wrote: 'Believe me, the Station of a Moderate Independent Man is no Post of Envy & the Duty of a Representative of Bristol requires every hour of the day a constant attendance in Parlt, an extensive & regular Correspondence, an attention to every Branch of Trade, an universall solicitation in all Offices & with all persons in power, to whom an honest man must [sic] be obnoxious who pursues the real interest of his Country.'

and his papers reveal in some detail the sort of demands that were made of him. He was asked to obtain adequate convoys for local shipping during the War of Jenkins's Ear, to pressure the Royal Africa Company to maintain its forts on the Guinea Coast, to oppose the Virginia Assembly's proposals on currency exchange, to resolve a few legal technicalities surrounding drawbacks. Many of these requests were thinly disguised orders, for attorneyship had long been a feature of Bristol politics. Indeed from 1585 until 1695 the Bristol Corporation had paid its MPs for their services. No wonder men like Edmund Burke, who had more grandiose ideas about the status and role of elected representatives, should have found Bristol business 'vexatious and sometimes humiliating'.[12]

Without doubt, trade was a central preoccupation of Bristol politics. It was a subject which no representative could afford to neglect. Predictably, the principal arbiters of the city's interests were the merchants. Powerfully placed within the city's economy, they were able to preside over its future. Not only did they invest heavily in local industry, but Bristol's manufacturing and distributive trades were very dependent upon overseas markets in Europe, Ireland, and the New World. What is more, merchant influence in Whitehall and Westminster was second to none. Organized through the Society of Merchant Venturers, merchants were effectively able to determine the town's economic priorities and to marginalize competing interests. Such was the case with the local ironmongers over the Iron Act of 1751.[13] Not until the late eighteenth century, when the Society's interests became heavily concentrated in the West Indian trade and its members increasingly interconnected by marriage, did its economic authority in Bristol wane.

The merchants were not only the economic leaders of Bristol society. They were also able to fuse political with economic power. Mercantile representation among mayors and sheriffs increased during the eighteenth century, from 43 per cent in

---

[12] Burke to duke of Portland, 3 Sept. 1780, in J. A. Woods (ed.), *The Correspondence of Edmund Burke*, 10 vols. (Cambridge, 1958–78), iv. 274.

[13] *Commons Journals*, 25, p. 1061. For the background, see R. A. Pelham, 'The West Midland Iron Industry and the American Market in the 18th Century', *University of Birmingham Historical Journal*, 2 (1949–50), 141–62.

the Jacobean era, to 52 per cent in the late Stuart, to 56 per cent in the period 1702–39. Among the forty-three councillors on Bristol's closed Corporation the picture was much the same, with an élite corps of Merchant Venturers comprising 30–40 per cent of total membership in any one year.[14] This formal political authority was not effectively challenged from other potentially prestigious sources. Unlike other provincial towns, Bristol lacked a resident nobility, and as a principal Atlantic port it was never especially dependent upon gentry or aristocratic patronage. To be sure, local magnates such as the duke of Beaufort, the Berkeleys, and the Codringtons, periodically graced the annual meetings of Bristol's political clubs and charities like the Gloucestershire Society, whose central function was to place county boys in Bristolian apprenticeships. But the landed presence in Bristol society was largely symbolic, part of the conventional theatre of hospitality. County gentlemen might provide coals for the Bristol poor during a hard winter or finance lying-in hospitals;[15] they might add a little cachet to a political meeting or a royal visit; but their political influence was not crucial. The last time Beaufort attempted to intervene in a Bristol election was in 1685, when he joined forces with the bishop, the lord chancellor, and lord treasurer, in the sponsorship of the town clerk. His parliamentary candidate 'was so treated . . . the first day of voting, that for the peace of the city and avoiding of bloodshed, he and three hundred of his friends forebore to appear, for of about two hundred that had voted for him, many were so beaten and trod under foot that he rather chose to send in a protest against their tumultuous behaviour'.[16] The crux of the matter was that Beaufort had crucially miscalculated the Bristolian response to the Bloody Assizes, especially Jeffrey's damning indictment of the civic hierarchy for manipulating the Clarendon Code to

[14] Walter Minchinton (ed.), *Politics and the Port of Bristol in the Eighteenth Century* (Bristol Rec. Soc., 23; Bristol, 1963), p. xvii. My calculations are based on the data in the Peter Muggleworth MS (Avon Lib., B 5330).

[15] For the landed presence and gentry paternalism see *Gloucester Journal*, 26 Feb. 1740 (Berkeleys); *Bristol Journal*, 4 Mar. 1769 (Ancient Britons-Welsh gentry); *Bonner and Middleton's Bristol Journal*, 23 Sept. 1775 (Gloucestershire Society).

[16] *HMC Ormonde*, v. 404–5.

their own mercenary advantage. Contingencies aside, this by-election proved to be a turning point in town–county relations. After 1685, as wealthy Bristol merchants purchased county residences, landed magnates had to worry more about the Bristol presence in the shire than city merchants had to worry about the county presence in the town.

If the landed aristocracy posed little threat to the political authority of the merchants in eighteenth-century Bristol, ·neither did the Church. Bristol's clergymen periodically complained about the lack of piety in merchant circles and urged them to a great sense of responsibility in the interests of social harmony. But their criticisms were always grounded upon the necessity of merchant leadership. In a sermon preached before the corporation in 1742, the Reverend Alex Catcott, rector of St Stephen's, urged his audience to 'regard not the clamours of the giddy multitude, nor endeavour to acquire popularity at the expense of your own integrity'. In another context he urged all 'in a low condition of life' to bear their 'station with humility' and not to repine or envy 'the dignity of the rich and powerful'. Like other clergymen, Catcott admired commerce as the bearer of refinement, learning, urbanity, and civility. It was, he said, 'the first mover, the mainspring . . . which gives life and motion to the whole, and sets all the inferior wheels to work'.[17] Such encomiums to trade were typical of the Bristol clergy, some of whom were related to merchant families as well as being dependent upon their patronage.

Of course the Mitre might have proved a counterpoint to merchant power as it did, to some extent, in Exeter. But in fact this was not the case at all. The Bristol see was the most poorly endowed in England, bringing in revenues of only £300 a year. By the standards of the day this was an episcopal pittance, scarcely enough to uphold the dignity of the office, even when held *in commendam*. One cleric complained to Walpole when he was offered the see in 1738 that it was 'not very suitable

---

[17] A. S. Catcott, *The Antiquity and Honourableness of the Practice of Merchandize* (Bristol, 1744), p. 15; *Sermons by the Late Reverend A. S. Catcott* (London, 1753), pp. 443–4, 466. See also John Gibb, *The Mutual Duties of Magistrates and People: A Sermon Preached at St. Mary Redcliffe 29 May 1721* [Bristol, 1721].

either to the condition of my fortune or of the circumstances of
my preferment, nor as I should have thought to the recommendation with which I was honoured'.[18] Consequently, ambitious clerics strove to make their tenure in Bristol as brief as
possible, viewing their poor western see as a stepping stone to
greater rewards. No fewer than twelve bishops passed through
Bristol between 1710 and 1761. Few had the time to build up a
political interest in the city, and the one that might have,
Joseph Butler, bishop from 1738 to 1750, was said to have
wafted to his see 'in a cloud of metaphysics and remained
absorbed in it'.[19] When he was not contemplating the
Almighty, he appears to have been organizing the rebuilding of
the Bishop's Palace, at a cost of between £3,000–5,000, in
addition to a gift of cedar from the merchants.

The pre-eminent position of the merchants within Bristol
society, which the clergy did little to dispel, helps to explain
why they tended to regard the constituency as their own and
why they were disposed to electoral compromise within their
own ranks. But to suppose that Bristol politics were incurably
and totally under merchant control would be misleading; for
Bristol was always subject to popular pressures. Every major
crisis in national politics reverberated through the constituency, sometimes wrecking merchant calculations and unsettling their plans. In the 1734 election, for example, the popular
will ran counter to the mainstream of merchant opinion; and
successfully too, for the principal merchants had hoped to
dissociate the general opposition to the Excise from Walpole's
unpopularity. In 1756, and again in 1774, merchant priorities
were compromised by sources beyond their control. So while
the merchants were always an important force in Bristol
politics, they could never count on the unquestioning support
of their fellow constituents. There were other important
factors in Bristol politics besides merchant dominance, and
ones to which the merchants themselves were party.

One of the salient characteristics of Bristol politics through

[18] Cited in Elizabeth Ralph, 'Bishop Secker's Diocese Book', in Patrick
McGrath (ed.), *A Bristol Miscellany* (Bristol Rec. Soc., 37; Bristol, 1985), p. 24.
[19] DNB under Joseph Butler; see also Lewis, *Walpole's Correspondence*, xx.
167, and William Barrett, *The History and Antiquities of the City of Bristol*
(Bristol, 1789), p. 285.

much of the eighteenth century was the resilience of its political divisions. Until very recently at least, historians have seen party strife reaching its apogee during the Augustan era, ebbing perceptibly during Walpole's ascendancy, and finally disintegrating during the 1750s. London's experience, I have argued, ran essentially along these lines, facilitating the formation of a bipartisan opposition to Whig oligarchy. But the Bristol experience was rather different. As late as 1754 voters were being encouraged to 'honour the Cause of True Blue' and 'Ne'er join with Dissenters', while honest Whigs were advised 'It's plain and most certain there is a Banditti / Of Nonjurors and Jacobites inhabits your City'. Even those who sought the middle ground and despaired of the 'stale and invidious' distinctions of 'High Church or Low Church', reluctantly acknowledged their vibrancy: 'As Party often infuses itself more or less into all Communities . . . so you may be sure, on this Occasion, all the Filth and Rubbish than can be raked together will be plentifully thrown at those who on either Side clash with or oppose the Interest of the Party they respectively espouse.'[20] Indeed, party rhetoric survived George III's accession. As late as 1774 Edmund Burke commented on the 'Capital divisions of Whigg and Tory' in Bristol, although by this time the changing climate of both high and low politics had complicated local alignments.

It would be tempting, of course, to regard these divisions as basically habitual, if not obsolescent, were it not for the continuing evidence of both party organizations and voting patterns. During the first half of the century Bristol sported a series of party clubs, the Tory Loyal Society being followed in 1737 by the Stedfast Society, the rival Hanoverian by the Union. Even the charity societies associated with Bristol's foremost philanthropist, Edward Colston, were divided along party lines, the mid-century seeing the formation of the Tory Dolphin Society and in 1768 the Whig Anchor.[21] Nor were these affiliations simply a feature of polite society, a by-product

---

[20] *The Bristol Contest 1754*, p. 71. See also the 1754 electoral broadsides, *Diversion upon Diversion* (Avon Lib., B 10950) and *Instructions Recommended to the Freemen of Bristol* (Avon Lib., B 10973).

[21] John Latimer, *The Annals of Bristol* (3 vols; Bristol, 1893; repr. 1970), ii. 280.

of the continuing rivalry of well-established families. Throughout the Georgian era a high proportion of the electorate was prepared to forfeit a vote in accordance with party loyalties. In 1722, for example, when the Tory William Hart ran alone against two Whigs, 84 per cent of Hart's supporters were plumpers. In 1734, in an election fought over the Excise, 74 per cent of the opposition voters plumped for the Tory candidate, Thomas Coster, rather than pair him with the anti-Excise Whig, Sir Abraham Elton.[22] Twenty years later, when Robert Nugent stood against the Tory Sir John Philipps and the sugar-planter Richard Beckford, Whig voters polled overwhelmingly for their only official candidate. As Nugent reported to Hardwicke on 30 April: 'We have this day obtained a complete Triumph over the Tories . . . Mine have been, almost all, single votes, and besides those which our Friends, for *reasons of zeal*, would divide with Beckford, there were near two hundred unpoll'd who would have been single with me.'[23] Given the importance of the slave and sugar trade to Bristol's economy and Beckford's broadly based connections—through his elder brother, William, he had links with the dukes of Bedford and Shaftesbury as well as with metropolitan Tories—this can only be regarded as extraordinary.

How can one account for the persistence of party divisions in Bristol politics? A look at the social geography of the town and its hinterland provides us with some clues. Bristol was one of the leading Atlantic ports. It had strong cultural links with the New England colonies, becoming a haven for American loyalism after the War of Independence. And it traded in areas where nonconformist associations were something of an advantage. It also served the local woollen industries of Gloucestershire and, to a lesser extent, North Somerset and Wiltshire, districts which had traditionally been breeding grounds for Dissent. Not surprisingly, Bristol gained a reputation for religious heterodoxy. By the 1680s six different congregations had been established in the city and during the

[22] My calculations, derived from the 1722 and 1734 poll-books located at the Avon Library, B 8766–7, *An Exact List of the Voters of the Freeholders and Freemen of the City and County of Bristol . . .* (Bristol, 1722) and *A List of the Free-Holders and Free-Men who Voted at the Election . . . for the City and County of Bristol begun Wednesday, May 15, 1734* (Bristol, 1734).
[23] BL, Add. MS 35,592, fo. 339.

next forty years their numbers and prosperity increased. Augustan Bristol featured the largest Quaker meeting in England. Its 1,700-strong assembly was led by a formidable phalanx of merchants and manufacturers whose collective wealth was said to be in excess of £500,000.[24] Two of the Presbyterian congregations were also wealthy. The Lewin's Mead congregation had some 1,400 hearers in 1715, together worth £400,000. It included a number of city councillors and ex-sheriffs as well as 'several other men of condition, divers many rich, many more substantial, few poor'.[25] Together the nonconformists made up nearly 20 per cent of the Bristol population, over twice the national average, and a disproportionately large section of the bourgeoisie. According to John Evans's inquiry, about 700 nonconformists voted in Bristol elections, but 'many of these by their Estates & Interest in trade can make many 100 more votes'. In his estimation 'the strength of all the Dissenters in Bristol may justly be reckon[e]d much more than that of all the Low Church Party there'.[26]

Yet the West Country was traditionally Tory territory, and its Toryism became more pronounced after the Civil War when the lesser gentry abandoned Puritanism. Only the textile towns and villages, as the Monmouth rebellion revealed, retained a nostalgia for the Good Old Cause. This polarization of West Country society tended to produce political extremism, with the gentry, clergy, and older, established merchant families intransigently Tory, if not Jacobite. Certainly, the West was noted for its clerical nonjurors, its October Club politicians, its general level of disaffection to the Williamite regime, as well as for its neo-republican nonconformity. And the Bristol area was no exception to the rule. Monmouth had held high hopes of support from the city's radical Whigs. Amongst his closest advisors was the Bristol lawyer, Nathaniel Wade, the son of a puritan officer in the Civil War, who had

---

[24] Dr Williams's Library, John Evans MS 34.4, fo. 147; William Braithwaite, *The Second Period of Quakerism* (Cambridge, 1961), pp. 100–8.

[25] Dr Williams's Lib., John Evans MS 34.4, fo. 147.

[26] Ibid. See also Watts, *The Dissenters*, table xii. A stranger commented in the *Bristol Gazette*, 31 Oct. 1771: 'Dissenters are numerous at Bristol; in one parish are 9 places of worship for different persuasions; in elections their votes chiefly preponderate, and those who canvass are not a little assiduous to gain their favour.'

organized an armed band of sectaries in Bristol during the Exclusion crisis and had been implicated in the Rye House plot. He was one of the rebel officers who opposed the proclamation of Monmouth as King.[27] By contrast, Bristol's MPs at the Convention Parliament, Sir Richard Hart and Sir John Knight II, both voted against the offer of the crown to William and Mary; both insisted that the Commons should observe the anniversary of Charles I's martyrdom in January 1689, and both were arrested in 1696 as Jacobite conspirators.[28] This political extremism continued into the eighteenth century. In 1716, in the aftermath of the Coronation-day riots, a local clothier, John Chisild, was fined two marks for justifying the execution of Charles I.[29] Two years later a tide-waiter testified before the mayor that the Reverend Edward Bisse had delivered a Jacobite sermon at Pill bemoaning the last thirty years' 'usurpation'. The nation had 'been brought into a Snare by a Snake in the Grass, accompanied by some Thousand of Dutch Boors,' Bisse asserted, 'who, instead of doing us good did involve us in a bloody and expensive war, and instead of our lawful and rightful sovereign, we [had] a poor diminutive worm, the Prince of Orange, set up in his place'. The government moved quickly to bridle this demagogue, but not before Bisse thundered his sedition in several other counties. Brought to King's Bench, fined £400, and imprisoned for four years, he remained an unrepentant Jacobite, for in Newgate he is said to have given a printer 'a copy of verses upon the people's numerous attendance of the pretender abroad' as well as a parcel of songs.[30]

What gave particular edge to Bristol politics was the sharpness of its religious antagonisms. Local ballads commemorated religious repression with unsavoury exuberance. One 'Prentices' Ditty' of 1656 urged the lads:

[27] Latimer, *Annals of Bristol*, i. 398, 418, 429, 432–3, 447–8; Peter Earle, *Monmouth's Rebels* (London, 1971), p. 30; Robin Clifton, *The Last Popular Rebellion* (London, 1984), *passim*.
[28] B. A. Henning (ed.), *The History of Parliament: The House of Commons 1660–1690* (3 vols.; London, 1984), ii. 502–3, 696–7.
[29] Bristol RO, Bristol Quarter Sessions Docket, 22 June 1715, and Tolzey Books, 1703–16, which shows that Chisild was from Barton Hundred, Gloucestershire.
[30] *Annals of George I*, iv. 351–2; *The Weekly Journal, or Saturday's Post*, 6 Dec. 1718; Latimer, *Annals of Bristol*, ii. 121; *London Evening Post*, 30 Mar.–2 Apr. 1734; PRO SP 35/7/214. For the 'Prentices Ditty', see Rose E. Sharland, *Ballads of Old Bristol* (Bristol, n.d.), p. 41.

Come! hasten we to High Cross to see the fun o' the fair,
For Quaker Naylor's pilloried and offering up a prayer
And better than bull-baiting, or squailing cocks, meseems,
To see the rascal suffer, and hear his saintly screams.

This sectarian hatred broke out with even greater ferocity after 1660, fanned by royal policy and approval. Over 900 Dissenters and Quakers were taken up in the first enforcement of the Conventicle Act. In August 1681, some 1,500 were said to be under prosecution and the fines on Quakers alone in this wave of repression amounted to £16,440. Nor was this all. Imprisonment and privation killed tens of nonconformists, including Mr Fownes, the minister of Broadmead Chapel. Six men and three women were even sentenced to seven years' transportation to Barbados and, but for a compassionate crew, would have been sent there. In this society there was little room for clergymen of a more moderate hue. When Thomas Jekyll, the vicar of Rowden in Wiltshire, lectured in Bristol in 1675, he was quickly taken to task for his easy-going sentiments. 'I was in a very rude manner clamour'd against', he recalled, 'and sent for before the Mayor, and accus'd of such crimes as would have taken my life in the most ignominious manner.'[31]

This sectarian persecution informed Bristol politics for over a generation. Many of the leading members of the nonconformist congregations belonged to families which had been victims of the Restoration purges. The Harfords, for example, prominent merchants and soap-manufacturers, two of whom were trustees of the Quaker meeting-house in 1718, led the Friends' resistance in the 1680s'.[32] Understandably, the legacy of the early years took a long time to die. Well into the 1720s the Bristol Friends were asked by their London compatriots whether there had been any 'Sufferings'.[33] This vigilance was sustained by the continuing discrimination against nonconformity during the eighteenth century. In the High Church

---

[31] Sir Thomas Jekyll, *Peace and Love, Recommended and Persuaded in Two Sermons Preached at Bristol 31 January 1675* (London, 1675), preface. For the hostility towards Quakers see Latimer, *Annals of Bristol*, i. *passim*. See also Anon., *The New and Strange Imprisonment of the People Called Quakers in the City of Bristol* (n.p., 1682) and Anon., *A letter to the Men's Meeting of the People Called Quakers in Bristol* (London, 1732), pp. 10–18.

[32] Latimer, *Annals of Bristol*, i. 408: see also Bristol RO, SF/CAT/1 (trustees of Quaker meeting-house, 1718).

[33] Bristol RO, SF/A1/5 (Men's Meeting (1716–27)), *passim*.

revival of 1710, Quakers were banned from joining the Society of Merchant Venturers. In the following year the Tories on Common Council insisted upon a strict enforcement of the Occasional Conformity Act, a demand that led to the resignation of three Presbyterians. Both of these actions were rescinded in the next decade, but the possibility of further proscriptions if ever the Tories came to power riveted the nonconformist interest to the Whig party. Unlike Hertfordshire, where there is evidence of a desertion of the Whig party once the religious priorities of Walpole's government became clear, Bristol's Quakers voted overwhelmingly in favour of the Whig candidates. Not one trustee of the meeting-house cast his vote for William Hart, the Tory candidate in 1722. Thirty-two years later, the picture was much the same. Prominent Quakers opted conclusively for Robert Nugent, the government Whig candidate. Of thirty-four voters, only one supported Nugent's opponents, Philipps and Beckford, and only two declined to plump for Nugent alone.[34]

This record can be seen to typify the nonconformist vote as a whole. The Presbyterian congregation at Lewin's Mead was solidly Whig in the twenties, thirties, and fifties, 48 out of 55 voters plumping for Nugent in 1754 and a further 5 pairing him with Beckford. Similarly, the Broadmead Baptists backed Whig candidates, 18 out of 20 voting for Robert Nugent. These figures, drawn from the rolls of members from extant denominational records, reflect tendencies that can be corroborated in other ways. If we investigate the electoral geography of Bristol, for example, we find that the parishes noted for their nonconformist presence were those where the Whig vote was strongest. St James's parish, for example, which housed several influential meeting-houses as well as a high proportion of nonconformist residents, remained a Whig stronghold right down to the 1780s. Save for a brief deviation in 1734, so also did St Philip and St Jacob, a large suburban, industrial parish which Secker noted had 'many presbyterians and quakers'. Moreover, if we look at what might be termed the party

---

[34] I have used SF/CAT/1 and SF/A1/9a to locate the leading Quakers and have traced their voting behaviour in the poll-books for 1722 and 1754. For my later remarks about the political proclivities of other Dissenting denominations, I have used the following records to locate Dissenting voters: Bristol RO, MS 6687 (1), Lewin's Mead Presbyterian Minute Book 1692–1774, and Bd/R1/2–3, Broadmead Baptist Church, Members' Roll 1727–46 and 1734–74.

zealots, the men who were prepared to sign petitions against the return of Tories in the 1734 and 1756 elections, we find many an influential Quaker and Dissenting family and a disproportionate number from the principal nonconformist parishes and trades. Of the 386 signatories of the two petitions against Thomas Coster in 1734, 230 (60 per cent) were nonconformists, the great majority being either Presbyterian or Quaker.[35] Many came from St James and the textile parishes of Temple and St Philip and St Jacob. Several can be identified as members of leading nonconformist families. Among them are to be found Jacob Elton of Queen Square, master of the Merchant Venturers in 1728 and mayor in 1733; Jeremiah Ames, a Presbyterian grocer and merchant in Peter Street, who died worth £70,000; Richard Farr, a Dissenting merchant who was nominated to the Common Council in 1746 and who became a leading light in the Union Club; James Hillhouse, another Queen Square merchant of Presbyterian origin, master of the Merchant Venturers in 1730; and Christopher Devonshire, a Quaker merchant and Union Club member whose premiums for apprentices ranged between £315 and £525.[36] Such wealth and influence was also apparent in 1756.[37] Among those who protested to Jarrit Smith's election were fifteen representatives of the Lewin's Mead congregation. They included John Wraxall, the city sword-bearer; three members of the Union Club, two of whom were also members of the city Council; several wealthy soap-manufacturers; and at least two merchants who were soon to become masters of the Merchant Venturers. By this time, in fact, the Presbyterians were very well placed on Bristol's closed Corporation. Between 1734 and 1754 they accounted for no less than 40 per cent of the 41 vacancies on the Common Council.[38] In terms of commitment

[35] *A List of All the Names that Sign'd the Two Petitions against Thomas Coster, Esq.* (n.p., n.d.): this list (Avon Lib., B 15163) was very probably printed in Bristol in 1735. It is annotated, noting those petitioners who were Baptists, Quakers, and Presbyterians.

[36] Latimer, *Annals of Bristol*, ii. 462; Alfred B. Beaven, *Bristol Lists: Municipal and Miscellaneous* (Bristol, 1899), pp. 126–7, 226–7; Bristol RO, Apprentice Books, 1740–60, fos. 8v, 174; Avon Lib., Jefferies Collection, x, fo. 10; BL, Add MS 32,867, fos. 203–7.

[37] For the petition see Bristol RO, Jarrit Smith papers, AC/JS 90 (2).

[38] Ronald Quilici, 'Turmoil in a City and an Empire: Bristol's Factions 1700–1775', Ph.D. diss. (University of New Hampshire, 1976), pp. 221–2.

and activism, as well as wealth, the nonconformists were the backbone of the Whig party.

Sectarian affiliations were crucial to the Whig party, and they fuelled, in reaction, Tory partisanship. Many of the traditionalists in Bristol society greatly resented the rise of Dissent to a position of social and economic prominence. The very *visibility* of Dissent, the fact that its sword-bearers were prominent Presbyterians, that mayors, sheriffs, and recorders frequented conventicles, that one Recorder and MP, John Scrope, was the grandson of a regicide, must have been galling to High Churchmen. Tory preachers fanned these flames with their references to Dissenting Ministers as the 'Usupers of the Ephod' and to their flocks as fanatics undermining a providential hierarchical order.[39] The Tory divines also made much of their support for a traditional ceremonial order in which charity added 'a new lustre to Persons eminent for their Rank and Dignity'.[40] George Smalridge, bishop of Bristol from 1714 to 1719, was especially insistent upon the social conventions of hospitality. 'By the Liberality of the Wealthy,' he argued, 'abounding in Plenty and Rich in good works, the Holy Scriptures, those Fountains of everlasting life, are open'd to the Poor.'[41] Predictably, the Tories strove to capitalize upon the munificence of Edward Colston, whose benefactions to churches, charity schools, hospitals, and almshouses were said to have surpassed £70,000.[42] With some success. The Tory tolerance of popular recreations and its tradition of open hospitality was not shared by the Dissenters in Bristol, nor by Whig clergymen like the Reverend Arthur Bedford, the vicar of Temple. Bedford was a leading light of the Society for the Reformation of Manners in Bristol. Along with prominent Whig merchants, the Bristol MPs, Sir Thomas Day and Robert Yate (both Whigs), and the redoubtable Major Nathaniel Wade

[39] See [Henry Abbot], *Unity, Friendship and Charity Recommended in a Sermon Preach'd before the Gloucestershire Society 27 August 1713* (Bristol, 1713), pp. 8–11.

[40] George Smalridge, *Twelve Sermons Preach'd on Several Occasions* (Oxford, 1717), p. 213.

[41] Ibid. 231.

[42] James Harcourt, *A Sermon Preach'd in the Church of All Saints in Bristol October 21, 1721, upon the Death of Edward Colston Esquire* (London, 1721), *passim*.

(now enjoying a quieter life as steward of the Sheriff's court), Bedford cracked down on alehouse tippling, fairground booths, gambling dens, and riverside traffic on the Sabbath.[43] Not everyone shared the reformers' enthusiasm for battling iniquity, nor Bedford's indefatigable zeal. In orchestrating the campaign in 1706 to suppress a theatre on St Augustine's Back, for example, Bedford produced a book which cited 7,000 passages from acting dramas that offended no fewer than 1,400 texts in the Bible. Indeed, the minutes of the society hint at considerable resistance to reformist vigilance, notably in All Saints, Edward Colston's native parish, and St Mary Redcliffe, also something of a Tory stronghold.[44] But hostility to the Reformation Society extended beyond the vestry to a trading world which maintained a lively interest in the rougher pastimes of the day, cock-fighting especially, and resented the restrictions upon Sunday trading. Consequently, Tories were quick to insist that the Reformation Society was a Whig enterprise and to extol their own tolerance of popular recreations.[45]

I do not wish to exaggerate the politics of conviviality; simply to suggest that during the reforming wave of the early eighteenth century Tory paternalism had some popular purchase. Nor do I wish to exaggerate the sectarian dimensions of mid-century Toryism, for there are reasons to believe that old-style Toryism began to decline in the 1720s. Clerical support for the Blues fell away as Crown and Corporation installed Whig divines in Bristol benefices. During the 1730s only 50 per cent of the clergy voted Tory whereas 70 per cent had done so in 1722. Furthermore, as Tory preachers modulated their pitch in a Whig world, high-flying sentiments became rather eccentric. The Reverend Hugh Waterman, the rector of St Peter and St Mary Port, had been singled out by the *Flying Post* in 1718 as a man who 'pronounced the word *Church* with great loudness in Season'. Upon his death in 1746, it was remarked, in a

---

[43] Avon Lib., Minutes of the Society for the Reformation of Manners 1699–1705 (B10162); see also T. C. Curtis and W. A. Speck, 'The Societies for the Reformation of Manners: A Case Study in the Theory and Practice of Moral Reform', *Literature and Society*, 3 (Mar. 1976), pp. 45–64.

[44] Latimer, *Annals of Bristol*, ii. 61–2.

[45] Ibid. 25, 86, 140, 170, 179, 432, 469: J. F. Nicholls and John Taylor, *Bristol Past and Present* (3 vols.; Bristol, 1881), iii. 146, 156–7.

somewhat caustic obituary, that 'he had not learnt the fashionable practice of putting the specious mark of moderation on the face of his disaffection'.[46] But, as a full-blown Tory, Waterman was not seen as a threat but rather as an odd, principled gentleman; 'high tory, plain, honest, exemplary, 75 years old' was how Bishop Secker described him in his diocese book. In fact, such was the temper of the times that Tory curates were being taken on by Whig vicars, as Secker noted in St Nicholas, something that would have been unthinkable two or three decades earlier.

Equally important in this transition was the changing pattern of Tory leadership in Bristol. Some royalist families disappeared or declined in economic importance. Others like the Canns, Creswicks, and Clutterbucks trimmed their sails to the prevailing wind and joined the Whig establishment, leaving only a rump of Tory die-hards. A look at the leading members of the Stedfast Society reveals that there were three or four of old Tory stock, men whose ancestors had been prominent in Tory politics. These included Robert Bound, a merchant and 'man of substance', a property-developer whose father had been a member of the City Council from 1696–1715, mayor in 1709, and whose grandfather had been involved in a royal conspiracy in Bristol in 1643.[47] The Stedfast members also featured Arthur and William Hart, senior and junior, whose family hailed from Devonshire, rose in fortune during the seventeenth century through marriage and the Newfoundland fishery, and represented the city between 1681 and 1695.[48] But, aside from the Harts, whose family stood again for the Tories in 1722, the driving force of the Stedfast Society came from men outside the local establishment. Comparatively few of the founding members belonged to the Merchant Venturers or came from old Bristol families. By and large they were well-to-do wholesalers, manufacturers, or professionals,

[46] *Flying Post*, 9–11 Oct. 1718; *Farley's Bristol Advertiser*, 26 July 1746; Ralph, 'Bishop Secker's Diocese Book', pp. 40, 43.

[47] For the members of the Stedfast Society see the records of the club in the possession of the Society of Merchant Venturers, Merchants' Hall, President's Accounts 1737–54. On Bound see *The History of the Antient Society of St. Stephen's Ringers, Bristol* (Bristol, 1928), pp. 18–19; PRO, PROB 11/795/147.

[48] On the Hart family see W. R. Williams, *The Parliamentary History of the County of Gloucester* (Hereford, 1898), pp. 120–1 and Henning, *Commons 1660–1690*, ii. 502–3.

men who asked high premiums from prospective apprentices and could attract applicants from polite society. Some were quite wealthy. John Brickdale, for example, a woollen-draper in a family business, was left £100,000 by his father in 1761. Joseph Percival, a merchant who traded in Jamaica, Ireland, and Europe, bequeathed £70,000.[49] Thomas Holmes, a merchant who joined the society in 1747, left lands and messuages in Cardiff, Glamorganshire, Hereford, and Bristol, as well as a £3,000 dowry to his daughter, Elizabeth. But few amassed fortunes which could compare with the richest merchants. Wealthy or not, they were not the cream of Bristolian society.

The establishment of the Stedfast Society in 1737 marked a new phase in Bristol Toryism. Its predecessor, the Loyal Society, had been a self-consciously High Church organization. Formed in 1710 to commemorate Edward Colston's electoral victory in Bristol, it had attempted to rally churchmen to his standard, emphasizing Colston's local munificence and his antipathy to Dissent. The annual dinners on Colston's birthday were always conducted with a great deal of gusto; in fact members were said to be 'very officious on all High Church festivals, and [to] make more Noise, drink more Beer and swear more Oaths than half of the rest of their Fellow Citizens'.[50] On Colston's birthday the High Churchmen gathered in hundreds for a service at the Cathedral before processing to Colston's school for their banquet. Their meetings were graced by prominent dignitaries from the neighbouring counties. The duke of Beaufort and ten MPs attended the celebrations in 1713.[51] And there was the predictable batch of clerical high-flyers. Twenty-three were noted in 1714 by a hostile observer, who believed they had 'assembled chiefly to affront the Magistrates and interrupt the Peace of the City'. None of these clergymen, he continued, attended the magistrates at the proclamation of King George, and their studied absence was thought to have encouraged the disorders which broke out on Coronation day.[52]

Like the Loyal, the Stedfast Society continued the tradition

---

[49] Latimer, *Annals of Bristol*, ii. 462; see also PRO, PROB 11/869/355 (Thomas Holmes); and PROB 11/885/138 (Joseph Percival).
[50] John Oldmixon, *The Bristol Riot* (London, 1714), p. 4.
[51] *The Post Boy*, 7–10 Nov. 1713.
[52] *Flying Post*, 9–11 Nov. 1714.

of inviting local magnates to its deliberations.[53] Its honorary roll included some of the stars of the Tory party, while its regular roll featured a handful of West Country MPs including the county representatives of Gloucestershire and Somerset. But the White Lyon Club, as the Stedfast was sometimes called, was always more than a political society that commemorated Tory anniversaries and nominated candidates for parliamentary contests. It held weekly meetings and forged links with parish clubs, the basis of its electoral strength. Through its member MPs, who by the mid-century included the Beckfords and Sir John Philipps, it maintained contact with important extra-parliamentary groups in the metropolis, for example, the Independent Electors of Westminster. Significantly, the clergy were absent from the new organization. A correspondence was also opened with dissident Whigs in Bristol, men like Alderman Nathaniel Day and the Quaker Henry Hobhouse, something that would have been impossible in the Loyal. The Stedfast Society, in other words, broke with High Church tradition and sought to co-ordinate the more heterogeneous opposition to official Whiggism that had emerged since Walpole's accession to power.

The event which made this new departure in Bristol politics possible was the Excise crisis and the subsequent return of Thomas Coster at the 1734 election. The initial reaction of Bristolians to the proposed excise was one of unanimous opposition. The port was a leading importer of wine and tobacco, and the prospect of a new tax on both of these commodities was opposed by the merchant community in general, especially since Bristol's overseas trade had entered a period of uncertainty, with declining tobacco imports and a rise in bankruptcies.[54] The clothiers were also against the excise, for they feared a disruption in woollen exports at a time when they were campaigning for a reduction in the duty upon oil used in their manufacture.[55] As soon as it was rumoured

[53] The honorary members of the society, and those invited to dine with it, can be ascertained from the Rules and Orders 1737–1802.

[54] W. E. Minchinton (ed.), *The Trade of Bristol in the Eighteenth Century* (Bristol Rec. Soc., 20; Bristol, 1957), pp. 15, 177, 184–5. Between 1722–31 Bristol imported 12% of the total tobacco imports for Britain. It re-exported far less (c.39%) than most ports.

[55] *Fog's Weekly Journal*, 30 Dec. 1732; *HMC Egmont Diary*, i. 128.

that Walpole was contemplating an excise, the Society of Merchant Venturers and the Whig-dominated city council instructed its MPs to oppose any legislation and agreed to share the costs of mobilizing support against the measure. When Walpole ultimately withdrew his bill, the mayor declared a general holiday, 'erected a battery of seven guns behind his house' to fire celebratory salvos, and distributed 108 gallons of beer at the High Cross at civic expense. In the anti-Excise festival that ensued, Sir Robert was burnt in effigy before the Excise Office in Broad Street.[56] Two months later, the homecoming of Sir Abraham Elton, the Whig MP who opposed the Excise, was wildly celebrated. According to one account, his entry to the city was 'attended by a numerous train of Coaches and Gentlemen on Horseback with gilt cockades of Tobacco in their Hats'. What is more, 'all Ranks and Degrees of People' and 'all Parties' toasted his conduct.[57]

The Bristol opposition to the Excise was thus a bipartisan affair. The Whig merchants regarded the issue as central to the town's prosperity, one that transcended party considerations. Consequently, their defection on this occasion was not intended to have any major political ramifications. Bristol's other representative, John Scrope, a lawyer and secretary to the treasury, offered a public apology for his support of the bill explaining that his government responsibilities really gave him no choice. This statement promptly restored him to favour with the Whig hierarchy. Before the Excise scheme, Scrope had shown himself attentive to the trading interests of his native city. He had defended Bristol's interests in the slave trade against those of the Royal Africa Company in 1730. In the following year he had supported the weavers' petition against the illegal export of Irish wool to the continent.[58] These activities and Scrope's general commercial experience made merchants reluctant to abandon him. But the Bristol electors refused to differentiate the politics of interest from the politics of party, and despite the solid backing of the Corporation, the nonconformists, and the Merchant Venturers,

[56] *Fog's Weekly Journal*, 20 Jan. 1733; Latimer, *Annals of Bristol*, ii. 184; *London Magazine*, 2 (1733), 213.

[57] *Gloucester Journal*, 26 June 1733.

[58] Sedgwick (ed.), *Commons 1715–54*, ii. 413; for Scrope's public apology see *Daily Post*, 11 Sept. 1733.

Scrope was defeated at the general election of 1734 by just over 200 votes.[59]

This so incensed the Whigs that they considered tinkering with the franchise, either eliminating the freeman vote altogether, which would have meant a loss of 2,700 votes, or excluding those who did not pay scot and lot. In the event they dropped this proposal in favour of two petitions complaining of electoral irregularities.[60] But while the managers mustered their evidence of almsmen-voters and impersonations in the spring of 1735, Walpole pressed Scrope to abandon the struggle. The lawyer was 'very angry with Sir Robert for making him give up,' Lady Cowper recalled, but 'Sir Robert's friends say that the mob are so exasperated against Mr. Scrope for having voted for the excise that they are resolved not to have him there and if he carried his petition were determined to rise and stone his friends.'[61] To compensate Scrope, Walpole found him another seat at Lyme Regis.

The Stedfast Society attempted to build upon this popular victory in order to mobilize the growing dissidence to Walpolean rule. It supported a Country programme of place and pension bills to curb electoral influence; it advocated a return to triennial parliaments. It also demanded an impartial inquiry into Walpolean corruption. In local government the Stedfast sought to restrict the influence of the closed Corporation in favour of more accountable administrative bodies, as the Board of Guardians had been since 1696.[62] Admittedly, this was party politics. An increase in corporate responsibility inevitably benefited the Whig party, for of the 55 men elected to the closed Council during the period 1710–30, at least 39 were Whigs, the proportion increasing among the aldermen.[63] But

[59] Of the Bristol Corporation, 33 voted for Elton and Scrope and only 2 for Elton and the Tory, Thomas Coster. Of the Merchant Venturers, 55 voted for Scrope and 18 for Coster. See 1734 poll, and Latimer, *Annals of Bristol*, ii. 189.

[60] Avon Lib., Jefferies Collection, x, fo. 9, the petitions of 20 Mar. and 11 Apr. 1735; see also the petition of Alderman Henry Walter, passed by Common Council (Bristol RO, Council Proceedings (1722–38), fos. 368–9, 374–5); Cambridge Univ., Cholmondley Papers, C (H) 60/20/1 ('A Short Case of the Bristol Election').

[61] Herts. RO, Cowper (Panshanger) MS (Lady Cowper's Diary, 24 Apr. 1735), cited in Sedgwick (ed.), *Commons 1715–54*, i. 245.

[62] E. E. Butcher (ed.), *Bristol Corporation of the Poor 1696–1898* (Bristol, 1932).

[63] Of the 20 aldermen elected 1710–30, 18 were Whigs. My figures are from Beaven, *Bristol Lists*, pp. 210–12.

the demand for a decentralized structure of local government did conform to the principle of constitutional dependency, to a balance of powers which inhibited the accretion of oligarchical power. Richard Beckford argued the case forcefully in the debate over the Bristol Night Watch Bill in 1755. It was 'the spirit and beauty of our constitution to divide the exercise of power into as many channels as possible, in order to prevent its gathering into such a torrent as must bear down everything before it'.[64] Such principles attracted support from those sectors of Bristol society who found the Corporation overbearing, petty, and unduly subservient to ministerial directives. Certainly, the Corporation's Addresses to the Crown on such occasions as Dettingen and, in the next decade, Minorca, left little doubt that it was a ministerial mouthpiece.[65]

In other ways, too, the Stedfast Society sought the support of independent opinion, sought to broaden its base beyond the Blues' traditional constituency. When Thomas Coster died in 1738 the club chose as his successor a man who was not closely identified with the Tory party. He was Edward Southwell, a country gentleman whose family seat was at Kingsweston, to the north east of Bristol on the Gloucestershire side of the Avon. Southwell was of Tory lineage: his father had been secretary of state for Ireland, closely associated with the duke of Ormonde. But like his father Edward Southwell had married into a prominent Whig family, the Rockinghams, and in the early Hanoverian era these links became more pronounced. Southwell described himself as a 'Moderate Independent Man' and when he ultimately took his place in the Commons he was introduced by William Pulteney and Sir John Barnard.[66] Some Bristol Tories suspected him of Court sympathies. They were troubled by the fact that he was 'known to Great Men'.[67] It was only after he had pledged himself to support a Country programme and to defend the

---

[64] Cobbett, *Parliamentary History*, xv. 481–2.

[65] Bristol RO, Council Proceedings (1738–45), fos. 171–3; (1754–62), fos. 101–2.

[66] *London Evening Post*, 18–20 Dec. 1739; Avon Lib., Southwell Papers, v (15 Oct. 1739), and Southwell to John Berrow, 11 Dec. 1740. For advertisements on Southwell standing in the Country interest see *London Evening Post*, 13–15 Nov. 1739, 5–7 May 1741.

[67] Avon Lib., Southwell Papers, vi (Southwell to John Brickdale, 15 Feb. 1742).

Test Act that the Stedfast Society agreed to back him at all.
Indeed, his political line during Walpole's final years created
problems for his Bristol friends, who continually had to placate
their more intransigent colleagues and a local public vociferously hostile to Walpole. After Southwell had opposed Samuel
Sandys's motion for Walpole's dismissal, for example, he was
advised 'to relate the whole case to some of the Principal men
in your Interest here, sending them a list of the Pro's and
Con's . . . It will be work enough between this and the Election
[of 1741] to clear up the matter.'[68] The Stedfast electoral agent,
Jarrit Smith, informed him that

the town was in a flame abt your voting for Sir Robert Walpole which
gave me great uneasiness, so that I went that evening to the Club
where was the greatest appearance I ever saw without a general
summons. I think there was about forty present full of expectations of
hearing your Speech. About eight that evening Mr Smith came there,
your Speech read, and notwithstanding several of us were sure . . .
[that] you thought & acted according to conscience, yet we blame you
for Dividing with the majority, you well knowing what your friends
have said and think of that great man.[69]

The club, Jarrit added, resolved 'to make it our business to keep
& make the Common people as easy as we can, and I hope we
shall succeed'. Clearly, Southwell's politics were too moderate
for Bristol's rank and file and exposed the difficulties of co-
ordinating the diverse forces which the Stedfast Society sought
to represent.

But who, we might ask, were these forces? Who were the
voters who rejected the politics of interest in 1734 and again in
1739, when Edward Southwell stood against the well-heeled
merchant Henry Combe, a member of the closed Corporation
and Merchant Venturers, whose commercial experience and
connections were vigorously promoted before the electorate?
In what ways did the 1730s see a departure from early
Hanoverian patterns of voting? The survival of four poll-books
between 1715 and 1739 provide us with some clues.[70] To begin

---

[68] Avon Lib., Southwell Papers, vi (John Harper to Southwell, 16 Feb. 1741).

[69] Ibid. vii (Jarrit Smith to Southwell, 20 Feb. 1741).

[70] The four poll-books are for 1715 (Tory only), 1722, 1734, and 1739: *A List
of the Inhabitants . . . who Poll'd for Mr. Freke and Mr. Edwards* (ts in Bristol
RO); *An Exact List of the Voters . . . Taken at the Election of Members of
Parliament* (Bristol, 1722); *A List of the Free-Holders and Free-Men who Voted
at the Election . . . for the City and County of Bristol Begun Wednesday May*

with, it is clear that Coster and Southwell were able to rely on a solid base of Tory voters. Despite the rapid turnover of the electorate and a level of absenteeism that reached 36 per cent among merchants in 1739, there is a high level of consistency among those who voted in consecutive elections—around 80 per cent.[71] There is also evidence of familial continuity among the few instances that can be identified. On the other hand, the voting-patterns by trade show few regularities, save among merchants, mariners, sugar-refiners, distillers, and weavers, all of whom voted predominantly for the Whig-Corporation candidates between 1722 and 1739. This is predictable. Bristol had few large employers and a rich diversity of artisanal trades, over 150 appearing in the 1754 poll-book.[72] One should not expect to find the kind of occupational patterns one might anticipate in a nineteenth-century town dominated by a few major industries.

But what is revealing about these elections is the shifting base of Country-Tory support. In the first Hanoverian contest the Tories could still count on the vote of many of Bristol's most substantial citizens. Whether we isolate this vote by parish or occupation the result is the same. During the next decade, however, Bristol's wealthy drifted decisively towards the Whigs. Only as Walpole's unpopularity increased do we see any reversal of this trend, a response to Walpole's excise proposals and to his pacific policy towards Spain, which began to disrupt trade in Caribbean waters from the late 1720s onwards.[73] In this context it is significant that those merchants who voted for Southwell in 1739, or who publicly

15 1734 (Bristol, 1734); *The Poll-Book, Being a List of the Freeholders and Freemen who Voted at the Last Election for the City and County of Bristol* (Bristol, 1739).

[71] My conclusions are based on three different samples: (a) a random 5% sample of the 1734 poll; (b) the 308 masters mentioned in the apprenticeship books 1735–40, omitting those who took on charity boys; and (c) the 138 merchants who voted in 1734. Of those who voted in 1734, 61–4% voted in 1739 (including several merchants who publicly declared their neutrality). Among active voters, changes in allegiance were rare. This holds for the earlier elections as well as for the 1730s.

[72] *A Genuine List of the Freeholders and Freemen who Voted at the General Election for Members to Serve in Parliament for the City and County of Bristol* (Bristol, 1754).

[73] Between Mar. 1729 and Feb. 1739 the Merchant Venturers petitioned Parliament or the government against Spanish depredations on five occasions: see Minchinton (ed.), *Politics and the Port of Bristol*, pp. 26–7, 39, 45, 47, 48–50.

declared their neutrality, were by and large heavily engaged in the tobacco and sugar trade.[74] Even so, the bulk of the merchant élite still voted for the Corporation candidate, Henry Combe, as did the gentlemen. Support for Southwell from these quarters never achieved 1715 levels.

Yet outside the merchant élite there was a discernible swing towards the opposition in the 1730s. This is even noticeable among trades in which nonconformist connections were strong; among weavers, for example, where Whig majorities were slimmer than they had been in 1722. But it is particularly evident elsewhere. For the first time in many years apothecaries, surgeons, and soap-makers voted strongly for opposition candidates. Even the freeholders, regarded in 1735 as safely Whig, gave Southwell a majority in 1739, polling 322 to 270 in his favour. It was among the middling citizens, in other words, that the opposition made substantial gains. This view may be corroborated by a more sensitive index of the vote, a survey of approximately 300 masters whose premiums are listed in the apprenticeship books for the period 1735–40. The figures (Table 8.1) show that the Whigs drew proportionately more of their votes from the richest and poorest employers while their opponents fared better in the middle range.

TABLE 8.1. *Distribution of Wealth among Bristol Masters who Voted in 1734 and 1739*

Premium	% in sample	% of Whig vote	% of Country/Tory vote
£1–19	36.0	35.8	30.3
£20–99	48.1	42.1	53.2
£100 plus	15.8	22.2	16.5
Nos.	308[a]	95	109

[a] 308 masters are in the apprenticeship books, although they did not all vote.

[74] In the 1739 by-election the merchant vote was as follows: Combe, 46; Southwell, 30; neutral, 14. Of the sugar-merchants, or those trading in sugar (some are listed under different occupational denominations in the poll), 28 voted for Combe, 18 for Southwell and 5 were neutral. Of the tobacco-traders, 5 voted for Combe and 8 for Southwell. Of the Irish and German linen-importers, 18 voted for Combe and 7 for Southwell, with 1 neutral. In other words, relative to the total mercantile vote, the tobacco-traders showed a clear disposition towards Southwell, the linen-importers towards Combe, while the sugar-merchants and traders showed a marginal preference for Southwell. The

The elections of 1734 and 1739 revealed the strength of anti-Walpolean sentiment in Bristol and a deep suspicion of the closed Corporation whose oligarchical impulses emerged clearly in 1735. As one 'Freeman' cautioned his fellow citizens in 1739, 'If any Candidate be set up and supported by the Interest of a Set of Men, who subscribed and carried on the Petition contriv'd for cutting off, for ever, no less than TWENTY-SIX HUNDRED of your Voices, . . . you will certainly shew a resentment suitable to such an *injurious Design*.'[75] Consequently, voters were encouraged to reject Combe, despite his commercial experience. They were urged to insist upon Liberty as much as Trade, and Combe's attitudes were found wanting. Samuel Pye, one of the members of the Stedfast Society, publicly swore that Combe had been amenable to the Excise, and despite Combe's denial, the charge was damning. Hostility to Walpole ran high in Bristol. 'The great man's fall', Joseph Lewis reported in February 1742, 'was received with almost universal joy, and was attended with ringing of Bells, Bonfires, & Burning & hanging him in Effigy.'[76] In a letter to Southwell he continued: 'The Calamity & dishonour he has brought upon ye Nation, your best friends think, requires a strict Parliamentary enquiry, for should his retreat be Easy & Safe, his successors may be encouraged to act what part they please.' Samuel Pye concurred. He told Southwell that the Tories

hope and expect you'll go on in the same way to make a publick example of those persons who have so infamously involved their Country in this calamitous & Lamentable a state. Their cry is everywhere for a Thorough Enquiry and publick Justice, and many of their friends here are under no small concern lest that Human Tenderness so interwoven in your constitution may lead you to wink on the side of compassion and mercy. They say slabbering over an affair of this consequence will draw severe reflections and censure on those who offer at any palliative of Crimes so enormous. The bare

trading orientations were derived from the Bristol port-books, PRO, E 190/ 1215/4. In a constituency in which religion and politics were closely intertwined, the results reveal some sectoral voting by trade.

[75] 'A Necessary Caution humbly Offered to the Freemen of the City of Bristol', in *The Bristol Contest* (1739), p. 1.
[76] Avon Lib., Southwell Papers, vi (Joseph Lewis to Southwell, 8 Feb. 1742).

changing of hands is no satisfaction for the Injuries we all suffer, and that screening such impiety is in some degree sharing in the Guilt.[77]

Instructions were issued to the Bristol MPs in February 1742 urging a strict inquiry into Walpole's conduct as first minister. Yet the Southwell papers reveal there had been a good deal of heated debate within the Stedfast Society about their scope and temper. Colonel Martin, who must have represented one of the parish clubs at the meeting, urged Instructions in the London style, with talk of 'exemplary punishment' and a further call for place and pension bills and a repeal of the Septennial Act.[78] But these proved too radical for most Tories, and the Instructions published in the newspapers, probably penned by Pye, focused upon the inquiry itself, save for a brief reference to the decay of the woollen industry.[79] Indeed, in the aftermath of Walpole's fall, Bristol's moderate line became more pronounced. Unlike the City of London and a few other towns, Bristol did not send further Instructions to its MPs criticizing the inquiry and the change of government without a comprehensive measure of parliamentary reform. Bristol's 'Country moment' proved of short duration. Tory-radicalism began to lose its momentum, even though the Tories captured both seats upon Sir Abraham Elton's death in November 1742, when Robert Hoblyn, Coster's son-in-law, replaced him. By 1747, when Southwell and Hoblyn offered themselves for re-election for the 'Peace, Quiet and Satisfaction of the City' and thanked the Whig Corporation for offering no opposition, a clear, though fragile, consensus prevailed in Bristol circles— one that foreshadowed the gentlemanly agreements of the next decade. Why, in a popular constituency like Bristol, seemingly riven by sectarian animosities and exuberantly anti-Walpolean, did this state of affairs come about?

One factor which pushed Bristol's party élites towards some sort of agreement was the rising cost of elections. Bristol contests had never been inexpensive; Joseph Earle is said to have spent £2,257 in 1713. Yet in the early eighteenth century

---

[77] Avon Lib., Southwell Papers, vi (Samuel Pye to Southwell, 15 Feb. 1742).
[78] Ibid. (John Brickdale to Southwell, 15 Feb. 1742).
[79] Ibid. (John Brickdale to Southwell, 15 Feb. 1742; and Samuel Pye to Southwell, 17 Feb. 1742); x (William Cox to Southwell, 16 Feb. 1742).

they were better known for their violence than their venality. In 1713, for example, the Tories nailed up the door of St George's Chapel where the Whigs had congregated, and 'rais'd a mob to obstruct their coming out to give their votes, and threw stones at them in the Streets and through the Windows'.[80] But from 1727 onwards hundreds of new freemen were recruited before the poll: 778 in 1727; 245 in 1734; 878 in 1739; over 600 in the anticipated contest of 1747. Precisely who created this precedent is uncertain, but it seems likely that it was the Whig Corporation, for it was the Tory, William Hart, who abandoned the poll in 1727 when he was expected to win. According to James Pearce, Abraham Elton had agreed to contribute £1,000 towards Hart's electoral expenses if he agreed to stand down. 'The people who sold their votes have received from one to five guineas per man', he reported, 'so that had Hart money and resolution to have stood it out, 'twould have proved the dearest election in England.'[81]

In any event, once the purchase of freedoms began it became difficult to discontinue. Although the parties agreed to disqualify new freemen admitted after the writs of the election had been received, they felt honour-bound to pay for the poor man's franchise. This batch of new voters, however, provided neither party with a permanent electoral interest. It proved a strictly one-time affair. The mechanics and mariners who sold their votes in return for a city freedom (which cost the equivalent of a week's wages) did so because they wished to work in the city without harassment—a real incentive down to 1760 when the regulations against foreigners were relaxed. Alternatively, artisans used elections to by-pass long apprenticeships. Once these objectives were satisfied, and followed perhaps by a popular 'divorce'—for mechanics who 'married' freemen's daughters soon disengaged themselves[82]—Bristol's sponsored freemen disappeared into the industrial suburbs and

[80] *Flying Post*, 15–17 Sept. 1713.

[81] Morice MS (James Pearce to Humphrey Morice, 9 Sept. 1727), cited in Sedgwick (ed.), *Commons 1715–54*, i. 245.

[82] Latimer, *Annals of Bristol*, ii. 411. Freedoms-by-marriage constituted 28% of the new burgesses in 1734 and 34% in 1739. These figures are derived from a 10% random sample of the freemen admitted in the final weeks before the elections.

down the hatches of merchantmen. Rarely did they trouble to vote again.[83]

One cannot resist the impression that both parties became the victims of their own venality. As the electorate grew, from approximately 3,600 in 1713 to around 4,900 in 1739, to over 5,900 by 1781—more than doubling in the century after 1688—so also did the costs. A formidable posse of managers and agents was required to solicit the votes of prospective freemen, to ensure that the Chamberlain admitted legitimate voters, whose freedoms had to be clipped every election, to ascertain whether voters had accepted poor relief or parish doles. Nor should treating be omitted, for it became customary to provide regular voters with some sort of electoral supper, or alternatively to disburse what was termed 'polling money' for those who wished to take their custom elsewhere.[84] Bristol elections demanded deep pockets and hefty subscriptions. Few candidates after 1750 could expect to get away with less than £10,000, so that the costs of frequent contests, particularly where the outcome was uncertain, came to be seen as prohibitive.

These circumstances explain why the Whigs were reluctant to contest the constituency at the height of the agitation against Walpole. But there were other factors that induced a new spirit of equanimity in Bristol politics. Neither Southwell nor Hoblyn neglected Bristol's mercantile interests. Southwell occasionally complained about the demands that were made upon him. In a letter addressed to William Berrow, which (instructively) he did not send, he bemoaned the fact that 'the Duty of a Representative of Bristol requires every hour of the

---

[83] Only 8% of the new freemen in my 1734 sample voted in 1739, a decade when the usual participation rate was over 60%.

[84] On electoral practices see *The Bristol Poll Book* (publ. Wm Pine: Bristol, 1774), pp. 155–69, and *An Authentic Report of the Evidence and Proceedings before the Committee of the Hon. House of Commons Appointed to Try the Merits of the Bristol Election of October 1812* (Bristol, 1813), pp. 63–76. For the 15 taverns opened for Beckford and Philipps in 1754 see *The Bristol Contest* (Bristol, 1754), app. For an eighteenth-century comment on rising electoral expenses see Barrett, *History and Antiquities*, p. 147: Barrett noted that Colonel Daines spent only £2,256 in 1713, and compared it to 'the enormous sums that are now advanced and expended in bringing in votes from the most distant parts in coaches, and treating and maintaining them all during any long election'.

day a constant attendance in Parlt., an extensive and regular correspondence, an attention to every Branch of Trade, an universall solicitation in all Offices & with all persons in power'.[85] To a man who prided himself upon his independence and held high offices of state in Ireland, this was all rather demeaning. But he accepted the responsibility, however irksome it seemed, and the merchants thanked him for his efforts. As early as 1740 Southwell's opposition to daggering, the insuring of ship's bottoms at an advanced premium, won him commercial respect. Michael Becher, an alderman and former warden of the Merchant Venturers, reported that 'many of considerable Interest who opposed ye before are now become yor staunch Friends'.[86] This recognition by the mercantile élite was sustained throughout the 1740s. Hoblyn and Southwell failed to break the Hudson's Bay monopoly in 1749, but they did ensure that Bristol was well represented in the slave trade when the Royal Africa Company was finally wrapped up in 1750. Bristol's long-standing battle with the company over the status of separate traders on the Barbary Coast ended to the West's advantage.[87]

Generally speaking, then, Bristol's Whig-dominated merchant community welcomed Hoblyn and Southwell's attention to trading issues, and this helped smooth political differences between them. Certainly, there were occasions when this tolerance dissolved. The Bristol Corporation resented the fact that the Whigs were under-represented on the new Turnpike Trust of 1749, and although Southwell protested that this was an oversight, the civic assembly refused both Members the customary pipe of wine.[88] But by and large the political stance of Bristol's MPs provoked little offence. Southwell, in particular, was sometimes irritated by his dependence upon the Stedfast Society. He swore he would 'never be a slave to Party'. What the country required, he argued, was 'cool heads and moderate men. Our Parties & the

[85] Avon Lib., Southwell Papers, v (Southwell to William Berrow, 11 Dec. 1741).

[86] Ibid. (Michael Becher to Southwell, 31 Oct. 1740).

[87] Patrick McGrath, *The Merchant Venturers of Bristol* (Bristol, 1975), pp. 132–4, 148.

[88] Latimer, *Annals of Bristol*, ii. 281; Avon Lib., Southwell Papers, x (Robert Hoblyn and Southwell to Francis Fane, spring 1749).

Violence of them are our Ruin.'[89] In fact his private papers suggest that he assiduously courted the middle ground in Bristol politics, mediating between the Stedfast Society and the Corporation over the Street Lighting Bill of 1748.[90] During the Jacobite rebellion of 1745 he firmly supported the subscriptions for volunteer troops and refused to qualify his endorsement of the government, believing that public credit and confidence were of the utmost importance in this hour of crisis. In so doing he distanced himself from the Tory-radicals of London and elsewhere and lent weight to the bipartisan loyalist campaign that was vigorously pursued in Bristol. This attitude was warmly applauded by the Whigs. During the celebrations of Culloden in 1746 Alderman William Jefferies, a Whig who had voted against Southwell in 1739, assured him that among the toasts 'yours & your Brother member's will certainly be remembered by the Company'.[91]

The Country-Tory representation of Bristol from 1742 to 1754 thus did little to fuel local party animosities. Both Southwell and Hoblyn, a Cornish industrialist who supplied alloys for Bristol's brass industry, were on good terms with the merchant community. Both stayed out of the limelight on controversial issues like the Naturalization Bills of 1751 and 1753. Their partnership, in fact, both facilitated and reflected the cautious but perceptible convergence of interests within the Bristol élite. Whigs and Tories joined forces to finance privateers during the wars against Spain and France. One 300-ton ship, the *Southwell*, with 24 guns and a crew of 200 men, was fitted out by two Whig aldermen and two members of the Stedfast Society, William Berrow and Michael Miller. Berrow, a linen-draper by trade, also had an interest in the *Phoenix*, a 150-ton sloop which he shared with fellow Stedfast member, John Brickdale, and one of the leading lights in the rival Union Club, Richard Farr.[92] These inter-party links were also extended to Bristol's first bank in 1750 and to the Theatre

---

[89] Avon Lib., Southwell Papers, vii (Southwell to Joseph Percival, 24 Feb. 1741).

[90] Ibid. x (petition of the Principal Inhabitants of the City parishes, c.1748; letter of Southwell to William Hart, 30 Mar. 1749).

[91] Ibid. ix (William Jefferies to Southwell, 24 Apr. 1746).

[92] PRO, HCA, 26/30/147, 26/32/45.

Royal.[93] They were also extended to the altar. In 1747 the *Bath Journal* reported the marriage of Michael Pope, the eldest son of a former Whig sheriff, to Miss Martin, 'a lady of distinguished beauty and merit', the daughter of the rabidly Tory Colonel Martin of College Green, whose fiery Instructions against Walpole had been voted down by the Stedfast Society some five years earlier.[94]

Business partnerships and society weddings encouraged a mutual respect between the leaders of Bristol's two parties and a greater tolerance of political differences. So also, ultimately, did the experience of riot. In 1727 and again in the 1730s the peace of Bristol and its environs was rocked by turnpike riots. Led by the unruly colliers of Kingswood Chase, who resented the tolls on their coal carts and the erosion of their rights to collect furze on the commons, crowds pulled down the toll-gates and, despite tough legal recriminations, effectively frustrated the full operation of the turnpikes for over a decade. The development of good road communications connecting Bristol to its hinterland none the less remained a strong commercial priority. In 1749 efforts were launched to extend Bristol's turnpike roads, but to exempt coals (as in 1731) in an effort to placate the 'ungovernable' colliers. This strategy proved a partial success. The Kingswood miners were slow to rise against the new turnpikes and showed little of their former militancy. But disagreements over the management of the Turnpike Trust polarized Bristol's business community along party lines. Angered by Tory over-representation, the Whig Corporation and the Merchant Venturers withdrew their financial support, forcing the Stedfast Society to invest £1,000 of its own money in the new venture.[95] Furthermore, the Whig magistrates were laggard in calling for troops, leaving the Tory turnpike commissioners to protect the toll-gates at Bedminster, where a crowd of country people had assembled, and to pursue the rioters into Somerset. Nor did matters end there, for the Bristol mayor went on to denounce the initiative, complaining to the secretary of state of the 'indiscreet warmth

[93] Charles H. Cave, *A History of Banking in Bristol from 1750 to 1899* (Bristol, 1899), pp. 9–12; Latimer, *Annals of Bristol*, ii. 282, 364.
[94] *Bath Journal*, 26 Oct. 1747.
[95] Stedfast Society, Rules and Orders 1737–1802, p. 47.

& precipitate measure of the acting Trustees in carrying the Act for erecting the Turnpikes into Execution'.[96]

The 1749 turnpike riots revealed how fragile the unity of Bristol's business community could be, even when their own economic interests were involved. But suitably chastened by a government inquiry and the acquittal of many of the rioters, the two parties once more began to repair their differences. Four years later they had an opportunity to show their unity. In May 1753 'a mob of many hundred colliers and other country people headed by a captain and colours' entered Bristol by Lawford's Gate and proceeded to the Council House to protest to the Corporation about the high price of grain and to urge that all exportation of wheat should be stopped. The Corporation made some assurances, but, unconvinced of their sincerity, miners boarded the *Lamb*, whose cargo of corn was bound for Dublin, and proceeded to unload it. Constables intervened, and a scuffle broke out, escalating into a full-scale riot in which the windows of the Council House were smashed and rioters were rescued from the custody of the constables. At this point the magistrates promised prompt redress and the colliers departed, but not before giving notice that 'they would arm themselves and repeat their Visit'.[97]

In the next few days Bristol's wealthier citizens strove to keep the colliers out of the city. At first they succeeded, but on 25 May a large company of miners, weavers, and country people entered the city by Milk Street and advanced to Bridewell to rescue a rioter from custody. Hard on its heels came a troop of soldiers from Gloucester. A bloody confrontation ensued in which four rioters were killed and at least thirty wounded. In this affray the colliers managed to capture a number of gentlemanly constables who had fired upon their fellows. Three of these gentlemen, Thomas Knox, a tobacco-merchant and a member of the Whig Union Club, Michael Miller, a jeweller cum merchant of the Stedfast Society, and his colleague, John Brickdale, were rescued from the colliers at Lawford's Gate. But Brickdale and Miller were subsequently

---

[96] Robert Malcolmson, 'A Set of Ungovernable People: The Kingswood Colliers in the Eighteenth Century', in John Brewer and John Styles (eds.), *An Ungovernable People: The English and their Law in the Seventeenth and Eighteenth Centuries* (London, 1980), p. 111.

[97] Malcolmson, 'A Set of Ungovernable People', p. 119; Latimer, *Annals of Bristol*, ii. 303–5; Avon Lib., Jefferies MS xii, fo. 231.

indicted for murder by a coroner's jury. Thanks to the intercessions of the Whig Corporation, their indictments were quashed at King's Bench and other specials were pardoned.[98] This intervention was publicly welcomed by the Stedfast Society, one of its members leading a deputation of citizens 'of every Rank and Persuasion' to thank the mayor and Corporation for their efforts in quelling the riots and bringing the ringleaders to justice.[99]

The united front of Tory and Whig merchants against the colliers in 1753 set the scene for pre-electoral negotiations. The Union Club first suggested that the two parties share the representation of Bristol in November 1753. Once it was clear that Hoblyn and Southwell would not stand again the Stedfast Society agreed to discuss the matter. But it quickly became apparent that the prospects of reaching an amicable settlement were slim. The Whigs wanted either Lord Barrington or Robert Nugent. The former was the son of a well-known supporter of the Dissenters, an opposition Whig who went over to the government in 1745 and was subsequently made a lord of the admiralty at the recommendation of Lord Cobham; the latter was an Irish adventurer who had risen to Parliament on the purse-strings of a wealthy widow, had entered the service of the Prince of Wales in 1747, and upon the Prince's death had gravitated to the Pelhams. An able speaker as well as negotiator, he had come to the attention of the Union Club as a campaigner for the naturalization of foreign Protestants in 1747 and the opening of the Levant trade in 1753. But the religious proclivities of both Barrington and Nugent were too heterodox for the Stedfast Society, as was their proximity to the Court. The club rejected both nominees, suggesting as alternatives Lord Egmont, the leading politician of Leicester House until Prince Frederick's death in 1751, and a kinsman of Southwell, Mr Cox of Stone-Eaton, or even Robert Hoblyn. In other words, candidates who were closer to the political temper of the out-going members, if not the same.[100] These terms were probably too high to begin with, but they were

---

[98] Latimer, *Annals of Bristol*, ii. 305.

[99] Bristol RO, Roslyn Papers, 11944 (2); *Felix Farley's Bristol Journal*, 2–9 June 1753.

[100] For these negotiations see Stedfast Society, Rules and orders 1737–1802, pp. 60–5; BL, Add. MS 32, 732, fo. 233.

driven even higher by the Stedfast's insistence on *carte blanche* for its own candidate, especially when it became clear that the club's choice would probably fall on Sir John Philipps, a well-known lawyer and country gentleman from Pembrokeshire. Philipps had achieved a notoriety for his opposition to volunteer associations during the Forty-Five and for his protests against the suspension of Habeas Corpus during the invasion scare of 1744. He had also been an active member of the Westminster Independents, had supported Alexander Murray in his contest with the Commons in 1749, and had defended customary rights of access to Richmond Park the following year. In short, he was a man with deep libertarian sympathies, befriended by Tory-radicals in London and Bristol and Jacobite squires in Wales—without a doubt a *bête noire* of the Whigs. His candidature alone would have prompted a contest, without the additional aggravation of Tory intransigence.

So, in one of the least contested general elections of the century, Bristol prepared for a trial of strength. Lord Barrington declined the offer to stand for the Whig interest in Bristol. Nugent, by contrast, agreed, although he soon fell out with the Whigs over his election expenses. They hoped that he would pay half of his electoral costs; he hoped nothing would be expected of him 'than the Credit of his Name', and he was so angry at the prospect of footing the bill that he initially turned back at Marlborough.[101] Only a promise of £10,000 towards his expenses, arranged through the Quaker banker, Capel Hanbury, induced him to come at all.[102] Against Nugent ranged Sir John Philipps, already a member of the Stedfast Society,[103] and Richard Beckford, a lawyer and wealthy sugar-planter whose Jamaican estates were worth £120,000. He was one of four brothers standing in the general election of 1754.

The Bristol contest of 1754 turned out to be a raucous, scurrilous affair, full of party invective and caustic aspersions about caucus politics. The Tories reminded the electorate that the Corporation had attempted to reduce the electorate in 1735

[101] BL, Add. MS 4,319, fo. 230.
[102] BL, Add. MS 32,735, fo. 48.
[103] Stedfast Society, Rules and Orders, p. 32. Philipps was admitted on 12 Aug. 1747.

and contrasted its sponsorship of a Court hireling with the broad, libertarian sympathies of their candidates. They invited the freemen to consider 'a Courtier and Placemen scattering before you the Promises of a Pittance of Court-Favours, which if not rejected at best can affect but very few of you for the present' and 'must infallibly in the End enslave you all'.[104] They combined this tack with traditional Tory prejudice. Philipps's honest churchmanship was compared to the specious Anglicanism of his opponent, whose conversion from Catholicism was viewed as flagrantly careerist. At the same time Sir John's opposition to Naturalization Bills was set against Nugent's warm advocacy. Under Nugent and his drones the very word Dissent would soon be 'a Word scarce comprehensive enough to include the Variety of Religions which will then start up amongst us'.[105] Thus the slogan 'Philipps and Beckford' was linked to the acclamations 'No Placemen! No Pensioners! No Jews! No Scum of Foreigners to eat up the Bread of Englishmen!'[106]

Against Tory nativism the Whigs presented Nugent's more positive qualities. In his electoral procession, carefully orchestrated by Josiah Tucker, voters were treated to many of his commercial virtues: his opposition to the privileges of the Royal Africa Company, the Levant Company, the Hudson's Bay Company; his opposition to the importation of French wine in bottles, a measure pitched at Bristol's glass industry. Pamphleteers even suggested that his affiliations at Court would benefit rather than prejudice Bristol's commercial lobbying. Merchants and tradesmen frequently wanted 'Favours of the Government, at the Boards of Treasury, Trade, Customs and Excise'. Could they expect them 'if they elect Representatives who (Right or Wrong) oppose it?'[107] But in an effort to neutralize the potentially damaging effects of Nugent's religious 'liberalism', an issue that inevitably evoked deeper, local, sectarian memories, the Whigs focused upon Philipps's Jacobite proclivities. Great play was made with Philipps's association with the Pembrokeshire Sea Serjeants, a convivial society notorious for its Jacobite revelling, and of his

---

[104] *The Bristol Contest* (1754), p. 37.
[105] Ibid. 16.
[106] Ibid. 46.   [107] Ibid. 51.

purported friendship with Counsellor David Morgan, the Welsh lawyer executed for treason at Kennington Common in 1746. Eyebrows were raised about his defence of Alexander Murray, whose bold exposure of Court chicanery in the Westminster election of 1749 incurred the wrath of the Commons and eventually forced him into the dissident world of Stuart politics. Finally, Philipps's opposition to the loyalist subscriptions of 1745 was emphasized. This piece of information had been discovered by Tucker, who was quite elated, assuring his informant, the Reverend Thomas Birch that 'good use . . . would be made of it'.[108] As indeed it was. Bristol had been vigorously loyal during the Jacobite rebellion, enthusiastically subscribing to the volunteer regiments and raising more money than the City of London. In fact the Tory-radical critique of these expedients had scarcely been mentioned in this western port, let alone the demand for an inquiry into the state of the nation which Philipps had moved in the Commons.[109] Consequently, Sir John's explanation of his actions cut little ice among some Bristolians and tainted his credibility as a libertarian. In a smear campaign masterminded by Tucker, Philipps was no Cato but a well-wisher to the 'Glanbucket Plaid Cause'.[110]

Despite the Whig claim that Nugent would advance the commercial prosperity of Bristol, a majority of merchants outside the closed Corporation voted for his opponents. Philipps and Beckford also enjoyed the strong support of the gentlemen and of the city clergy and churchwardens.[111] Like Coster and Southwell they also attracted the middling voter, particularly the surgeons, soap-makers, and linen-drapers; although they did lose some ground among some of the industrial trades, the distillers, glassmakers, and sugar-refiners, for example. Even so, there is good evidence that they did capture a higher percentage of the middling vote than the Whigs. As Table 8.2 reveals, the Tory candidates fared well

[108] BL, Add. MS 4,319, fo. 227.
[109] For Philipps's motion see ch. 3.
[110] *The Bristol Contest* (1754), p. 51.
[111] Of the 45 churchwardens listed for 1754 in the visitation returns, 40 voted for Philipps and Beckford, 1 for Nugent and Beckford, 2 remained neutral, and 2 did not vote. For the returns see Bristol RO, EP/V/1.

TABLE 8.2. *Distribution of Wealth among Bristol Masters who Voted in 1754*

Premium	% of sample	% of Whig vote	% of Tory vote
£1–19	34.8	41.5	31.6
£20–99	46.8	43.9	48.8
£100 plus	18.2	14.6	19.5
Nos.	175	41	56

Note: I located 175 different masters who registered apprentice indentures for the period 1753–6, and checked their names against the 1754 poll. Most of the voters for Nugent were plumpers; a few voted for Nugent and Beckford. I have regarded both as Whig votes.

among the middling-to-rich employers, confounding Whig rhetoric that property and money was all on its side.

But Tory influence and appeal was no match for the combined interest of the Corporation–Dissenting caucus. Lubricated by huge sums of money and abetted by the Council House, the Whigs were able to muster a substantial client vote. Tory journalists complained of the numbers of apprentices, journeymen, and servants who were forced to vote for Nugent under duress. Victuallers were threatened with the loss of their licences if they did not vote for the Corporation candidate.[112] Freedoms-by-marriage were partially distributed and the credentials of many suspect Nugent supporters were not investigated. The Tories always worried that they were vulnerable to a flood of new freedoms at election time, and not without reason. 889 new voters were admitted in March and April 1754, many after the teste of the writ, and the bulk of those who actually voted buoyed up Nugent's support (the freemen admitted in April, by a ratio of 8 : 3). As Tucker remarked to the Reverend Thomas Birch, 'the Mob is all of our side, great numbers of low & middling Tradesmen of theirs'.[113] By the final days of the election the Whigs had at least 500 votes in hand. 'We have only to consider which of ye two Candidates in the opposition it is best for us to chuse,' Tucker wrote to Dr

[112] *The Bristol Contest* (1754), p. 52; *Felix Farley's Bristol Journal*, 6–13 Apr. 1754.
[113] BL, Add. MS 4,319, fo. 227.

Forster on 27 April.[114] The general opinion was that Beckford was the lesser of two evils, even though there was considerable opposition to his candidature from the Quakers and a more general feeling that this wealthy planter would subordinate provincial interests to metropolitan. Besides, confessed Tucker to Birch, 'it would be quite inconsistent in us first to rouse ye People against Philipps as a Jacobite & then choose him Ourselves'.[115]

The Bristol election of 1754 was one of the most expensive of the eighteenth century. The Whigs alone spent over £30,000.[116] After it the two parties were more disposed to compromise. In February 1756, as Beckford's health declined, the Whigs once again proposed an arrangement whereby the two parties shared Bristol's representation. The relations between the parties were still difficult, however, soured by a recent dispute over the Night Watch Act which vested executive power in the hands of the Whig Corporation. There were also continuing recriminations about who was responsible for the exorbitantly expensive contest of 1754. And so while Nugent favoured a sharing of Bristol's representation, and the Tory candidate, Jarrit Smith, expressed his support for such a compromise, the negotiations fell through. Josiah Tucker attributed the breakdown to 'a club of low tradesmen among ye Dissenters' who 'were taught to believe that it would redound to ye Honour of ye Dissenting Cause that they should make a Member for ye Second City in ye Kingdom'.[117] He was incensed that his own conciliatory overtures, which had received the blessing of Newcastle and influential Presbyterians, should have been undermined by sectarian politics. In the ensuing contest he refrained from casting his vote even though he was 'pressed prodigiously to break [his] Neutrality'.[118] Nevertheless, Tucker was a lonely voice. Once the challenge had been made, the Whig political machine swung

---

[114] BL, Add. MS 11,275, fo. 129; *Felix Farley's Bristol Journal*, 18–25 May 1754.

[115] BL, Add. MS 4,319, fos. 246–7.

[116] BL, Add. MS 35,596, fo. 207, cited by P. T. Underdown, 'The Parliamentary History of the City of Bristol 1750–1790', M.A. thesis (Bristol, 1948), p. 54.

[117] BL, Add. MS 11,275, fos. 147–8.

[118] Ibid. 154–5.

into action and the usual accusations about electoral corruption followed, embellished this time by the complaint that the Whig magistrates had allowed the press gang to sweep up Smith's supporters. Tucker doubted that the Whigs would win 'unless Mr. Spencer's men get leave for ye Carpenters, Mariners, Soldiers & Saylors now in ye King's Service to leave their Stations at this critical juncture & come to Bristol to vote'.[119] And he was right. In a surprisingly high poll—'where such Numbers can be picked up is a matter of surprise to everybody',[120] Tucker observed—the Whigs lost the election by 52 votes. Spencer's friends demanded a scrutiny, but 'ye Blue Mob without became violent and outrageous, vowing that ye Sheriffs should not come out alive unless they made a fair return, that is, returned Mr. Smith'.[121] The sheriffs complied. In the victory celebrations that followed in the neighbouring county villages, sheep were roasted whole, and local dignitaries were chaired in imitation of Bristol's victory parade.[122] In Bristol itself Tory voters expressed their jubilation with toasts to Sir John Philipps and William Beckford. Their humiliation in 1754 was behind them.

The elections of 1754 and 1756 proved to be a turning point in Bristol politics. In the next twenty years neither the Union Club nor the White Lyon showed any inclination to disrupt the political equipoise of the mid-1750s. Gentlemanly agreement became the order of the day. The two societies became so habituated to electoral compromise that the very idea of a contested election became something of an inconvenience, a challenge to their presumptive right to manage the constituency. Provided that Bristol's commercial interests were adequately represented in the corridors of power, so the argument went, change seemed unnecessary. Indeed, the notion that the politics of interest were best served if party divisions were brought under control received more emphasis. This was Josiah Tucker's basic message to the Bristol electors in his defence of Lord Clare (Nugent) in 1775. And as the Address

---

[119] Ibid. fo. 153.
[120] Ibid. fos.154–5.
[121] Ibid. 154–5.
[122] *Felix Farley's Bristol Journal*, 13–20, 20–7 Mar. 1756.

lamenting Clare's withdrawal in 1774 revealed, Bristol's commercial élite, including many old stalwarts of the Union and Stedfast societies, concurred with this view.[123]

In any case, the leading Whigs and Tories found little to quarrel about. After the 1756 by-election the strain of libertarianism in Bristol Toryism became increasingly rhetorical. This emerged within months of Jarrit Smith's victory. Although the Tories could not ignore the popular demand for a public inquiry into the loss of Minorca in the summer of 1756, their leaders were embarrassed by the move. Jarrit Smith even refused to sign the petition calling for an investigation into the government's responsibility, arguing that its sponsors had acted 'from no other purpose but to distress the present administration and raise feuds among his Majesty's innocent subjects'.[124] In the event the Tory leaders tempered the terms of the Address, leaving the field open for pro-ministerial resolutions from the other side.[125] Even so, the Stedfast Society was unable to prevent a group of 'loyal and independent' citizens from drawing up Instructions urging an inquiry before supply and reforms to preserve the 'Constitutional Independency' of Parliament. Nor could it suppress a satirical Address to both Bristol MPs thanking the administration for its prudence in abandoning Minorca, failing to defend America, and opposing triennial Parliaments and a 'Constitutional Militia'.[126]

Yet if the Stedfast Society failed to muzzle independent opinion on these occasions, in the long run it proved more successful. While the Farleys kept Bristol in touch with London developments, there was no move to emulate the City.

[123] Josiah Tucker, *A Review of Lord Viscount Clare's Conduct as Representative of Bristol* (Gloucester, 1775), pp. 25–32.

[124] BL, Add. ms 32,867, fos. 203–4.

[125] The three Addresses, one from the Corporation, one from the 'gentlemen, clergy, merchants & others', and a third from the Tories, were printed in the *London Evening Post*, 7–9, 16–18 Sept. 1756. The Tory Address emphasized the need for an inquiry into Minorca, for a strict appropriation of supply, and for a militia. It also criticized the government for its mismanagement of the defence of the American colonies. The Whig-sponsored Addresses were respectful to the king and deferential to the government, expressing the blessings of Hanoverian rule and the prudent measures of the administration.

[126] *Felix Farley's Bristol Journal*, 11 Dec. 1756; *London Evening Post*, 11–13 Jan. 1757.

The Blues did not press for a civic freedom for Pitt in 1757. There was no attempt to reinstate him to popular favour after his resignation in 1761. Nor were the Blues publicly critical of the Peace of Paris, even though their former rivals on the Corporation had drawn up a highly complimentary Address to the Crown, commending the administration for a 'definitive' treaty which secured 'an honourable and advantageous peace'. As Josiah Tucker remarked, Bristol was 'less infected with ye Pittian Madness than ye good Folks within ye sound of Bow-Bell'.[127] The political élite so asserted its authority over the city, treating its inhabitants to patriotic junkets, firework displays, and annual doles, that there was very little evidence of anti-Butite sentiment in Bristol circles, even over issues which affected its prosperity such as the Cider Tax of 1763.[128] The priorities of the two caucuses, now ideologically indistinguishable, held sway. After 1763 the Stedfast Society no longer monitored the Corporation's activities. It became increasingly a convivial society; its only business, the ritual of an electoral negotiation. On the other hand, the Union Club found its rivals so congenial that it admitted a few to the Common Council: men like Michael Miller junior, a merchant-banker who had married a daughter of the Elton dynasty, one of the foremost Whig families in the city. Miller's father had helped to found a political society to take on the Presbyterian Eltons and the Corporation clan. Those differences no longer mattered.

So what can we learn from the Bristol experience of the early Hanoverian era? Was Namier right? Were Bristol politics intrinsically oligarchical, with a level of electoral morality and political consciousness that approximated a rotten borough? Not really. Bristolians were always aware that their city was the metropolis of the West and they were not prepared to abandon it willingly to private interests. To be sure, there was an abiding assumption that the merchants were the best arbiters of the city's interests, and in a boom-economy this proved remarkably difficult to dispel. This acceptance of

---

[127] Common Council Proceedings (1762–72), 30–2; BL, Add. MS 4,319, fo. 271.
[128] The Merchant Venturers did petition against the cider tax, however: see Minchinton (ed.), *Port of Bristol*, p. 97.

mercantile power was necessarily reinforced by the absence of real alternatives. The merchants dominated the economy of this western port, controlled its trade, organized its charities, and had a strong collective presence in the Society of Merchant Venturers. Although there was some opposition to Bristol's closed Corporation, there was no tradition of civic democracy which could serve as a check to merchant power and a platform for urban populism. Bristol lacked the habit of civic service and electoral participation which gave the London citizenry a powerful voice in local politics. Consequently, Bristol politics were always vulnerable to private arrangements within the mercantile élite.

At the same time there was a volatility to Bristol politics that could fracture merchant control of the constituency. Part of this volatility stemmed from a long history of sectarian strife, sustained in the eighteenth century by the very visible presence of nonconformity. Sectarian rivalries not only fuelled party politics; they also checked merchant urbanity and consensus, and forced merchants to seek support beyond their own boundaries. Among other things, they encouraged electoral venality, a development that certainly impaired the growth of an open, independent politics. On the other hand, the purchase of a large, shifting, and calculating electorate was an enormously expensive proposition, and so merchants sometimes sailed in the libertarian wind that periodically blew through the political nation. This meant that libertarian politics gained a fragile foothold in Bristol among the middling tradesmen and artisans, and periodically exposed Bristol to the sorts of popular pressures and argument that enlivened metropolitan circles.

The impact of these pressures was most explicit in the 1730s when the merchant élite miscalculated the strength of anti-Walpolean sentiment. But popular anti-ministerialism, embodying a critique of Whig oligarchy, national and local, did surface on other occasions: in the critique of electoral compromise in 1754; in the espousal of Phillips, which was libertarian and True-Blue; in the Instructions over Minorca. I do not wish to exaggerate its salience in Bristol politics. It was a marginal force, constrained within the prevailing economic and political structures of this Atlantic port. Local clubs of independent freemen, first evident in the mid-century decades, had yet to challenge the leadership of the dominant caucuses, as they did in 1781. Similarly, the critique of electoral venality in the mid-century decades was never as sharp as it was during the radical era, when James Thistlethwaite depicted Tory plebeians processing the town on election day 'With dirty shirt, blue-wig and hungry face, / The miserable emblem of disgrace, / . . . Shewing his master's *hospital* cheer, / Under the meagre type of sour small beer.'[129] The anti-ministerialism of these decades set precedents more than anything else. It is no accident that the Bristol radicals, in formulating their Instructions for shorter parliaments in 1772, should have recalled the Country Tory Instructions against Walpole some thirty years earlier.[130]

[129] James Thistlethwaite, *Corruption* (London, 1780), canto iv, 252–7.
[130] *Bristol Gazette*, 20 Feb. 1772; *Bristol Journal*, 22 Feb. 1772.

9

Norwich: City of Whigs and Weavers

NORWICH was the second largest city in England in the late seventeenth and early eighteenth century. Numbering approximately 20,000 inhabitants in 1650, its population grew to approximately 30,000 by 1700 and 35,000 by 1740, when it was overtaken by Bristol and then subsequently by the industrial towns of the North.[1] Although it continued to be a service and administrative centre for the county of Norfolk, Norwich chiefly owed its pre-eminence to the manufacture of worsted cloth, first introduced to the city by the Dutch and Walloon refugees during the reign of Elizabeth. This was the foundation of its growth during a period generally noted for urban stasis or decline. From the mid-seventeenth century onwards, Norwich stuffs—says, bays, shalloons, and then crapes, camlets, damasks, satins, and bombazines—dominated the town's economy and provided work for thousands both within and without its walls. In the 1720s Defoe reckoned that 120,000 people were engaged in the various production-processes of the Norwich silk and woollen industries. Arthur Young's figure of 72,000 some fifty years later is probably closer the mark, with some 12,000 looms serving a steadily expanding domestic and export market.[2] But, whichever estimate we choose, it is clear that textiles were the life-blood of the town, employing probably half the population.[3] 'If a stranger was only to ride through or view the city of Norwich for a day,' wrote Defoe, 'he would

---

[1] The best discussion of Norwich's population is to be found in Penelope J. Corfield, 'A Provincial Capital in the Late Seventeenth Century: The Case of Norwich', in Peter Clark and Paul Slack (eds.), *Crisis and Order in English Towns 1500–1700* (London, 1972), pp. 263–70, and her 'Social and Economic History of Norwich 1650–1850: A Study in Urban Growth', Ph.D. thesis (London, 1976), ch. 1.

[2] Defoe, *A Tour through the Whole Island*, p. 85; Arthur Young, *A Farmer's Tour through the East of England* (4 vols; London, 1771), ii. 80.

[3] Freeman admissions show that the textile trades rarely accounted for less than 40% of all admissions in any one decade between 1650 and 1750, and these ignore the activities of women and children. In 1700–19 they accounted

have more reason to think there was a town without inhabitants than there is really to say so of Ipswich; but on the contrary, if he was to view the city either on a Sabbath-day, or on any public occasion, he would wonder where all the people could dwell, the multitude is so great. But the case is this, the inhabitants being all busy in their manufactures, dwell in their garrets at their looms, and in their combing-shops, so they call them, twisting-mills, and other work-houses; almost all the works they are employed in being done within doors.'[4]

As Herbert Heaton once remarked, Norwich was the 'Worstedopolis' of the eighteenth century.[5] It was the premier textile town in England in the century after the Restoration, generating over £1m. in business per annum by 1770. Predictably, its political reputation rested in large measure upon its production of Britain's cherished staple and its ability, as an incorporated, ancient city, to represent that trade in Parliament. As one petition from the Corporation stressed, Norwich was 'the chief seat of the chief manufacture of the realm' and 'next to London . . . the most rich and potent city in England'.[6] But Norwich's claim to be the second city in the kingdom was also enhanced by its remarkably open constitution. Unlike Bristol and Exeter, Norwich was not run by a self-perpetuating oligarchy. Since the fifteenth century its constitution had allowed for a large measure of freeman participation in government, a state of affairs only temporarily disrupted by the *quo warranto* proceedings of the 1680s. After 1688 Norwich's freemen retained the right to nominate and elect the sixty Common Councilmen of the Assembly and one of the two Sheriffs on an annual basis (the other Sheriff was chosen by the incumbent Mayor, Sheriffs, and Aldermen). The freemen also elected the twenty-four Aldermen who held their offices for life and nominated the two candidates for the mayoralty from

for 58% of all admissions; and in 1720–39, 53%. See Corfield, 'A Provincial Capital', pp. 275–7. Poll-books also reveal that weaving was a frequent by-employment for men.

[4] Defoe, *A Tour through the Whole Island*, p. 86.
[5] Herbert Heaton, *The Yorkshire Woollen and Worsted Industries* (Oxford, 1920), p. 264.
[6] *The Humble Petition of the Mayor, Sheriffs, Citizens and Commonalty of the City of Norwich*, cited by Sidney and Beatrice Webb, *English Local Government* (2 vols.; London, 1908), ii. 530.

the eligible pool of Aldermen, a right that was so liberally exercised in the eighteenth century as to be tantamount to direct mayoral elections.[7]

This meant that Norwich was more democratic than the City of London, at least before 1714 when the City instituted direct aldermanic elections. And it was arguably more democratic thereafter, for the qualifications for office-holding were more liberal and the franchise less restrictive. Unlike London, where the property qualifications for office-holders were quite specific, Norwich simply insisted that its principal representatives be 'suffisaunt' citizens, a requirement that put aldermanic office within the realizable ambitions of prosperous, public-spirited burghers.[8] And whereas London's municipal and parliamentary franchise differentiated liverymen from freeman householders, Norwich's franchise rested upon a uniform freeman-base which even included prisoners and almsmen.[9] Indeed, because the freedom of the city was of some economic importance as long as the Corporation regulated trade, the franchise was broadly based. In the late seventeenth and early eighteenth century it grew at roughly the same rate as the population as a whole, rising from 2,000 in 1690 to over 3,300 in the mid-1730s. It probably encompassed about a third of the adult male population and included such unlikely participants as a muck-man, a bellman, and a chimney-sweep.[10] Only after

---

[7] In 1710 there were only two candidates for mayor, but there was a contest in which the Tory Alderman Beaney (Bene) defeated the Whig Alderman Cockman by 1703 : 1471: see *Norwich Gazette*, 29 Apr.–6 May 1710. To all intents and purposes this was a direct mayoral election, even though strictly freemen only nominated candidates, leaving the final choice to the Court of Mayoralty: see S. and B. Webb, *English Local Government*, ii. 532.

[8] The expense of civic hospitality could nevertheless curb such ambition in practice. Generally speaking, aldermen were among the wealthier sections of the citizenry, although not necessarily the wealthiest. Of the 77 richest citizens cited in the poor-rate assessments of 1725, only 9 were aldermen: see Daniel S. O'Sullivan, 'Politics in Norwich 1701–1835', M.Phil. thesis (University of East Anglia, 1975), p. 9.

[9] *Commons Journals*, 21, p. 478.

[10] The 1730 figure excludes those voters who were entitled to vote in parliamentary elections in Norwich by virtue of their freeholds in the city and its hamlets. For the lowly voters see *An Alphabetical List of the Polls . . . 1734–5* (Norwich, 1735), pp. 44, 57, 61, 73. For estimates of the ratio of voters to adult male inhabitants see John T. Evans, *Seventeenth-Century Norwich* (Oxford, 1979), pp. 12–13; John A. Phillips, *Electoral Behavior in Unreformed England* (Princeton, 1982), p. 201.

1750 did Norwich's electorate fail to keep pace with urban growth, constituting roughly 22 per cent of the adult male population at the end of the century.

So Norwich had an extraordinarily open, popular constitution by the standards of the day. This had two important ramifications. In the first instance it meant that major shifts in the economy were likely to be quickly registered in Norwich politics. From the early seventeenth century, in fact, textile-workers began to be admitted to the freedom in increasing numbers, constituting 40 per cent of all admissions from the 1650s onwards and within two decades a similar proportion of the electorate.[11] At the same time textile-merchants and manufacturers began to climb the civic hierarchy. By the early eighteenth century the textile trades made up 36 per cent of the common councilmen and 41 per cent of the aldermen.[12] Their predominance in civic politics was unparalleled. It was not replicated in other textile towns.

Norwich's open structure of politics also meant that it was deeply embroiled in the extra-parliamentary struggles of the seventeenth and early eighteenth century. Indeed, because of Norwich's close commercial and religious affiliations with London and its abiding conviction that both cities shared a common political heritage (Norwich's charter was modelled after London's), it was highly sensitive to developments in the capital. Royalist and Puritan battled for control of this East Anglian town in the 1640s, Tory and Whig during the Exclusion crisis. Upon entering his deanery in 1681, Humphrey Prideaux described Norwich as 'divided into two factions, Whigs and Torys; the former are the more numerous, but the latter carry all before them as consisting of ye governing part of ye town, and both contend for their way with the utmost violence'.[13] The same observation about the virulence of party allegiances was made in 1705. 'Never was a City in this miserable kingdom so wretchedly divided as this,'

---

[11] Evans, *Seventeenth-Century Norwich*, p. 20. By 1710 the proportion of weavers within the electorate (excluding out-voters) was 37.8%. In 1715 it was 41.3%, rising to 43.1% in 1734, and 43.3% in 1735. These figures do not take into account the combers and finishers in the textile industry.

[12] O'Sullivan, 'Politics in Norwich', pp. 51, 53.

[13] Edward Maunde Thompson (ed.), *Letters of Humphrey Prideaux to John Ellis 1674–1722* (Camden Soc., NS 15; 1875), p. 90.

declared the *London Post*, 'Never were such divisions carried on with such feud, such malice, such magisterial tyranny and such defiance of laws of government.'[14]

Religious tensions lay at the root of party divisions in Norwich. The main bone of contention was the rising prominence of the nonconformist community which had profited from the growth of the textile industry, one of its traditional breeding grounds. After 1660 the nonconformist sects had been largely insulated from the rigours of the Clarendon Code because conservative magistrates had been unwilling to pursue stridently interventionist policies which might undermine the city's autonomy and its popularist temper.[15] But in 1678, with the encouragement of the lord lieutenant, Viscount Yarmouth, these reservations were cast aside. The Quakers in particular, felt the wrath of Royalist-Anglican policy. 'Great and many have been our trials', they complained to the secretary of state in 1683, 'being for many weeks kept out of our meetinghouse in the street and upwards of 70 of us have been committed to prison where we have been very severely treated by the jailer.'[16] Yet despite the change in climate, the Dissenters managed to hold on to their electoral support in Conesford and Northern wards, and benefited from Anglican divisions over the surrender of the Charter and James II's renunciation of Anglican support after 1686. In subsequent decades they rose in economic and civic prominence. Between 1720 and 1750, in fact, no fewer than 25 members of the leading Presbyterian meeting-house entered corporate office. Together with the Quakers, who were well represented among Norwich's manufacturers, they were an important mainstay of the Whig party.[17]

[14] The *London Post*, 14 May 1705, cited by Speck, *Tory and Whig*, p. 77.

[15] Evans, *Seventeenth-Century Norwich*, chs. 6, 7.

[16] *Calendar of State Papers: Domestic Series 1 July–30 Sept. 1683* (London, 1934), xxv. 232.

[17] O'Sullivan, 'Politics in Norwich', pp. 221–3; my conclusions about the Quakers are derived from an annotated poll of the 1734 and 1735 elections by the Whig agent, Nockold Thompson, which lists those 84 voters who affirmed. I have traced their names in the 1734 Land Tax, which reveals (a) that a higher proportion of Quakers were rated than of the electorate as a whole, and (b) that the Quakers were disproportionately represented among the upper echelons of the taxable population. For the poll see *An Alphabetical Draught of the Polls . . . 19 Feb. 1735* (Norwich, 1735), in Norwich Central Lib. (N 328.42:8172).

Norwich remained predominantly Tory in the immediate aftermath of the Glorious Revolution, but the party's ascendancy was far from unassailable. Support for the Tories among the city's 36 vestries remained fairly strong with some 30 churchwardens voting for the 1710 candidates, Robert Bene and Richard Berney, out of an identifiable total of 45. The party also continued to do well in the traditionally royalist and affluent ward of Mancroft, especially among the wholesalers and retailers. It also retained a narrow majority on the Court of Mayoralty. But by the turn of the century the Tories had lost the patronage of the Paston (Yarmouth) family, which had gravitated to the Whigs. And more important, it lost the patronage of the Cathedral with the promotion of Charles Trimnell in 1708. Trimnell was a protégé of Sir John Trevor, the Master of the Rolls, and he had been a domestic chaplain to one of the leading Augustan Whigs, the earl of Sunderland. He was also a prominent Whig controversialist, defending the rights of the Crown against convocation in 1701, supporting the impeachment of Sacheverell, and delivering sermons on 30 January that managed to avoid all reference to Charles I's martyrdom.[18] His elevation to Norwich during the Whig ministry of 1708–10 was clearly designed to boost the Whig cause there, and judging from his inaugural charge to the Norfolk clergy he clearly meant business, for his sermon insisted upon the subordination of the church to the state whatever its original apostolic status. Within a few years, in fact, he was harrying Henry Crossgrove, the printer of the Tory *Norwich Gazette*, for his uncompromising opposition to the Hanoverians.[19]

Trimnell's promotion to Norwich boded ill for the Tories, for much of the ecclesiastical patronage of the city was centralized in his hands and those of the Dean and chapter. Even so, it was not insurmountable in a city with a large measure of civic democracy, and it was some time before the Whigs were able to exploit their control of the church hierarchy. In the Augustan era the Tories retained their narrow majority on the Court of Mayoralty and remained in control of

[18] See DNB and Charles Trimnell, *A Sermon Preach'd at the Parish Church of St. James's Westminster 30 January 1708* (London, 1709).
[19] Charles Trimnell, *A Charge Deliver'd to the Clergy of the Diocese of Norwich 1709* (London, 1710); BL, Add. MS 5853, fo. 107.

the Assembly. Norwich's Address to the Crown during the Sacheverell trial was unrepentantly Tory, condemning the doctor's prosecutors for professing to uphold the royal prerogative 'even whilst they were loudly contending for their Darling Privilege of Resistance'. Similarly, the city's Address to the Crown on the peace negotiations of 1712/13 left no doubt as to its politics. The Assembly applauded the efforts for peace and wished Her Majesty every success, 'notwithstanding the close conspiracy and the secret Artifices of an Ill-designing and Factious Party both at Home and Abroad'.[20]

The Tory control of civic politics was not, however, echoed at the parliamentary level. Here the two parties were more evenly matched. In the seven general elections between 1701 and 1715 each party won both seats on three occasions and shared them in the other. This meant that the Whigs fared better in Norwich than in other open constituencies, although only marginally, for the Tories won the one by-election of the Augustan era, Captain Thomas Palgrave defeating Edward Clarke by a mere 80 votes. Norwich politics were thus keenly contested, swinging from Tory to Whig to Tory during Anne's reign and finally to Whig under George I.

In this topsy-turvy era the Tories' greatest victory was in 1710 when they picked up 54 per cent of the popular vote. This triumph came in the wake of a fiercely contested mayoral election in which Alderman Bene defeated the worsted-weaver, William Cockman, the next alderman below the Chair and by convention the favoured candidate. It was a contest that was strongly influenced by the Sacheverell trial, for during the poll the *Norwich Gazette* reported that 'the chief Cry was the Church and BEANY, the Church and BEANY, and Dr. Sacheverell's Picture being hung out at a Window facing the Hall, the People huzza'd the same, hallowing and shouting, HIGH CHURCH and Sacheverell, Sacheverell and BEANY Huzza!'[21] This High Church militancy was again evident in the shrieval election of August, when to cries of 'The CHURCH and QUEEN, the CHURCH and DOCTOR', the Whigs quickly abandoned the poll.[22] And it resonated through

---

[20] *Norwich Gazette*, 6–13 May 1710, 5–12 July 1712.
[21] Ibid., 4–6 May 1710.
[22] Ibid., 26 Aug.–2 Sept. 1710.

the hustings during the general election two months later. In the Norfolk county election (which was also held at Norwich) the Whig candidates were trounced. Walpole, in particular, felt the weight of High Church opinion, for he had been one of the managers of the Sacheverell trial. He had the humiliation of coming bottom of the poll, trailing his Whig partner by almost 400 votes. In the city election, too, the Tories triumphed. When their candidates were chaired around Market Cross, the *Norwich Gazette* reported, 'The Pictures of the Royal Martyr King Charles I, Her Majesty Queen Anne and the Reverend Dr. Sacheverell being all three put on boards together, were advanced on a Pole, and carried all the Time before them, as also were the Pictures of the 6 Loyall Bishops that voted for Dr. Sacheverell, with the Doctor's Picture between them on another pole.'[23]

1710 marked the high tide of Tory influence in Norwich. Defeated at the parliamentary polls in 1705 and 1708, the High Church party now dominated both parliamentary and municipal politics. This supremacy continued for the rest of Anne's reign, although it showed signs of faltering in 1713 when the opposition of the textile trade to the eighth and ninth clauses of the Anglo-French commercial treaty redounded to Whig advantage. Even so, the Tories held Norwich in the parliamentary election of 1713 by a comfortable, if reduced, majority. As one Tory correspondent reported in elation, 'our Whiggs are all going into Black and White Crapes, decently to bemoan their loss'.[24] With the advent of George I, however, the Tories' parliamentary fortunes slipped. In the first Hanoverian general election the Whigs swept the polls, winning 56 per cent of the vote and revenging their humiliation of 1710. As the poll-book shows, this victory was not attributable to any dramatic shift in élite allegiance. The civic hierarchy remained politically divided, while the gentlemen, esquires, and clergy remained predominantly Tory. Rather, it owed much to the Whig mobilization of the textile vote which constituted some 48 per cent of its supporters as opposed to 37.8 per cent of its opponents (or 27 per cent of the total vote as opposed to 16.6

[23] Ibid., 14–21 Oct. 1710.
[24] *Post Boy*, 24–6 Sept. 1713.

per cent) and to the Whigs' greater hold over the out-voters, especially the freeholders.[25]

The Whig victory of 1715 appears to have taken the Tories by surprise. Before the election Henry Crossgrove, the editor and printer of the staunchly Tory *Norwich Gazette*, had thought the Whig party too divided to win. Writing to the antiquary, John Strype, he had described his Norvicensian opponents as 'a strange compound Body of False Churchmen, Presbyterians, Independents, Anabaptists, Antinomians and Quakers, each of whom have Separatists for them, & all Conventicles to assemble in. These now think', he continued, 'they have got the Ascendant, & threaten destruction to all who jump not with their Republican notions of Government.'[26] The 1715 election clearly left him perplexed. 'The Church Interest', he wrote again in March, 'is strangely thrown here, for the Whigs have carried their members both for City and County.' And he went on to emphasize the violence with which his opponents had carried the day, predicting further harassment at the hands of the newly constituted Artillery Company, which was 'all of the Oliverian cant', and 'strangely insult & dragoon us, & stab Gentlemen's horses who are of a contrary Kidney to themselves'.[27]

In the aftermath of the 1715 election the Tories fought hard to retain their standing in Corporation politics. By 1717 they had lost their majority on the Assembly, but they still managed to hold their own in aldermanic contests. Henry Crossgrove was pleased that the brewer Richard Lubbock replaced Sir Peter Seaman as one of the Aldermen in Northern ward notwithstanding divisions within the High Church party and stiff opposition from the Dissenters. He was elated when this 'True Son of the Church' rose rapidly in the civic hierarchy, becoming mayor in 1717 at the comparatively young age of 41.[28] Unfortunately, Lubbock died in office, but in the contest that followed the Tories again triumphed, a former captain of the militia, Thomas Bubbin, defeating the well-

---

[25] For an occupational breakdown of the 1715 poll see Speck, *Tory and Whig*, app. b, pp. 119–20.
[26] BL, Add. MS 5853, fo. 107.
[27] Ibid. 107v.
[28] *Norwich Gazette*, 14–21 Jan. 1716, 27 Apr.–4 May 1717.

known alderman and ex-mayor, John Hall, whose son ran the Artillery Company. These elections revealed that Toryism was still a force in civic politics. It also suggested that the Artillery Company was far from popular.

The activities of the Artillery Company achieved considerable notoriety because of the highly emotive street-anniversaries that informed Norwich politics in the early accession years. As in London, Norwich had witnessed an upsurge of political festival after the Sacheverell trial, especially from the Tories, with bells and bonfires on Stuart anniversaries and streets strewn with sand and flowers. Crossgrove noted such exuberance on Restoration day 1717, bells ringing until midnight, cannonades from Castle Hill, 'and musketeers and wheel-guns kept firing all day in the streets'. At St Margaret's, he reported, the church was topped with oak boughs and the churchyard strewn with thyme; at St James and the contiguous hamlet of Pockthorpe beyond the walls, 'the outsides of the houses were hung with pictures and Garlands across the streets, particularly there were Pictures of the Church and the Rev, Dr. Sacheverell bower'd over a vast many Doors, and people sat there Loyally Drinking Prosperity to the CHURCH and KING'.[29] In the highly charged atmosphere of the accession when Tory disappointment ran high and accusations of Tory perfidy were rife, such anniversaries could easily provoke violent partisanship. Disturbances were reported on Coronation day when a Tory crowd disrupted a Whig celebration to the cry of 'Bene and Berney . . . God d—n King George, pull off their Knots'.[30] Further confrontations occurred in the next few years, fanned by Crossgrove's detailed accounts of popular sedition in London and elsewhere as well as by the interventions of political clubs and societies.

The Artillery Company was very much a player in this theatre of politics. Formed in response to the 1715 rebellion, its partisanship was never seriously in doubt. On the first anniversary of the coronation, the company defied the order of the Tory lord mayor, Peter Attlesey, to confiscate effigies of

[29] *Norwich Gazette*, 25 May–2 June 1717. For a similar discussion of popular political culture in Norwich see Kathleen Wilson, 'The Rejection of Deference', ch. 7.

[30] *Political State of Great Britain* (1714), viii. 366–7.

the Pretender and Mar, and publicly officiated over their auto-*da-fé* at Market Cross. It also complemented the activities of the Whig mug-house-men of the Roebuck and Crown in curbing Tory exuberance, especially any defiant display of Jacobite symbolism. 'We have had here for several days no small disorder about wearing White Roses', reported the *Gazette* in June 1716, 'which it seems gives great Offense to our Artillery Men. On Sunday last one of them drew his Sword on a White Rose Man at the Great Church in Sermon Time, but the Fellow laid him on his Back, took his sword from him, and broke it. And on Monday they push'd the Jest so far, that there was a great Mobb up in the Market, till [a] Proclamation was made for them to disperse.'[31] More controversial still, the Artillery Company actively intervened at elections on behalf of Whig candidates, forming a veritable bruising-militia. 'Never was so much Party-Heat seen in any Election here before', recalled Crossgrove during the mayoral contest of 1716, when the Whig musketeers were much in evidence, 'nor so many Bloody Noses and Broken Heads . . . They began at first with Head and Fist, and so proceeded to Club Law . . . they then began to pelt each other with Sheeps Horns, Brick Ends, and great Paving Stones by which many People received sad Cuts and Contusions. Several Constables had their Heads crack'd and their staves broke, and the very sheriffs were impudently insulted and mobb'd.'[32]

The operations of the Artillery Company were thus provocative. They were bitterly detested by the Tories because they enjoyed government protection, as Mayor Attlesey discovered when he attempted to indict two members of the company for a riot on Restoration day 1715.[33] On the other hand, the Whigs could plausibly argue that the zeal of their most militant supporters was not unwarranted. Norwich Toryism had a distinctly Jacobite hue. White roses were defiantly paraded on Stuart anniversaries and Guild days. Six men from Norwich were indicted for drinking the Pretender's health at Caister-on-Sea. A barber from Fakenham, 15 miles north-west of the city in the heart of Walpole–Townshend territory, was com-

[31] *Norwich Gazette*, 23–30 June 1716; see also *Flying Post*, 23–6 June 1716.
[32] Ibid., 12–19, 19–26 May 1716.
[33] PRO, SP 44/116/341.

mitted to Norwich Castle for celebrating King George's cuckoldry on his royal birthday.[34] In January 1716, as the Preston rebels awaited trial in London, a loyalist farce was staged at the New Inn, Norwich, entitled 'The Earl of Mar marr'd.' On the first night the gallery cheered when the Pretender was proclaimed, much to the consternation of Captain Hall and his Whig militia-men, and the performance ended in an uproar. On subsequent nights the gallery hiss'd every time King George's name was mentioned.[35] These incidents might be dismissed as high spirits or as an expression of Tory defiance in the face of encroaching Whig power. But it is important to note that Norwich had strong nonjuring associations. The diocese of Norwich probably had more nonjurors than any other, including Bishop William Lloyd, who succeeded Sancroft as the nonjuring primate in 1692. At the Hanoverian accession the city still had a 'great congregation' of nonjurors, presided over by notable preachers such as Dr Nathaniel Spinkes, the celebrated bishop of Norwich who was taken into custody in October 1716.[36] Not surprisingly, Norwich spawned a militant, nonjuring tradition that produced high-class dissidents like Christopher Layer. Indeed Layer's own list of likely Jacobite supporters included five aldermen and a number of other Tory notables including the former MP Richard Berney.[37]

Perhaps the best example of Tory extremism was Henry Crossgrove, the indefatigable printer of the *Norwich Gazette* and for some years a councillor of Mancroft ward. The son of a pro-Stuart Irishman who lived in Stepney, Crossgrove was very conscious of treading in his father's footsteps. 'Passive Obedience & Non-Resistance is what I contend for as a striking Doctrine of our Church', he wrote to the Reverend John Strype in August 1715, '& happy had it been for Britain if her

[34] *Norwich Gazette*, 23–30 June 1716, 12–19 Jan., 3–10 Aug. 1717, 31 May–7 June 1718.

[35] Ibid., 14–21 Jan. 1716.

[36] Ibid., 22–9 Sept., 6–13 Oct. 1716; John H. Overton, *The Nonjurors* (London, 1902), pp. 467–96; G. M. Yould, 'Two Nonjurors', *Norfolk Archaeology*, 35 (1972), 364–81. For more on the character of Norwich Tory-Jacobitism see my 'Popular Jacobitism', pp. 123–41.

[37] Paul S. Fritz, *The English Ministers and Jacobitism between the Rebellions of 1715 and 1745* (Toronto, 1975), pp. 71, 145. For nonjurors see *Norwich Gazette*, 22–9 Sept., 6–13 Oct. 1716, and Overton, *The Nonjurors*.

members had practised as well as preached that doctrine . . .
but if ever an usurper should happen to be crouded into the
Throne by men of Latitudinarian Principles (which I hope will
never happen here)' all would be lost.[38] Crossgrove clearly did
think all was lost or at least in the balance under Hanover,
although he was pleased 'that Norwich is not altogether
Germanized'. We 'have Persons here, & in Norfolk too, &
many of no mean Station & Circumstance,' he confided to
Strype, 'who are real Englishmen, & can never cease to be so'.[39]
From his printing house in St Peter Mancroft, and later St
Giles, Crossgrove sought to stiffen their resistance to the
Hanoverian regime. Stuart anniversaries were commemorated
in his paper with an audacious enthusiasm; Whig political
folklore was reviled; London disaffection was pointedly detailed. There was scarcely a seditious outburst in the London
press that escaped his eye, and the more outrageous it was, the
more extensive its coverage.[40] At the same time the City of
London's opposition to the new government was held up as an
exemplary point of reference for Norwich's own Tories.

Crossgrove faced considerable harassment from the authorities for his intrepid Toryism. In early 1716 the Whiggish
Lieutenancy had ransacked his house for treasonable papers
and arms. The previous summer he had been accused of
planning to 'head up a Body of 80 stout fellows with Horns on
their Heads on the first of August next, & [to] attack the
Whiggish Artillery Company, take their arms from them, and
down with the Conventicles'.[41] Neither of these actions
silenced him and they probably boosted the fortunes of the
Norwich Tories at a time when the party was nationally in
considerable disarray. Certainly, they did little to inhibit Tory
festival or to undermine the Tories' continued control of the
Court of Mayoralty.

---

[38] BL, Add. MS 5853, fos. 108–9.
[39] Ibid. 108.
[40] For example, Crossgrove devoted considerable space to Bisse's sermon at
St George Portbury, which maligned Nassau and Hanover and declared that
'things are now worse than in the days of Good old NOLL, for a man cannot
put his Hand to his Hat now but if it touch his Brow Imprisonment must be his
portion', a reference to the crackdown on political festival and merriment:
Norwich Gazette, 3–10 May 1718.
[41] BL, Add. MS 5853, fo. 108v.; *Norwich Gazette*, 21–8 Jan. 1716; *Weekly
Journal*, 23 July 1715.

By 1720, however, the political tide appeared to be turning. In that year the Whigs captured both the Assembly and the Court of Mayoralty for the first time in decades. Within seven years they had also consolidated their grip on the parliamentary constituency. In 1722 the Tories failed to muster candidates with the financial resources to challenge Whig power. Five years later they failed to make any headway against the incumbents Bacon and Britiffe, winning only 43.5 per cent of the poll, their lowest turnout in decades. Yet in spite of these victories Whig confidence remained fragile. In May 1722 the Tories won the mayoral election, the old campaigner Robert Bene and his nephew Thomas Newton defeating Aldermen John Coshold and Daniel Fromanteel. In the same month Edward Weld defeated John Harvey in an aldermanic contest for Conisford ward, forcing a scrutiny upon a reluctant Whig mayor. And in the shrieval election of August Weld came close to defeating the well-known Dissenter, Nathaniel Paul, losing only by virtue of a highly contentious scrutiny.[42] These setbacks so bothered the Whigs that they considered tampering with the constitution. If the Whigs continued to lose civic elections, opined one of their leaders to Townshend in August 1722, 'it will give such a turn to the constitution as will not easily be helped without taking away the Charter and granting it on another foot, viz. by confirming the present Court of Aldermen, who have a majority firmly in the interest of the present Government, and granting to them a power to choose sixty Common Councilmen who shall remain so for life'.[43] Curbing the city's democratic traditions remained on the Whig agenda for the rest of the decade, becoming a matter of pressing concern when the Tories resumed control of the Assembly in 1728 and 1729.

The Whigs' response to these civic reversals was doubtless extreme, an indication of their beleaguered mentality. It reflected a lingering insecurity about their standing in an area of the country that had traditionally been a bastion of Toryism, notwithstanding Walpole and Townshend's ascendancy at Court. But Whig anxiety was also generated by a depression in

[42] *Norwich Gazette*, 28 Apr.–5 May, 26 May–2 June, 2–9 June, 25 Aug.–1 Sept., 22–9 Sept. 1722.
[43] Cited from the State Papers Domestic 22 Aug. 1722, by S. and B. Webb, *English Local Government*, ii. 545–6.

the woollen industry and by the series of scandals that had rocked Whig-Hanoverian rule. Since the 1690s the Norwich textile industry had been concerned with the importation of printed calicoes into England and had campaigned hard for their prohibition. This was achieved in 1700, but the act was quickly circumvented by the practice of importing undyed calicoes which were then dyed and finished at home. Norwich weavers petitioned to close this loophole in 1710, and in the next decade, as a depression in domestic sales coincided with an overseas recession, these protests reached fever pitch, with further petitions from weavers, dyers, wool-combers, dressers, and freeholders.[44] Riots broke out in Norwich in 1719, to which the Corporation quickly responded with promises of further action. They recurred the following year, this time fuelled by the South Sea Bubble and a growing hatred of the moneyed companies. As William Massey reported on 13 December: 'This day a mob in Pockthorpe in this city rose in a tumultuous manner, complaining of the want of trade and the wear of Calicoes and making outcries against the Managers of the South Sea Company as plunderers of the country.'[45] It was only with the intervention of the Artillery Company that order was restored.

A new Calico Act was passed in 1721 addressing the weavers' grievances. It was welcomed by the Assembly, which at the same time publicly thanked the king for restoring financial confidence after the South Sea Scandal and declared that it was 'fully satisfied that not any the least part of this misfortune can be imputed to your Majesty'.[46] But some of the rank and file remained dissatisfied with the way in which the Whig hierarchy handled the crisis of 1719–21. It found political expression in electoral defeats of John Croshold and John Harvey, the two men who as sheriffs had been responsible for the suppression of the Pockthorpe riot in 1720. Together with

---

[44] For Norwich petitions against calicoes see *Commons Journals*, 16, p. 336; 19, pp. 176–7, 182, 192, 253. In Dec. 1721 the Corporation of Norwich was also complaining about the growing use of paper rather than woollen hangings: see *Commons Journals*, 19, p. 693.

[45] Cited by Basil Cozens-Hardy and Ernest A. Kent (eds.), *The Mayors of Norwich 1403 to 1835* (Norwich, 1938), p. 115.

[46] Norwich and Norfolk RO, Case 16 c.8, Assembly Book 1714–31, fos. 131–2.

the return of Robert Bene, a former Tory MP and well-known benefactor, a civic politician of nearly thirty years' standing whose age probably precluded his continued parliamentary candidature (he was 69 in 1722), the Norwich voters served notice on the Whigs not to take them for granted.

The shrieval contest of 1722 was especially disturbing to the Whigs because, coming in the wake of disclosures about the Layer conspiracy, it should have put their electoral supremacy beyond doubt. It prompted them to consider new ways to boost their popularity. In January 1723 the Assembly petitioned Parliament for a new Election Act which would force all resident adult males engaged in the textile industry to take up the freedom, regularize electoral polls and scrutinies, and specify property qualifications and fines for Sheriffs appointed by the Court of Mayoralty.[47] The ostensible reason for this act was to increase the city's declining revenue, an issue that had been troubling the Corporation for some time.[48] But it is clear that the Whig-dominated Assembly was looking for some political advantage from this seemingly innocuous bill. Increasing the textile vote would very probably improve Whig political prospects (as in fact, it appears to have done).[49] Regularizing the electoral process would improve the Whig party's image, somewhat tainted by its illegal mobilization of the prison vote, of scores of dependent electors who were pressured into polling in both Wymer and Mancroft wards during the crucial contests of the Hanoverian era.[50] Indeed, some Whigs felt that tighter electoral procedures would ultimately benefit their party. William Chase, the printer of the *Norwich Mercury* and a councilman of Wymer ward, was

[47] Assembly Book 1714–31, fos. 118–19; see also 9 Geo. I, c.9.

[48] In 1721 an Assembly committee had reported on the city's financial problems, recommending a retrenchment in civic fees and salaries and cuts in the 'extravagant rates' for Corporation contracts: Assembly Book 1714–31, fos. 137–40.

[49] Of the first 50 worsted-weavers and 50 wool-combers admitted under the act, 40 voted in the 1734/5 elections. 28 polled for the Whig candidates, 11 for the Tory: see O'Sullivan, 'Politics in Norwich', p. 92.

[50] See *Norwich Gazette*, 22–9 Mar. 1718 and Assembly Book 1714–31, fos. 188–9. The petition to the Commons, 7 Jan. 1723, declared that 'A great many prisoners' were 'taking the liberty to vote in two several Wards under pretense that the Gaol is situated in both, besides the Ward wherein their families inhabit'.

of this opinion. According to his calculations, the Whigs would have won the aldermanic election of 1722 in Conesford ward had they persevered with the scrutiny and avoided a peremptory declaration on behalf of the Whig candidate by the mayor.[51]

The Tories went along with this electoral bill. Two of their aldermen, Thomas Harwood and Edward Weld, were on the committee which prepared the presentation to the Commons. And for a brief time civic politics in Norwich were remarkably quiet. But this equanimity quickly evaporated in 1728 when the Tories won majorities in Mancroft and Wymer wards and consequently controlled the Assembly. 'Upon this success', reported Chase, the Tories were 'so elevated that they ordered the bells to be rung and the Pott Guns to be fired, and made Publick Rejoicings as if they had obtained some Signal Victory or Deliverance. But their Mob, grown giddy even with a distant view of Power, were so insolent as to insult Gentlemen of the contrary party in the streets and at their own Doors.'[52] This breakthrough was followed by a successful mayoral contest, when the Tory Thomas Harwood defeated his opponent, Captain John Black, a prominent member of the Artillery Company, by 28 votes. Amid accusations of electoral intimidation and chicanery, and jubilant demonstrations by Tory supporters inside the civic chamber, party strife intensified. Scuffles between the Artillery Company and Tory supporters were reported on Restoration day, and the contentious, protracted scrutiny of the mayoral struggle was followed by an equally contentious one in August, when the Whig John Spurrel was returned as the freemen's Sheriff, defeating his opponent by 92 votes.[53] By December party spleen had reached such a pitch that the Whig aldermen decided to abandon the Assembly, sabotaging civic business for over a year.[54] In the mean time they considered further ways to reform the city's electoral structure.

The fruit of these deliberations, the Norwich Elections Act of 1730, was highlighted by the Webbs because it inaugurated a

---

[51] *A Copy of the Polls taken at an Election for an Alderman for the Great Ward of Conesford in the City of Norwich on the 19 Day of May 1722*, printed by W. Chase (Norwich, [1722]).

[52] *Norwich Mercury*, 6–13 Apr. 1728.

[53] Ibid., 27 Apr.–4 May, 25 May–1 June, 24–31 Aug. 1728; *Norwich Gazette*, 7–14 Sept. 1728.

[54] S. and B. Webb, *English Local Government*, p. 546.

novel experiment in municipal politics, a bicameral legislature. In their account of its origins they claimed that the act was a compromise between the city's warring factions, a solution to the impasse of 1728.[55] In fact, this was not so. Although the heads of the bill were set down in the Assembly Book records, and although it was presented to Parliament as emanating from the 'mayor, sheriffs, citizens and commonalty', it never received official approval, as Crossgrove reminded voters in March 1729.[56] From the very beginning it was a Whig project. It was a private bill pushed through the Commons by Bacon and Britiffe, Norwich's Whig MPs. Its architects included two prominent members of the Artillery Company, Mayor John Black and Timothy Balderstone, Alderman of St Giles's ward; Daniel Fromanteel, an attorney and alderman of Walloon descent; John Custance, a prominent textile-manufacturer who had acquired a country estate at Weston, Norfolk in 1726; two other aldermen and textile manufacturers, John Harvey and Jeremiah Ives, whose families played leading roles in Norwich politics for the rest of the century; Francis Arnam (or Arnham), soon to be mayor; and Philip Meadows, one of the up-and-coming Dissenters in Norwich politics, a governor of several children's hospitals in the city and a leading Presbyterian.[57] All these men were Whig in politics; they were, in fact, members of the inner Whig caucus.

The ostensible intention of the bill was to curb the electoral irregularities and violence which continued to plague Norwich politics. The real object was to immobilize civic Toryism and deplete its parliamentary resources. In the first place the bill insisted upon a stricter registration of voters: a six-month residential qualification for freemen who elected civic representatives; and a twelve-month qualification for freemen who participated in parliamentary elections. This was because 'the Freedoms of great number of poor Men have been

---

[55] Ibid.

[56] Assembly Book 1714–31, fos. 295–7; *Commons Journals*, 21, p. 429; *Norwich Gazette*, 15–22 Mar. 1729. The official air with which the bill was presented may well have been in response to Tory criticisms.

[57] The sponsors are listed in the *Norwich Mercury*, 15–22 Mar. 1729. For information about them see Cozens-Hardy and Kent (eds.), *Mayors of Norwich*, and *passim*.

purchased by other People at a very low Price'.[58] This appeared reasonable enough. Electoral venality was an issue of rising concern and its elimination self-evidently libertarian. But the regulation certainly gave the Whig party an edge over their opponents. Poor voters in the Whig party were very likely to be weavers or wool-combers, and the 1723 Act had insisted upon their registration as freemen, so that the qualification clauses were more likely to prejudice the petty artisans of the Tory party. Moreover, the regulations were in the civic context restrictive, as the Tories insisted.[59] Voters were mobile. Many freemen were journeymen whose residential stability was contingent upon their employment prospects. The scrutiny of voters in the 1730 Wymer ward elections revealed that several were 'constant removers', and the turnover in parliamentary, let alone civic, elections was relatively high, amounting to nearly 19 per cent in 1734/5.[60] The problem of electoral venality might have been tackled in other ways without disfranchising some of these poor voters.

So the 1730 Elections Act did narrow the civic electorate. It also compromised Norwich's tradition of popular political participation in two other ways. In order to reduce the duration of the annual Assembly elections, the number of Councillors chosen by each ward was reduced to three, and these three then co-opted the rest. Given the intensity of party strife in Norwich this was probably not a very dramatic change. In all likelihood it increased the partisan coloration of each individual ward. But it did curb the freemen's right of choosing a full quota of local representatives. More controversial was the clause which gave the Common Council and the aldermen a veto over any acts or ordinances of the Assembly. This clause replicated that of the City of London's Elections Act of 1725; in effect it was an aldermanic veto, a restraint upon Norwich's most democratic and representative institution. As long as the Whigs held a majority on the Court of Mayoralty, which they now did by a substantial margin of 20 : 4, they could muzzle

[58] *Commons Journals*, 21, p. 478; for the final act see 3 George II c.8 and Francis Blomefield, *An Essay towards a Topographical History of the County of Norfolk* (11 vols; London, 1805–10), iii. 451.

[59] *Norwich Gazette*, 15–22 Mar. 1729.

[60] *Norwich Mercury*, 11–18 Apr. 1730. The turnover figures are based on my calculations from the combined 1734/5 poll.

any dissident voices on Council, any embarrassing Address or set of Instructions bearing the civic seal.

The Tories opposed the 1730 bill. Crossgrove thought the Whig rationale of electoral peace specious. He warned the electorate that the bill was an 'underhand, irregular scheme' designed to undermine freemen's rights. 'If ye sacrifice your Consciences for a Trifle, your Integrity for Lucre, and barter your Birth-Rights for a mess of Pottage', he warned voters, 'many ye not expect with Esau to lose your Blessings and find the Termination of those valuable Privileges ye now enjoy for your final Reward.'[61]

How far the Norwich electorate heeded these warnings remains difficult to determine. The Tory party appears to have been demoralized by the Whig initiative. It offered no opposition to the Whig application to Parliament, unlike its counterparts in London some five years earlier. And this defeatism inevitably undercut popular resistance to the bill. Not that this resistance was insubstantial. In the ward elections of 1730 and 1731 the Whigs only just scraped home. Six votes separated the two parties in Wymer ward in 1730, only one in 1731.[62] Had these results gone the other way the Tories would have continued to control the Assembly, for they emerged with convincing majorities in the other large ward (that is, Mancroft), while the Whigs retained Northern and Conesford wards.[63] But these results left the Tories increasingly dispirited. It discouraged them from canvassing in other civic contests. As the *Gazette* reported after the mayoral election of 1731, 'the poor Freemen of the High Church party polled of their own accords . . . without any Incouragement from the Gentlemen of that Interest'.[64]

The Norwich Elections Act of 1730 thus achieved its immediate objective: it immobilized civic Toryism. By 1732 the Whigs were comfortably in control of the Assembly as well

[61] *Norwich Gazette*, 15–22 Mar. 1729.

[62] *Norwich Mercury*, 14–21 Mar. 1730, *Norwich Gazette*, 3–10 Apr. 1731.

[63] Wymer returned 20 councillors to the Assembly, Mancroft 16, and Northern and Conesford 12 apiece. Thus a Tory victory in Wymer in 1730 and 1731 would have given them 36 seats and the Whigs 24.

[64] *Norwich Gazette*, 1–8 May 1731. See also issue for 25 Apr.–2 May 1730, where it was reported that the Tory candidates did quite well, 'seeing no Interest was made in Time to promote their Election'.

as of the Court of Mayoralty, and breathed a new confidence. In their eyes the electoral will had vindicated their policy and established beyond all doubt the loyalism of most Norwich citizens to the Hanoverian–Whig regime. As William Chase had argued after the first crop of Whig victories, it was 'now evident (notwithstanding the vain boast of the Tories which have been so often rung in our Ears, that they have the Hearts of the People) that the Freemen of the City are zealously affected to the present government'.[65]

Whig confidence was expressed in a number of ways, but it was most evident in the zeal with which the Norwich faction supported Walpole. During the Excise crisis, for example, the Norwich Corporation showed no sign of abandoning the first minister or of trimming its sails to the national mood. Chase was contemptuous of the patriot coalition which agitated against the Excise scheme, emulating the *Daily Courant* in portraying it as an unholy alliance of Jacobites, republicans, and malcontents.[66] And his fellow councillors and aldermen were unabashedly pro-Walpolean, toasting the Great Man's health on Accession day, 1733, amid salvos from the Artillery Company. In fact, precisely a month later, some three months after the abandonment of the Excise bill, the Whig-dominated Corporation presented Sir Robert with the freedom of the city in a gold box.[67] This ceremony was not conducted in the Council chamber, but publicly, in the market-place. It was a clear counterpoint to the anti-Excise demonstrations which had rang through the country and had been faithfully reported in the Tory press.

Sir Robert's visit to Norwich in 1733 was also the occasion for inducting his brother, Horace Walpole, as one of the Whig candidates for the city in the next general election. He was to replace Robert Britiffe, a Norwich lawyer who acted for the Townshend and Walpole families and who had agreed to stand down. The move was part of an expansion of Walpolean ambitions in Norfolk.[68] Sir Robert's son, Edward, was to take over 'old' Horace's seat in Great Yarmouth, and Sir Robert

---

[65] *Norwich Mercury*, 25 Apr.–2 May 1730.
[66] Ibid., 31 Mar.–7 Apr. 1733.
[67] Ibid., 9–16 June, 7–14 July 1733.
[68] Langford, *The Excise Crisis*, pp. 41–2.

himself had contemplated a second try for the county, although the agitation over the Excise dissuaded him. None the less, the Norwich part of the plan was pursued. The *douceur* for the city was greater attentiveness to the textile industry. For some time there had been complaints that the government had neglected the trade. 'The People's Expectation, if you mean the Manufacturers,' wrote one spokesman 'is seldom under Consideration with the Great, or we should not have seen, in former Parliaments, so little action taken of the annual and numerous petitions from these unhappy artizans, nor St. Stephen's Chappel so often and so suddenly grown thin at the same mention of wool or woollen Manufacturers.' Party and local rivalries were impediments to change, he went on, and he held out little hope that the current grievances, owling (or the smuggling of wool from England) and the constraints upon the import of Irish yarn, would be addressed.[69] But Walpole did address these issues. He publicly expressed his support for a bill to allow Irish wool into the country duty-free. And he might well have informed his audience of his brother's own efforts for the local textile industry, if they needed reminding. In April 1731, Horace Walpole had moved a bill for the free importation of Irish yarn into England, only to see it flounder in the Lords. And the following year he had seconded a bill which removed a concession allowing Irish seamen to carry forty-shillings worth of woollen goods, arguing that it prejudiced the English woollen industry.[70] Support for the Walpoles in Norwich was never simply a question of political snobbery, of associating with Whig celebrities. It was based on material considerations, on the welfare of its primary industry and the general prosperity that was said to have flowed from the government's fiscal and pacific foreign policy.

While the Norwich Whigs were busily regaling the Walpoles and applauding the benefits of the present government, the Tories were reconstituting their forces for the upcoming general election. On the defeat of the Excise bill, demonstrations of joy had broken out in the Tory quarter of Mancroft

[69] Anon., *A Letter from a Weaver at Norwich to a Member of Parliament Concerning the Present State of our Woollen Manufactures* (London, 1734).

[70] Sedgwick (ed.), *Commons 1715–54*, ii. 509.

and the principal traders in the ward sent a message of thanks to the Norfolk Tory, Sir Edmund Bacon, for opposing the measure in Parliament.[71] Crossgrove kept his readers abreast of developments elsewhere, and he made a good deal of Lord Mayor Barber's impassioned defence of London's agitations against the bill.[72] He also kept them well apprised of the political developments in Norfolk, where Sir Edmund Bacon and William Wodehouse were canvassing hard on an anti-Excise ticket. Yarmouth gave the Country candidates a stirring reception in September, with the harbour littered with 'No Excise' bunting. And the following month their entry into Wymondham, a market town only six miles from Norwich, was accompanied by 600 gentlemen, clergy, and freeholders, and a standard bearer displaying a flag with a tobacco leaf, pipe, and 'No Excise' slogan painted upon it.[73] This progress compared favourably to that of their opponents, who were greeted with stones and other missiles in Yarmouth and shouts of 'No Pensioners! No Excise!'. According to the *Gazette*, the onlookers 'broke the Glasses of some of the Coaches and . . . bespattered several of the gentlemen with dirt'.[74] This rough treatment bode well for the Tories.

Within Norwich, too, there were signs that the anti-Excise furore might bite into Whig ranks. The wool-combers' Bishop Blaize procession displayed a certain scepticism that Walpole's promises would ring true. It featured two boys with woollen crowns on which were fastened favours representing the redoubtable John Barber, scourge of the Whigs and the Excise scheme. Spectators were urged to 'congratulate his Fate / Who trimm'd the City and who shar'd the State'.[75] Two months later, the anniversary of the defeat of the Excise bill saw another flurry of oppositionist fervour. 205 candles—one for each MP who opposed the Excise—illuminated several steeples and an anti-Excise banner was raised at St Peter Mancroft. Chase thought the anniversary a forced affair, directed from London rather than generated locally. Only the staunchest Tory parishes, he claimed, rang bells. 'The whole

[71] *Norwich Gazette*, 7–14, 14–21 Apr. 1734; the *Craftsman*, 26 May 1733.
[72] *Norwich Gazette*, 12–19 May, 29 Sept.–6 Oct. 1733.
[73] Ibid., 15–22 Sept., 6–13 Oct. 1733.
[74] Ibid., 24 Nov.–1 Dec. 1733.
[75] Ibid., 2–9 Feb. 1734.

public Rejoycings amounted to no more than a few Candles set upon the steeples of four of the seven churches where the Bells were rung.'[76] In his eyes it compared poorly with the Whiggish celebrations of the marriage of the king's eldest daughter to the Prince of Orange the month before. He was far from convinced that the political disposition of the citizenry had changed.

The 1734 general election served to test these calculations. In a closely fought contest in which 218 votes separated the four candidates, out of a total of 3,363 votes, the Whigs emerged as the victors. Crossgrove complained that the returning officers closed the polls early to the detriment of the Tories and that the numbers reported for Walpole and Waller Bacon were different on the following morning from what they had been on the night before.[77] This cannot be ruled out. Horace Walpole's letter to Newcastle hints at some sharp practice. 'We have carried it for both,' he wrote on 15 May, 'Great expenses made, great threats usher'd in the day, but a due provision to repel force by force made it a quiet Election.'[78] But in view of the pre-electoral speculations that Sir Edward Ward would not stand for the Tories in Norwich,[79] it seems more likely that superior resources and organization gave the Whigs their narrow victory. Certainly the poll-book suggests this was the case. As in 1715, the Whigs fared well among the growing ranks of out-voters, especially those that travelled from London and the Norfolk towns of King's Lynn and Yarmouth where the Walpole interest was firmly established. Within Norwich itself the Whig majority was narrower. Here the Court party did well in the predominantly nonconformist wards of Northern and Wymer, where the turnout appears to have been exceptionally high. In Northern ward they won the support of 30 of the 33 Quakers who voted, including 7 leading worsted-manufacturers, 3 of whom were Gurneys.[80] By contrast, they lost narrowly in Conisford and more decisively in the Tory quarter of Mancroft.

Despite this slim victory it is none the less clear that the

---

[76] Ibid., 6–13 Apr. 1734; *Norwich Mercury*, 16–23 Mar., 6–13 Apr. 1734.
[77] *Norwich Gazette*, 11–18 May 1734.
[78] BL, Add. MS 32689, fo. 241.
[79] *Norwich Mercury*, 23–30 Mar. 1734.
[80] 5 of these were worsted-weavers, 2 combers. All had personal property rated at £100 or more in the 1734 Land Tax. All save one lived in St Augustine: see *An Alphabetical Draught of the Polls*.

Whigs did not lose much support as a result of the Excise. The Whig vote in Norwich was not ruptured as it was in some other large urban constituencies. Even among the freemen resident in the city itself it remained at 1730/1 levels. The point emerges clearly by comparing the Norwich return with that of the county. Few expected the Whigs to lose the 1734 county election. Lord Bathurst assumed that it would 'be carried (one way or another) as the great Man wou'd have it'. Even Horace Walpole, in the aftermath of his victory at Norwich, thought 'the County a much more secure game'.[81] But in fact events proved otherwise. In another close contest in which Sir Robert Walpole is said to have spent £10,000 of his own money,[82] the Tories edged out their opponents by a mere 6 votes. Only in Norwich (among freeholders resident in the city but with freeholds elsewhere) and other Walpolean strongholds did the Whigs chalk up some majorities.[83]

The Tories were suitably elated by this victory and it served to compensate in part for their disappointing showing in Norwich. The *London Evening Post* reported that 'the Day after the Election, the Bells rang throughout the City, and the Streets were finely strown with Sand, Flowers, and Greens'.[84] Hopes for a political regeneration in the wake of this victory were again raised in November on the death of Waller Bacon. But they were blunted by the defection of Thomas Vere, an alderman and Norwich merchant who had stood for the Tories in the 1730 and 1731 mayoral elections. Since the spring of 1734 Vere had been gravitating towards the Whigs and had opened a correspondence with Horace Walpole. Late in 1734 the mayor and some of the principal merchants and manufacturers in the city asked him to stand in the government interest.[85] Vere agreed to do so, bringing with him some

[81] Cartwright (ed.), *Wentworth Papers*, p. 506; BL, Add. MS 32689, fo. 241.
[82] William Coxe, *Memoirs of the Life and Administration of Sir Robert Walpole*, 3 vols. (London, 1798), i. 456.
[83] The votes for the freeholders resident in Norwich were as follows: Bacon, 146; Wodehouse, 144; Coke, 154; Morden, 160: see *A Copy of the Poll for the Knights of the Shire for the County of Norfolk, Taken at Norwich May 22 1734*.
[84] *London Evening Post*, 25–8 May 1734.
[85] *Norwich Mercury*, 28 Dec.–4 Jan. 1734–5; on Vere's correspondence with Walpole see J. H. Plumb, *Sir Robert Walpole* (2 vols.; London, 1956–60), ii. 320n.

worsted-weavers in the process. These developments laid the foundations for a convincing Whig victory in the February 1735 by-election. In another large poll—3,246 voters turned out—Vere won by nearly 400 votes. Significantly, he did well in the city and hamlets, securing large majorities in the parishes within Wymer and Northern wards and reducing the Tory's majority in Conisford. Only the High Church parishes of St Peter Mancroft, St Stephen's, St Andrew's, St John Maddermarket, and those within the sub-ward of Berstreet resisted the onward march of Whiggery.

The survival of the poll-books of 1734 and 1735, together with those of the Augustan era, allows us to chart the emergence of the Whig ascendancy in some detail. Not that such a venture is without its problems: like Bristol, Norwich's voters were asked their occupations at the hustings; they were not required to state their affiliation with particular companies, as in London and Newcastle. For the purposes of sociological analysis this is a real advantage. Even so, the occupational ascriptions in the poll-books still have to be organized into meaningful social categories. In the case of grocers, for example, one of the wealthier groups in the seventeenth century, one has to attempt to differentiate wholesalers and fairly substantial distributors from retailers. In the case of weavers, a large portion of the electorate, journeymen, small masters, and large manufacturers are indistinguishable. Not until the second half of the century do directories provide any clues about such critical distinctions.[86] Hence it is necessary to supplement the occupational clusters with rate-book and apprenticeship data, and (where possible) combine them so that they at least differentiate large-scale employers, middlemen, and the emergent professions from the small masters and journeymen.

Throughout the first three decades of the century the partisan vote in Norwich elections remained high. In 1710 96.4 per cent of the electors voted for one or other of the party slates; in 1734 93.6 per cent did so. Even if one includes those voters who switched sides in 1735, the percentage of straight party voters remains extraordinarily high, at 92.1. Not until

---

[86] For a discussion of how city directories and rate-books might supplement the occupational data of the poll-books in the second half of the century see Phillips, *Electoral Behavior*, ch. 5.

the late eighteenth century did electoral partisanship attain these levels.[87] Moreover, the participation rates in Norwich elections were quite substantial. It is impossible to predict what precise proportion of the freeman and freeholder electorate actually turned out in any one election, but we know that of the 3,384 voters who polled in 1734, only 640 failed to appear nine months later. Allowing for mortality, this means that 81.7 per cent of the electorate participated in both elections and the vast majority voted consistently. This compares very favourably with the participation rates in some Augustan elections, although I would argue that it was not atypical for the large urban electorates.[88] Allowing for the mobility of the city—and it is probable that half the electorate disappeared in the course of five years—we are dealing with a substantial core of politically conscious, party-minded voters.

Rate assessments suggest that there was little to choose between the two parties in terms of wealth. As Table 9.1 reveals, there were no glaring disparities or skewed distributions. To be sure, the Tories appear to have a higher proportion of smaller voters in both 1710 and 1734/5, a fact which would certainly make the Whig insistence upon the

TABLE 9.1. *Distribution of Wealth within Parties: Norwich 1710 and 1734/1735*

	1710		1734/5	
	Tory	Whig	Tory	Whig
£0–9 (%)	24.5	21.0	31.0	26.7
£10–19 (%)	39.9	39.1	24.0	29.4
£20+ (%)	35.5	41.0	45.0	43.9
no.	301	261	229	221

Sources: 1710 and 1734/5 poll-books; 1708 Window Tax; 1734 Land Tax. For 1710, 28.4 per cent of total voters have been located; for 1734/5 19.5 per cent.

[87] Phillips, *Electoral Behavior*, p. 216. The straight party-vote was very high in 1784 and 1803, but there was more split voting in 1780 (12.6%), 1790 (24.6%), and 1796 (18.7%).

[88] The Augustan figures are provided by Phillips, *Electoral Behavior*, p. 95. Some very preliminary investigations of the Norwich polls, based on specific occupations within three parishes, suggests that 47% of the 1715 electorate had voted in 1710. Of these old voters, 88% voted for the same party.

registration of voters in 1730 more explicable. They also appear to have gained a somewhat richer clientele by the 1730s. But an examination of the personal stock of voters in 1734/5— arguably a more sensitive index of wealth than the rateable value of property which did not, at this stage in the century, differentiate owner from occupier—contradicts this judgment. Here (Table 9.2) we find that the proportion of Whig voters with personal stock of £200 or more was greater than that of their opponents. According to this assessment, the Whigs commanded the support of a higher proportion of rich voters, not vice versa, as in the assessments of property. Even so, the contrast between the two parties was not substantial. Just over half of the Tory voters (50.2 per cent) located in the records had personal stock of £100 or more. The corresponding figure for the Whigs was 55.8 per cent.

TABLE 9.2. *Distribution of Personal Stock among Norwich Voters 1734/1735*

	Tory	Whig	TOTAL
Stock under £60 (%)	31.7	30.1	30.8
£60–199 (%)	51.2	48.4	49.9
over £200 (%)	17.1	21.5	19.3
no.	211	233	444

Sources: 1734/5 poll-book; 1734 Land-Tax assessments.

The rate-books offer some rough parameters of wealth among Norwich voters. Their principal defect is that they cover a small section of the electorate (between 19 and 28 per cent), and we have little knowledge of how representative this section is. One would assume that it offers a general profile of the richer voters, particularly those whose businesses involved the use of large workshops, warehouses, breweries, and taverns. But it would exclude many lodgers, journeymen, and poor householders. Because of the geographical range of the tax records it would also exclude out-voters. Yet if one uses the Window- and Land-Tax records to isolate the wealthiest voters and to differentiate large employers and wholesalers from the rank and file of voting tradesmen and artisans, some interesting patterns emerge. As Tables 9.3 and 9.4 show, the most

TABLE 9.3. *Occupations of Voters 1710 and 1734/1735 (%)*

	1710		1734/5	
	Tory	Whig	Tory	Whig
Gentlemen/professions	2.5	1.3	3.7	5.5
Merchants/wholesalers/manufacturers	3.7	3.0	2.4	2.6
Craftsmen	32.1	34.0	27.8	35.7
Freeholders	8.5	5.8	5.9	6.0
Retailers	6.0	2.1	5.6	3.4
Others	0.7	0.2	0.6	0.7

Note: this Table excludes split voters.

TABLE 9.4. *Voting within Occupational Group: Norwich 1710 and 1734/1735 (%)*

	1710		1734/5	
	Tory	Whig	Tory	Whig
Gentlemen/professions	65.5	34.4	40.6	59.4
Merchants/wholesalers/manufacturers	55.1	44.9	48.4	51.6
Craftsmen	48.6	51.4	43.7	56.3
Freeholders	59.0	41.0	49.4	50.6
Retailers	74.1	25.9	61.9	38.1
Others	78.3	21.7	49.0	51.0

Note: this Table excludes split voters.

critical base of the Norwich electorate in the early decades of the eighteenth century was the craftsmen, and within this sector the textile trades were overwhelmingly preponderant. Artisans constituted 66.1 per cent of the active voters in 1710 and (in an electorate which expanded to over 3,000 by the 1730s) 63.5 per cent in 1734/5. At the high point of their influence, the Tories fared reasonably well in this sector, although they were never able fully to capture it. By the mid-1730s they were losing their foothold among the weavers, combers, and hot-pressers of the city and its industrial suburbs, and this crippled their chances of regaining the parliamentary representation of this thriving textile town. They also lost support among the city's new freeholders, and more importantly among the upper echelons of Norwich society. By the time of the Excise Crisis, the Whigs dominated the Court of Mayoralty and the Commission of the Peace by a majority of 23 : 7. The poll-books also reveal that the Tories could no longer count upon the clerical vote. Indeed, of the 71 clergymen voting in 1734 and 1735, only 24 voted for their candidates. Nor could they rely upon the churchwardens, who were fairly evenly divided between the two parties.[89] Their majority among the gentlemen (who by 1734/5 included a fair number of wealthy manufacturers with genteel aspirations) also slipped, as it did among big employers. Among the textile manufacturers, the Tories won over 24 to the Whigs' 71, a disappointing showing considering that they only lagged by 3 : 5 in 1710.[90] The inescapable conclusion is that the Tories failed to hold on to their support within the manufacturing sector, the real life-blood of the town, and as the Whigs assumed control of government and ecclesiastical patronage, the Tories also lost some of their traditional power-bases.[91] Only among the retailers did they retain their supremacy, and in this respect it is significant that their foremost supporters included a disproportionate number of brewers and grocers.

A brief look at the electoral geography of the city helps to supplement some of these conclusions. As the Appendix to this Chapter reveals, the principal sources of Tory support in Norwich itself were those parishes where there was a fairly dense clustering of retail trades. These included the busy shopping precinct of St Peter Mancroft, the headquarters of Norwich Toryism, and the contiguous parishes of St Andrew and St John Maddermarket to the north. Bordering the river Wensum, these parishes contained a higher proportion of weavers, but the food, drink, and clothing trades were by no means poorly represented. In 1710 the Tories also held

---

[89] The clerical vote in 1734/5 was 24 Tory, 45 Whig, with four splitting their votes or changing sides in the by-election of Feb. 1735. The churchwardens have been identified with the use of the visitation records for 1710 and 1735: see Norwich and Norwich RO, VIS 11 and 16/1, 2.

[90] My calculations for 1710 are 15 Tories (including one wealthy hot-presser) and 26 Whigs (including one dyer). I have taken every weaver and comber in the top tax bracket to be a substantial employer.

[91] Of the 38 civic and government officers noted by Nockold Thompson in 1735, all voted for Vere, the Whig candidate, and none for the Tories. See *An Alphabetical Draught of the Polls.*

a majority in the predominantly weaving parishes of St Augustine and St Helen's (the latter within the shadow of the Cathedral and electorally small), but they had lost them by 1734. Where the party did gain ground was in the retailing parishes of St Stephen, St John's Timberhill, and St John Sepulchre, the last two being the principal centres of the meat and leather trades.

The predominantly Whig parishes, by contrast, were those that had a high concentration of weavers. In 1710 the Whigs held majorities on the northern bank of the river Wensum, one of the leading textile quarters. They also did well in the poorer districts of Conisford close to the Wensum, another area where weavers were very numerous. By the 1730s the Whig party no longer held St Ethelred and St Julian, parishes with relatively few voters, but it continued to dominate St Peter Permountergate, where 60 per cent of the electors were linked to the textile industry. It also captured the populous parishes of East Wymer between the river and the Cathedral, and largely held its majorities in the parishes of Northern ward. Wherever weaving was combined with nonconformity, as it was in Colegate, Coslany, St Clement's, St Peter Permountergate, Whiggery was virtually unassailable. The only exceptions to this rule were (arguably) St James and St Paul's, both of which swung away from the Whigs in the 1730s despite the presence of dissenting congregations, some of which predated the Hanoverian Succession.[92]

The crucial importance of textiles to Norwich Whiggery may be illustrated in another fashion, by simply isolating the vote of the weavers and setting it against the record of the parishes in the four great wards. The results are set out in Table 9.5. They illustrate the very Whiggish disposition of the textile industry. Weavers showed a greater willingness to vote for Whig candidates than did the electorate as a whole. Whichever parliamentary election we chose, whether the Tory victory of 1710 or the subsequent Whig triumphs, the weavers' commitment to Whiggism was consistently higher than average. This tendency was as apparent in Tory parishes as it was in

[92] The geography of nonconformity in Norwich has been derived from the meeting-house certificates for the period and the comments on nonconformity in the visitation of 1784: see Norwich and Norfolk RO, DIS/1 and VIS/28.

TABLE 9.5. *The Total Vote and the Weavers' Vote 1710–1735 (%)*

| Ward | 1710 | | | | 1715 | | | | 1734 | | | | 1735 | | | |
| | Vote | | Weavers | | Vote | | Weavers | | Vote | | Weavers | | Vote | | Weavers | |
	Tory	Whig	Tory	Whig	Tory	Whig	Tory	Whig	Tory	Whig	Tory	Whig	Tory	Whig	Tory	Whig
Comisford	54.4	45.6	41.7	58.3	41.1	58.9	36.8	63.2	53.7	46.3	33.3	66.6	50.9	49.1	40.0	60.0
Mancroft	64.1	35.9	51.8	48.2	56.1	43.9	49.0	51.0	58.1	41.9	48.3	51.7	56.3	43.7	44.9	55.1
Northern	43.2	56.8	34.8	65.2	38.5	61.5	33.6	66.4	40.9	59.1	34.1	65.9	35.4	64.6	25.4	74.6
Wymer	59.3	40.7	53.4	46.6	49.9	50.1	41.7	58.3	46.5	53.5	37.2	62.8	42.5	57.5	34.3	65.7

Whig. It suggests that the interest of the trade was a very important determinant of political behaviour in eighteenth-century Norwich, transcending local, parochial identities and the sinews of patronage, and even weathering the storms of party strife. It was an aspect of Norwich politics that was keenly appreciated by the Whig hierarchy. In fact, it was central to its overall strategy of electoral reform and constituency management. When Walpole pledged his support for measures advocated by the East Anglian industry in 1733, he knew he would strike a responsive chord. As long as the Whigs delivered, and avoided policies detrimental to eastern-county textile interests, their popularity was more or less assured.

The careful cultivation of the textile interest thus proved to be a crucial ingredient of Whig success. Together with Walpolean largesse and the benefits of church and government patronage, the Norvicensian Whigs were able to ride in the eye of the Excise storm and consolidate their hold on the constituency. Their spirits were buoyed up by an increasingly confident and visible nonconformist community, itself deeply committed to the health of the textile industry, which preferred the tangible fruits of Whig toleration, however limited in principle, to the Tory alternatives. Crossgrove's continued disdain of Dissent and his trumpeting of Augustan anniversaries as late as 1735[93] hardly induced nonconformists to believe that much had changed in the High Church camp.

Crossgrove had none the less attempted to broaden the bases of Norwich Toryism with the inception of a new reign in 1727. Loyalty to Hanover was emphasized;[94] the Court–Country dichotomy was dutifully reproduced. But there were flagrant lapses. 'As to my Friend Zachariah Hopeful's Observations in his Letter as to Whigg and TORY,' he wrote in December 1739,

I must tell him he seems to mistake the matter very much; and he

[93] See *Norwich Gazette*, 2–9 Nov. 1734, 1–8 Feb. 1735, where Crossgrove makes some barbed references to the 'sober party', i.e. neo-Puritan Whigs, while privileging the 'MEMBERS of our NATIONAL CHURCH'. Crossgrove also made a good deal of the celebrations of Queen Anne's birthday in St Peter Mancroft.

[94] Ibid., 24 Feb.–2 Mar., 8–15 June 1728. For a somewhat different interpretation of Norwich Toryism after 1727, emphasizing the successful implantation of Country ideas, see Kathleen Wilson, 'The Rejection of Deference', pp. 425–8.

and I shall never agree on that Head, as long as I am in my Conscience convinced there are such things as Right and Wrong. I wish, as much as he, that there was no Distinction in this Nation but Churchmen and Dissenters: But while TORY and Whigg do exist, I hope I shall always enjoy that English privilege to vote at all times for which I like best; and that I do assure him will ever be for what he calls the TORIES, inasmuch as I firmly believe them as loyal subjects to his Majesty King George as they are real friends to the Church of England.[95]

Even so, the intrepid Tory was particularly attentive to political developments in the capital where the opposition coalition was eroding Court power. The mayoral controversies of 1739–41 were closely reported in the *Norwich Gazette*, and Crossgrove did all he could to keep the debate over the Spanish Convention before the public eye. Predictably, Vernon's exploits received extensive coverage. 'Our merchants now can carry on their Trade to America', he wrote in July 1741, 'without the apprehension of being interrupted . . . since Fort Chagre, Porto Bello and all the Forts belonging to Cartagena . . . have been destroyed by the brave Admiral VERNON.'[96] As elsewhere in the opposition press, Vernon's victories were commemorated for restoring national pride and the spirit of true patriotism:

> BRITONS, with Awe, this Son of Freedom view,
> Excell'd by none, and equall'd but by few;
> Who Midst Corruption uncorrupted stood
> His Heart and Hand devoted to your Good:
> O BRITONS, while an ardent Joy you feel
> At Vernon's image, catch his Patriot zeal
> And let the venal tribes of Hirelings see
> There are still Britons who still dare be free.[97]

Crossgrove was still harping on this theme in 1744, contrasting Vernon's public integrity with the careerism of Pulteney and Walpole.[98] Without doubt, Crossgrove sought to project the admiral as an East Anglian counterpoint to the notorious squire of Houghton.

Crossgrove's endeavours met with limited success. Norwich

---

[95] *Norwich Gazette*, 8 Dec. 1739.
[96] Ibid., 18–25 July 1741.
[97] Ibid., 14–21 Nov. 1741.
[98] Ibid., 8–15 Dec. 1744.

celebrated the City of London's stridently oppositionist Address to the Crown applauding the capture of Porto Bello, and honoured the admiral on his victory at Bocca Chica and his birthday.[99] Porto Bello and the brave Vernon graced alehouse signs.[100] But the lasting political impact of this patriotic festival proved negligible. Stuff exports to British North America and the Caribbean had not been adversely affected by the *guardacostas*; in fact, the exports to America had risen in the period 1730–40.[101] More importantly, the prosperity of the Norwich stuff industry rested upon the domestic market and upon the market in Northern and Central Europe and, from the Hanoverian accession onwards, in Spain. Exports through Rotterdam were unlikely to be affected by Anglo-Spanish tensions (and these accounted for 40 per cent of overseas traffic); exports through Leghorn, Trieste, Naples, Genoa, Cadiz, Lisbon, and Barcelona clearly were.[102] But it was peace, not war, that Norwich desired. Norwich might applaud Vernon's restoration of a firm British presence in the Caribbean, but it had far less of a stake in a bellicose mercantilism than the western ports and the metal industries of the Midlands.

Consequently, the Vernon celebrations had very little electoral impact in Norwich, despite the fact that Horace Walpole had been one of the warmest advocates of the Spanish Convention and that the other Whig incumbent, Thomas Vere, had voted for it as well. The 1741 contest, in fact, betrayed the debility of Norwich Toryism. Unable to field any of their own candidates, the Tories attempted to divide the Whig interest by inviting Edward Bacon and Alderman William Clarke to stand. The former was the son of Waller Bacon, who had represented Norwich in the period 1705–10, and from 1715 until his death in 1735. The latter was a Whig who as sheriff in 1725 had successfully challenged the right of the St George's Company

---

[99] *Champion*, 27 Mar. 1740; *London Evening Post*, 23–8 May 1741; *Norwich Gazette*, 8–15, 15–22 Nov. 1740.

[100] BL, Add. ᴍs 27960, fos. 232–3.

[101] Corfield, 'Social and Economic History of Norwich', table 9, p. 99, citing E. B. Schumpeter, *English Overseas Trade Statistics 1697–1808* (Oxford, 1960), table xliv, p. 69.

[102] On the geography of Norwich trade see Corfield 'Social and Economic History of Norwich', ch. 2; Arthur Young, *A Farmer's Tour*, ii. 76–7.

to control the organization and financing of the inaugural dinner on Guild day.[103] But Horace Walpole bought off Bacon by promising him a seat at King's Lynn, and the Tories were unable to muster much support for Clarke, a politician whom they had opposed as Alderman for Northern ward in 1729 despite his civic record.[104] The result was the worst-ever showing for the Tories, for Clarke picked up only 829 votes before he abandoned the poll. Their only consolation was a satirical poem highlighting Vere's time-serving qualities and the corrupt practices of the Whig machine.[105]

Poetry aside, the 1741 election began the rout of the Norwich Tories. The Jacobite rebellion of 1745 completed it. When the news of the rebellion first broke, the Norwich citizenry quickly organized a loyalist association. As the preamble to its declaration revealed, Norvicensians prepared to defend themselves from internal as well as external threats. With the memory of Jacobite revels still stamped in their minds, the signatories declared they would 'use their best endeavours for the suppressing, quelling or dispersing such rioutous persons in order to preserve His Majesty's Peace'.[106] Predictably, the Whig hierarchy was very active in promoting the association. The vast majority of the Whig-dominated Court of Mayoralty appear to have joined, as did most of the rising stars of the affluent Presbyterian congregation. At least ten of the leading members of the future Octagon Chapel penned their names, including Mayor Simeon Waller, Aldermen Philip Meadows, Benjamin and John Nuthall, and the town clerk, Nehemiah Lodge. But the association was not exclusively a Whig affair. Thomas Churchman, the son of a former Tory alderman and a future sheriff, signed. So too did the Tory aldermen John Goodman and William Lovick and members of the Harwood and Helwys families. Only the most die-hard Tories from Mancroft ward—men like tailor Mark

---

[103] See Norwich and Norfolk RO, MS 79 (a contemporary history by Benjamin Mackerell, *History of the City of Norwich Both Ancient and Modern* (2 vols.; 1739)), pp. 77–88.

[104] *Norwich Gazette*, 12–19 Apr. 1729.

[105] Anon., *The Norwich Cavalcade and Opposition: A Satire Addressed to 829 Uncorrupted Freemen and Freeholders* (London, 1741).

[106] Norwich and Norfolk RO, Case 13 d(2) (Loyalist Association, 26 Sept. 1745).

Addey, grocer Daniel Ganning, and the draper Isaac Schuldham who sat on Council and were active members of St Peter's parish—refused to sign. In their view,· one suspects, the association was a licence to persecute Tories.

Without doubt, the local preparations for the Forty-Five became something of a celebration of Whig confidence. Thomas Gooch, the bishop of Norwich, struck the appropriate note at a county meeting in October when he urged Protestants of all denominations to unite against the Papist threat and to remember how their fellow Huguenots had been forced to flee from Catholic persecution.[107] This was an astute privileging of nonconformity, and one that encouraged greater denominational co-operation. It set the tone for some forthright demonstrations of Whig conviviality on royal anniversaries, with the Artillery Company and the newly formed Constitutional Club very much to the fore.[108]

The Tories clearly felt upstaged by these proceedings. The *Gazette* was upset by the exposure given to 'that matchless political club stiled by themselves the Constitution', and its account of the celebrations which accompanied the news of Culloden and other anniversaries was formulaic.[109] In fact, the exuberance of Whig festival so piqued the Tories that the vestry of St Peter Mancroft resolved that there would be 'no Ringing of Bells on any Publick Days at the Expense of the Parish'.[110] This hardly blighted Whig spirits. After a summer of celebrations, Norwich prepared for magnificent thanksgiving for the suppression of the rebellion in October. 'Norwich may be said to have outdone,' recalled William Arderon,

any city in England considering its magnitude and far more than ever was seen in it before. Imprimis, we had the greatest part of the Nobility & Gentry of ye County here as well as Multitudes of people of lower life. And for their Amusement we had a general illumination through the Whole City and in ye Market Place was erected a Triumphal arch wch cost at least 100 pounds. In imbelishing [sic] it was used 96 yards of persian silk painted with the Kings Arms &c. In the

---

[107] *Norwich Mercury*, 5–12 Oct. 1745.
[108] Ibid., 18–25 Jan., 12–19 Apr., 19–26 Apr., 19–26 July, 26 July–2 Aug. 1746.
[109] *Norwich Gazette*, 19–26 Apr. 1746.
[110] Norfolk and Norwich RO, PD 26/73 (s) (St Peter Mancroft, Churchwarden's accounts, 1707–52, p. 815).

insides were placed multitudes of Candles and thro' the above mentioned silk appeared Trophies of Honour, Mottos, & many other devices too long to mention.[111]

The arch had 'Religion and Liberty' inscribed on the front and a crown of laurel and an olive branch with the words 'Victory and Peace'. It was dedicated to the duke of Cumberland, 'the Deliverer of His Country'.[112]

Religion and Liberty, Peace, the benefits of Hanoverian deliverance: this was, in truth, a familiar script to the Norwich Whigs. Thanksgiving day was not strictly partisan, but the local context made it a celebration of triumphant Whiggery. The election the following year was a foregone conclusion. The only matter of debate was which Whig candidates would run. Eventually, Thomas Vere, who does not appear to have won the confidence of the local Whig caucus, was ousted in favour of Lord Hobart, a young cub just returned from the Grand Tour, the son of the Lord Lieutenant of the county who had organized Norfolk's response to the Forty-Five. Together with old Horace Walpole, who had survived his brother's fall, despite his very dubious undertakings as auditor of the plantations, the future heir of Blickling sat for Norwich in the next Parliament.

Did the uncontested election of two Norfolk grandees in 1747 inaugurate a new era of oligarchy in Norwich? To some extent this was the case. Hobart and Walpole were returned without a contest in 1754 and upon their elevation to the peerage in 1756 they were replaced by men with whom they had close, or at least tangible, links. Harbord was cousin of Hobart (later the first earl of Buckinghamshire). Edward Bacon, who succeeded old Horace, was the local landowner who had deferred to his predecessor in 1741; he was also a practising barrister who had ingratiated himself in Corporate circles, firstly as steward of Norwich and then as recorder. There was thus a smooth succession to Parliament of men from county society—but men, it should be stressed, who would respect the existing power-structures in Norwich, especially the rise to prominence of merchant-manufacturers such as the Harveys, the Ives, and the Gurneys. These wealthy families not only

---

[111] BL, Add. MS 27966, fo. 68.
[112] *Norwich Mercury*, 4–11 Oct. 1746.

controlled the distribution of the textile industry and diversi-fied their assets into other profitable enterprises, they so dominated civic life that aldermanic office became something of an heirloom.[113] The parliamentary arrangements of 1747–69 were thus homologous to the civic. Electoral ossification and élite nomination were the order of the day. The mid-century decades saw a close partnership between the rising Whig bourgeoisie of Norwich and the county families who had helped consolidate the Whig ascendancy.

The aristocratic representation of Norwich was thus less a reassertion of territorial rule than a working arrangement between the dominant forces that had made this provincial capital a haven of Whiggery. In the long term such an alliance had only been made possible by the Whig leadership's willing-ness to attend to the welfare of the city's dominant industry. The Walpoles had worked assiduously to protect the Norwich stuff industry and this gave their civic allies a tremendous electoral advantage. Reductions in the duty on Irish yarn, the prohibition of Indian calicoes and Irish woollen goods—these issues were of great importance to a city of weavers. In the end, these palpable benefits blunted any critique of corruption that the Tories could offer. Not that the Tories' ideological inheritance helped. Unlike the Bristol Blues, Norwich's Tories were never able to shed their High Church cloth sufficiently to broaden their constituency. As the 1752 disturbances revealed, when Tory mobs beseiged a new Methodist sect to the cry of 'Church and King, and down with the meeting houses,' they remained locked in the sectarian world of an earlier era.[114] These 'Hell-Fire clubbers', and the Jacks before them, served to rivet the powerful nonconformist community to the Whig party, however tepid its policy of toleration. It was not until the second half of the century, when the health of the textile industry became more dependent upon American markets and nonconformists more insistent for their civic rights, that the political climate would radically change. It is no accident, in

[113] The Gurneys were more active as parliamentary organizers, beginning in 1734 when the founder of the fortune helped Sir Robert Walpole with the Norfolk scrutiny. The Ives and the Harveys provided no fewer than 14 mayors between 1727 and 1801 (20% of the total).

[114] Anon., *A True and Particular Narrative of the Disturbances and Outrages . . .* (London, 1752), p. 13.

fact, that the very first signs of dissension from the orthodox Whig camp occurred in the context of Minorca and the support given Pitt during the Seven Years War.[115] But in the first half of the century Whiggery spelt religious peace and material prosperity. It was an intoxicating brew that dulled any talk of Robinocracy and exonerated the Norfolk colossus from the accusations of his opponents. As the *Mercury* mused:

> Happy are we, since they on WALPOLE wait,
> Walpole who guides the Helm and steers the Ship of State.[116]

[115] Norwich thanked Pitt for his services in 1757 and lamented his departure in 1761. Consternation about Minorca in Norwich also prompted Sir William Harbord to sign the Norwich Address urging an inquiry, fearing that his failure to do so would prejudice his son's imminent by-election. For details see ch. 3.

[116] *Norwich Mercury*, 8–15 June 1734.

APPENDIX: The Electoral Geography of Norwich 1710–1735

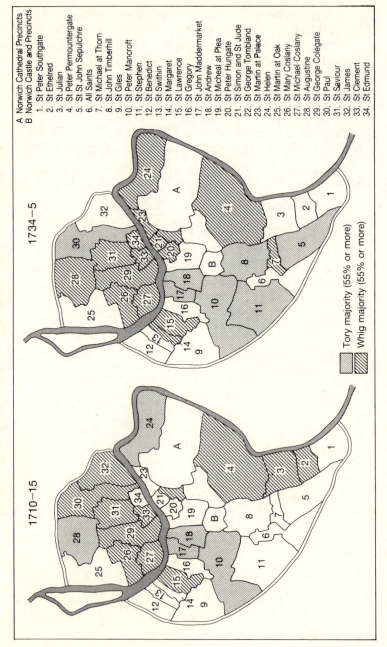

A Norwich Cathedral Precincts
B Norwich Castle and Precincts
1. St Peter Southgate
2. St Ethelred
3. St Julian
4. St Peter Permountergate
5. St John Sepulchre
6. All Saints
7. St Michael at Thorn
8. St John Timberhill
9. St Giles
10. St Peter Mancroft
11. St Stephen
12. St Benedict
13. St Swithin
14. St Margaret
15. St Lawrence
16. St Gregory
17. St John Maddermarket
18. St Andrew
19. St Micheal at Plea
20. St Peter Hungate
21. St Simon and St Jude
22. St George Tombland
23. St Martin at Palace
24. St Helen
25. St Martin at Oak
26. St Mary Coslany
27. St Michael Coslany
28. St Augustine
29. St George Colegate
30. St Paul
31. St Saviour
32. St James
33. St Clement
34. St Edmund

1734–5

1710–15

▨ Tory majority (55% or more)

▧ Whig majority (55% or more)

PART IV
Exploring the Crowd

10
The Crowd in Urban Politics
c.1710–1760

The 'CROWD' is, at best, an evanescent theme. Like the Cheshire Cat it is there, it is almost there, then it is not there, and then it is there again.

> [Richard Cobb], 'Overcrowding', *Times Literary Supplement*, 30 December 1965, p. 1205.

A blunt Country Bumpkin came lately to London
In King Street near Guildhall he saw a great throng
He gaized, he star'd and he feared he was undone
To see such distraction as he past along.
The Mob got about him and cry'd, honest Roger
What makes you be frightened, you tremble & shake,
He shrugg'd up his shoulders & said Sturdy Fellows,
Excuse me at present, *Ize meddle nor make.*
Come along say the multitude, join in our clamour,
For Liberty, Property and no Excise,
For tho you but lately come from your Cammer
We'll show you new fancies and open your Eyes.

> *West Country Roger's Remarks upon London.*[1]

While sports, festivals, merriments, shews, entertainments of every kind engross the mind, people by degrees lose sight of liberty, and think not of it any more.

> Jean-Paul Marat, *The Chains of Slavery*
> (London, 1774), p. 32.

ONE of the major thrusts of the new social history of the 1960s and 1970s was the insistence that the history of the subaltern classes could only be recovered 'from below'; that is, that historians had to move beyond the administrative categories that imprisoned ordinary people in official discourse and made

[1] Cambridge Univ. Lib., Madden Collection, 6/1915.

them an object of state action in order to reconstruct popular experience in more imaginative and creative ways. The notion liberated labour history from its institutional moorings and restored a historical and cultural dimension to the class struggles of the early industrial era. But it also sent historians on a quest for less formal collectivities. In the context of the eighteenth century the notion prompted a new examination of the phenomenon of riot and disturbance whose tracks lay scattered throughout the State Papers Domestic and the records of the courts. The crowd was recovered from the condescension of posterity, and the boundaries of the political dramatically widened. Whether one focused upon the problem of scarcity, or agrarian custom, or crime, or popular ideology, the crowd consistently obtruded upon the scene. However evanescent its appearance, it has reshaped the way in which we view eighteenth-century social relations.[2]

Precisely what the status of the crowd was in late Stuart and Hanoverian politics remains, none the less, disputed territory. The pioneering work of George Rudé did much to uncover the social anatomy of the crowd and to formulate a new method-ological strategy for dealing with well-documented, dramatic confrontations with authority. But Rudé's explorations were consistently metropolitan, and they were largely devoted to charting the lineaments of the 'revolutionary crowd' and the contribution of the common people to the democratic up-heavals of the late eighteenth century. Indeed, Rudé's priorities in his definitions tended to concentrate upon proto-radical crowds engaging in direct action at the expense of other forms of popular political activity, and marginalized the more festive side of the popular idiom and those actions not conforming to an oppositionist, radical canon.[3] The result was a rather

---

[2] Even those who wish to reassert the notion of popular deference or traditionalism have been forced to come to terms with this new body of literature: see Ian R. Christie, *Stress and Stability in Late-Eighteenth Century Britain* (Oxford, 1985), pp. 33–5, 150–5. The exception to the rule is J. C. D. Clark, whose comments on English society rarely leave the terrain of high theory. He rests his case with the following comment: 'We still know remarkably little about the world view of the inarticulate millions—the unskilled; the illiterate; the really poor; those who thought they found dignity and meaning in their relations to things they did not create—their religion, their country, their rulers', *English Society*, p. 42.

[3] Rudé's methodological and theoretical presuppositions can best be gauged

episodic history of disturbance, diachronically arranged, reaching a climacteric in the revolutionary era.

If Rudé's definition of the crowd was teleological, leading irrevocably to the revolutionary *journées*, it was also reductionist. His early efforts to probe the relationship between crowd action and social unrest were crudely mechanical, often based on highly problematic correlations between political disturbance and grain prices. This search for an underlying social cause tended to take the mind out of the crowd, to discount its symbolic gestures and slogans in favour of more tangible, class-based impulses. To emphasize the pulsating sense of social grievance which lay behind popular interventions, Rudé contrasted the social status of the assailants with those of their targets. He also emphasized the imprecations against the rich which periodically surfaced in popular demonstrations. In this way the religious or political passions of the crowd were subordinated to the rudimentary egalitarianism of the street.[4]

Rudé was correct in detecting the undeferential behaviour which surfaced in street riots and so troubled the more respectable citizenry. But whether these incidents could bear the explanatory weight of his interpretation remained in doubt. As anthropologists and anthropologically-minded historians were quick to point out, what Rudé understood to be social protest could equally be described as carnivalesque licence. Crowds were derogatory, transgressive, and critical of authority—but within an established pattern of festive time

---

from his collection of essays *Paris and London in the 18th Century* (London, 1970) and from *The Crowd in History* (New York, 1964). His *Ideology and Popular Protest* (New York, 1980) represents a refinement of his earlier formulations of the role of ideology in popular movements, giving greater weight to the complex of derived and indigenous ideas and attitudes in the creation of popular political consciousness. This synthesis makes greater allowances for the persistence and reaffirmation of reactionary popular movements, but it still shows a linear-progressive bias. For a perceptive critique of Rudé's presuppositions see Robert J. Holton, 'The Crowd in History: Some Problems of Theory and Method', *Social History*, 3/2 (May 1978), 219–33.

[4] This line of argument is most explicit in Rudé's interpretation of the Gordon riots, his first foray in British popular history: see 'The Gordon Riots: A Study of the Rioters and their Victims', in *Paris and London*, pp. 268–92.

and space.[5] Was this protest or popular catharsis, a challenge to the authorities or a ruse of power? The question could only be resolved by attending to the cultural dimensions of popular politics, to the familiar terrain in which crowd interventions took place.

The French historian, Georges Lefebvre, made some gestures in this direction before the crowd really gripped the imagination of social historians. Countering Le Bon's pathological interpretation of popular unrest which saw crowds as degenerate, animalistic hordes at the beck of unscrupulous demogogues and pillagers, whipped to a frenzy by crude prejudice and excitement, Lefebvre emphasized the cultural bases of popular action and the modes of sociability which sustained them.[6] In recent years this emphasis upon the quotidian, upon the everyday roots of collective action, has been taken up with a vengeance.[7] Historians have become increasingly aware of the cultural affinities of riot and ceremony in the pre-democratic era, of the way in which festivals and popular rites provided both a focus and context for tumultuous assembly as well as a plausible source of social integration and ruling-class hegemony. This cultural dimension is of particular relevance, for it suggests that the examination of the crowd should begin within a specific political terrain, marking out the place (street, market-place) and occasion (anniversary, thanksgiving, public sentence or enactment) as a site of contention among

---

[5] The most explicit exposition of this line of argument within the English context came from John Brewer, who drew much insight from the work of Victor Turner in his analysis of the Wilkite riots: see his *Party Ideology*, ch. 9.

[6] Lefebvre's major works on the crowd have been published in English: *The Great Fear of 1789* (London, 1973), edited by George Rudé; and 'Revolutionary Crowds' in Jeffrey Kaplow (ed.), *New Perspectives on the French Revolution* (New York, 1965), pp. 173–90.

[7] The bibliography on this subject is immense. In the French context see Natalie Zemon Davis, 'The Rites of Violence: Religious Riot in Sixteenth-Century France', *Past and Present*, 59 (May 1973), 51–91; Emmanuel Le Roy Ladurie, *Carnival: People's Uprising at Romans 1577–80*, trans. Mary Feeney (New York, 1979); and Yves-Marie Berce, *Fête et révolte: Des mentalités populaires du XVIe au XVIIIe siècle* (Paris, 1976). On the Anglo-American see Thompson, 'Patrician Society', *Journal of Social History* (1974), 382–405; Brewer, *Party Ideology*, ch. 9; and Alfred F. Young, 'English Plebeian Culture and Eighteenth-Century American Radicalism', in Margaret and James Jacob (eds.), *The Origins of Anglo-American Radicalism* (London, 1984), pp. 185–213.

different social groups, all of whom have a stake in mobilizing the 'people' and underscoring the consent (or dissent) of the nation at large. In this way the dangers of classifying popular politics as exclusively plebeian, may be suitably counter-balanced by a recognition that the 'crowd-in-politics' signifies a set of activities whose organization, participation, and mobilization is complex, variable, and not easily reducible to 'plebeian versus patrician' formulations. Certainly street politics can reveal important features of popular mentalities and structures of authority; but it would be more appropriate to see them as a terrain in which ideology, culture, and power intersect.

Such a perspective is of particular relevance to an understanding of the early eighteenth century where there has been substantial disagreement about the sophistication and autonomy of crowd action. While Edward Thompson has emphasized the self-activating nature of the eighteenth-century crowd, tetchily defensive of custom and scornful of authority,[8] and George Rudé the proto-radical tendencies of the London populace, others have been more sceptical. Geoffrey Holmes, for example, interpreted the Sacheverell riots of 1710 as a clerically led protest to the Whig ministry, fuelled by fears of growing religious nonconformity. Together with W. A. Speck, he has cast the crowd as an essentially surrogate force in British politics, whipped up by party propaganda and electoral practice.[9] The line of argument has been taken still further in recent years, to a point where the persistence of popular Toryism and Jacobitism has been interpreted as conclusive evidence of the deep, ideological sedimentation of Anglicanism in eighteenth-century society, and by extension the deference of the common people to their social superiors.[10]

---

[8] Thompson, 'Eighteenth-century English society', *Social History* (1978), 152–64.

[9] Geoffrey Holmes, 'The Sacheverell Riots: The Crowd and the Church in Early Eighteenth-Century London', *Past and Present*, 72 (Aug. 1976), 55–85, repr. in Paul Slack (ed.), *Rebellion, Popular Protest and the Social Order in Early Modern England* (Cambridge, 1984), pp. 232–62; Geoffrey Holmes and W. A. Speck (eds.), *The Divided Society: Parties and Politics in England 1694–1716* (New York, 1968), pp. 77–82.

[10] See Clark, *English Society*, pp. 15–41, and his 'Politics of the Excluded: Tories, Jacobites and Whig Patriots 1715–60', *Parliamentary History*, 2 (1983), pp. 209–22. Linda Colley adopts a similar perspective, although she is less

Such views cannot be dismissed out of hand. Historians of popular politics have to come to terms with the substantial evidence of clerical incitement of disorder, especially in the early years of the Hanoverian succession.[11] They also have to address the way in which gentlemen and clergy were able to mobilize anti-Methodist mobs by appealing to prevailing modes of sociability and to the role of the Church in sustaining the traditional fabric of life.[12] Equally crucial is some consideration of the client-crowds which periodically intervened at the hustings. In the Taunton election of 1722, for instance, the Whigs were said to have organized

a Gang of loose Fellows called the Bloody Blacks of North Town [who,] being armed with Clubs, and led by a Captain of their Clan, marched in a riotous Manner into the Borough, committing Batteries and Outrages, and seized many of Deane and Mr. Earle's voters, some in the Street, others in their Houses, and dragged them away Captives to their Captain's House. Here they were kept intoxicated with Brandy and other Liquors till the time of the Election, when they were brought to Poll against their Neighbours, Mr Deane and Mr Earle, who were deny'd their Check on the Poll.[13]

Electoral intimidation such as this, and the continuing incidence of electoral mobs parading under party colours and even occasionally sporting the livery of their superiors, is too commonplace to be dismissed as aberrant behaviour or excluded from the ambit of popular political culture.[14] We need a

emphatic about plebeian deference. She sees the Tory party playing upon voter dissidence, voter venality, and religious intolerance, and solidifying its cultural affinities with the poor: see *In Defiance of Oligarchy*, chs. 5, 6.

[11] See my 'Riot and Popular Jacobitism', p. 73.

[12] John Walsh, 'Methodism and the Mob in the Eighteenth Century', in G. L. Cuming and Derek Baker (eds.), *Popular Belief and Practice* (Studies in Church History, 8; Cambridge, 1972), pp. 213–27.

[13] *Political State of Great Britain* (1722), xxiii. 499–503. For an example of a mob organized by the territorial grandee, Sir William Watkins Wynn, on behalf of Sir Robert Grosvenor in the Chester mayoral election of 1732, see Sedgwick (ed.), *Commons 1715–54*, i. 203–4. For further examples of gentry-led riots at elections see PRO, KB 1/2 part 2 (9 George I, Michaelmas term 1722) and KB 1/4 (7 & 8 George II, Trinity term 1734). The depositions refer to the Carmarthenshire election of 1722 and the Cheshire and Newcastle-under-Lyme elections of 1734.

[14] Rudé deliberately excludes electoral mobs from his definition of the crowd, although this has not satisfied historians, even those of the left. See his *Paris and London*, pp. 293–4, and the review of *The Crowd in History* by

framework that will encompass these surrogate activities as well as the more 'self-activating' crowds explored by Rudé and Thompson. Otherwise, we will simply trade examples in an unending quest for *the* quintessential eighteenth-century crowd.

The study of festival and popular rites has conventionally been associated with ethnography or folklore; that is, with disciplines preoccupied with the recovery of lost cultures, or with cultures that appear to have retained a sense of organic unity in an increasingly alienated, modern world. Set in an almost timeless context, festival has been seen to be a more appropriate subject for rural than urban settings, or at the very least for the medieval city with its guilds, fraternities, and demonstrable hierarchies than for the thriving manufacturing centre or bustling port. When we think of eighteenth-century urban culture we tend to think of the world of Defoe, not Dekker; the coffee-house, the assembly room, the Georgian square, not the fair and the market-place. Yet, in fact, even in London the older conventions of urban life commingled with the new in critical and creative ways. Through the new medium of journalism, urban festival reached an expanding audience. With the changing urban prospect and the new dimensions of space, the carnivalesque lost its older territoriality and spread beyond the market-place. The relationship of print to oral culture was not simply one of displacement.[15] The new did not immediately supplant the old or render it vestigial.

Certainly, the eighteenth-century calendar lacked the unity of its medieval counterpart, with its maskings and merry-makings, its religious processionals and cognate festivities. As John Stow's *Survey* makes clear, such a calendar provided Londoners with a visual résumé of the social order, stratified by

Gwyn Williams in *New Society*, 27 May 1965, pp. 30–1. Edward Thompson recognizes that client crowds are a problem, but he does not address them in his generalizations on popular political culture: see 'Eighteenth-Century English Society', *Social History* (1978), 163n.

[15] Peter Burke's illuminating study of 17th-century popular culture uses a paradigm of modernization to explain the purported demise of such a culture in the 18th; I would cavil at this formulation. See Peter Burke, 'Popular Culture in Seventeenth-Century London', the *London Journal*, 3/2 (Nov. 1977), 143–62.

guild and parish fraternity, and also opportunities for institutionalized ridicule and social integration.[16] Nevertheless,
eighteenth-century London was not without its moments of
theatre, its symbols of power and prestige, its conventions of
merriment. To be sure, certain royal ceremonies declined in
the first quarter of the century: William III was the last
monarch to wash the feet of the poor on Maundy Thursday; the
Royal Touch fell into abeyance, disappearing from the prayer
book in the 1730s.[17] But London's civic calendar had changed
little since the Tudor era. There were over twenty occasions
during the year when the City aldermen traversed the streets,
opening the fairs and the Old Bailey sessions, soliciting alms
for the poor in the markets, patronizing the charity-school
processions; this reached a climax during the Lord Mayor's
show, which was an affirmation of both civic pride and
merchant grandeur.[18] The annual perambulations were still
observed on Ascension day, when the youths of the parish beat
the bounds and were regaled with cakes and ale. And although
profane rites had long lost official approval, the calendar of
youthful revelry had not altogether been extinguished. The
mayings survived the years of puritan proscription: even with
the disappearance of the Strand maypole in 1717, May day
customs were observed by milkmaids and chimney-sweeps.[19]
Shrovetide holidays continued to be revelrous, with cock-
shuing, shrew-baiting, and whore-hunting. On St James's day

---

[16] John Stow, *The Survey of London* (London, 1912), p. 93; Joseph Strutt,
The Sports and Pastimes of the People of England (London, 1833), p. 347.

[17] Rosamond Bayne-Powell, *Eighteenth-Century London Life* (New York,
1938), p. 315; Horton Davies, *Worship and Theology in England 1603–1690*
(Princeton, 1975), p. 233. The Archbishop of York washed the feet of the poor
at Whitehall until 1727; thereafter Maundy Thursday became a day of royal
charity. In 1768, 30 poor men and women were each given three ells of Holland
cloth, a pair of shoes and stockings, 30 shillings in a purse, 30 silver twopences
and threepences, a loaf of bread, and a platter of fish: see *Northampton
Mercury*, 4 Apr. 1768.

[18] See William P. Treloar, *A Lord Mayor's Diary 1906–7* (London, 1920),
pp. 230–59, which includes the diary of Micajah Perry during his mayoralty,
1738–9.

[19] A. R. Wright, *British Calendar Customs* (3 vols.; London, 1940), ii. 239;
Bayne-Powell, *Eighteenth-Century London Life*, pp. 301–3; George L. Phillips,
'May-Day is Sweeps' Day', *Folklore*, 60/1 (Mar. 1949), 217–27. For the survival
of perambulations in the 18th century see Guildhall Lib., MS 4117/1 (St
Andrew Undershaft 1711–44); MS 1061/22 (St Ann Blackfriars 1718–20); MS
1313/2 (St Martin Ludgate).

children asked for contributions for their grottoes, i.e. arrangements of oyster shells lit by rush lights. St Crispin's day was celebrated by shoemakers; St Clement's day by blacksmiths. As new modes of sociability and institutional care emerged, other features were added to this traditional calendar. Charity children had long been visible at Eastertide to attend the Spital sermons, but the emergence of the charity-school movement gave rise to lengthier and more elaborate processions celebrating London's munificence.[20] Even more secretive organizations had their moment of theatre and, indeed, were parodied for it. Thus in 1741 and 1742 several Westminster Independents organized a mock procession of the freemasons' annual parade in the city.[21]

The urban calendar was clearly not a vestige of the past surviving into a more secular and literate society. It was a dynamic entity, shaped by new forces and new sources of civic pride. But what was especially significant about its development in the eighteenth century, in London and the provinces, was its political orientation. The year was replete with royal and national anniversaries, and, because Britain waged a series of successful wars throughout the century, with victory celebrations. The politicization of the calendar was not a new development. It had its roots in the Tudor era, when pageants and progresses extolled the virtues of royal authority and the nation's deliverance from Rome, themes reinforced by sermons and popular works like Foxe's *Book of Martyrs*. It received a boost after 1660, when Caroline London witnessed a grand revival of the King's Touch and the establishment of the political festival *par excellence*, Oak Apple day, which combined the traditional mayings with royalist folklore commemorating Charles II's escape after the battle of Worcester in 1651 and his restoration 9 years later. By the turn of the century there had been a steady accretion of political anniversaries to the calendar. State services were held to commemorate the accession of the reigning monarch, the martyrdom of

[20] For London festive life see Wright, *British Calendar Customs*, *passim*. For the charity-school processions see *Post Boy*, 1–3 June 1710, *Flying Post*, 25–7 Aug. 1713, *Northampton Mercury*, 29 May 1727.
[21] *London Evening Post*, 19–21 Mar. 1741; Hugh Phillips, *Mid-Georgian London* (London, 1964), p. 166.

Charles I (30 January), the restoration of monarchy (29 May), and the discovery of the Gunpowder Plot and William's landing at Torbay in 1688 (5 November). In addition to these anniversaries it was customary to celebrate a number of others. Queen Elizabeth's accession (17 November), first commemorated in the 1570s and revived in 1640, was regularly observed as a symbol of Britain's national identity and Protestant heritage, at least until 1730 and in some parishes as late as the 1750s. So also was the birthday of William III (4 November). To these one should add a more varied list of anniversaries celebrating the coronation and birthdays of the royal family. In 1689/90, for example, the bells of St Martin-in-the-Fields were rung on the birthdays of William and Mary, the Queen Dowager, and Princess Anne of Denmark, upon the monarchs' arrival in London from Hampton Court, upon their visit to the City on the Lord Mayor's Day, and upon the news that Princess Anne had given birth to a son.[22]

Officially, these anniversaries were intended to legitimize the political order, to imbue it with drama and dignity. Richard Hooker reminded his Puritan critics during the formative years of the political calendar that no nation ever tolerated 'public actions which are of weight . . . to pass without some visible solemnity, the very strangeness whereof . . . doth cause popular eyes to observe and mark the same'.[23] And his words were echoed by modernists like Defoe who saw public commemorations as making 'deep impressions upon the minds of the people'.[24] Consequently, political anniversaries were staged

[22] Westminster Pub. Lib., St Martin-in-the-Fields, Churchwarden Accounts, 1689/90, F6. On Queen Elizabeth's Accession day see Roy C. Strong, 'The Popular Celebration of the Accession Day of Queen Elizabeth I', *Journal of the Warburg and Courtauld Institutes*, 21 (1958), 86–103; O. W. Furley, 'The Pope-Burning Processions of the Late 17th Century', *History*, 44 (1959), 16–23. In 1730 it was reported that Queen Elizabeth's accession was observed 'with the usual demonstrations of joy': see *Farley's Bristol Newspaper*, 21 Nov. 1730. The churchwarden accounts of several London parishes suggest, however, that it was not officially observed beyond the second decade of the century. However, in All Saints, Bristol, Queen Elizabeth's day was celebrated well into the 1750s: see Bristol RO, All Saints parish, Churchwardens' Accounts.

[23] Richard Hooker, *Of the Lawes of Ecclesiastical Politie* (London, 1594–7), 7; repr. Scholar Press, 1969), p. 170. I would like to thank Neal Wood for this reference.

[24] Daniel Defoe, *The Royal Progress* (London, 1720), p. 65.

with appropriate ceremony—civic parades, court levees, can-nonades, bonfires, and illuminations. They were special holi-days which reminded the nation of its common heritage, recalled the momentous events in its creation and preser-vation, and pertinently defined that heritage in particular ways.

In addition, public anniversaries assumed the social func-tions that had been associated with royal progresses and older civic processionals and, at a more modest, local level, with parish wakes or grandee marriages and *rites de passage*. That is, they provided set occasions for ruling-class liberality and display. George I's triumphal entry into London in 1714 took three hours, so that due respect could be paid to social rank. Even at Frome, where the local hierarchy of gentlemen and clothiers organized a formal coronation-day parade, there was some disagreement about the order of precedence.[25] Such occasions were rounded off with appropriate tokens of munifi-cence—beer and wine before the celebratory bonfire, with perhaps a roasted ox to mark a special event. At Northallerton the Coronation-day celebrations of 1714 were financed by the local patron, Cholmey Turner, Esquire, who had his servants roast an ox and set up a beer tent. 'No less than 100 anchors of the best ale, Two hogheads of French Claret, and one of the truest Brandy', one correspondent reported, were made into punch for the occasion.[26] In Bristol, Gloucester, and Liverpool, the Hanoverian junkets were laid on by the local Corporations. By contrast, in London such celebrations appear to have been organized on a local basis, by a ward club, livery company, or a vestry, for the churchwardens' accounts of several London parishes itemize payments 'for drink at the bonfire'.[27] In

---

[25] *The Annals of King George* (6 vols.; London, 1716–21), i. 161–7; *Flying Post*, 20–3 Nov. 1714.

[26] *Flying Post*, 28–30 Oct. 1714.

[27] Ibid., 23–5 Sept., 23–6 Oct., 30–2 Nov. 1714; Guildhall MS 4825/2. The accounts for St Michael's Queenhithe show that the parish supplied 50 faggots for the bonfire when the king made his entry in 1714 and a further 50 at his coronation and on Guy Fawkes's night. On Queen Anne's birthday in 1715 an unspecified sum was 'Pd to the boys for faggots and drink'. In St Martin-in-the-Fields, five shillings was paid 'for drink at the bonfire' when the king visited the lord mayor on 29 Oct. 1714. In 1715 the parish purchased 5,000 billets, 200 faggots, and a further 200 small shrubs for celebratory bonfires: see West-minster Pub. Lib., Churchwardens' Accounts, F 71, 73.

Westminster, of course, the nobility and gentry were expected to contribute their fair share. And ambassadors, too, where appropriate. Thus on the State General's thanksgiving for the Peace of Ryswick, the Dutch Ambassador 'made a very noble bonfire before his house in St. James' Square, consisting of about 140 pitch barrel, placed pyramidically on 7 scaffolds, during which the trumpets sounded, and 2 hogsheads of wine were kept running continually amongst the common people'.[28]

Political festivals, then, combined the traditional functions of ceremonialism, the transmission of power through pageantry and beneficence, with an explicit didacticism. They sanctified the political order and at the same time elevated the status of its principal guardians. The stabilizing effects of such practices, however, rested upon two essential preconditions: the existence of permanent dependencies linking rich and poor, for public display and intermittent largesse could at best reinforce class mutualities, not serve as their basis; and a high degree of political consensus. Neither were particularly present in the Augustan and Hanoverian era.

To begin with, the craft-solidarities which had underpinned the old ceremonial order eroded as companies fell under the domination of merchant capital and abandoned or surreptitiously subverted the traditional policy of guild exclusivism. By the early eighteenth century, if not before, many urban artisans were reduced to a semi-proletarian status, working for large manufacturers or dependent upon merchant-middlemen for raw materials and credit. Except for key luxury-trades, the prospects of becoming independent masters were fewer, a situation that was reflected in the rise of journeymen combinations and the increasing disposition of craftsmen to protest against reductions in wages, piece rates, unemployment, and the abuse of the apprenticeship laws.[29] In other words, new forms of association were emerging, ones which redefined

---

[28] Narcissus Luttrell, *A Brief Historical Relation of State Affairs from September 1678 to April 1714* (6 vols.; Oxford, 1857), iv. 298

[29] For these developments see John Stevenson, *Popular Disturbances in England 1700–1870* (London, 1979), ch. 6; Max Beloff, *Public Order and Popular Disturbances 1660–1714* (Oxford, 1938); Sidney and Beatrice Webb, *The History of Trade Unionism* (London, 1902), pp. 26–7; C. R. Dobson, *Masters and Journeymen* (London, 1980), ch. 1; Robert W. Malcolmson, 'Workers' Combinations in Eighteenth-Century England', in M. and J. Jacob

labour relations and broke down the older patterns of sociability associated with the guild.

If the mutualities of the guild had disappeared, the forms of dependency which bound the poorer sections of the community to the urban bourgeoisie and gentry became less encompassing. As urban economies became more complex and specialized, so they were less reliant upon the patronage of a few notables and increasingly subject to market forces. Even the relations between masters and domestic servants became more impermanent, for the interrogatories of the Consistory Court of London reveal that very few servants remained in the same household for more than one year and most lasted less than six months. At the same time the social authority of the Church was on the wane. Despite its admonitions to the rich to care for the needy, its pastoral responsibilities became increasingly intermittent and ceremonial. It is no accident that Methodism took hold in urban centres. To be sure, there were some parishes like St Botolph Bishopsgate in London that were extremely attentive to the needs of its residential poor and regularly promoted feasts to bond the community together. The activities of charitable societies, moreover, could advance vertical solidarities by providing educational opportunities and apprenticeships for the sons of poor parents (such was the case in eighteenth-century Bristol where nearly 30 per cent of all apprenticeship indentures were financed by charitable aid).[30] But the paternalistic penetration of the Church and allied organizations in urban society was rarely deep. Indeed, it became increasingly socially discriminatory. The forms of dependency which bound the labouring poor to their social superiors in the closed, nucleated villages of England—the command that landowners could have over the labour, shelter, and leisure of relatively self-contained agrarian communities—were largely absent from the larger towns and cities.[31] At

(eds.), *Origins of Radicalism*, pp. 149–61; John Rule, *The Experience of Labour in Eighteenth-Century Industry* (London, 1981), ch. 6; Alfred Plummer, *The London Weavers' Company* (London, 1972), chs. 11–14.

[30] For St Botolph Bishopsgate see Guildhall MSS 4525/12, 31. The Bristol evidence is based on a survey of the apprenticeships for 1735–40 located in the Bristol Record Office: see Apprenticeship Books 1724–40.

[31] For some penetrating insights on rural dependencies see Howard Newby, 'The Deferential Dialectic', *Comparative Studies in Society and History*, 17/2 (1975), pp. 139–64, and *The Deferential Worker* (Harmondsworth, 1977), ch. 8.

least, they could only be replicated in those urban centres dominated by one or two major industries.[32]

The shifting nature of urban reciprocities between rich and poor, employer and worker, changed the dynamics of popular festival. While officially organized from above, political anniversaries could easily generate popular licence and self-assertion. Instead of sanctifying the benefactors, festive largess could translate into a demand for festive rights. Such transgressions had always been part of the carnivalesque, but in the new social context they rose in intensity, beginning in the metropolis. Particularly troublesome were the November holidays of Gunpowder Plot and Queen Elizabeth's day when plebeian revels were likely to get out of hand. As early as 1652 John Evelyn had recalled the 'great insolencies'[33] that were committed on the streets of London. By the 1670s, when these gambols assumed a new vigour with regular pope-burnings and mock-ceremonials, they appear to have generated a great deal of lawlessness. In 1674 it was claimed that 'divers rude and disordered Young-Men, Apprentices and others had terrified women and children with their squibs and serpents', and that 'almost all Persons of Quality . . . being so frequently assaulted in their Coaches in that rude manner' had been 'driven and kept out from the City to secure themselves from those dangers'.[34] During the next three decades similar complaints were brought before the Lord Mayor, and by the end of the century Guy Fawkes's day had become very much a plebeian event. New Ward recalled car-men and porters ridiculing popery with paper mitres and rosaries, and how 'towards the Evening, Men and Boys / Fill'd every Street with hideous Noise, / All threatening by their brutish Rudeness, / Much Mischief and excessive Lewdness'.[35] By this time, plebeian self-assertion, with its demands for festive doles, was very

[32] One should not discount the strength of industrial paternalism in some mining communities and domestic ports such as Newcastle: see J. S., *Memoirs of the Public Life of Sir Walter Blackett* (Newcastle, 1819), pp. xxix–xxxvii, 31–3; and Kathleen Wilson, 'The Rejection of Deference', pp. 196–204. For a 19th-century example see Patrick Joyce, *Work, Society and Politics: the Culture of the Factory in Later Victorian England* (Brighton, 1980).

[33] E. S. De Beer (ed.), *The Diary of John Evelyn* (6 vols.; Oxford, 1955), iii. 71.

[34] Houghton Lib., Harvard Univ., Precept of Lord Mayor against the throwing of squibs, firebrands and fireworks, 3 Nov. 1674.

[35] Edward War, *Hudibras Redivivus*, 4th edn. (London, 1710), pp. 7–8.

much a feature of London anniversaries. In 1706 a freeman wrote to the Lord Mayor imploring him to reconsider the policy of ordering illuminations on public festivals. 'It gives ye Rude Rabble', he declared,

Liberty to Doe what they list . . . they Breake windows with stones, fire Gunns with Pease in our Houses to ye Hazard of Peoples Lifes or Limbs because they doe not comply to thare Humours and abusing People in ye Streets yt will not give money to the Bonfire as they call it, which is a very Bad fire and of dangerous consequence all soe mutch swareing, cursing and Blasphemy is occasioned thare by.[36]

Festivals marked by such a vociferous and irreverent plebeian presence did not necessarily have any serious political ramifications. But in periods of acute controversy, when the divisions within national politics reverberated throughout society, they were likely to become explosive situations. The authorities were certainly alive to this possibility, and during the 1680s and again during the second decade of the eighteenth century, the London militia was called out to patrol the streets on public holidays. Very occasionally bonfires were banned. But this policy of policing was never very successful. Militiamen frequently shared the sympathies of the crowd, and the official proscription of bonfires was a virtual admission of unpopularity. Even the royalists of the Stuart era feared the consequence of depriving the poor of their holidays.

In short, governments and parties had to live with the crowd, and with crowds they had helped to politicize. Since the 1640s, when Pym had first mobilized the London apprentices against the Laudian regime, politicians had become increasingly sensitive to the plebeian presence and had attuned their propaganda accordingly. During the Exclusion crisis one sees this most clearly: not only in the well-known pope burnings of the Green Ribbon Club, which represented a new departure in popular mobilization and political spectacle, derived from popular festival; but also in the Tories' attempt to orchestrate loyalism in a popular idiom. Hence the plan to burn the Rump on Oak Apple day, 1680, recalling former celebrations of its dissolution in 1660.[37]

---

[36] Bodleian Lib., MS Rawl. D 862, fo. 83.
[37] K. H. D. Haley, *The First Earl of Shaftesbury* (Oxford, 1968), pp. 557–8, 572–3, 681, 694–5; J. R. Jones, 'The Green Ribbon Club', *Durham University*

By the turn of the century this new iconography had become a regular feature of political ritual, attuned to a calendar that assumed a more explicit party coloration as the succession issue once more absorbed English politics. The most cherished days in the Whig year were the November festivals commemorating England's anti-Catholic heritage and William's landing in 1688. These anniversaries saw Whig iconography in full bloom, with ceremonial burnings of popes and pretenders and uncompromising sermons on the virtues of the Revolution settlement. Contrariwise, the martyrdom of Charles I became the classic occasion for High Church sermons on the iniquities of Whigs, republicans, and regicides. John Dunton complained that 'the 30th January is more religiously observed by some sort of people than is the Sabbath; every little curate in the country must upon that day give his People an account of the Martyr and must rail at the Whigs'.[38] Restoration day, on the other hand, gave the same curates a chance to commemorate their triumph over the Rump and to laud the virtues of hereditary monarchy. Even seasoned Whig preachers like Benjamin Hoadly were hard pressed to divest the day of its Stuart connotations. Accompanying these two were the Augustan anniversaries, those of the last Stuart queen, which in some London parishes were celebrated as late as 1730.[39] Finally, there was the anniversary of 10 June, the Pretender's birthday, which was specifically reserved for the Jacobites or for anyone who wished to commit political blasphemy.

Associated with these anniversaries was a repertoire of symbols, colours, and songs. The royal oak had long been the motif of Restoration day, and oak sprigs and green ribbons were regularly worn by Tory stalwarts. The party's favourite song appears to have been 'The King shall enjoy his own again', which first appeared in 1659, was subsequently appropriated

---

Journal, 49 (1956–7), 17–20; John Miller, *Popery and Politics in England 1660–1688* (Cambridge, 1973), pp. 183–7; *Cal. State Papers Domestic 1679–80*, pp. 422–4.

[38] [John Dunton], *The Shortest Way With the King* (London, n.d.), p. 62.

[39] Westminster Pub. Lib., B14 (Churchwardens' accounts, St Clement Danes). Queen Anne's accession was celebrated until 1727, her birthday until 1731; by contrast, the commemoration of George I's anniversaries lapsed soon after his death.

by Monmouth's supporters, and was reappropriated by the Tories in the 1690s. Those who disapproved of its seditious sentiments, or who feared prosecution, could simply have whistled it, for the Whigs revamped its verses with Hanoverian doggerel in 1714 and inadvertently gave it a plausible legality. Several ballad singers argued this out with a London constable in 1723.[40] By contrast, orange was the favourite Whig colour, Sweet William its seasonal emblem, and 'Lillibulero' its favourite tune, suitably retitled 'Over Hanover' before George I's accession. Jacobites normally took pains to conceal themselves and in many instances would have been indistinguishable from Tories, save for the odd toast to JOB, James–Ormonde–Bolingbroke, and indiscreet songs like 'Jemmy, dear Jemmy'. On 10 June, however, they might have been more visible, parading white roses or blue, green, and white rosettes. Each party, finally, had its emblem of derision, although the way in which one chose to celebrate an anniversary, whether bells were pealed or tolled, whether rue and thyme were substituted for celebratory symbols, was often telling enough. And one could, of course, parody the symbols of one's opponents, as a Shoreditch housekeeper did in 1716, when he placed an owl in an egg-basket covered with oak leaves, and placed it over his door with a Catholic cross and a pair of wooden shoes.[41] But the Whigs' principal symbol of derision was the warming-pan, which cast doubts upon the Pretender's legitimacy, or the more unorthodox calf's head, which denied Charles I his martyrdom. In reply, the Tories baited the Whigs with Jack Presbyter or an effigy of Oliver Cromwell. After 1714, however, when Tory symbolism converged with Jacobite, the most profane image was a turnip or a pair of horns, sometimes conjoined, as in a broadsheet doing the rounds at the time of the South Sea Bubble, which recounted how Sir George came up from 'Turnipshire' and was cuckolded by that errant knight Sir James.[42]

This theatre of politics, with its oaths, riddles, rhymes, and ribald balladry, its folklore and iconography, might seem to modern understandings to be droll if not frivolous. But in an

---

[40] *Weekly Journal, or Saturday's Post*, 29 June 1723.
[41] *The Shift Shifted, or Robin's Last Shift*, 28 July 1716.
[42] PRO, SP 35/24/241.

age when ceremonialism was of decisive importance in fostering political allegiances and dignifying the political order, it was played in deadly earnest. In the final years of Queen Anne, Whigs and Tories took to the political stage with a new urgency, broadening the very boundaries of the political realm in the process. Dr Sacheverell opened the act with a triumphal tour of the West Midlands in the summer of 1710 to mark his partial deliverance from Whig retribution. His progress facilitated a gathering of the clans in this stridently Tory region of the country, and save for Worcester (where he was rebuffed by Bishop Lloyd), he was rapturously received by cavalcades of gentry, clergy, and freeholders, although some Whigs in Bridgnorth baited him by carrying 'Oranges on Sticks', assuring his supporters that 'it was the best fruit that ever came to England'.[43] Predictably, there was a good deal of Tory rejoicing on the expiry of his sentence in March 1713. At Norwich, the bells began ringing at five in the morning and continued all day, with 'the Mob' singing 'songs to the Doctor's Honour and in Reflection on the Whiggs'. Similar celebrations were reported in Wells, Frome, 'and all the considerable Towns in Somersetshire', while in some places, the *Flying Post* reported, 'the Musick play'd the old Tune . . . Let the King enjoy his own again'.[44]

Sacheverell's popularity piqued the Whigs, and there were persistent rumours that they planned to burn him in effigy.[45] But while the Tories rode high on the Doctor's political fortitude and capitalized upon the Peace of Utrecht, the Whigs sought to enhance Marlborough's visibility, to promote an official visit to London by Prince Eugene, and to reshape the political calendar by adding days which emphasized England's deliverance from Stuart rule or Popish atrocities.[46] In addition

---

[43] H. Owen and J. B. Blakeway, *A History of Shrewsbury* (2 vols.; London, 1825), i. 503–4; the *Flying Post*, 18–20, 20–2 July 1710.

[44] *Flying Post*, 31 Mar–2 Apr., 7–9 Apr. 1713.

[45] In London, on the day of George I's entry (20 Sept. 1714), some gentlemen were brazen enough to hang a picture of Sacheverell with a rope around his neck out of a tavern window in Charing Cross. This so exasperated the mob that it smashed the windows and threatened to pull the place down. The landlord of the tavern, a Mr Curtain, successfully claimed damages from the gentlemanly pranksters at the Court of Common Pleas: see the *Weekly Journal*, 2 July 1715.

[46] *Flying Post*, 10–12 Feb. 1712. The paper emphasized that 13 Feb. was the

they played the old Shaftesburian card. From 1711 onwards the rising stars of the party, together with their allies in the City, financed a series of elaborate pope-burning processions through the main thoroughfares of the metropolis. The one promoted by the Kit-Kat Club on Queen Elizabeth's day 1711 cost £200 to stage. It featured monks, friars, cardinals, as well as effigies of the Pope, Devil, and Pretender. According to Swift, an effigy of Sacheverell was also scheduled to accompany the execrable triumvirate. Flanked by innumerable linkmen hired from Clare market, and dozens of watchmen and beadles, it was to march from Drury Lane to St James, then along the Strand and through the City, culminating in a ceremonial burning of the effigies before Queen Elizabeth's statue at Temple Bar.[47]

The secretary of state, Lord Dartmouth, had the effigies confiscated on the night of 16 November, but it proved difficult to ban pope-burnings indefinitely. They had become such a part of popular tradition that their continued proscription would have been counter-productive as well as ideologically suspect. Predictably, there was a ruckus when the trained bands attempted to stop a chimney-sweep heaving 'a Paper scull'd Pastboard, low-priced Pope' around Holborn the following year.[48] Within three months Whig-sponsored pope-burnings were back. On the Queen's birthday, popes and pretenders were burnt at the Three Tuns and Rummer in Gracechurch Street and by the Hanover Club before Jenny Man's

day of Prince William's proclamation in 1688, and that 11 Dec. was the day upon which James II 'abdicated'. The Hanover Club also commemorated 23 Oct. in 1715, the anniversary of the 'popish massacre of 1641'. See *The Englishman*, ed. Rae Blanchard (Oxford, 1955), for 19 Oct. 1715. For the controversy surrounding Prince Eugene's visit, promoted by Whig aldermen, see Reginald R. Sharpe, *London and the Kingdom* (3 vols.; London, 1894–5), ii. 645–6.

[47] *Political State of Great Britain*, ii. 667–9; Anon., *An Account of the Mock Procession of Burning the Pope and the Chevalier de St. George Intended to be Perform'd on the 17th Instant, Being the Anniversary of Queen Elizabeth* (n.p., 1711); Anon., *A True Relation of the Several Facts and Circumstances of the intended Riot and Tumult on Queen Elizabeth's Day Gathered from Authentic Accounts*, 2nd edn. (London, 1711); Ryland (ed.), *The Prose Works of Jonathan Swift*, ii. 283; *HMC Dartmouth*, i. 307–8.

[48] *Flying Post*, 6–8, 18–20 Nov. 1712.

coffee-house in Charing Cross.[49] Within a year anti-papal processionals were in full bloom, enjoying official approval after the accession, and spreading beyond the metropolis to the provinces. Pope-burnings were reported at Axminster, Chichester, Frome, Northallerton, Norwich, Stony Stratford, Trowbridge, and Weymouth.[50]

The final years of Queen Anne thus saw an upsurge of political festival, a more partisan appropriation of the calendar, and a growing incidence of disorder. With the advent of Hanover, the political calendar became a calendar of riot. Disturbances were reported in 26 English and Welsh towns on Coronation day; and the next five years saw clashes between troops and inhabitants, attacks upon meeting-houses, and seditious demonstrations in a further 31, if we include London and Westminster.[51] Virtually every town with a population of 10,000 inhabitants or more was implicated in this rash of disorder, Colchester and Great Yarmouth excepted; and very few towns with over 5,000 remained unscathed. To be sure, the geographical incidence of disturbance provides us with only a rough index of the scale and intensity of disaffection to the Hanoverian regime and its Whig allies. Even so, popular hostility to the new reign was a good deal more widespread than most historians have allowed.[52] While it did not precipitate a popular uprising on the scale of 1685—for the Scottish Jacobites proved unable to muster a sizeable popular following south of the border—it was not without its insurrectionary

[49] Ibid., 7–10 Feb. 1713; *The Englishman*, p. 509. The Hanover Club had approximately 30 members, including Joseph Addison, Richard Steele, Paul Methuen, Thomas, Lord Pelham, William Pulteney, Horace Walpole, the duke of Montagu, and the earl of Lincoln.

[50] *Flying Post*, 26–8, 28–30 Oct., 30 Oct.–2 Nov., 2–4, 16–18, 18–20 Nov. 1714, 8–10 Nov. 1715. For the London pope-burnings see my 'Popular Protest', *Past and Present* (1978), 77–9.

[51] These conclusions are based on an intensive search through the contemporary newspapers and periodicals and upon information found in the State Papers Domestic.

[52] The most notable exception is Thompson, *Whigs and Hunters*, pp. 164–6, 199–202: yet even he remains cautious about the extent of disaffection, arguing, rather, that its translation into Jacobitism served Whig repression and spoilation. Those historians who wish to restore Jacobitism to the centre of the political stage tend to emphasize its importance in subsequent decades and play down its popular manifestations in 1715–18: see Cruickshanks, *Political Untouchables*.

impulses and sectarian violence. In the West Midlands and Lancashire, in particular, the government proved powerless to contain massive reprisals against Dissenting chapels, the principal centres of Whig support in this staunchly Tory region.

What, then, do these disturbances disclose about the nature of crowd politics in the early eighteenth century? In the first place, they suggest that we are no longer in the world of metropolitan precocity and provincial bumpkinism which the Excise ballad with which I began this Chapter implies. They also suggest that the forces of localism and regional identity no longer prevented anyone from forming a perception of national politics outside the social parameters of the gentry, bourgeoisie, and small masters. Provincialism, in its current revisionist formulation, had long disappeared. It no longer denoted élite politics and popular passivity, or indeed élite control over popular allegiances.[53] Decades of party strife in an era of declining patriarchalism had broadened the boundaries of politics to encompass petty artisans, servants, and labourers, straining the bonds of political deference in the process.[54] Not that the politics of the meaner sort were necessarily very sophisticated. Political allegiances were personalized around figures such as Sacheverell, Ormonde, Marlborough. They involved, even in their visceral denunciations of George I, a certain reverence for monarchy and good lordship (hence the idealization of the House of Stuart and the comparison of Hanover with local grandees).[55] But that said, we should not presume a pre-political mob mustered by superiors to act on

[53] Jonathan Clark has attempted to apply such a notion to 18th-century political developments, largely as a counter to class-based analyses: see his *Revolution and Rebellion* (Cambridge, 1986), ch. 4. In fact provincial or regional perspectives are perfectly compatible with national and even with class-nuanced studies, as the work of David Underdown, in particular, suggests. For Underdown's specific reflections on this theme see his 'Community and Class: Theories of Local Politics in the English Revolution', in Barbara C. Malament (ed.), *After the Reformation: Essays in Honour of J. H. Hexter* (Manchester, 1980), pp. 147–65.

[54] Outside London, the best evidence of the composition of the crowd is for the West Midlands: see PRO Assi 4/18. In the riot at Canterbury on Coronation day, the leading rioters were identified as two maltsters, a tailor, a silk weaver, a cordwainer, and Lawrence Bridgen, a gentleman. For London, see my 'Popular Protest', *Past and Present* (1978), 84–7.

[55] See e.g. the comment of a Newport, Monmouth nailer in 1715, who was

their behalf, drawn into the fray by material inducements. Certainly, there is some evidence of this sort in the depositions on the Cambridge riot of 10 June 1715, where a crowd of 'young lads' outside the Three Tuns, hallowing for Cotton and Slater, were encouraged to drink the health of James III.[56] Yet the very fact that festive largess so frequently failed to curb contention should make us wary of exaggerating the venality of the poor. Customary doles on political anniversaries were taken for granted. They could at best consolidate, not create, political loyalties.

Even so, one should not assume that crowds always acted autonomously. As we have already emphasized, the popular right to heckle, huzza, and riot operated within conventions which facilitated intervention from above. Clergymen had plenty of opportunity to inflame political passions on anniversary sermons, and there is no doubt that they did so, to a point where Defoe believed that the pulpit had become 'a Trumpet of Sedition' where 'Treason and Rebellion' were preached 'at pleasure'.[57] Nor were dissenting attitudes confined to the pulpit. The rector of St Nicholas in Liverpool refused to participate in the thanksgiving service for the peaceful accession of Hanover and the same evening 'headed about 40 Mob, who roar'd out the Church and Dr. Sacheverell'. Later on he entertained them at the George tavern 'where they swore and curs'd, threaten'd to break all the Windows, and having placed his Rectorship in a Chair, . . . carried him about in the House as if he had been chose Member of Parliament'.[58] Similarly, civic dignitaries and local patrons could orchestrate violence by connivance or a studied disrespect for anniversary

brought before the summer assizes for saying 'that if the Duke of Beauford had been now living he was a fitter man to be King than King George': PRO, Assi 4/18/478.

[56] PRO, SP 35/3/185–96.

[57] [Daniel Defoe], *Bold Advice* (London, 1715), p. 29. For an example of a seditious sermon see W. R. Ward, *Georgian Oxford: University Politics in the Eighteenth Century* (OUP, 1958), p. 54. Thomas Hearne noted that the sermon, preached by Abel Evans of St John's, hinted 'at some of our modern tyrants and usurpers . . . meaning particularly ye present Elector of Brunswick'. See also the information against Willoughby Myners, the curate of Shoreditch, who preached a scurrilous sermon against the king at St Ethelburga, within Bishopsgate, in Sept. 1715: PRO, SP 44/118/1, Oct. 1715.

[58] *Flying Post*, 28–30 Sept. 1714.

occasions. At Abergavenny a local revenue officer's wife burnt a wig on the bonfire on Coronation day, and several notables refused to illuminate their houses. At Taunton, the mayor's party stood by while the 'Sacheverellites' took firebrands from the celebratory bonfire and threw them at their opponents in the Castle tavern. According to one account, the mayor and recorder cried 'Sound for the Church and Sacheverell, Sound for Portman and Warre', but said 'not one word for King George'.[59]

There are plenty of examples, then, of incitement from local notables, especially during the Coronation-day riots of 1714. These sometimes took place in open constituencies where there were fierce party rivalries and where the Hanoverian succession threatened to tip the balance in favour of the Whigs. Canterbury, Chichester, Cirencester, Gloucester, Hereford, and Salisbury, for example, all experienced disorders during the Coronation-day festivities, and all had a record of disputed elections during the Augustan era. So too did Worcester and Norwich, where the High Church party refused to join in the official festivities and instead led a mob to the market-place to the cry of 'Bene and Berney', the standing Tory members.[60] In towns like these, riots sometimes resembled pre-electoral show-downs, fanned by Tory élites who resented the way in which their rivals had transformed Hanoverian celebrations into Whig fanfares.[61]

But not all disturbances were so obviously orchestrated from above (and even where they were, they should not preclude the possibility of genuinely held convictions by humbler participants). Many of the demonstrations had a distinctly plebeian flavour. In London, in particular, crowds drew upon an independent tradition of street politics for their momentum, drawing support from local youth groups such as the Bridewell Boys and countering the anti-papal parades of the Whig mughouses by burning Whig heroes in effigy and flamboyantly traversing their opponents' territory. Similarly, in Manchester and the West Midlands, scores of nailers, buckle-makers, and

[59] PRO, SP 35/74/6–7; *Flying Post*, 26–8 Oct. 1714.
[60] *Flying Post*, 26–8 Oct. 1714.
[61] For clerical criticism of this tendency see the complaints of a Trowbridge parson cited in the *Flying Post*, 30 Oct.–2 Nov. 1714.

colliers carried out a massive purge of Dissenting chapels and defiantly confronted troops with a raucous celebration of Tory anniversaries and toasts to the Pretender and the rebel army. As the legal record reveals, very few gentlemen were implicated in these proceedings, despite the intensive search for well-to-do ringleaders and the rumours of roving mobs in the pay of their superiors. Most of the attacks upon Dissenting chapels, in fact, involved local men, and were captained by such: in Manchester by a blacksmith; in Worcester, a butcher; in Shrewsbury, a skinner, one Henry Webb, alias Captain Rag.[62]

Even further south, where the authority of the government was better represented on the bench, disaffection was often couched in a popular idiom. Thus at Bedford the maypole was dressed in mourning on Coronation day. More flamboyantly, the common people at Frome Selwood confronted the loyal parade of the clothiers and textile manufacturers with a 'Hanoverian' fool, whose turnip-topped wand and chalked hat mimicked the celebratory emblems of their superiors.[63] Instances such as these may well have enjoyed unofficial Tory licence, but they drew on the resources of the populace itself, its ability to adapt older traditions of misrule to political contexts and to rattle Whig confidence. Indeed, it is difficult to account for the persistent undercurrent of disaffection, at a time when the Tory party was reeling from the impeachment of its leaders, without some appreciation of the self-generating aspects of plebeian culture. Predictably, this was most advanced in London, where it proved extremely difficult to suppress the evanescent charivari-like disturbances of the populous out-parishes, and even harder to probe the network of vestries, alehouses, and markets that served as the bases of collective protest.[64] A Middlesex presentment in 1716, for instance, condemned the constables for permitting 'idle and disorderly Persons to assemble in the Publick Streets, Lanes and Passages,

[62] For these and other examples see my 'Popular Protest', *Past and Present* (1978), 70–100, and 'Riot and Popular Jacobitism', pp. 74–7. Of the 500 rioters mentioned in the process book of the Oxford circuit, only eight were gentlemen (one was found guilty): see PRO, Assi 4/18.

[63] *Flying Post*, 30 Oct.–2 Nov., 18–20 Nov. 1714.

[64] For evidence of Tory alehouses, printers, and nonjuring chapels as sources of disaffection see *Political State of Great Britain*, xii. 130, and PRO, SP 44/79A/34, 145.

and to sing and disperse seditious Songs, Ballads and Pamphlets reflecting on his Majesty and his Government'. But none of these orders, nor the crackdown upon disaffected alehouses, proved capable of curbing the seditious balladry which taunted the government well into the 1720s.[65] Even outside London, market-place disaffection was extremely difficult to suppress. In 1720 the government managed to track down a Tory balladeer in Cleobury Mortimer who had declared that 'King George was Gone over to Hannover to eate Turnip Tops & for that Cuckoldy King George & the Whiggs he cared not a fig'. Investigations revealed the man to be a journeyman weaver from St Giles-in-the-Fields, who 'had Noe other way to gett his Liveing but by singing of songs in the streets at severall Markett townes'. In the last four months he had been to Oxford, Gloucester, Hereford, Ludlow, and to various small market towns in Wales and Worcestershire.[66] Even in years not punctuated by street demonstrations, the tramping artisan could keep the spirit of disaffection alive. As James Montague told the grand jury of Dorset in 1720, the countryside buzzed with the 'most daring and insulting Behaviour, both in Words and Actions, perhaps that ever was heard of, towards our Great and Good King'; especially, he noted, 'amongst the ignorant and meanest of the People'.[67]

The four decades after 1680 thus saw a significant broadening of the boundaries of the political nation to encompass wide sections of the labouring populace. Years of acute party strife, in a social context which allowed the common people greater cultural space, had created a dynamic and contentious political culture, centred around royal and national anniversaries, in which the populace itself was a vigorous participant. The crowd had come of age. It entered political discourse as a phenomenon that had to be cultivated, nurtured, and contained. Robert Ferguson claimed that the first years of George I's reign saw a higher incidence of riotous disturbance than

---

[65] GLRO, MSP/1716/Oct/58. See also Whitlock Bulstrode's charge to the Middlesex Grand Jury in Apr. 1718, printed in *Annals of George I*, iv. 393–413, where he complains of 'Apprentice Boys' who 'pretend to determine the Title and Right of Kings'; and the informations to the government, PRO, SP 35/11/33–7, 35/31/12, 233, 281, 296; 35/43/147.

[66] PRO, SP 35/22/166–7.

[67] *Weekly Journal of British Gazetteer*, 18 June 1720.

ever before, and he was probably correct.[68] To be sure, contemporary commentators continued to regard the mob as an essentially subaltern force, gullible, credulous, manipulable. But in the Accession crisis they also sensed its unpredictable, volatile power. For in these years we see not only the crowd as the hustings institutionalized, a force called upon to act on behalf of external interests, but also intimations of a more popular impulse. Fuelled by fears of another war, by a deep-rooted aversion to a German-born monarch whose commitment to Britain was suspect, and by a legacy of sectarian strife, crowds transformed the official calendar into a carnival of sedition and riot. Ridicule, laughter, and the popular retribution of transgressors against the community had long been part of the tradition of misrule. They were adapted to new social and political contexts, questioning the very authority of the Hanoverian regime and its Whig, often Dissenting, allies.

The calendar of sedition which had marked the early years of the Hanoverian accession survived until the early 1720s. Its survival was admittedly uneven. In Norwich, for example, Jacobite revels punctuated local electoral contests and Hanoverian anniversaries well into the 1730s, while in Bristol there was a major anti-Hanoverian riot in 1735. In the Midlands, moreover, Jacobite symbolism was defiantly displayed upon Lord Gower's defection to the Court in 1747, and the Hill Top lads of Walsall annually defiled an effigy of George I until 1751.[69] But these outbreaks of Jacobitical revelry tended to register the rhythms of local conflicts rather than of national, and the flamboyant display of Stuart sympathies was increasingly territorial. After the Atterbury plot, as hopes of the Tory

---

[68] [Robert Ferguson], *The History of All the Mobs, Tumults, and Insurrections in Great Britain from William the Conqueror to the Present Time* (London, [1715]), p. 53. For a greater awareness of the political presence of the mob see [Daniel Defoe], *Captain Tom's Remembrance to his Old Friends the MOBB of London, Westminster, Southwark and Wapping* (London, 1711); [id.], *A Hymn to the Mob* (London, 1715), [id.], *A Humble Address to our Sovereign Lord the People* (London, 1715). See also Anon., *An Account of the Riots, Tumults and Other Treasonable Practices since his Majesty's Accession to the Throne* (London, 1715), and Anon., *An Account of a Dreadful Mob at Manchester and Other Places in England* (Edinburgh, 1715).

[69] See my 'Riot and Popular Jacobitism', pp. 82–5.

revival declined, so Stuart holidays lost some of their contentious, if not symbolic, resonance. White roses were last
reported in London on the Pretender's birthday in 1723. Even
the anniversary of the Restoration, described in 1722 as a 'Day
of Riot, Mischief and great disturbance', lost some of its
partisan connotations.[70] Save for high-flyers like Henry Crossgrove, who continually celebrated the holiday by reverencing
Stuart rule, it was gradually assimilated into a political
calendar which combined a respect for established monarchy
with a conservative Revolution heritage. At the same time, the
last vestige of the Good Old Cause, the annual re-enactment
of Charles I's execution, became an eccentric pursuit, last
celebrated by the Calves Head Club in 1735.[71] Thereafter the
calendar increasingly reflected the political dispositions of the
Revolution settlement.

The decline of the Hanoverian–Stuart dyad did not necessarily mean, of course, that political anniversaries *per se* were
any less contentious. The emergence of a patriot opposition to
Walpole led to a redefinition of the traditional holidays of 4 and
5 November. Whereas ministerial Whigs commemorated the
nation's deliverance from popery and arbitrary rule, their
opponents added a further dimension—William's so-called
restoration of triennial parliaments.[72] In addition, the patriots
attempted to achieve maximum publicity from official anniversaries, celebrating those of the reversionary interest with
usual vigour when Leicester House was at odds at St James.
Thus in January 1741, as the opposition mobilized against
Walpole, the City of London went out of its way to congratulate the Prince and Princess on the birth of a daughter, a visit
that set the stage for a joyous celebration of the Prince's
birthday a few days later.[73]

But what transformed the calendar in the 1730s and 1740s
were the extraordinary celebrations of opposition victories

---

[70] PRO, SP 35/31/241.

[71] John Doran, *London in the Jacobite Times* (2 vols.; London, 1877), i. 433,
ii. 62–5.

[72] See e.g. the *London Evening Post*, 5–7 Nov. 1741. King William, it was
claimed, 'came to redeem us from STANDING ARMIES in time of peace, from
LONG PARLIAMENTS, and other ENCROACHMENTS of the Prerogative,
and restor'd to us that inestimable blessing of TRIENNIAL PARLIAMENTS'.

[73] *London Evening Post*, 31 Jan.–2 Feb. 1741.

against the Court. The news of the withdrawal of the Excise Bill, for instance, was celebrated in at least twenty towns outside the metropolis. At Nottingham 'no sooner was the News heard . . . but the Bells in all the Churches began to ring and continued to do so all Day, and at Night the Inhabitants met at several Houses in the Town and drank their Majesties and Royal Family's Healths, the worthy Patriots who voted against the extension of the Excise Laws, and to the Trade and Liberties of the Subjects of Great Britain'. In Newcastle the principal merchants and traders met at the Crown Tavern where they lighted 204 candles to the 'WORTHY PATRIOTS, who for the LIBERTY of their COUNTRY, and the GOOD of TRADE, made so glorious a STAND against the Increase of Excise Laws'.[74] At Coventry, the Liverpool courier was greeted to a more raucous cacophony of 'Trumpets, Drums, French Horns, Warming Pans, and every thing that would make a Noise'.[75] Here, as in Bristol, Liverpool, Maidstone, and Warwick, effigies of Excisemen and Walpole were put to flame, in some cases upon a bonfire before the local Excise office.

The symbolism of the Excise crisis, the gilded tobacco leaf, the celebrated number 204 (or 205), denoting the opposition division on the bill, resonated across the urban hustings in 1734. In a few places it was invoked at subsequent opposition triumphs, especially in London, where Alderman John Barber, the man who mobilized the City against the bill, remained a very popular figure.[76] But probably the most popular opposition festival of the mid-eighteenth century was the birthday of Admiral Edward Vernon, war-hero, patriot, and unremitting opponent of Walpole. In ballads and broadsides he was portrayed as 'a true cock of the game', the intrepid son of old England who cared for his men and refused to truckle before the Catholic powers of Europe or powerful politicians at

---

[74] *Newcastle Courant*, 21 Apr. 1733.

[75] *London Evening Post*, 14–17, 17–19, 21–4 Apr. 1733; *Craftsman*, 21, 28 Apr., 5 May 1733.

[76] Barber was acclaimed by the crowd when Mayor Humphrey Parsons went to Westminster in November 1740 to take the oaths of office. 'They cannot forget', claimed *Common Sense* (1 Nov. 1740), 'his great services to them and his Country by his strenuous opposition of the Excise Scheme'.

home.[77] After his victory at Porto Bello in 1740, his birthday was celebrated in at least thirty major towns and cities—according to the *London Magazine*, 'in most of the chief places in the kingdom'.[78] In the next two years it eclipsed royal anniversaries in the popular, as opposed to official, calendar. 'Admiral Vernon's birthday', remarked Richard West with a certain amazement as well as hyperbole, 'has been kept all over the globe two or three times over.'[79] Not surprisingly, even the rumour of another Vernon victory could generate considerable enthusiasm. As the *London Evening Post* reported on 7 May 1741: 'Yesterday all the Town was alarm'd at the firing of the Town Guns, and a Report was immediately spread that News was come of Cartagena's being taken. But all that Joy was soon dampen'd by hearing the Guns was fir'd for *No Victory* obtain'd, but for his Gracious Majesty's going down the River in order to proceed to his German Dominions.'[80]

The popularity of Vernon reached dizzy heights and it is important to gauge his appeal. To the merchants and manufacturers engaged in the rapidly expanding transatlantic trade, Vernon's victories constituted an important turning-point in the mounting campaign for a more aggressive blue-water policy, one which Walpole had been reluctant to pursue. But Vernon's attraction, as we have already seen in Chapter 7, always transcended such sectional interests. He was the intrepid admiral in the tradition of Drake and Raleigh, the Britannic bane of the great Catholic powers. He was the quintessential patriot, combining naval heroism with political integrity. Vernon never played politics for preferment; he remained adamantly anti-ministerialist throughout his career, and very critical of the Admiralty, even though this certainly delayed his promotion. These qualities were widely respected among Countrymen in what was regarded as a mercenary, venal age. But what particularly caught the popular eye was Vernon's paternalism, his concern for naval welfare; his willingness to flout authority; and his contempt for foppery and fashion. Vernon shared with the populace a disrespect for

---

[77] *Vernon's Glory, Containing 14 New songs, Occasion'd by the Taking of Porto Bello and Fort Chagre* (London, 1740).

[78] *London Magazine*, 9 (1740), 558.

[79] Lewis (ed.), *Correspondence of Walpole*, xiii. 236.

[80] *London Evening Post*, 5–7 May 1741.

rank, haughtiness, and servility. Or at least he was projected as sharing those sentiments, just as he was cast, rather problematically, as a buccaneering gallant. There was always an element of machismo about the portrait of Vernon's exploits, an explicit sexuality that won broad appeal.[81]

The varied interpretations of the character of Admiral Vernon, the different dimensions of his personality and career, help to explain his immense popularity. One does not have to indulge in notions of false consciousness, or emphasize the crudely material attractions of another festival, to explain why he was acclaimed by a plebeian as well as a middling audience. The same line of argument can be advanced for the Excise demonstrations. Objectively, one could say that the agitation against the Excise was very sectional. It affected first and foremost mercantile fortunes, and specifically those commission merchants and wholesalers involved in the wine and tobacco trade. Even the *Craftsman* admitted as much.[82] But the campaign against the Excise was successfully promoted as a campaign against Liberty. It became a symbol of government corruption and authoritarianism, of obtrusive, arrogant officials and illiberal laws. As such, it had some purchase among shopkeepers and craftsmen who continually had to reckon with the press-gang, the crimp, and petty officialdom, and who saw the author of the scheme glorying in his own political success while levying heavier taxes upon the poor. 'Liberty, No Excise' was a protest against disreputable politics, against corrupt officials, and in some sense against a legacy of Whig authoritarianism. 'Damn your laws and proclamations', cried the crowd before the Commons at the second reading of the bill, when JPs attempted to read the Riot Act. George II and Walpole were 'Rogues and Villains', declared a man from Ratcliff Highway several days earlier. It is no accident that Sir Robert was burnt in several places in conjunction with Sarah Malcolm, a murderess hanged at Mitre Court, near Newgate, in March 1733.[83] In a manner reminiscent of *Jonathan Wild* and the *Beggar's Opera*, both were equally criminal.

[81] See *Vernon's Glory*, p. 19, where the capture of Porto Bello is portrayed as a sexual conquest.

[82] The *Craftsman*, 21 Apr. 1733.

[83] CLRO, M/SP/1733/Ap./76; *Northampton Mercury*, 12 Feb., 12 Mar. 1733; *HMC Egmont Diary*, i. 361–2.

It may be argued, then, that the demonstrations against the Excise and in favour of Vernon had a genuinely popular base and were not simply the product of client-based politics or the captive propaganda of mercantile factions. Morley's belief that the opposition to the 1733 bill was based on 'popular ignorance, prejudice and passion', that it constituted 'an epidemic of unreason',[84] glosses over popular grievances and twists the pent-up anger against Walpole into paranoia. Even so, Morley and successive historians were correct in noting how skilfully the opposition orchestrated the protest, playing upon popular fears of oppressive taxation and state vigilance with the image of the Monster Excise devouring the people, and co-ordinating the local celebrations with constituency instructions against the bill. Only in London—where the mob jostled Sir Robert, broke the windows of the Post Office and 'of all other houses not illuminated', and 'stopt every coach that came by, and made them cry "No Excise," '—did the protests threaten to get out of hand.[85] The same was true of the Vernon demonstrations. The opposition and its middling allies carefully laid the groundwork for the new bellicosity by highlighting Spanish atrocities upon merchant seamen, organizing petitions and Addresses against the Convention, and staging pageants depicting Vernon's triumph over Don Blas de Lezo.[86] Its newspapers gloried in Vernon's triumphs, over both the Spanish and ministerial intrigue, while its provincial supporters translated the admiral's birthday into anti-ministerial rallies.[87] As in 1733, so in the 1740s, the opposition sought to emphasize the decorum of popular jubilations, and to cast the crowd as both a guardian and weathervane of Liberty. 'Public blessings naturally produce publick Rejoicings', claimed the *Craftsman*, and whatever transgressions were committed on the streets were put down to libertarian exuberance.[88]

---

[84] John Morley, *Walpole* (London, 1913), pp. 171–2.

[85] *HMC Carlisle* MSS, p. 108; *HMC Egmont Diary*, i. 361.

[86] For the Chancery Lane pageant see the *London Magazine*, 7 (1740), 558.

[87] For an interesting commentary on the political import of Vernon see the pre-election feature by *Common Sense*, 6 June 1741. For the anti-ministerial rallies see ch. 7.

[88] *Craftsman*, 21 Apr. 1733. For the emphasis upon the decorum of Vernon festival and for some acknowledgement of popular transgressions see *Common Sense*, 29 Nov. 1740, and *Northampton Mercury*, 8–15 Nov. 1740.

During the final decade of Walpole's leadership the crowd helped to create the space for a libertarian politics. In its joyous support for Admiral Vernon, in particular, it had helped sustain the momentum of opposition politics and to underscore the un-popularity of Walpole and his policies. Even so, the politics of the crowd did not necessarily follow an opposition script. The particular convergence of opposition and plebeian politics disin-tegrated over the Forty-Five. Or, more specifically, the nascent nationalism of the populace threw critical divisions within the opposition itself into high relief. Similarly, in 1756, the popu-lar rage over Byng's retreat from Minorca critically delayed the opposition's critique of government strategy. During both crises, in 1745/6 and 11 years later, it was the government which profited most from the popular mood. Both incidents reveal that crowds did not necessarily follow an oppositional cum radical vector. Indeed, they illustrate that popular sympa-thies could conceivably bolster rather than challenge oligarchic regimes. By extension, they raise once more the general question of whether street politics can be cast in terms of plebeian–patrician polarities rather than as a site of struggle among different groups for popular representation.

At first sight, the shift in popular political sympathies between 1715 and 1745 might seem surprising. At the Hanoverian accession the crowd tended to be Tory rather than Whig, and Tory anger and disillusionment could easily trans-late itself into Jacobitism. To be sure, Whiggery was not without some popular purchase. In the textile towns in particular, where Dissenting affiliations ran deep, the Whigs consistently mustered a popular clientele. In London, too, Whig mobs were visible. Early in June 1715, one was reported attacking Lloyds coffee-house in Charing Cross and a chocolate-house in Piccadilly, moving on to threaten the house of the duke of Ormonde.[89] But the sympathies of the metro-politan crowd were usually of the other stamp, as Whig mug-house-men were very much aware. And this was emphatically the case in the West Midlands and Lancashire, where Tory-Jacobitism was so deeply entrenched as to survive well into the 1740s. 'Down with the rump—Down with the Hanoverians, Presbyterians—Down with the k—g, is so familar to us', wrote

[89] *Weekly Journal*, 18 June 1715.

one Manchester correspondent in 1746, 'that we expect it as soon as daylight is over.'[90]

Yet the very areas which saw a massive purge of Dissenting meeting-houses in 1715 witnessed threats upon Catholic chapels in 1745 and 1746. At Stourbridge, it was reported that the nailers, colliers, and bucklesmiths of the area, the very same groups active in 1715, were only with difficulty restrained from pulling down all the mass-houses in the locality and seizing priests and papists. In April 1746, a 'prodigious number' of carpenters and sailors attacked a Catholic chapel in Liverpool. Three weeks later they directed their fury upon a private chapel, and 'altho the mayor and town clerk both appear'd in order to read the riot act, they drove them both away and set fire to the house'.[91] In London also there were threats upon Catholic property and warnings of dire retribution if Catholics armed or fired the town.[92] Indeed, as the prosecutions for Jacobitism in the metropolis show, men and women from all walks of life were prepared to bring the disaffected to account. What the court records reveal is that by 1745 London Jacobitism had assumed a marginal, ethno-religious character. It was to be found among Catholics, principally the London Irish, but had lost ground among the wider community.[93]

How can one account for the vigour of popular anti-Catholicism during the Forty-Five, which in some areas amounted to a Catholic *peur*? Clearly, one factor was the strident propaganda of the government and its allies. The Bishop of London encouraged his clergy to deliver sermons affirming 'a just Abhorrence of Popery' and, in an open letter to the people of his diocese, warned Catholics not to provoke dissension, 'for their declared Disaffection to the Government makes them so liable to be suspected'.[94] In prints, ballads, and

---

[90] *Whitehall Evening Post*, 11 Oct. 1746, cited in the *Gentleman's Magazine*, 16 (1746), 579. For some insights into Jacobite culture in Manchester see Overton, *The Nonjurors*, pp. 354–60.

[91] *True Patriot*, 31 Dec. 1745; *Gentleman's Magazine*, 16 (1746), 324. According to the *Bath Journal*, 2 June 1746, the Liverpool rioters went on to a chapel at Ormskirk, and threatened to go to Wigan.

[92] *General Evening Post*, 19–22 Oct. 1745; *St. James's Evening Post*, 19–21 Oct. 1745.

[93] See my 'Popular Disaffection', *London Journal* (1975), 5–27.

[94] [Edmund Gibson], *The Bishop of London's Pastoral Letter to the People of*

cheap tracts specifically directed at 'the lower Sort of People',
government writers emphasized the dangers of a Jacobite
restoration to English liberty, noting the country's inevitable
subservience to France and the bloody Catholic inquisition
that would follow. Lengthier pamphlets retold the familiar
stories of past Catholic atrocities; broadsides resurrected the
Smithfield fires; and a subscription was launched to build an
obelisk to the Marian martyrs.[95] This flurry of anti-Catholic
propaganda also saw a revival of pope-burnings. At Deptford,
the parade featured a Highlander carrying a pair of wooden
shoes, a Jesuit heralding the Inquisition, two friars selling
indulgences for murder, adultery, and rebellion, the Pope
riding upon a bull, and the Pretender 'with a green Ribbon,
Nosegay of Thistles &c, riding upon an Ass, supported by a
Frenchman on the Right and a Spaniard on the Left'. It was
closed 'by all sorts of rough musick'. According to the *London
Evening Post*, the actors 'played their parts with great Droll-
ery'.[96]

Horace Walpole believed that the literature 'setting forth
popery and slavery in their true colours' had 'a wonderful
effect upon the minds of the commonalty', and there seems
little doubt that the anti-Catholic pageants, which were also
reported at London, Bristol, and Wrotham in Kent, were
celebrated with gusto.[97] Even so, one is still left with the
nagging question of why anti-Catholicism struck such a
responsive chord in 1745 when it did not in 1715.

Part of the reason, I would suggest, is conjunctural. Anti-
Catholicism was so deeply embedded in the English consciousness that it almost approximated to a *mentalité*. But, for it to
be a political force, much depended upon its articulation. In
the 1680s anti-Catholicism assumed such urgency because it
was linked in the popular mind with subversive forces at Court
and with the genuine threat of invasion. But during the early

his Diocese . . . *Occasion'd by our Present Dangers* (London, 1745), p. 26; J. J.
Majende, *A Sermon Preach'd at the Cathedral Church of St. Paul, London, on
Sunday Morning the 10th of November 1745* (London, 1745), p. iv.

[95] See my 'Popular Disaffection', the *London Journal* (1975), 15–16, 23–4.
[96] *London Evening Post*, 2–5 Nov. 1745; *Felix Farley's Bristol Journal*, 9
Nov. 1745.
[97] BL, Add. MS 9183, fo. 94; *St. James's Evening Post*, 12–14 Nov. 1745; *Bath
Journal*, 11 Nov. 1745; *True Patriot*, 3 Dec. 1745.

years of the Hanoverian accession this particular set of linkages was ruptured. First, anti-Catholicism was invoked in a highly partisan manner, by a Whig party closely identified with 'foreigners', whether Dissenting, Dutch, or Hanoverian. By contrast, the image of the Stuarts was still suffused with a nostalgia for Queen Anne, and because it was widely believed that she was sympathetic to a restoration of her brother, the exiled House of Stuart was not regarded as especially alien. Indeed, James III was regularly toasted as the 'Best Born Briton', and to many appeared a more suitable choice than the German Elector whose bearing and culture did not make him a very charismatic alternative.[98] Secondly, the threat of a foreign invasion from the Catholic powers of Europe was not as urgent after the War of Spanish Succession, and there was some justification in believing that a Tory-Jacobite regime would keep France at arm's length. Despite Whig propaganda, the treaty of Utrecht was not a capitulation to French power.

By the 1740s, however, the chain of associations which had made anti-Catholicism such a potent political force had returned. Britain was now locked in an armed struggle with France and Spain in which the future of the imperial economy was at stake. Moreover, there was every reason to believe that a Stuart restoration would tip the balance in favour of the Bourbon powers. Few sections of the crowd had much love for George II; the furore over Dettingen had revealed that. But Protestantism, patriotism, and empire was an intoxicating mix. On the eve of the rebellion, Lord Chesterfield noted how public bellicosity had centred around Cape Breton. It had become 'the darling object of the whole nation, it is ten times more so than ever Gibraltar was, and people are laying in their claims, and protesting already against the restitution of it upon any account'.[99] Admiral Vernon, of course, had done much to create this mood, and he remained very much in the public eye. As commander of the Channel fleet, he was responsible for keeping France at bay during the invasion scares of 1744 and 1745. In fact, he retained his visibility during the early months of the Forty-Five by flying the colours off the Downs.

[98] See my 'Popular Protest', *Past and Present* (1978), 97–7.
[99] HMC Trevor MSS, p. 127.

When he did finally strike his flag in December 1745, Fielding reported, 'the Spirits of the Nation' sank with it.[100]

The Forty-Five thus saw a resurgence of popular loyalism. The government, and indeed influential sections of the opposition, successfully mobilized the anti-Catholic, libertarian, and chauvinist sympathies of the crowd against the rebels. At Newcastle, for example, where Jacobite sentiments were openly expressed in 1715, the king's birthday was celebrated in 1745 'with Ringing of Bells which continued the whole Day'. An 'inexpressible Joy and Satisfaction appear'd in the Face of the Inhabitants of the Town', reported the Tory *Courant*, 'All Sorts of People seem'd to treat with a just Indignation any Attempts of an Invasion from our Enemies.'[101] When the news that the Jacobite army was in retreat reached Altrincham, near Manchester, in February 1746, a mock pretender dressed up in plaid was carried through the streets and ceremoniously executed. Similar effigy burnings were reported on Cumberland's birthday two months later, together with joyous celebrations of Culloden, to a point where the royal duke vied with Vernon in popularity.[102] In this militant mood there was little room for equivocal loyalism, and even less for the conditional loyalism of those Tories and independents who had preferred militias to volunteer regiments and had campaigned for political reform to reconcile the nation to the Hanoverian regime. Such reservations were regarded as disruptive, if not subversive, and were remembered in the 1747 election and beyond. Before the large electorates of Bristol and the metropolis they cut little ice.

Yet, if the crowd rallied to the Crown during the Forty-Five and its aftermath, it did not do so indefinitely. Its chauvinist

---

[100] *London Evening Post*, 12–15 Oct., 31 Oct.–2 Nov. 1745; *True Patriot*, 7 Jan. 1746.

[101] *Newcastle Courant*, 26 Oct.–2 Nov. 1745: two men in the town, Daniel Farnes and James Bristowe, were detained 'on suspicion of treasonable practices', but there is no further evidence of disaffection in the Quarter Sessions record. See Tyne and Wear Archives, 540/5 (Quarter Sessions Order Book 1743–7).

[102] *London Evening Post*, 13–15 Feb., 22–4 Apr., 1–3 May 1746; *Newcastle Courant*, 12–19, 19–26 Apr., 26 Apr.–3 May, 19–26 July, 4–11 Oct. 1746; Lewis (ed.), *Correspondence of Walpole*, xix. 255, xxxvii. 266. Kathleen Wilson first drew my attention to Cumberland's popularity in the provinces.

and libertarian instincts proved too volatile a mix to ensure the government unquestioned allegiance. The demonstrations that accompanied the Westminster contest of 1749 revealed that the Court could not take the crowd for granted and that aristocratic arrogance and a flouting of popular justice could badly backfire. Similarly the ruckus over the Jew Bill revealed how tetchy the populace could be about its national and religious identity. To be sure, the hostility to Jewish naturalization was probably most intense in the metropolis, where the issue was fuelled by an antipathy to the moneyed interest and to the intrusion of Jewish hawkers in the marketplace. Samuel Martin reported to Thomas Birch 'that the clamour against the Jew Bill is much greater in London than amongst the Gross of the people whom he had met with in his Journey to Cornwall'.[103] And he was probably right. Not only did the Southwark mob burn a jew in effigy, but the City rank and file rejected a hitherto popular alderman and brewer who had supported Jewish naturalization in Parliament. Even so, the letters to Philip Yorke reveal that the clamour had penetrated the provincial towns and countryside, with bishops besieged by angry clergy, and hostile Addresses or Instructions coming from centres such as Bristol, Coventry, Devizes, Gloucester, Exeter, and York, not to mention those penned at the Midland and Home County assizes.[104] As Thomas Secker noted, the Jew Bill had 'not only raised very great clamours amongst the ignorant and disaffected, but hath offended great numbers of both understandings and disposition'.[105]

In 1753 the political dispositions of the street were in line with the middling councillors and petitioners of the large, independent towns, as they had been during the agitation of war and over Vernon in 1739–42. In the run-up to the next war, however, the politics of the crowd and the middling sort diverged. Following the loss of Minorca to the French in 1756, the government published edited dispatches incriminating Admiral Byng, and were happy to witness his burning in effigy

---

[103] BL, Add. MS 35,398, fo. 178.
[104] Ibid., fos. 120, 125, 128. *London Evening Post*, 7–9 Aug., 20–3 Oct., 3–6, 8–10, 15–17, 17–20 Nov. 1753; *Read's Weekly Journal*, 27 Oct. 1753; *Public Advertiser*, 7 Nov. 1753; *Jackson's Oxford Journal*, 29 Sept., 17 Nov. 1753.
[105] BL, Add. MS 35,592, fos. 84, 102.

at several places along the south coast, at Whitechapel,
Newgate, and Tower Hill in London, at Higham Ferrers,
Bewdley, Dudley, and as far north as Leeds and Tynemouth.[106]
At the north-western port the captains

got a Tar-Barrel dressed up as the Effigy of a certain person, with a
laced Coat and Hat, fine Wig, &c, and having exposed him thro' the
Place in a very ignominious Manner, burnt him at the high End of the
Town, in view of a prodigious Number of Spectators, who expressed
the highest Satisfaction, drank Confusion to him, and all such
Traitors to their King and Country.[107]

Similarly, up the river at Newcastle-upon-Tyne,

an admirable Admiral was carried through this Town in Effigy, riding
on an Ass, preceded by a White Standard, on which was the following
Inscription: *Oh! back your Sails, for G—d's Sake, a Shot may hit the
Ship.* On each Side of his Hat was *Bung*; and round his Waist was, *This
is the Villain that would not fight.* The Procession ended in the Flesh
Market (to which Place it was with the Greatest Difficulty they got
him, the Populace pulling him several Times from the Ass) where a
Gallows was erected, and a large Fire kindled; and after hanging some
Time in the most disgraceful Manner imaginable, amongst a number-
less Crowd of Spectators, he was let down and burnt to Ashes, and
even those very Ashes strew'd about the Streets.[108]

As these and other reports reveal, Byng was ceremoniously
executed as a traitor in many places, most, though not all,
being ports. His rough treatment drew upon the same passions
that had brought Vernon popularity: a nascent nationalism; a
strong strain of anti-Catholicism, accentuated by fears of a
French invasion and an impending struggle for the Atlantic
world; a love of naval valour and gallantry; even a contempt for
political intrigue and duplicity, for just as Vernon was thought
to transcend factionalism, so it was rumoured that Byng hoped
to use his connections to evade culpability.[109] It was only as
further disclosures about the fall of Minorca and ministerial

---

[106] *York Courant*, 3 Aug. 1756; *Northampton Mercury*, 23 Aug. 1756;
Boddely's Bath Journal, 2, 9, 16, 23 Aug. 1756.
[107] *Berrow's Worcester Journal*, 5 Aug. 1756.
[108] Ibid., 12 Aug. 1756.
[109] See the epigram ibid., 15 July 1756, in which Byng declines to engage the
French, saying 'Sudden death I abhor; while there's life, there is hope: / Let me
'scape but the Gun, I can buy off the Rope'.

disinformation became known that the opposition was able to focus public attention upon government culpability. Even then sections of the crowd were not prepared to let Byng off the hook. As the story broke in London, West End society was entertained by ballad-singers chanting 'To the block with Newcastle, and the yard arm with Byng'.[110] Outside Portsmouth, thousands assembled with pitchforks and clubs 'in hopes of paying their respects to Admiral Byng' as he was escorted to London.[111] As Dr Johnson observed, 'The very mob discovered the name of Byng to be bandied round the kingdom only as a bubble to their proper indignation.'[112] Thanks to popular credulity and a vociferously chauvinist crowd, the government won critical time to rally its own parliamentary forces. It successfully mobilized the nationalism of the crowd in an effort to forestall a full Patriot critique of the crisis. Unlike what happened in the row over Jenkins's Ear, anti-Catholic fervour and gut chauvinism did not converge with the reformist inclinations of the parliamentary opposition and its urban allies.

What particular role, then, did the crowd play in early eighteenth-century politics? What impact did its interventions have on the character and pattern of extra-parliamentary politics in the Augustan and Georgian eras?

Clearly, we cannot relegate the crowd to a marginal role in this period. Its cumulative presence was very visible before the advent of Wilkes, even in the provinces. The demonstrations that beset England at the Hanoverian accession reveal that crowd actions were not a metropolitan problem alone: politics engaged the attention of artisans and labourers in most large centres as well as in the manufacturing districts of the South-West, East Anglia, the Midlands, and the North. Wilkes, in other words, was not the first to mobilize the meaner sort. The boundaries of the informal political nation had broadened dramatically long before that political adventurer taunted the Establishment. Wilkes simply perfected the art of playing to

---

[110] W. J. Smith (ed.), *The Grenville Papers* (4 vols.; London, 1852), i. 172; see also the ballad *The Block and the Yard Arm*, particularly the lines 'Nor can his vile Treason to you be strange News / Since so lately he sold his God to the Jews / The block for Newcastle and the yard arm for Byng.'

[111] *Berrow's Worcester Journal*, 12 Aug. 1756.

[112] Cited by Tunstall, *Admiral Byng*, p. 183.

the popular gallery. He knew how to play the fool in a ceremonial age.[113]

Ceremonialism, in fact, provides the key to understanding plebeian politics in the eighteenth century. If we concentrate upon the 'hostile outburst' alone, we lose much of the texture of street politics and the particular power-structures which at once defined and constrained plebeian interventions. Crowd actions were often closely synchronized to a well-defined but flexible calendar of political anniversaries or to the electoral process. They were regularly cast in a festive idiom which resembled the earlier traditions of misrule, within conventions which anticipated popular approval or disapproval, tolerated a certain amount of carnivalesque licence, and at the same time sought to dignify the political order and reaffirm reciprocities between rich and poor. These basic structures remained part of the popular canon for over a century. They were not substantially displaced until new forms of extra-parliamentary association, developed first by middle-class radicals and democrats, were taken over by artisans during the age of revolution.

Yet, if there were crucial continuities in the forms of collective action, its political significance changed. Crowd interventions may have harked back to earlier forms of misrule, but they did so within a very different class context. Older patterns of paternalism were breaking down. The growth of the putting-out system and the decline of the guilds gave the labouring trades considerable control over the labour process and their leisure time, and facilitated, as Edward Thompson has emphasized,[114] a revival of plebeian culture and a re-assertion of customary perquisites as rights. Plebeian self-assertion is most evident in the demands for a moral economy of subsistence and in the efforts to bargain for better working conditions within a modified system of industrial protection. Within the terrain of politics, where a divided political élite had itself created and courted a broader audience, such assertiveness was embodied in the tradition of the free-born

[113] See John Brewer's excellent treatment of this theme in *Party Ideology*, ch. 9.
[114] Thompson, 'Patrician Society', *Journal of Social History* (1974), 382–405.

Englishmen which legitimized rights of assembly and redress. Given the propertied classes' own suspicion of standing armies, the libertarian impulses of the crowd had perforce to be tolerated.

The theatre of politics which blossomed in the eighteenth century thus involved a complex dynamic of social forces. It cannot be written off as a simple ruse of power, a licensed opportunity for plebeian catharsis. Certainly every national anniversary was a potential poor man's holiday; and the opportunities for festive venality sometimes threatened to be diversionary, as Marat's remark at the opening of this Chapter suggested. Moreover, political ceremonial afforded opportunities for upper-class grandeur and for the expression of strong local dependencies. Client crowds were, after all, part of the political theatre. They sometimes epitomized the vibrant force of subject economies as much as the crude purchase of plebeian muscle. Yet at the same time the demystifying potential of misrule could be subversive. It could unsettle the assurance of England's rulers, and strip the political order of its symbolic supports. In the early part of the century, in particular, the Hanoverian-Whig supremacy was perilously fragile, rocked by a sea of sedition, and for several years both parties may be said to have lost control of the popular constituency they created. Between 1710 and 1722 political disaffection proved extremely difficult to accommodate by ceremonial means. It required a continual resort to coercive measures and stronger legal sanctions against riotous assembly. It was not until the mid-decades of the century that the dominant classes regained some of their assurance in dealing with the crowd, and then in terms that recognized its crucial presence. As Lord Egmont reminded the Commons in 1751 when it was taunted with the spectacle of crowds hallowing for 'Murray and Liberty', 'a general popular opinion, however founded, ought never to be neglected by those in authority; and a wise magistrate will never persist in a measure if not absolutely necessary, which he finds to be against the general bent of the people'.[115]

[115] Cobbett, *Parliamentary History of England*, xiv. 1070.

Henry Fielding, like Egmont, recognized the critical position of the crowd in extra-parliamentary politics.[116] But he also noted that the interventions of the crowd were essentially reactive, defining the limits of the possible. In fact, his remarks serve to remind us that we may overplay the autonomy of plebeian politics. Profane, sacrilegious, the crowd remained dependent upon groups above it for its politics. It proved incapable of breaking out of the libertarian tradition which constrained it and allowed it a subaltern role. Crowds challenged political authority, but their challenges tended to be transgressive rather than subversive, and were often inspired by other dissident groups. Thus while street politics were shaped in part by a class 'field of force' in which polite culture was pitted against plebeian, it cannot be reduced to those polarities.[117] Popular politics was not the people's own; it was a site of struggle between contending groups, Whig and Tory, Court and Country, middling and patrician, for popular allegiances, and its boundaries were being transformed by market practices. Vernon's popularity, for example, may in large part be attributable to the success of the patriot press in bringing his exploits to the public attention and interpreting their significance for a socially diverse audience. Hence it is crucial to understand the particular way in which political ideology was formulated and the purchase it may have had. Without some sense of the ideological terrain of the popular, we fall into an essentialist fallacy. The plebeian crowd was not intrinsically oppositionist or anti-establishment, even if it showed a hearty disrespect for the polite world and its immediate local rulers. Strongly nativistic, it could be mobilized for King and Country or for a very different kind of patriotism. Much depended upon the projection of political ideas and personalities and the particular resonance this had in the plebeian imagination and experience. On the whole, the crowd helped create the space for a libertarian politics in the first half of the eighteenth century, one from which the urban middling sort could profit.

[116] *Covent Garden Journal*, 13, 20 June 1753; see also the comments of Arthur Murphy in the *Gray's Inn Journal*, 16 Mar. 1756.

[117] See Thompson, 'Eighteenth-Century English Society', *Social History* (1978), 133–66.

It was not until 1780, when anti-Catholic crowds threatened to discredit the new forms of associational power that the radicals had created, that popular interventions were eyed with a new scepticism. By then radicals heeded Marat's words about the idolatry of power and political revelry. Mobs recalled an older, ceremonial order, not the new dawn of Liberty.

Conclusion

Iᴛ is currently fashionable to minimize the significance of urban politics in the early Hanoverian era. Despite the continuing research on electoral politics and the varied forms of extra-parliamentary action, historians have been remarkably reluctant to accord the large cities, with the exception of London, any salient role in the reign of the first two Georges. Part of the reason for this lies in the weight of historiographical tradition, the continuing obsession with the high political manœuvres in Parliament, with but token glances at what was happening outside. Part of it may be attributed to the interpretative orthodoxy laid down some twenty years ago by Holmes and Plumb which saw the vitality of the Augustan era ossify with the growth of political stability under Walpole and the resurgence of landed political power. Within this framework, opposition to Whig oligarchy was largely a matter of 'mutinies within the guarrison', ins versus outs, or it was confined to those declining forces in society—the minor gentry for example, or the rump of Tory patricians—who were increasingly excluded from influence and preferment. Even those who have objected to this sociological analysis, whether on grounds of the continued resonance of dynastic conflict or the resilience of landed Toryism, have obscured the political contribution of the cities. Scarcely a factor in J. C. D. Clark's reverential, patriarchal world, they are firmly subordinated to Tory electoral strategy in Linda Colley's. Both stress voters' dependence upon landed grandees and deference to their leadership.

Yet the political experience of the cities, I have argued, was both vital and complex. Judged by the usual psephological criteria more seats were contested in the towns and cities with 1,000 voters or more in the Hanoverian era than in the Augustan. Relatively few of these 28 constituencies were dominated by landed patrons (Chester, Gloucester, Newcastle,

Northampton, and Nottingham being the principal exceptions), and those that were, required firm and vigorous management and considerable attention to constituent wishes. Most of the large towns and cities were open, independent boroughs in which voters were tuned in to national as well as local issues. In the few cases where I have been able to gauge the participation of voters, it appears to have been extraordinarily high—in London, Bristol, and Norwich, in the region of 60–80 per cent. In the hurly-burly of city politics patron–client relations were conditional and reciprocal, complicated by strikingly rapid turnovers and strong partisanship. Even in the more venal constituencies heavy purses could not guarantee allegiance, as Chandos discovered in Hereford.

The large towns and cities, then, hardly conform to the accepted pattern of electoral deference and lethargy. Contemporaries understood them to represent, along with the counties, the independent voice of the electorate, the true sense of the political nation at large, and self-consciously differentiated them from the petty boroughs under ministerial or landed patronage.[1] Indeed, cumulatively, the large urban constituencies registered the growing alienation of the nation from the Walpolean regime after the Excise crisis and the recovery of Whig popularity after the Forty-Five, when the stigma of Jacobitism and irresponsible libertarianism plagued the opposition.

But the large towns did not simply reflect the sense of the political nation at large. At critical moments, they were also important sites for the creation of a major challenge to the Whig regime. Following the lead of London, the large towns and cities petitioned Parliament and issued Instructions to their Members, demanding a purification of the political system and a return to the more open politics of the Augustan era. The scale and frequency of these Instructions has often been underestimated by historians. So, too, has the thrust of their demands. The Instructions of 1739–41 and 1756 were not simply designed to secure the independence of Parliament from executive influence and control. They were also intended to make the representatives themselves more accountable to the electorate, to revive the rights of smaller men in playing an

[1] See the *Craftsman*, 25 July 1741.

active role in the political process. 'It is a happy thing for a
Country, when their Governors are governed by the Voice of
the People;' wrote one commentator at the time of the Excise
crisis, 'but still more happy when the Constitution of their
Government is such that their Governors must necessarily
regulate their Measures by the Inclinations of the People.'[2]
True, urban spokesmen were reluctant to advance demotic
politics beyond insisting upon frequent parliaments, greater
safeguards against bribery and dependency, and the right to
instruct members. Their demands did not usually extend to
the disfranchisement of rotten boroughs or to a redistribution
of seats. Nor indeed, to an extension of the franchise, although
John Shebbeare, one of the early authors of the *Monitor*, noted
that whereas 'every Subject' had 'an equal Claim to Freedom
and the Privileges of the Realm', not more than a third had 'the
Right of voting for their Representatives'.[3] Like some post-
1760 radicals, mid-century reformers were rather ambivalent
about extending the vote to individuals whose poverty and
dependence might simply augment the influence of the
powerful. But some of these demands, notably the under-
representation of London, the enfranchisement of important
manufacturing centres, and the disfranchisement of the 'beggarly corrupt boroughs', were certainly mooted at the time.[4] It
was not that urban reformers lacked vision or a rudimentary
radical consciousness. It was rather that until the 1750s, at
least, they were still unconvinced that such radical, controversial, and potentially divisive demands were necessary.
Government majorities did dwindle in 1734 and 1741. The
notion that mid-eighteenth century governments were electorally unassailable took time to take root. Urban politicians
might be accused of a certain naïvety and optimism, but we
should not ignore their reforming impulse.

One of the most interesting aspects of this agitation was the
willingness to temper party differences in the pursuit of a
common goal, the elimination of Walpole and the system he

---

[2] *Political State of Great Britain*, v. 440–1. I would like to thank Kathleen
Wilson of Harvard University for this reference.

[3] [John Shebbeare], *A Fifth Letter to the People of England* (London, 1757),
p. 17.

[4] *Common Sense*, 10 Jan. 1741; *Protester*, 22 Sept. 1753; *London Evening
Post*, 7–9 Nov. 1754.

epitomized and helped to create. This was not an easy task. The religious conflicts of the late seventeenth and early eighteenth century remained very much a battleground in the large towns and cities, particularly in constituencies where nonconformity was socially and politically visible. They created strong patterns of party partisanship, sustained through neighbourly, familial, and craft affiliations, as well as through friendly societies and political clubs, that were abandoned only with reluctance. Indeed, despite Walpole's refusal to grant full citizenship to Protestant Dissenters, the memory of the High Church attack upon occasional conformity and Dissenting academies was strong enough to keep the Dissenting communities officially loyal to the Whig regime.[5] But in 1734 and 1741 opposition Whigs did ally and support Tory candidates and vice versa. The particular nature of this Country alliance varied from town to town. It depended upon the availability of suitable candidates, the strategies of political societies such as Bristol's Stedfast Society and the Independent Electors of Coventry and Westminster, and the sensitivity of the electorate to calls for the abandonment of party voting by such newspapers as the *Craftsman* and the *London Evening Post*. But there was something of the Country moment in the towns, as there was in the counties, and it was not simply confined to the South-East.[6] In some instances it did breed voter truculence, a willingness to question older patterns of influence that could be as threatening to Tory patrons as it was to Whig. This Country experiment has been overlooked by recent historians in their eagerness to stress the longevity of party allegiances. The point is not that party affiliations were unimportant down to 1750; rather, that their survival was uneven, susceptible to ruptures, and by no means synchronized to developments with Parliament. Historians tend to read party from the top down.[7] We ought to investigate the particular concordance between high and low, between Westminster and the localities.

[5] Langford, *The Excise Crisis*, p. 117.
[6] Ibid. 114–15.
[7] J. C. D. Clark, 'The Decline of Party, 1740–1760', *English Historical Review*, 93 (July 1978), 499–527, and 'A General Theory of Party, Opposition and Government, 1688–1832', *Historical Journal*, 23/2 (1980), 295–325.

What was particularly important about this Country moment was its sociological and ideological dimension. The Country moment was not a politics of nostalgia, a desire by a backwoods gentry to return to an Arcadian world of unquestioned landed authority.[8] The main impetus for reform came from the large towns and cities, generated in the first instance by the merchants and the middling sort. There were several reasons why this was so. The oligarchical drift of Whig politics was most keenly felt in the larger towns and cities where there had been dramatic attempts to narrow the franchise and cobble freeman democracy. In Liverpool, the leading advocate of the freeman of Common Hall, Thomas Bootle, was defeated by the sharp practice of the Whig-dominated Corporation interest in alliance with a Whig-dominated Commons. In Shrewsbury, the electorate was ruthlessly pared down from 1,900 to 300 voters, making it a Whig haven. As we have seen, Whigs advocated a reduction of the electorate in Bristol, Norwich, and London. In these last two cities they also sought to buttress patrician authority by allowing the aldermanic courts a veto over the freemen's assemblies. Pelham's comment in 1745 that it was absolutely necessary to ensure that the 'chief Magistrates [were] vested with a Power to give a check to the Extravagances of the People' struck hard at freemen's rights and their sense of dignity.[9]

In London, of course, the question of the aldermanic veto was closely associated with the rise of the moneyed interest and its political and economic ramifications. Londoners were not irrevocably opposed to the institutions of public credit. They did not reject *tout court* the values of an exchange society. Indeed, they believed that good business practice and fair trading not only were compatible with civic responsibility but were its essential complements. Sir John Barnard argued as much in the debate on the aldermanic veto in 1745, noting that the Common Council was the epitome of public spiritedness because the trade and business of most of its members 'must always in a great measure depend upon the love and esteem of their neighbours in the city'.[10] Men like Barnard had a good

---

[8] For this view see Kramnick, *Bolingbroke and His Circle*.
[9] Almon, *Debates and Proceedings*, ii: 97.
[10] Cobbett, *Parliamentary History of England*, xiii. 1146.

regard for 'the real and honest Creditors of the Publick', and would have shared Defoe's hope that public stock could attain the same solidity as landed wealth. What they deplored was the speculative spirit of the Exchange and its pernicious effects upon private credit and civic felicity. In their eyes the financial revolution not only devalued merchanting and turned trading heads to quick profits, but also reinforced political oligarchy. Most plutocrats with political ambitions soon quit the hurly-burly of city politics for the safer havens of smaller, manageable boroughs, providing the ministry with a solid phalanx of supporters. Those that did stay strove to circumscribe the still resonant traditions of civic democracy that made the City a paradigm of political independence.

The struggle between the moneyed interest and the City informed London politics for at least two generations and shaped, as we have seen in Chapter 4, its social configurations. Outside London the financial scandals of the Walpolean era and the activities of financial interlopers in parliamentary elections certainly added to anti-ministerial rancour and exposed for many the degradation of public standards that was regarded as the hallmark of Robinocracy. But the political effects of the financial revolution in the provinces were largely symbolic and indirect. As Julian Hoppit has recently shown, before 1770 the British economy remained too regional and unintegrated for one to be able to talk of national financial crises.[11] Consequently, the tensions between land and credit, or high finance and trade, were strongly mediated by local factors and did not generate nation-wide movements for their resolution.

However, there were issues upon which opposition groups in London and the provinces could build. One pertinent problem was the relative tax advantages that traders and merchants might win from the state. The attempt by Walpole to extend the taxes on excise to include wine and tobacco in 1733 was strongly resisted by a wide variety of traders in towns as diverse as Bristol, Nottingham, and Lewes, and certainly took the first minister by surprise. He likened the country gentle-men to their sheep, who 'layd down to be taxed at quietly and

---

[11] Julian Hoppit, 'Financial Crises in Eighteenth-century England', *Economic History Review*[2], 39/1 (1980), 39–58.

complain no more than they when they are shorn;' but 'touch
only a bristle of the hog of trade', he went on, 'and he is sure to
squeal and bite till all his neighbours believe him ill treated
whether in reality he is or not'.[12] Despite the often conflicting
interests of trading and manufacturing lobbies and the pull of
religious affiliation—the Dissenters, for example, did not
desert the administration over the Excise Bill—the 1733 crisis
saw a noticeable flexing of political muscle by the middling
sort. In Bristol the crisis saw the first signs of a shift in
traditional political alignments and a rejection of the leadership of the Merchant Venturers. Only in places like Norwich
where Whig brokerage paid economic dividends in the dominant textile industry, did the furore over the Excise have a less
dramatic impact.

The other issue which animated the towns in the mid-
century era and served to alienate wide sections of the
middling merchants and tradesmen from the Whig regime was
the future of American and Caribbean trade. In his early years
in office Walpole had managed to satisfy a wide range of
trading and manufacturing interests with his tariff reforms and
strategic concessions to sectional interests. However ruthless
Walpole's quest for power, many tradesmen identified with his
policy of peace, prosperity, and dynastic stability. But as the
transatlantic trade rose in importance, many baulked at the
government's foreign policy which seemed unnecessarily
expensive, Byzantine, deferential to Hanover, and neglectful of
Britain's emerging trade in the West. In London the issue was
raised in the early years of George II's reign and was taken up
by the opposition press as a tactical challenge to Walpole's
leadership. But it was not until ten years later, as the
transatlantic economy began to progress in leaps and bounds,
that the merchants' frustrations prompted vigorous protests
against the government's accommodating attitude to the
Bourbon powers.

The opposition to the tax proposals of 1732 and 1733 and the
demand for a more bellicose mercantilism might have been
interpreted simply as sectional campaigns had it not been for

[12] Cited by John Styles, 'A Landed Ruling Class? Interest Groups, Lobbying
and Parliament in Eighteenth-Century England' (unpublished paper, 1986),
p. 1; Langford, *The Excise Crisis*, pp. 113–14.

their overall political significance and the way in which they were projected in the press. The Excise and to a lesser extent the Salt Tax of 1732 were successfully portrayed as a massive assault upon English liberties as much as impositions upon the 'productive' classes that brought dubious benefits to the landed proprietors. Panic-mongering aside, this articulation played upon the government's oligarchical record and the series of scandals which sullied its political integrity. Similarly, the campaign for a war with Spain in 1738 and 1739 exploited the anti-Catholicism and nascent nationalism of the average Englishman and went a long way towards impugning the ministry's oft-repeated claim to be the guardian of Protestantism and liberty. Equally significant, the Excise Bill and the government's response to mercantile militancy, the Convention of El Pardo, were both pushed through Parliament in the face of public clamour by exploiting every ounce of patronage at the government's disposal. Although the government remained reliant upon some country gentlemen for its majorities, in the popular mind the government's insensitivity to public wishes became associated with the sinews of patronage and the need for political change. It is no accident that the major crises of the 1730s led to demands for political reform, especially since the eventual defeat of the government over the Excise challenged, but did not topple, its electoral supremacy.

The Country programme of the 1730s and 1740s, then, was not simply an opportunistic sortie by Bolingbroke and opposition Whigs to harness the support of country gentlemen and disaffected merchants and manufacturers by serving up a traditional medley of political demands with a blue-water militancy. Patriotism, nationalism, and commercial expansion were more closely intertwined than this interpretation suggests and continued to resonate into the 1750s.[13] Admiral Vernon's immense popularity underlined the way in which patriotism and bellicose mercantilism could be intoxicatingly

[13] H. T. Dickinson, in his important biography of Bolingbroke, tends to downplay the importance of commercial expansion in Country reasoning, although his recent discussion of popular politics goes some way towards revising his early views: see his *Bolingbroke* (London, 1970), ch. 12, and 'Popular Politics in the Age of Walpole', in Black (ed.), *Britain in the Age of Walpole*, pp. 45–68.

mixed, just as Pitt's subsequent career emphasized its continued relevance to the political nation.

What is also important about these colourful personalities is the light they shed upon urban political culture in mid-eighteenth century England. The nation-wide demonstrations in favour of Vernon would not have been possible without a buoyant and resilient press in London and the provinces which brought to a wide audience the Caribbean exploits of the admiral, and the songs, poems, acrostics, pageants, and demonstrations which these adventures generated. Equally, the celebration of Vernon's birthday and victories could not have been so vigorous or colourful without the existence of a political calendar of state and royal anniversaries upon which it could draw for inspiration. What one sees in the Vernon demonstrations of the 1740s is the adaptation and secularization of political festival, hitherto polarized around dynastic loyalties and local rivalries, and the attempt to create a rival calendar to Whig orthodoxy. Although some of these demonstrations were redolent of gentry hospitality at election time, organized by local anti-ministerial grandees such as Sir Watkin Williams Wynn, others were promoted by a range of middling groups and societies outside Corporate circles, and very occasionally by poor neighbourhoods. All in all, they were evidence of the increasing complexity of urban political culture.

I do not wish to exaggerate the sophistication of this culture. Outside London, urban politics continued to centre upon the traditional sites of church vestry, chapel, and town hall and revolved around long-standing civic rivalries under the leadership of well-entrenched merchant families. But the opportunities for political discussion and organization were widening. The number of provincial newspapers grew erratically, from around 24 in 1723 to reach a high point of 41 at the time of the Forty-Five, falling to 37 during the Seven Years War. Over the same period their geographical incidence was extended to the North, and some of the principal cities, such as Bristol, Norwich, and Newcastle, featured two rival papers.[14] The circulation of these papers was small—rarely more than 440 copies by week—but provincial readers could avail

[14] G. A. Cranfield, *The Development of the Provincial Newspaper 1700–1760* (Oxford, 1962), p. 21.

themselves of the London tri-weeklies and weeklies, either by subscription or by resorting to the handful of coffee-houses which provided them for their clientele.[15] Alehouses and taverns were also sites for political discussion and controversy, as numerous depositions reveal, and they were much thicker on the ground, constituting 1 house in every 10 in mid-century Bristol.[16] In addition to these obvious centres for sociability, some large towns sported a number of important political clubs, such as the Stedfast and Union in Bristol, both of which appear to have had extensive parochial networks, as well as a cluster of friendly societies, masonic lodges, and charitable societies, many of which had political affiliations.[17]

By the mid-century there were a growing number of sites for political discussion and debate and the potential, at least, to challenge the prevailing conventions of custodial politics. Even so, this potential was not always realized. The large towns and cities remained vulnerable to gentlemanly agree-ments. After 1745, when rival élite factions became increas-ingly disposed to political compromise, or at least unwilling to sustain high electoral expenses, the provincial towns shared some of the characteristics which typified the era as a whole. Even the flourishes of support for Pitt had few local ramifi-cations. It was not until the Wilkite controversies that new clubs and organizations emerged to challenge local hierarchies. In Bristol, for example, the campaign for Wilkes saw the emergence of the Independent Society and a radical platform openly critical of the electoral agreements of the old oligarchy. By 1781 independent freemen were urging their fellows 'not to be bought and sold like Cattle in Smithfield market' and to reject the pressures of the Union and Stedfast clubs and that of

[15] Brewer, *Party Ideology*, ch. 8; for Bristol's coffee-houses see Latimer, *Annals of Bristol*, ii. 240–1.

[16] Latimer calculated that there were 625 alehouse licences issued in 1754, at a time when there were no more than 6,250 houses in the city: see Latimer, *Annals of Bristol*, ii. 235. For evidence of political controversy in alehouses see my 'Popular Disaffection', *London Journal* (1975), 5–27, and 'Popular Jacobitism', pp. 123–41.

[17] On Whig friendly societies in Norwich see my 'Popular Jacobitism'. On the importance of masonic lodges and voluntary hospitals as sites for political action see the essays by John Money and Kathleen Wilson in Eckhart Hellmuth (ed.), *The Transformation of Political Culture in Late Eighteenth-Century England and Germany* (Oxford, forthcoming).

their employers. 'All we can get from them is a scanty maintenance for ourselves and our families, and scarcely that; whilst *they* live in all manner of luxury and get Fortunes besides by the sweat of our brows.'[18] Such class-conscious rhetoric was new to Bristol's political scene, as it was to Newcastle and Norwich.[19] In Bristol, the Walpolean and Pittite eras had seen some interesting departures in popular mobilization and some resistance to the resumption of closed caucus-politics, but little assertiveness on the part of small masters and journeymen.

Even within the metropolis, the electoral presence of the small proprietor remained fragile before Wilkes and the American Revolution. In Westminster the contests of the 1740s saw a dramatic rejection of Court and magnate dependence and a demand for a more open, accountable style of politics. Thus an independent elector from Soho insisted in 1749 upon a candidate 'who will have such a Regard to the Importance of us, his Constituents, as not to attempt to dare to partake of any Amusements or Diversions but such we shall prescribe to him'.[20] But despite this truculence on the part of voters and the mobilization of the popular vote by the middling dissidents of the Independent Electors, Westminster politics once more relapsed under control by grandees. Nor did the initiatives in this West End constituency have substantial reverberations for urban voters elsewhere. Baltimore was nearly toppled in the Surrey by-election of 1742, but largely due to the efforts of the rural rather than urban freeholders. The same was true of Cooke's victory in Middlesex, following the second great Westminster contest of the mid-century. In this instance, Cooke's standing in the county enabled him to tap the resources of old Tory Hundreds and the county townships of Brentford, Enfield, and Ealing.

Psephological analysis is necessarily an imperfect guide to the level of political articulateness in the metropolis. If we

[18] *The Bristol Contest* (Bristol, 1781), p. 9.
[19] Thomas R. Knox, 'Popular Politics and Provincial Radicalism: Newcastle-Upon-Tyne, 1769–85', *Albion*, 11/3 (autumn 1979), 224–41; Albert Goodwin, *The Friends of Liberty* (Cambridge, Mass., 1979), p. 213.
[20] *A True and Impartial Collection of Pieces in Prose and Verse . . . Written and Published on Both Sides . . . during the Contest for the Westminster Election* (London, 1749), p. 6.

look for the broader indices of political engagement in greater London we can show that it involved all walks of life. De Saussure noted that 'workmen habitually begin the day by going to coffee rooms in order to read the latest news', and by 1732 there were 551 coffee-houses for them to frequent, not to mention the common alehouses which also catered to the insatiable appetite for political journalism.[21] By 1722 there were 41 newspaper editions a week, with four dailies, four tri-weeklies, and five weeklies. There was also a heavy trade in broadsides and ballads in local markets, many of them scurrilously critical of government, to a point that one ministerial supporter recommended that 'proper persons be employed to make sevl Ballads & Storys as might Engage ye Ears of ye mob, and those sold by Proper hands to all persons such as Chandlers, Grocers, market people & in short to all Persons yt have anything of Retail trade'.[22] This pulsating world of patterers and garret-printers proved enormously difficult to control. A German visitor to London in 1725 regularly saw a balladeer at Cranbourne Alley off the Strand 'bawling out his Pye Corner pastorals in behalf of Dear Jemmy, Lovely Jemmy'. He was 'astonished at the remissness or lenity of the magistrates in suffering the Pretender's interest to be carried on and promoted in so public and shameful a manner'.[23] What he failed to appreciate was that since 1716 the government had attempted to root out the cells of disaffection, breaking up nonjuring congregations, and harrying Jacobite printers into exile. Without effect. At a time 'when Apprentice Boys pretend to determine the Title and Right of Kings',[24] the government could do little more than prosecute the main offenders and ride out the storm by subsidizing its own propaganda.

The warrants and depositions in the state papers during the

---

[21] Cesar De Saussure, *A Foreign View of England in the Reign of George I and George II*, trans. and ed. Madame von Muyden (London, 1902), pp. 162–3; Maitland, *London*, ii. 719; for common alehouses as sites for political information, see PRO, SP 35/31/296.

[22] PRO, SP 35/30/167–8.

[23] Anon., *A View of London and Westminster, or The Town Spy*, 2nd edn. (London, 1725), cited by William Chappell, *The Ballad Literature in the Olden Time* (3 vols.; London, n.d.), ii. 524.

[24] See charge of Whitlock Bulstrode to the Middlesex Grand Jury, 21 Apr. 1718, printed in *Annals of George I*, iv. 393–413.

reign of George I throw some light on this Jacobite underground and, by extension, upon the politics of the alehouse and market-place. They tend to confirm John Dennis's remark that 'from Westminster to Wapping, go where you will, the conversation turns upon Politics'.[25] But what always sharpened the edge of urban politics in the metropolis and focused its energies was the leadership of the City of London. The City was an enormously complex entity with a strong tradition of independence from Crown and aristocracy that was sustained from the grass roots by the active participation of its freemen and liverymen at all levels of government. Despite the declining economic importance of the civic freedom, its principal representative institutions were vigorously supported. Together with an impressive range of clubs, organized by ward and on a city-wide basis,[26] London remained a vibrant political community, proud of its independence and not amenable to the usual arts of aristocratic influence. Neither Walpole nor his successors were able to control the City, and it remained a constant thorn in the side of government as well as an exemplary, open constituency. Armed with special rights of address to the Crown, its political interventions were crucial to the mobilization of the political nation. And because it was the premier port, its pronouncements assumed a special significance in an era of incipient imperialism and commercial expansion. 'The City of London is so commodiously situated for Trade and hath long carried it on to so considerable an Height', wrote the *Craftsman*,

that it hath always been look'd upon, not only as the *Metropolis*, but the very *Heart* of the Kingdom, from whence the Blood circulates through all Parts of the Body-Politick; and therefore it would be as ridiculous for the Generality of the Nation not to concur with the City of London in all essential Points of Trade as it was for the Limbs, in the Fable, to complain of the Belly's receiving all the Food and Nourishment.[27]

[25] E. N. Hooker (ed.), *The Critical Works of John Dennis* (2 vols.; Baltimore, 1939–43), i. 293.

[26] 'Not a Ward within the City Gates but has its Club, and some two or three', *Fog's Weekly Journal*, 11 Mar. 1732. For the existence of city-wide clubs see Horwitz (ed.), *London Politics*, pp. 1–61, and my 'Centenary of Cheapside', *London Journal* (1985), 51–8.

[27] *Craftsman*, 13 Oct. 1739.

The City's Addresses and Instructions thus assumed a double significance. They represented the voice of the independent sectors of the political nation in an age when such independence was constrained by the structures of government and aristocratic influence. They also represented those commercial interests outside the privileged circle of financiers and trading monopolies who wanted freer trade and greater access to and protection of the transatlantic economy. Although there were always manufacturers and merchants who preferred to approach the government as pressure groups and lobbyists, there were many who approved of a more confrontational approach, especially in periods when the government's larger political priorities appeared to impede progress.

London's stature as the urban vanguard depended a great deal upon this double articulation, but just how this was played out in the cities and large towns varied a good deal. In Norwich Walpole's active promotion of local manufacture effectively constrained the forces of freemen democracy and prevented a Jacobitical Tory party from exploiting the diminution of freemen rights. Norwich only followed London's lead when its growing American trade seemed imperilled by Old Corps policies. In Bristol there was a continual tension between demotic and custodial politics, with a substantial section of the mercantile élite believing that the town's interests were best served by electing MPs with substantial commercial experience and easy access to the corridors of power. Indeed, the rival claims of libertarianism and clientage resonated across the hustings in 1739 and 1754, before the Whig and Tory caucuses closed ranks to immobilize the electorate and promote their own style of oligarchic politics. The concordance of interest and demotic politics, so apparent during the late Walpolean era, proved in retrospect a contingent affair. But it was one that would set precedents for the future, as the politics of discontent during the American war would reveal.

What conclusions, finally, does the urban experience permit about the relationship between politics and social class in the mid-eighteenth century? Can one see, in this era of contested urban elections and substantial popular agitations, the advent of a middle class? Crudely formulated, the answer must be 'No'. The emergence of middle-class politics was essentially the product of the nineteenth-century battle over cash and corn, of a battle between industrial and agrarian capitalism over state protection and economic growth. Even then, it was highly mediated by the symbiotic relationship between high finance and land ownership which dated back to the mid-eighteenth century and by the slow, uneven development of the factory system. In the age of manufacture (as opposed to the factory), the interests of land, trade, and credit were still too regional and particularist for such polarities to occur. Even so, it would be misleading to claim that the mid-century urban experience did not register a growing middling presence in national politics. From the Excise crisis onwards, the interests of the merchants and tradesmen increasingly became part of the political agenda, especially as the transatlantic economy rose in importance. At the same time, the urban opposition to government triggered a debate about the prevailing conventions of political leadership and the rights of middling townsmen to question government policies and, by implication, the boundaries of the 'deliberative constituency' in national politics, both within and outside Parliament. In the 1730s and 1740s, in particular, ministerial spokesmen condemned the presumption of shopkeepers and tradesmen in challenging parliamentary authority and dictating to their representatives through Instructions and Addresses. Could they pretend, asked Lord Egmont, to 'a knowledge of political affairs superior to that of the best, the wisest, the greatest Men of this and former Ages, whom their Education, and whole Turn of Life have adapted and dedicated to the Study of Politics?'[28] Whether they did or not, the middling townsmen, like the mob, were not about to forsake their rights as Englishmen: 'All degrees of people who have leisure and abilities', contended the *Liveryman*, had the right to discuss public affairs and the right to redress, and 'great men of estate' could no longer command allegiance by personal influence and 'artful discourse'.[29]

---

[28] Perceval, *Faction Detected*, p. 109; for a similar line about the political ineptitude and credulity of the people and their susceptibility to opposition panic-mongering see [Horace Walpole], *The Interest of Great Britain steadily Pursued* (London, 1743), p. 59.

[29] Anon., *The Liveryman, or Plain Thoughts on Public Affairs* (London, 1740), p. 9.

If one detects a new assertiveness on the part of urban townsmen in the middle decades of the eighteenth century, to what extent did it entail a challenge to the class parameters of political power? The answer seems to be that the principal focus of discontent was *political* oligarchy. There was no fundamental questioning of aristocratic power and privilege, save perhaps among a minority of crypto-republicans in the metropolis, whose activities were the subject of Lord Egmont's pamphlet in 1743.[30] As long as aristocrats acted responsibly and did not lord it over citizens, they were above criticism. 'While *Great Men* behave with *Propriety* and *Decency*', claimed the *London Evening Post*, 'they are ever treated with all the *Deference* and *Respect* that is *due* to them; not only in a *Time* of *Prosperity*, but even when *Public Affairs* go crosly.'[31] Yet it was increasingly recognized that many aristocrats were the supports for and beneficiaries of a political system that occluded popular rights and liberties. Despite Bolingbroke's endorsement of aristocratic trusteeship, there was a growing feeling that the decadence of the aristocrats had discredited their leadership and encouraged the growth of corruption and servility in political life. Hence urban spokesmen could be quite scornful of the 'genteel sinecures' of army commissions and the venality of Court preferment. 'The Clamour that is rais'd against the exorbitant Salaries annex'd to many Places is at this time particularly most just', wrote 'Anglicus' at the time of Minorca and widespread bread rioting: 'How unreasonable is it that Gentlemen should receive a Thousand Pounds per annum for riding in their Coaches two or three times a week to an Office, when many of their Fellow Creatures are starving for want.'[32] Before 1760 'corruption' was still identified with the Court rather than with the aristocracy, but the identification was by no means clear-cut. In the urban milieu anti-aristocratic invective was beginning to fuel libertarian argument, just as it was beginning to inform the demands for a moral regeneration of the nation by middle-class evangelicals.

---

[30] Perceval, *Faction Detected*, pp. 8–10. Egmont said that the republicans were generally 'Men of an inferior class'.

[31] *London Evening Post*, 7–9 Oct. 1756.

[32] Ibid., 30 Nov.–2 Dec. 1756; see also ibid., 7–9 Oct. 1756 and the satirical Bristol address of 11–13 Jan. 1757.

In one other way mid-century urban politics conflicted with the realities of aristocratic rule. That was in its striving for a more open style of politics. Firmly grounded in a civic tradition of governance, which in London and Norwich involved annual council elections, urban Instructions and Addresses implicitly challenged the custodial politics of the aristocracy by emphasizing attorneyship rather than trusteeship. Similarly, the demands for responsible magistrates and due process, issues raised by the aldermanic veto, the Maidstone affair, and the Habeas Corpus Bill of 1758, questioned aristocratic habits of rule. True, urban political practice did not always measure up to the ideal; not did judicial politics become part of the general urban agenda. But the groundwork was laid for the sharper articulation of these issues under Wilkes.[33] In this respect there is a need to emphasize the urban continuities to eighteenth-century reform, not its sudden efflorescence in the reign of George III, after decades of political stasis. Urban politics in the early Hanoverian era coexisted uneasily with the growth of oligarchy. The relationship between high and low politics was less symbiotic than contradictory, with the cities constituting the major sites of opposition to the Whig regime.

[33] See especially John Brewer, 'The Wilkites and the Law 1763–74; A Study of Radical Notions of Governance', in Brewer and Styles (eds.), *An Ungovernable People*, pp. 128–71.

Bibliography

I. Manuscripts

Avon Central Library, Bristol
  B 5330 (Peter Muggleworth MS)
  B 10162 (Minutes of the Society for the Reformation of Manners 1699–1705)
  Jefferies Collection
  Southwell Papers
Bedford Estate Office, Bloomsbury
  Bedford MSS
  Bedford Election Papers 1749
Bedfordshire Record Office
  Howe MSS
Bodleian Library
  Carte MS 175
  Dashwood MSS
  Rawlinson MSS
Bristol Record Office
  Apprentice Books 1724–56
  Bd/R1/2–3 (Members of Broadmead Baptist Meeting 1727–74)
  Books of Burgesses, vii–xi, 1726–54
  Common Council Proceedings 1722–63
  EP/V/1 (Visitation Books, Bristol, 1754)
  Jarrit Smith Papers
  'A List of the Inhabitants ... who polled for Mr. Freke and Mr. Edwards.' (Typescript of 1715 Bristol Poll)
  Quarter Sessions Dockets 1715–45
  Roslyn Papers
  SF/A1/5–9 (Quaker Men's Meeting 1727–60)
  SF/CAT/1 (Trustees of Quaker Meeting-House 1718)
  Tolzey Books 1703–16
  Vestry Minutes: All Saints, Bristol, 1722–39
                Christchurch 1733–9
                St James 1733–9
                St Philip and St Jacob 1723–39
                St Stephen's 1734–39
  6687 (1) (Lewin's Mead Presbyterian Minute-Book 1692–1774)

British Library
  Additional MSS
    4319 (Birch Papers)
    5853 (Strype Papers)
    9183 (Horace Walpole Papers)
    11275 (Tucker–Forster Correspondence)
    22202 (Strafford Papers)
    27825–6, 27849 (Place Papers)
    27966 (Arderon Papers)
    32689–32945 (Newcastle Papers)
    34712 (Astle Papers)
    35355–598 (Hardwicke Papers)
    43422 (Papers of Sir Benjamin Keene)
    51349–432 (Holland Papers)
    46967–47,137 (Egmont Papers)
  Egerton MS 1959 (Warburton Papers)
  Egerton MSS 3456–40 (Holdernesse Papers)
  Hargrave MS 139 (Notes on London Politics)
  Lansdowne MS 509 (Scrutiny to the Westminster By-Election 1749)
  Loan 29/204 (Harley Papers)
  Stowe MS 354
Cambridge University Library
  Cholmondley Papers
  Madden Collection
Chatsworth House, Derbyshire
  Chatsworth MSS
Corporation of London Record Office
  Apprenticeship Indentures of the Chamberlain's Court c.1720–40
  Books of Common Hall 1738–63
  Court of Lieutenancy Minute-Books 1710–63
  Journals of the Court of Common Council 1714–63
  Repertories of the Court of Aldermen 1714–63
  MS 64.1 (On the Manner of Holding Wardmotes)
  MS 64.2 (Notes of Committee Set Up to Investigate the Elections in Broad Street, Cheap, and Tower wards 1711–17)
  MS 70.2 (Accounts for Lord Mayor's Banquet 1727)
  MS 77.3 (Poll-Books for Common Council Election in Tower ward 1717)
  MS 186.7 (Subscription for Relief of Soldiers in HM Forces 1745)
  Misc. MS 25.18 (Notes Concerning Qualification of Ward Voters)
  Misc. MS 31.12 (Notes on Aldermanic Elections)
  Misc. MS 34.5 (Scrutiny Papers, Common Council Election, Queenhithe ward, 1710)

Misc. MS 83.3 (Ward Lists, 1721, and a Canvasser's List for Walbrook ward 1714)

Misc. MS 146.6 (Scrutiny Book, Cripplegate Without, 1722/3)

Misc. MS 149.12 (Letters addressed to James Hodges, Town Clerk, 1759–61)

Misc. MS 172.7 (Petition that Members of the East India Company Should be Compelled to Become City Freemen)

Misc. MS 241.1 (Report of Common Council Committee to Investigate Broad Street and Langbourn Elections 20 July 1714)

Misc. MS 248.1 (Scrutiny Books for Aldermanic Election in Langbourn ward, 1712)

Small Box MS 23, no. 31 (1702 Petition to Have Members of the United East India Company Take the City Freedom)

Small Box MS 25, no. 7 (Questions Addressed to City Recorder in 1724 Concerning Wardmote and Freeman Franchise)

Small Box MS 30, no. 9 (Proceedings of Committee to Investigate Common Council Election in Cheap ward 1711)

Companies Boxes, 1, 2, 3, and 12

Alchin Box D/32 (Subscribers to the Loyalist Declaration of 4 October 1745)

Alchin Box M/LX (Minutes of Committee to Investigate the Disrupted Election in Bread Street ward 1718)

Sessions Files

Sessions Papers

Dr Williams's Library

MS 34.4 (John Evans' List of Dissenting Congregations 1715–29)

MS 38.18 (Revd Samuel Palmer's account of the Dissenting Interest in London 1695–1731)

MS 73 (General Baptist Church, Barbican)

East India House, London

L/AG/14/5/328 (Ledgers on East India Stock and Bonds 1749–51)

Essex Record Office

D/DM A7 (Earl Fitzwalter's Household Accounts in London)

Q/SB (Quarter Sessions Papers)

Greater London Record Office

Acc. 790/81 (MS poll of Middlesex By-Election 1750)

Acc. 1085 (Election Diary of Sir Roger Newdigate 1747)

E/BER/CG/E/6–7 (Covent Garden Estate Rental, 1749–51)

Sessions Books

Sessions Rolls

Sessions Papers

Process Register Book of Indictments, xv (1745–6)

Guildhall Library

MSS 4, 100, and 6000 (Papers and Diary of Marshe Dickenson)

MSS 214 and 14,175 (Wilkes Papers)

MS 544/1 (Centenary Club, Register of Members, 1695–1806)

MS 592/4 (Baptist Congregation, White's Alley, Moorfields, 1733/4)

MS 1061/22 (Churchwarden's Accounts, St Ann Blackfriars)

MS 1313/2 (Churchwarden's Accounts, St Martin Ludgate)

MS 3038/1 (Minutes of the Dissenting Deputies 1732–67)

MS 4117/1 (Churchwarden's Accounts, St Andrew Undershaft)

MS 8674 (Hand-in-Hand Insurance Registers)

MS 8991 (Parish List of St Mary Aldermanry 1733, noting Dissenters)

MS 9537/33, and 34 (Visitation Books)

MS 9557 (Diocese of London Book, 1770–1812)

MS 11316 (Land Tax Assessments)

MS 11936 (Sun Fire Insurance Registers)

Stocken Collection

'The poll . . . March 1741/2 . . .' (Photostat of MS Poll for Surrey By-Election, MS 39291 in the British Library.)

Hoare's Bank, Fleet Street

Loan Books and Private Accounts

Norwich and Norfolk Record Office

Case 12 Shelf b (2) (Information and Examinations 1700–40)

Case 13 d(2) (Loyalist Association, 26 Sept. 1745)

Case 16 c.8 (Assembly Book 1714–31)

Case 16 Shelf b (27–30) (Court of Mayoralty 1709–46)

Case 23 a and b (Norwich, Window Tax 1708, Land Tax 1734)

MS 79, Benjamin Mackerell, 'History of the City of Norwich, Both Ancient and Modern' (2 vols.; 1739)

PD 26/73 (s) (St Peter Mancroft, Churchwarden's Accounts, 1707–52)

Public Record Office

Assi 4 (Assize Books)

E 190/1195, 1214–15 (Port Books, Bristol, 1734–42)

HCA 26/5–12, 26–31 (Letters of Marque)

KB 1/1–4 (King's Bench Depositions 1714–34)

PRO 30/8/6–83 (Chatham Papers)

PRO 30/29/1/11 (Granville Papers)

PROB 11 (Prerogative Court of Canterbury, Wills)

SP 35 and 36 (State Papers Domestic 1714–60)

SP 44 (Warrants)

TS 11 & 20 (Treasury Solicitor's Papers)

Society of Merchant Venturers, Clifton, Bristol

Stedfast Society, Rules and Orders 1737–1802

President's Accounts 1737–56

Tyne and Wear Record Office, Newcastle-upon-Tyne
    Quarter Sessions Order Book 1743–47
University College, London, Library
    Parkes MSS
University of London Library, Senate House, Malet Street
    Stuart MSS (Microfilm)
University of Nottingham Library
    Newcastle MSS
Westminster Public Library
    Churchwarden Accounts (c.1680–1720)
    Vestry Minutes (1744–49)
    E 3078 (Objections Made by Sir George Vandeput's Counsel for the
        Poll of St Margaret and St John, Westminster)
West Sussex Record Office
    Goodwood MS

II. Printed Sources

The place of publication is London, unless otherwise stated.

A. POLL-BOOKS (IN CHRONOLOGICAL ORDER)

*Exact Copy of the Poll at the Chusing of the Knights of the Shire for
    the County of Middlesex . . . Monday 28 May 1705* (1705).
    [Chiswick Public Lib.]
The Poll Taken at Brentford . . . 12 October 1710 (n.p., n.d.). [Chis-
    wick Public Lib.]
*The Poll of the Livery-Men of the City of London, at the Election of
    Members of Parliament* (1710).
*An Alphabetical Draft of the Poll of Robert Bene Esq. and Richard
    Berney, Esq., (and of Waller Bacon Esq. and Stephen Gardiner)
    Taken the 18th of October 1710* (Norwich, 1710).
*An Exact List of the Voters . . . Taken at the Election of Members of
    Parliament* (Bristol, 1722).
*The Poll of the Liverymen of the City . . . at the Election of Members
    of Parliament . . . April . . . 1722* (1722).
*A Copy of the Polls Taken at an Election for an Alderman for the
    Great Ward of Conesford in the City of Norwich on the 19th Day
    of May 1722* (printed by W. Chase; Norwich, [1722]).
Daily Post, 16 Mar. 1724. 'A List of the Members of the Several
    Companies that Polled for Sir Edward Bellamy to be Sheriff for
    London and Middlesex.'
Daily Journal, 20 Mar. 1724. 'A List of the Members of the Several
    Companies that Poll for Sir John Williams . . . to be Sheriff for . . .
    London and Middlesex.'

Daily Post, 7 Dec. 1724. 'A List of the Person who have Polled for Charles Goodfellow Esq., at the Late Election for a Member of Parliament to Represent the City of London . . . November 1724.'

Daily Journal, 7 Dec. 1724. 'A List of the Persons who have Polled for Sir Richard Hopkins at the Late Election for a Member of Parliament to represent the City of London . . . '

Daily Post Extraordinary, 9 Apr. 1734. 'A list of the Persons who have Poll'd for Mr. William Selwin (for City Chamberlain).'

Daily Post Extraordinary, 9 Apr. 1734. 'A List of the Persons who Poll'd for Mr John Bosworth, at the Late Election of a Chamberlain for the City of London.'

A List of the Free-Holders and Free-Men who Voted at the Election . . . for the City and County of Bristol . . . May 15 1734 (Bristol, 1734).

A Copy of the Poll for the Knights of the Shire for the County of Norfolk, taken at Norwich, May 22, 1734 (Norwich, 1734).

An Alphabetical Draught of the Polls . . . Norwich . . . 1734 (Norwich, 1734).

An Alphabetical Draught of the Polls for Sir Edward Ward . . . Miles Branthwayt . . . Horatio Walpole . . . Waller Bacon . . . May 1734 and Miles Branthwayt . . . and Thomas Vere . . . February 1735 (Norwich, 1735).

The Poll-Book, Being a List of the Freeholders and Freemen who Voted at the Last Election for the City and County of Bristol (Bristol, 1739).

The Poll for Members of Parliament for the Borough of Ipswich 8 May 1741 (Ipswich, 1741).

A Genuine List of the Freeholders and Freemen who Voted at the General Election for Members to Serve in Parliament for the City and County of Bristol (Bristol, 1754).

The Bristol Poll Book (Bristol, 1774).

B. NEWSPAPERS AND PERIODICALS

Bath Journal (1747).

Berrow's Worcester Journal (1756).

Boddely's Bath Journal (1756).

Bonner and Middleton's Bristol Journal (1775).

Bristol Gazette (1772).

Bristol Journal (1769–72).

Champion (1739–41).

Common Sense (1740–1).

Con-Test (1756–7).

Covent Garden Journal (1753).

Craftsman (1727–41).

Daily Gazetteer (1738–42).
Daily Journal (1724–7).
Daily Post (1722–42).
Dublin Post Man (1715).
Farley's Bristol Newspaper (1730).
Felix Farley's Bristol Journal (1745–53).
Fog's Weekly Journal (1732–3).
Free Briton (1734).
Freeholder's Journal (1721–2).
Flying Post (1710–15).
Gazetteer and London Daily Advertiser (1754–63).
Gray's Inn Journal (1756).
General Advertiser (1747).
General Evening Post (1747).
Gentleman's Magazine (1731–63).
Gloucester Journal (1733–40).
Gray's Inn Journal (1752).
Jackson's Oxford Journal (1753–6).
London and Country Journal (1741).
London Evening Post (1727–63).
London Gazette (1740).
London Magazine (1732–63).
Mist's Weekly Journal (1727–8).
Monitor (1755–62).
Morning Advertiser (1745).
Newcastle Courant (1733–46).
Northampton Mercury (1727–68).
Norwich Gazette (1710–46).
Norwich Mercury (1729–46).
Post Boy (1713–22).
Protester (1753).
Public Advertiser (1754–7).
Read's Weekly Journal (1753–4).
Remembrancer (1750).
Shift Shifted, or Robin's Last Shift (1716).
St James's Chronicle (1761–3).
St James's Evening Post (1745).
St James's Post (1715).
Test (1756–7).
True Patriot (1745).
Weekly Journal (1715).
Weekly Journal, or British Gazetteer (1718–20).
Weekly Journal, or Saturday's Post (1718–23).
Westminster Evening Post (1750–1).

Whitehall Evening Post (1751–8).
York Courant (1756).

C. PAMPHLETS, BROADSIDES, AND SERMONS

[Abbot, Henry], *Unity, Friendship and Charity, Recommended in a Sermon Preach'd Before the Gloucestershire Society, 27 August 1713* (Bristol, 1713).

An Account of a Dreadful Mob at Manchester and Other Places in England (Edinburgh, 1715).

An Account of the Riots, Tumults and Other Treasonable Practices since his Majesty's Accession to the Throne (1715).

An Account of the Mock Procession of Burning the Pope and the Chevalier de St. George Intended to be Perform'd on the 17th Instant, Being the Anniversary of Queen Elizabeth (1711).

An Address to the Livery of the City of London (1754).

Address to the Worthy Liverymen of the Free City of London (1754).

An Appeal to the People: Part the Second (1757).

BRADBURY, THOMAS, *The Necessity of Impeaching the Late Ministry* (1715).

The Bristol Contest (Bristol, 1739).

The Bristol Contest (Bristol, 1754).

The Bristol Contest (Bristol, 1781).

The Bristol Sailor's Discovery, or Spanish Pretensions Confuted (1739).

The Case of a Late Resignation Set in a True Light (1761).

CAMPBELL, THOMAS, *The London Tradesman* (1747).

CATCOTT, A. S., *The Antiquity and Honourableness of the Practice of Merchandize* (Bristol, 1744).

The Citizen's Procession (1733).

City Corruption Display'd (1739).

A Collection of Papers Pro and Con which have been Published during the Election of a Knight for the Shire for the County of Middlesex, 1750 (1750).

Considerations Humbly Offered, first, to the Inhabitants of the City and Liberty of Westminster, Secondly to the Worthy Liverymen of the City of London, with regard to the Nomination of Admiral Vernon to be their Representative in Parliament (1741).

[Copithorne, Richard], *The English Cotejo, or the Cruelties, Depredations and Illicit trade Charg'd upon the English in a Spanish Libel lately Published* (1739).

[Defoe, Daniel], *The Alteration in the Triennial Act Considered* (1716).

—— *An Essay in Praise of Knavery* (1723).

[Defoe, Daniel], *Bold Advice* (1715).

—— *Captain Tom's Remembrance to his Old Friends the MOBB of London, Westminster, Southwark and Wapping* (1711).

—— *The Compleat Tradesmen*, 3rd edn. (2 vols.; 1732).

—— *A Humble Address to our Sovereign Lord the People* (1715).

—— *A Hymn to the Mob* (1715).

—— *The Pernicious Consequences of the Clergy's Intermeddling with Affairs of State* (1715).

—— *The Royal Progress* (1720).

Diversion upon Diversion [Bristol, 1754].

[Dunton, John], *The Shortest Way With The King* (n.d.).

[Ferguson, Robert], *The History of all the Mobs, Tumults, and Insurrections in Great Britain, from William the Conqueror to the Present Time* [1715].

[Fielding, Henry], *A Dialogue between the Gentleman of London, Agent for Two Court Candidates and an Honest Alderman of the Court Party* (1747).

The Freeholder's Plea against Stock-Jobbing Elections of Parliamentary Men (1701).

GIBB, JOHN, *The Mutual Duties of Magistrates and People: A Sermon Preached at St. Mary Redcliffe 29 May 1721* [Bristol, 1721].

[Gibson, Edmund], *The Bishop of London's Pastoral Letter to the People of his Diocese . . . Occasion'd by our Present Dangers* (1745).

GORDON, THOMAS, *An Appeal to the Unprejudiced concerning the Present Discontents Occasion'd by the Late Convention with Spain* (1739).

—— *A Short View of the Conspiracy with Some Reflections on the Present State of Affairs* (1723).

The Groans of Britons at the Gloomy Prospect of the Present Precarious State of their Liberties and Properties, Compared with what it Has Been (1743).

HARCOURT, JAMES, *A Sermon Preach'd in the Church of All Saints in Bristol, October 21, 1721, upon the Death of Edward Colston Esquire* (1721).

HOLLAND, JOHN, *The Directors of the Bank of England: Enemies to the Great Interests of the Kingdom* (1715).

[Hornby, Charles], *The Second and Last English Advice to the Freeholders of England* (1723).

An Impartial Relation of the Proceedings of the Common Hall and the Court of Aldermen (1740).

The Independent Briton, or Free Thoughts on the Expediency of Gratifying the People's Expectations (1742).

Instructions Recommended to the Freemen of Bristol [Bristol, 1754].

JEKYLL, SIR THOMAS, *Peace and Love, Recommended and Persuaded in Two Sermons, Preached at Bristol, 31 January 1675* (1675).

The Late Excise Scheme Dissected (1734).

A Letter from a Weaver at Norwich to a Member of Parliament Concerning the Present State of our Woollen Manufactures (1734).

A Letter to a TORY FRIEND upon the Present Critical Situation of our Affairs (1746).

A Letter to the Men's Meeting of the People Called Quakers in Bristol (1732).

A Letter to the Right Honourable Author of a Letter to a Citizen (1762).

A Letter to the Worshipful Sir John Barnard . . . on the Act of Parliament for Naturalising the Jews (1753).

A List of All the Names that Sign'd the Two Petitions against Thomas Coster, Esq. [Bristol, 1735].

The Liveryman, or Plain Thoughts on Publick Affairs (1740).

The Lord's Protest, to which is Added a List of the MPs who Voted for and against the Hanoverian Troops in British Pay, January 18 1743/ 4 (1744).

[Lyttelton, George], *Farther Considerations on the Present State of our Affairs at Home and Abroad In a letter to a Member of Parliament from a Friend in the Country* (1739).

MAJENDE, J. J., *A Sermon Preach'd at the Cathedral Church of St. Paul, London, on Sunday Morning the 10th of November 1745* (1745).

MARAT, JEAN-PAUL, *The Chains of Slavery* (1774).

The Negotiators, or Don Diego brought to Reason (1739).

The New and Strange Imprisonment of the People called Quakers in the City of Bristol (n.p., 1682).

The Norwich Cavalcade and Opposition: A Satire Addressed to 829 Uncorrupted Freeman and Freeholders (1741).

Old England's Te Deum [1743].

[Oldmixon, John], *The Bristol Riot* (1714).

Opposition not Faction, or The Rectitude of the Present Parliamentary Opposition to the Present Expensive Measures (1743).

[Perceval, John], *Faction Detected by the Evidence of Facts*, 2nd edn. (1743).

Popular Prejudices against the Convention and Treaty with Spain Examined and Answer'd (1739).

The Proceedings of the Court of Hustings and Common Hall of the Livery of the City of London at the Late Election for Lord Mayor (1739).

Proceedings of the General Meeting of the Electors of Westminster in the Interest of Admiral Vernon and Charles Edwin Esq. (1741).

Public Discontent Accounted for, from the Conduct of our Ministers in the Cabinet and our Generals in the Field (1743).

[Robins, Benjamin], *A Narrative of what Passed in the Common Hall of the Citizens of London, Assembled for the Election of a Lord Mayor 29 Sept. 1739* (1739).

A Scheme of the Proportions Several Counties in England Paid to the Land Tax in 1693 and to the Subsidies in 1697, Compared with the Number of Members then Sent to Parliament (1698).

Sermons by the late Reverend A. S. Catcott (1753).

[Shebbeare, John], *A Fourth Letter to the People of England* (1756).

—— *A Fifth Letter to the People of England* (1757).

SMALRIDGE, GEORGE, *Twelve Sermons Preach'd on Several Occasions* (Oxford, 1717).

[Stanhope, Philip Dormer, (4th Earl Chesterfield) and Waller, E.] *The Case of the Hanover Forces in the Pay of Great Britain* (1743).

[Stanhope, Philip Dormer, (4th Earl Chesterfield)], *The Interest of Hanover steadily pursued since the A——n* (1743).

SYDNEY, ALGERNON, *Discourses concerning Government*, 3rd edn. (1751).

TRIMNELL, CHARLES, *A Sermon Preach'd at the Parish Church of St. James's Westminster 30 January 1709* (1709).

—— *A Charge Deliver'd to the Clergy of the Diocese of Norwich 1709* (London, 1710).

A True and Impartial Collection of Pieces in Prose and Verse . . . Written and Published on Both Sides . . . during the Contest for the Westminster Election (1749).

A True and Particular Narrative of the Disturbances and Outrages that Have Been Committed in the City of Norwich since November to the Present Time (1752).

A True Relation of the Several Facts and Circumstances of the Intended Riot and Tumult on Queen Elizabeth's Day Gathered From Authentic Accounts, 2nd edn. (1711).

TUCKER, JOSIAH, *A Review of Lord Viscount Clare's Conduct as Representative of Bristol* (Gloucester, 1775).

The Two Candidates, or Charge and Discharge [1749].

Vernon's Glory, Containing 14 New Songs, Occasion'd by the Taking of Porto Bello and Fort Chagre (1740).

[Walpole, Horace], *The Convention Vindicated from the Misrepresentations of the Enemies of Our Peace* (1739).

—— *The Interest of Great Britain steadily Pursued* (1743).

[Whitehead, Paul], *The Case of the Hon. Alexander Murray Esq.* (1751).

WRIGHT, SAMUEL, *The Church in Perils among False Brethren* (1733).

—— *A Sermon Preach'd on the Fifth of November in the Year 1719* (1719).

The Yellow Sash, or H——R BESHIT [1743].

D. OTHER PRIMARY SOURCES IN PRINT

Annals of George I.

An Alphabetical List of the Livery 1733 (n.d.).

Anon., *Number of Liverymen in London Wards and Neighbouring Counties 1751* (1751).

BARRETT, WILLIAM, *The History and Antiquities of the City of Bristol* (Bristol, 1789).

Boswell's London Journal 1762–3, ed. Frederick A. Pottle (1950).

BOYER, ABEL, *The Political State of Great Britain* (60 vols.; 1711–40).

Bristol Corporation of the Poor 1696–1898, ed. E. E. Butcher (Bristol, 1932).

Calendars of State Papers, Domestic Series.

CALAMY, EDMUND, *An Historical Account of My Own Life*, ed. John T. Rutt (2 vols.; 1829).

CAREW, THOMAS, *Historical Account of the Right of Elections* (2 vols.; 1755).

Collected Papers on the Jacobite Risings, ed. Rupert Jarvis (2 vols.; Manchester, 1971–2).

CHAMBERLAIN, HENRY, *A New and Complete History and Survey of the Cities of London and Westminster* (1770).

A Complete Collection of State Trials and Proceedings for High Treason, 4th edn. (10 vols.; 1778).

Correspondence of Alexander Pope, ed. George Sherburn (5 vols.; Oxford, 1956).

The Correspondence of Edmund Burke, ed. Thomas Copeland *et al.* (10 vols.; Cambridge, 1958–78).

Correspondence of William Pitt, Earl of Chatham, ed. William Stanhope Taylor and John Henry Pringle (4 vols.; 1838–40).

COXE, WILLIAM, *Memoirs of the Life and Administration of Sir Robert Walpole* (3 vols.; 1798).

The Debates and Proceedings of the British House of Commons . . . 1743–6, ed. John Almon (2 vols.; 1764).

DEFOE, DANIEL, *A Tour Through the Whole Island of Great Britain*, ed. Pat Rogers (1724/5; Harmondsworth, 1971).

DENNIS, JOHN, *The Critical Works of John Dennis*, ed. E. N. Hooker (2 vols.; Baltimore, 1939–43).

DE SAUSSURE, CESAR, *A Foreign View of England in the Reign of George I and George II*, trans. and ed. Madame von Muyden (1902).

The Diary of John Evelyn, ed. E. S. de Beer (6 vols.; Oxford, 1955).

The Englishman, ed. Rae Blanchard (Oxford, 1955).

GLOVER, RICHARD, *London, or The Progress of Commerce*, 2nd edn. (1739).

The Grenville Papers, ed. W. J. Smith (4 vols.; 1852).

Historical Manuscripts Commission:
    Carlisle MSS
    Dartmouth MSS, i.
    Egmont Diary, i–iii.
    Portland MSS, vii.
    Trevor MSS

The History and Proceedings of the House of Commons, ed. R. Chandler (7 vols.; 1741–2).

The History, Debates, Proceedings of Both Houses of Parliament, ed. John Debrett (7 vols.; 1792).

HOOKER, RICHARD, *Of the Lawes of Ecclesiastical Politie* (1594–71; repr. 1969).

The Journeys of Celia Fiennes, ed. Christopher Morris (1947).

A Journal of the Shrievalty of Richard Hoare (1815).

Journals of the House of Commons

Journals of the House of Lords

The Letters of Horace Walpole, Fourth Earl of Orford, ed. Mrs Paget Toynbee (16 vols.; 1903–5).

Letters of Humphrey Prideaux to John Ellis 1674–1722, ed. Edward Maude Thompson (Camden Society, NS 15; 1875).

A List of the Subscribers to the Veterans Scheme, ed. Samuel Smith (1748).

A Lord Mayor's Diary 1906–7, ed. William P. Treloar (1920).

LUTTRELL, NARCISSUS, *A Brief Historical Relation of State Affairs* (6 vols.; Oxford, 1857).

MAITLAND, WILLIAM, *The History of London from its Foundation by the Romans to the Present Time* (2 vols.; 1756).

Memorials of John Murray of Broughton 1740–47, ed. Robert Fitzroy Bell (Publications Scottish History Society, 27; Edinburgh, 1898).

'Minutes of a Whig Club 1714–1717', ed. Henry Horwitz, in *London Politics 1713–1717* (London Record Society Publications, 17; 1981).

NORTHOUCK, JOHN, *A New History of London* (1773).

The Parliamentary History of England from the Earliest Period to the Year 1803, ed. William Cobbett (36 vols.; 1806–20).

The Political Journal of George Bubb Doddington, ed. John Carswell and Lewis A. Dralle (Oxford, 1965).

Politics and the Port of Bristol in the Eighteenth Century, ed. Walter E. Minchinton (Publications Bristol Record Society, 23; Bristol, 1963).

The Prose Works of Jonathan Swift, ed. Frederick Ryland (2 vols.; 1913).

RALPH, ELIZABETH, 'Bishop Secker's Diocese Book', in *A Bristol Miscellany*, ed. Patrick McGrath (Publications Bristol Record Society, 37; Bristol, 1985).

A Selection from the Papers of the Earls of Marchmont in the Possession of the Rt. Hon. Sir George Rose (3 vols.; 1831).

STOW, JOHN, *The Survey of London* (Everyman edn. 1912).

Surrey Hearth Tax 1664, ed. C. A. F. Meekings (Surrey Record Society, 17; 1940).

THISTLETHWAITE, JAMES, *Corruption* (1780).

The Trade of Bristol in the Eighteenth Century, ed. Walter E. Minchinton (Publications Bristol Record Society, 20; Bristol, 1957).

Trial of Simon, Lord Lovat of the '45, ed. David N. MacKay (Edinburgh and Glasgow, 1911).

The Yale Edition of Horace Walpole's Correspondence, ed. W. S. Lewis and others (34 vols.; New Haven, 1937–70).

YORKE, PHILIP C., *The Life and Correspondence of Philip Yorke, Earl of Hardwicke* (3 vols.; Cambridge, 1913).

YOUNG, ARTHUR, *A Farmer's Tour Through the East of England* (4 vols.; 1771).

The Vernon Papers, ed. B. McL. Ranft (Publications Navy Records Society, 99; 1958).

WALDEGRAVE, JAMES, EARL WALDEGRAVE, *Memoirs from 1754 to 1758* (1821).

WALPOLE, HORACE, *Memoirs of the Last Ten Years of the Reign of George II* (2 vols.; 1822).

WARD, EDWARD, *Hudibras Redivivus*, 4th edn. (1710).

The Wentworth Papers 1705–1739, ed. James J. Cartwright (1883).

III. Secondary Works

The place of publication is London, unless otherwise stated.

A. BOOKS, ARTICLES, AND ESSAYS

ALLISON, K. J., 'Parliamentary Representation', in *Victoria County History of Warwickshire*, ed. W. B. Stephens, viii (Oxford, 1969).

Anon., *The History of the Ancient Society of St. Stephen's Ringers, Bristol* (Bristol, 1928).

BADDELEY, JOHN J., *The Aldermen of Cripplegate Ward 1276–1900* (1900).

BAUGH, DANIEL, *Aristocratic Government and Society in Eighteenth-Century England* (New York, 1975).

BAYNE-POWELL, ROSAMOND, *Eighteenth-Century London Life* (New York, 1938).

BEAVEN, ALFRED B., *The Aldermen of the City of London* (2 vols.; 1908, 1913).

—— *Bristol Lists: Municipal and Miscellaneous* (Bristol, 1899).

BECKETT, J. V., 'Regional Variation and the Agricultural Depression 1730–1750', *Economic History Review*, 2nd ser., 35/1 (Feb. 1982), 35–52.

BELOFF, MAX, *Public Order and Popular Disturbances 1660–1714* (Oxford, 1938).

BERÉ, YVES-MARIE, *Fête et revolte: Des mentalités populaires du XVIe au XVIIIe siècle* (Paris, 1976).

BLACK, JEREMY, 'Grain Exports and Neutrality: A Speculative Note on British Neutrality in the War of Polish Succession', *Journal of European Economic History*, 12/3 (winter 1983), 593–600.

BLOMEFIELD, FRANCIS, *An Essay towards a Topographical History of the County of Norfolk* (11 vols., 1805–10).

BRAITHWAITE, WILLIAM, *The Second Period of Quakerism* (Cambridge, 1961).

BREWER, JOHN, *The Misfortunes of Lord Bute: A Case Study in Eighteenth-Century Political Argument and Public Opinion; Historical Journal*, 16 (Mar. 1973), 7–43.

—— *Party Ideology and Popular Politics at the Accession of George III* (Cambridge, 1976).

—— 'The Wilkites and the Law 1763–74; A Study of Radical Notions of Governance', in *An Ungovernable People: The English and their Law in the Seventeenth and Eighteenth Centuries*, ed. John Brewer and John Styles (1980).

BROWNE, JAMES, *A History of the Highlands and the Highland Clans* (Glasgow, 1840).

BULLOCK, J. M., 'The Charitable Corporation', *Notes and Queries*, 160 (4 Apr. 1931), 237–41.

BURKE, PETER, 'Popular Culture in Seventeenth-Century London', *The London Journal*, 3/2 (Nov. 1977), 143–62.

BUTTERFIELD, HERBERT, 'George III and the Constitution', *History*, 43 (1958), 14–33.

CANNON, JOHN, 'The Parliamentary Representation of the City of Gloucester 1727–90', *Transactions Bristol and Gloucestershire Archaeological Society*, 78 (1959), 137–52.

—— *Parliamentary Reform 1640–1832* (Cambridge, 1973).

CARSWELL, JOHN, *The South Sea Bubble* (1960).

CAVE, CHARLES H., *A History of Banking in Bristol from 1750 to 1899* (Bristol, 1899).

CHANCELLOR, E. BERESFORD, *History of the Squares of London* (1907).

CHAPPELL, WILLIAM, *The Ballad Literature in the Olden Time* (3 vols.; n.d.).

CHRISTIE, IAN R., *Stress and Stability in Late-Eighteenth Century Britain* (Oxford, 1985).

CLARK, J. C. D., 'The Decline of Party, 1740–1760', *English Historical Review*, 93 (July 1978), 499–527.

—— 'A General Theory of Party, Opposition and Government, 1688–1832', *Historical Journal*, 23/2 (1980), 295–325.

—— *The Dynamics of Change: The Crisis of the 1750s and the English Party System* (Cambridge, 1982).

—— *English Society 1688–1832* (Cambridge, 1985).

—— *Revolution and Rebellion* (Cambridge, 1986).

CLIFTON, ROBIN, *The Last Popular Rebellion* (1984).

COLLEY, LINDA, 'Eighteenth-Century Radicalism Before Wilkes', *Transactions of the Royal Historical Society*, 5th ser., 31 (1981), 1–19.

—— *In Defiance of Oligarchy: The Tory Party 1714–1760* (Cambridge, 1982).

CORFIELD, PENELOPE J., 'A Provincial Capital in the Late Seventeenth Century: The Case of Norwich', in *Crisis and Order in English Towns 1500–1700*, ed. Peter Clark and Paul Slack (1972).

COWLES, VIRGINIA, *The Great Swindle* (1960).

COZENS-HARDY, BASIL, and KENT, ERNEST A. (eds.), *The Mayors of Norwich 1403–1835* (Norwich, 1938).

CRANFIELD, G. A., *The Development of the Provincial Newspaper 1700–1760* (Oxford, 1962).

CRUICKSHANKS, EVELINE, *Political Untouchables: The Tories and the '45* (1979).

CURTIS, T. C., and SPECK, W. A., 'The Societies for the Reformation of Manners: A Case Study in the Theory and Practice of Moral Reform', *Literature and Society*, 3 (Mar. 1976), 45–64.

DAVIES, HORTON, *Worship and Theology in England 1603–1690* (Princeton, 1975).

DAVIS, NATALIE, 'The Rites of Violence: Religious Riot in Sixteenth-Century France', *Past and Present*, 59 (May 1973), 51–91.

DAVIS, RALPH, 'English Overseas Trade 1700–1774', *Economic History Review*, 2nd ser., 15/2 (Dec. 1962), 285–303.

—— *Aleppo and Devonshire Square: English Traders in the Levant in the 18th Century* (1967).

DE BEER, E. S., 'Places of Worship in London about 1738', *Studies in London History*, ed. A. E. J. Hollander and W. Kellaway (1969).

DE KREY, GARY STUART, *A Fractured Society: The Politics of London in the First Age of Party 1688–1715* (Oxford, 1985).

—— 'Political Radicalism in London after the Glorious Revolution', *Journal of Modern History*, 4/4 (Dec. 1985), 591–7.

DICKINSON, H. T., 'The Tory Party's Attitude to Foreigners: A Note on Party Principles in the Age of Anne', *Bulletin of the Institute of Historical Research*, 40 (1967), 153–63.

—— 'The October Club', *Huntington Library Quarterly*, 33 (1969–70), 155–73.

—— *Bolingbroke* (1970).

—— 'Popular Politics in the Age of Walpole', in *Britain in the Age of Walpole*, ed. Jeremy Black (1984).

DICKSON, P. G. M., *The Financial Revolution in England* (1967).

DOBSON, C. R., *Masters and Journeymen* (1980).

DOOLITTLE, I. G., 'Walpole's City Elections Act (1725)', *English Historical Review*, 97 (July 1982), 508–28.

DORAN, JOHN, *London in the Jacobite Times* (2 vols., 1877).

EARLE, PETER, *Monmouth's Rebels* (1971).

ELDON, C. W., *England's Subsidy Policy Toward the Continent during the Seven Years War* (Philadelphia, 1938).

EMDEN, CECIL, *The People and Constitution* (Oxford, 1933).

EVANS, JOHN T., *Seventeenth-Century Norwich* (Oxford, 1979).

FISHER, F. J., 'The Development of the London Food Market 1540–1640', *English Historical Review*, 1st ser., 5 (1934–5), 46–64.

FISHER, H. E. S., *The Portugal Trade: A Study in Anglo-Portuguese Commerce, 1700–1770* (1971).

FITTS, JAMES L., 'Newcastle's Mob', *Albion*, 5/1 (Spring, 1973), 41–9.

FRITZ, PAUL, *The English Ministers and Jacobitism between the Rebellions of 1715 and 1745* (Toronto, 1975).

FRYER, W. R., 'King George III: His Political Character and Conduct 1760–84; A New Whig Interpretation', *Renaissance and Modern Studies*, 6 (1962), 68–101.

FURLEY, O. W., 'The Pope-Burning Processions of the Late 17th Century', *History*, 44 (1959), 16–23.

GEORGE, M. DOROTHY, *English Political Caricature* (2 vols.; Oxford, 1959).

GOODWIN, ALBERT, *The Friends of Liberty* (Cambridge, Mass., 1979).

GREAVES, R. W., *The Corporation of Leicester 1689–1836* (repr. Leicester, 1970).

HALEY, K. H. D., *The First Earl of Shaftesbury* (Oxford, 1968).

HANSON, LAURENCE, *Government and the Press 1695–1763* (Oxford, 1936).

HARTMANN, CYRIL H., *The Angry Admiral* (1953).

HEATON, HERBERT, *The Yorkshire Woollen and Worsted Industries* (Oxford, 1920).

HENDERSON, ALFRED J., *London and the National Government 1721–42* (Durham, NC, 1945).

HERTZ, G. B., *British Imperialism in the 18th century* (1908).

—— 'The English Silk Industry in the Eighteenth Century', *English Historical Review*, 24 (Oct. 1909), 710–27.

HILL, B. W., 'The Change of Government and the "Loss of the City" 1710–11', *Economic History Review*, 2nd ser., 24 (Aug. 1971), 395–413.

The History of Parliament: The House of Commons 1754–1790, ed. Sir Lewis Namier and John Brooke (3 vols.; 1964).

The History of Parliament: The House of Commons 1715–1745, ed. Romney Sedgwick (2 vols.; 1970).

The History of Parliament: The House of Commons 1660–1690, ed. B. D. Henning (3 vols.; 1984).

HOBHOUSE, HERMIONE, *The Ward of Cheap in the City of London* (1963).

HOLMES, GEOFFREY, *Political Stability in the Age of Anne* (1967).

—— 'The Sacheverell Riots: The Crowd and the Church in Early Eighteenth-Century London', *Past and Present*, 72 (Aug. 1976), 55–85.

—— *The Electorate and the National Will in the First Age of Party* (Lancaster, 1970).

HOLMES, GEOFFREY, and SPECK, W. A., *The Divided Society: Parties and Politics in England 1694–1716* (New York, 1968).

HOLTON, ROBERT J., 'The Crowd in History: Some Problems of Theory and Method', *Social History*, 3/2 (May 1978), 219–33.

HOPPIT, JULIAN, 'Financial Crises in Eighteenth-Century England', *Economic History Review*, 2nd ser., 39/1 (1980), 39–58.

HORN, D. B., *Great Britain and Europe in the Eighteenth Century* (Oxford, 1967).

HORWITZ, HENRY, 'Party in a Civic Context: London from the Exclusion Crisis to the Fall of Walpole', in *Britain in the First Age of Party 1650–1750: Essays Presented to Geoffrey Holmes*, ed. Clyve Jones (Leicester, 1987).

—— 'Testamentary Practice, Family Strategies and the Last Phases of the Custom of London 1660–1727', *Law and History Review*, 2/2 (autumn, 1984), 224–5.

HUNT, N. C., *Two Early Political Associations: The Quakers and the Dissenting Deputies in the Age of Sir Robert Walpole* (Oxford, 1961).

JAMES, REGINALD, 'Bristol Society in the Eighteenth Century', in *Bristol and its Adjoining Counties*, ed. C. H. MacInnes and W. F. Whittard (Bristol, 1955).

JENKINS, PHILIP, *The Making of a Ruling Class: The Glamorganshire Gentry 1640–1790* (Cambridge, 1983).

JOHN, A. H., 'War and the English Economy 1700–1763', *Economic History Review*, 2nd ser., 7 (1954–5), 329–44.

JONES, J. R. 'The Green Ribbon Club', *Durham University Journal*, 49 (1956–7), 17–20.

—— *The Revolution of 1688 in England* (1972).

JONES, P. E., *The Worshipful Company of Poulterers in the City of London* (1965).

JOSLIN, D. M., 'London Private Bankers 1720–1785', *Economic History Review*, 2nd ser., 7 (1954), 175–89.

JOYCE, PATRICK, *Work, Society and Politics: The Culture of the Factory in Late Victorian England* (Brighton, 1980).

JUBB, MICHAEL, 'Economic Policy and Economic Development', in *Britain in the Age of Walpole*, ed. Jeremy Black (1984).

KELLY, PAUL, 'Constituents Instructions to Members of Parliament in the Eighteenth Century', in *Party and Management in Parliament 1660–1784*, ed. Clyve Jones (New York, 1984).

KEMP, BETTY, *King and Commons* (1956).

KEMPE, ALFRED V., *Historical Notes of the Collegiate College of St. Martin le Grand* (1825).

KRAMNICK, ISAAC, *Bolingbroke and His Circle: The Politics of Nostalgia in the Age of Walpole* (Cambridge, Mass., 1968).

KNOX, THOMAS, 'Popular Politics and Provincial Radicalism: Newcastle-upon-Tyne, 1769–85', *Albion*, 11/3 (autumn 1979), 224–41.

LADURIE, E. LE ROY, *Carnival: People's Rising at Romans 1577–80*, trans. May Feeney (New York, 1979).

LANG, ANDREW, *Pickle the Spy* (1897).

LANGFORD, PAUL, 'William Pitt and Public Opinion, 1757', *English Historical Review*, 88 (Jan. 1973), 58–71.

—— *The Excise Crisis: Society and Politics in the Age of Walpole* (Oxford, 1975).

LATIMER, JOHN, *The Annals of Bristol* (3 vols.; Bristol, 1893; repr. 1970).

LEFEBVRE, GEORGES, 'Revolutionary Crowds', in *New Perspectives on the French Revolution*, ed. Jeffrey Kaplow (New York, 1965).

—— *The Great Fear of 1789*, ed. George Rudé (1973).

MAHON, LORD, *History of England* (7 vols.; 1858).

MALCOLMSON, ROBERT, 'A Set of Ungovernable People: The Kingswood Colliers in the Eighteenth Century', in *An Ungovernable People: The English and their Law in the Seventeenth and Eighteenth Centuries*, ed. John Brewer and John Styles (1980).

MALCOLMSON, ROBERT, 'Workers' Combinations in Eighteenth-Century England', in *The Origins of Anglo-American Radicalism*, ed. Margaret and James Jacob (1984).

MANNING, BERNARD LORD, *The Protestant Dissenting Deputies* (Cambridge, 1952).

MANNING, BRIAN, *The English People and the English Revolution* (1976).

MARCY, PETER T., 'Eighteenth Century Views of Bristol and Bristolians', in *Bristol in the Eighteenth Century*, ed. Patrick T. McGrath (Newton Abbot, 1972).

MASON, J. F. A., 'Parliamentary Representation', in *Victoria County History of Shropshire*, ed. G. C. Baugh, iii (Oxford, 1979).

MATHIAS, PETER, *The Brewing Industry in England 1700–1830* (Cambridge 1959).

McGRATH, PATRICK, *The Merchant Venturers of Bristol* (Bristol, 1975).

McLACHLAN, JEAN O., *Trade and Peace with Old Spain 1667–1750* (Cambridge, 1940).

MILLER, JOHN, 'The Militia and the Army in the Reign of James II', *Historical Journal*, 16/4 (1973), 659–79.

—— *Popery and Politics in England 1660–1688* (Cambridge, 1973).

MINCHINTON, WALTER, 'The Port of Bristol in the Eighteenth Century', in *Bristol in the Eighteenth Century*, ed. Patrick T. McGrath (Newton Abbot, 1972).

MITCHELL, A. A., 'London and the Forty-Five', *History Today*, 15/10 (Oct. 1965), 719–26.

MORLEY, JOHN, *Walpole* (1913).

MORRILL, J. S., 'Chester 1660–1832', in *Victoria County History of Cheshire*, ii (Oxford, 1979).

MUNBY, L. M., 'Politics and Religion in Hertfordshire 1660–1740', in *East Anglian Studies*, ed. L. M. Munby (Cambridge, 1968).

MURRAY, DAVID, *The York Buildings Company* (Glasgow, 1883).

NASH, ROBERT, 'The English and Scottish Tobacco Trades in the Seventeenth and Eighteenth Centuries: Legal and Illegal Trade', *Economic History Review*, 2nd ser., 35/2 (May 1982), 354–72.

NAMIER, SIR LEWIS, *The Structure of Politics at the Accession of George III*, 2nd edn. (1957).

NEWBY, HOWARD, 'The Deferential Dialectic', *Comparative Studies in Society and History*, 17/2 (1975), 139–64.

—— *The Deferential Worker* (Harmondsworth, 1977).

NICHOLLS, J. F., & TAYLOR, JOHN, *Bristol Past and Present* (3 vols.; Bristol, 1881).

OVERTON, JOHN H., *The Nonjurors* (1902).

OWEN, H., and BLAKEWAY, J. B., *A History of Shrewsbury* (2 vols., 1825).

OWEN, J. B., *The Rise of the Pelhams* (1957).

—— 'Political Patronage in 18th Century England', in *The Triumph of Culture: Eighteenth-Century Perspectives*, ed. Paul Fritz and David Williams (Toronto, 1972).

PARES, RICHARD, *War and Trade in the West Indies 1739–63* (1936).

—— *George III and the Politicans* (Oxford, 1953).

—— 'The London Sugar Market 1740–69', *Economic History Review*, 2nd ser., 9 (1756), 254–70.

—— 'A London West-India Merchant House 1740–69' in *Essays presented to Sir Lewis Namier*, ed. Richard Pares and A. J. P. Taylor (1956).

PEARL, VALERIE, *London and the Outbreak of the Puritan Revolution* (Oxford, 1961).

PELHAM, R. A., 'The West Midland Iron Industry and the American Market in the 18th Century', *University of Birmingham Historical Journal*, 2 (1949–50), 141–62.

PENSON, L. M., *The Colonial Agents of the British West Indies* (1924).

PERRY, T. W., *Public Opinion, Propaganda and Politics in Eighteenth Century England* (Cambridge, Mass., 1962).

PETERS, MARIE, *Pitt and Popularity: The Patriot Minister and London Opinion during the Seven Years War* (Oxford, 1980).

PHILLIPS, JOHN A., *Electoral Behavior in Unreformed England* (Princeton, 1982).

PHILLIPS, GEORGE L., 'May-Day is Sweeps' Day', *Folklore*, 60/1 (Mar. 1949), 217–27.

PLUMB, SIR J. H., *Sir Robert Walpole* (2 vols.; 1956–60).

—— *The Growth of Political Stability in England 1675–1725* (1967).

—— 'Political Man', in *Man Versus Society in Eighteenth-Century Britain*, ed. James L. Clifford (Cambridge, 1968).

—— 'The Growth of the Electorate in England from 1600 to 1715', *Past and Present*, 45 (Nov. 1969), 90–116.

PLUMMER, ALFRED, *The London Weavers' Company* (1972).

PORRITT, EDWARD, *The Unreformed House of Commons* (Cambridge, 1903).

PRICE, JACOB M., 'Capital and Credit in the British Chesapeake Trade, 1750–1775', in *Of Mother Country and Plantations*, ed. Virginia B. Platt and David C. Skaggs (Proceedings, 27th Conference in Early American History; Ohio, 1971).

—— 'The Excise Crisis Revisited: The Administrative and Colonial Dimensions of a Parliamentary Crisis', in *England's Rise to*

Greatness 1660–1763, ed. Stephen Baxter (Berkeley and Los Angeles, 1983).

PRIESTLEY, MARGARET, 'London Merchants and Opposition Politics in Charles II's reign', *Bulletin of Institute of Historical Research*, 29 (1956), 205–19.

QUINN, J. F., 'York Elections in the Age of Walpole', *Northern History*, 22 (1986, 175–97).

ROBERTSON, A. M., 'The Suburban Food Markets of 18th Century London', *East London Papers*, 2/1 (Apr. 1959), 21–6.

—— 'The Smithfield Cattle Market', *East London Papers*, 4/2 (Oct. 1961), 80–7.

ROBERTSON, J. M., *Bolingbroke and Walpole* (1919).

ROBBINS, CAROLINE, *The Eighteenth-Century Commonwealthman* (Cambridge, Mass., 1959).

ROBBINS, MICHAEL, *Middlesex* (1953).

ROGERS, NICHOLAS, 'Aristocratic Clientage, Trade and Independency: Popular Politics in Pre-Radical Westminster', *Past and Present*, 61 (1973), 70–106.

—— 'Popular Disaffection in London during the Forty-Five', *London Journal*, I/1 (May 1975), 5–27.

—— 'Resistance to Oligarchy: The City Opposition to Walpole and his successors 1725–47', in *London in the Age of Reform*, ed. John Stevenson (Oxford, 1977), 1–29.

—— 'Popular Protest in Early Hanoverian London', *Past and Present*, 79 (May 1978), 70–100.

—— 'Riot and Popular Jacobitism in Early Hanoverian England', in *Ideology and Conspiracy: Aspects of Jacobitism 1689–1759*, ed. Eveline Cruickshanks (Edinburgh, 1982), 70–89.

—— 'The Urban Opposition to Whig Oligarchy 1720–1760', in *The Origins of Anglo-American Radicalism*, ed. Margaret and James Jacob (1984), 132–48.

—— 'The City Elections Act (1725) Reconsidered', *English Historical Review*, 100 (1985), 604–17.

—— 'Clubs and Politics in Eighteenth-Century London: The Centenary of Cheapside', *London Journal*, 11/1 (summer 1985), 51–8.

—— 'Popular Jacobitism in Provincial Context: Eighteenth-Century Bristol and Norwich', in *The Jacobite Challenge*, ed. Eveline Cruickshanks and Jeremy Black (Edinburgh, 1985), pp. 123–41.

RUDÉ, GEORGE, *Wilkes and Liberty* (Oxford, 1962).

—— *The Crowd in History* (New York, 1964).

—— *Paris and London in the Eighteenth Century* (1970).

—— *Hanoverian London 1714–1808* (1971).

—— *Ideology and Popular Protest* (New York, 1980).

Bibliography 429

RULE, JOHN, *The Experience of Labour in Eighteenth-Century Industry* (1981).

S., J., *Memoirs of the Public Life of Sir Walter Blackett* (Newcastle, 1819).

SAVAGE, JAMES, *The History of Taunton* (Taunton, 1822).

SHARLAND, ROSE E., *Ballads of Old Bristol* (Bristol, n.d.).]

SHARPE, REGINALD R., *London and the Kingdom* (3 vols., 1894–5).

SHAW, JOHN STUART, *The Management of Scottish Society 1707–1764* (Edinburgh, 1983).

SHERIDAN, R. B., 'The Molasses Act and the Market Strategy of British Sugar Planters', *Journal of Economic History*, 17 (1957), 62–83.

—— *Chapters in Caribbean History* (1970).

SOLOMANS, ISRAEL, 'Satirical and Political Prints on the Jews' Naturalization Bill 1753', *Transactions of the Jewish Historical Society*, 6 (1908–10), 205–33.

SPECK, W. A., *Tory and Whig: The Struggle in the Constituencies 1701–1715* (1970).

—— *Stability and Strife: England, 1714–1760* (Cambridge, Mass., 1977).

STEVENSON, JOHN, *Popular Disturbances in England 1700–1870* (1979).

STRONG, ROY C., 'The Popular Celebration of the Accession Day of Queen Elizabeth I', *Journal of the Warburg and Courtauld Institutes*, 21 (1958), 86–103.

STRUTT, JOSEPH, *The Sports and Pastimes of the People of England* (1833).

Survey of London, ed. F. H. Sheppard (42 vols., 1900–86).

SUTHERLAND, LUCY, 'Sampson Gideon, 18th c. Jewish financier', *Transactions of the Jewish Historical Society*, 17 (1951–2), 79–90.

—— 'The City of London in Eighteenth-Century Politics', in *Essays presented to Sir Lewis Namier*, ed. A. J. P. Taylor and Richard Pares (1956), 49–74.

—— *The City of London and the Opposition to Government 1768–74* (1958 Creighton Lecture in History; 1959).

—— 'The City of London and the Devonshire–Pitt Administration 1756–7', *Proceedings of the British Academy*, 46 (1960), 147–93.

—— 'Edmund Burke and the Relations between Members of Parliament and their Constituents', *Studies in Burke and His Time*, 10 (autumn, 1968), 1005–21.

THOMPSON, E. P., *The Making of the English Working Class* (1963).

—— 'Patrician Society, Plebeian Culture', *Journal of Social History*, 7 (summer, 1974), 382–405.

THOMPSON, E.P., *Whigs and Hunters. The Origins of the Black Act* (1975).

—— *Whigs and Hunters. The Origins of the Black Act* (1975).

—— 'Eighteenth-Century English Society: Class Struggle Without Class?' *Social History*, 3/2 (May 1978), 133–66.

THRUPP, SYLVIA, *A Short History of the Worshipful Company of Bakers of London* (1933).

TRELOAR, WILLIAM P., *A Lord Mayor's Diary 1906–7* (1920).

TUNSTALL, BRIAN, *Admiral Byng and the Loss of Minorca* (1928).

TURNER, RAYMOND, 'The Excise Scheme of 1733', *English Historical Review*, 42 (Jan. 1927), 34–57.

UNDERDOWN, DAVID, *Pride's Purge: Politics in the Puritan Revolution* (Oxford, 1970).

—— 'Community and Class: Theories of Local Politics in the English Revolution', in *After the Reformation: Essays in Honour of J. H. Hexter*, ed. Barbara C. Malament (Manchester, 1980).

VERNON, WILLIAM F., *Notes on the Parish of Harefield, County of Middlesex* (1872).

WALSH, JOHN, 'Methodism and the Mob in the Eighteenth Century', in *Popular Belief and Practice*, ed. G. L. Cuming and Derek Baker (*Studies in Church History*, 8; Cambridge, 1972).

WARD, W. R., *The English Land Tax in the Eighteenth Century* (Oxford, 1935).

—— *Georgian Oxford: University Politics in the Eighteenth Century* (Oxford, 1958).

WARNER, OLIVER, *The Innholders Company* (1962).

WATTS, MICHAEL, *The Dissenters* (Oxford, 1978).

WEBB, SIDNEY and BEATRICE, *The History of Trade Unionism* (1902).

—— *English Local Government from the Revolution to the Municipal Corporations Act: The Manor and the Borough: Part Two* (2 vols.; London, 1908).

WESTERFIELD, RAY B., *Middlemen in English Business* (New Haven, Conn., 1915).

WILLIAMS, DAVID ALAN, 'Anglo-Virginia Politics 1690–1735', in *Anglo-American Relations 1675–1775*, ed. Alison G. Olson and Richard M. Brown (New York, 1970).

WILLIAMS, BASIL, *The Life of William Pitt, Earl of Chatham* (2 vols.; 1913).

WILLIAMS, W. R., *The Parliamentary History of the County of Gloucester* (Hereford, 1898).

WILSON, KATHLEEN, 'Empire, Trade and Popular Politics in Mid-Hanoverian England: The Case of Admiral Vernon', *Past and Present*, 121 (1988), 74–109.

WOODHEAD, J. R., *The Rulers of London 1660–1689* (1965).

WRIGHT, A. R., *British Calendar Customs* (3 vols.; 1940).

YORKE, P. C., *Life of Lord Chancellor Hardwicke* (2 vols.; Cambridge, 1913).

YOULD, G. M., 'Two Nonjurors', *Norfolk Archaeology*, 35 (1972), 364–81.

YOUNG, ALFRED, 'English Plebeian Culture and Eighteenth-Century American Radicalism', in *The Origins of Anglo-American Radicalism*, eds. Margaret and James Jacob (1984).

B. UNPUBLISHED PAPERS AND THESES

CORFIELD, PENELOPE J., 'The Social and Economic History of Norwich 1650–1850: A Study in Urban Growth', Ph.D. thesis (London, 1976).

DE KREY, GARY STUART, 'Trade, Religion and Politics in London in the Reign of William III', Ph.D. thesis (Princeton, 1978).

KELLETT, J. R., 'The Causes and Progress of the Financial Decline of the Corporation of London 1660–1694', Ph.D. thesis (London, 1952).

QUILICI, RONALD, 'Turmoil in a City and an Empire: Bristol's Factions 1700–1775', Ph.D. thesis (New Hampshire, 1976).

O'SULLIVAN, DANIEL S., 'Politics in Norwich 1701–1835', M.Phil. thesis (East Anglia, 1975).

STYLES, JOHN, 'A Landed Ruling Class? Interest Groups, Lobbying, and Parliament in Eighteenth-Century England', unpublished paper (1986).

UNDERDOWN, P. T., 'The Parliamentary History of the City of Bristol 1750–1790', M.A. thesis (Bristol, 1948).

WILSON, KATHLEEN, 'The Rejection of Deference: Urban Political Culture in England 1715–1785', Ph.D. thesis (Yale, 1985).

Index